D0492151

BUSINESS
ETHICS

2 4

BUSINESS **ETHICS**

PROBLEMS AND **CASES**

DAMIEN **GRACE** & STEPHEN **COHEN**

THIRD EDITION

OXFORD

UNIVERSITY PRESS

OXFORD

UNIVERSITY PRESS

253 Normanby Road, South Melbourne, Victoria 3205, Australia

Oxford University Press is a department of the University of Oxford.
It furthers the University's objective of excellence in research, scholarship,
and education by publishing worldwide in

Oxford New York

Auckland Bangkok Buenos Aires Cape Town Chennai
Dar es Salaam Delhi Hong Kong Istanbul Karachi Kolkata
Kuala Lumpur Madrid Melbourne Mexico City Mumbai Nairobi
São Paulo Shanghai Taipei Tokyo Toronto

OXFORD is a trade mark of Oxford University Press
in the UK and in certain other countries

National Library of Australia
Cataloguing-in-Publication data:

Grace, Damian, 1950–.
   Business ethics: Australian problems and cases.

   3rd ed.
   Bibliography.
   Includes index.
   ISBN 0 19 551727 X.

   1. Business ethics—Australia. I. Cohen, Stephen, 1947–.
   II. Title.

   174.40994

Typeset by OUPANZS
Printed by Bookpac Production Services, Singapore

Contents

Acknowledgments

We wish to express our gratitude to a number of people who assisted in the completion of this work. To Jane Martin for her skilled and intelligent research; to Jill Lane for advice; to Rosi Benninghaus, Kaz Kazim and John Cheong Seong Lee for bibliographic and other assistance in preparing the text; and to Shirley Cohen for establishing the required American avenues for us to reproduce some advertising materials. Greg Goodman has offered valuable information and advice about the state of play of formal compliance and corporate governance regimes within the Australian context.

Debra James provided the stimulus—and convinced us of the rationale—for the different format of the third edition. Lucy McLoughlin exercised considerable care and good judgment of layout and clear expression. The text is better for her work on it.

We wish to thank the following colleagues, who made comments on the earlier editions and suggestions for improvement: Andrew Brian, Pam Byde, Ted Cohen, Conal Condren, Glyn Hardingham, Michael Jackson, John Lawrence, Kathleen MacDonald, Bryan Maher, Ian Marsh, Noel Preston and members of our classes in the Graduate Diploma in Professional Ethics at the University of New South Wales.

Thanks are also due to Saatchi and Saatchi, Toyota Australia, Style Counsel, Chrysler Corporation, Bozell Worldwide Inc. and Behrens Brown for supplying material and allowing its reproduction.

Damian Grace
Stephen Cohen

Personal thanks are due to Conal Condren and Michael Jackson and Denise Quay. I am grateful for the hospitality of the Philosophy Department of McGill University in Montreal and to the University of New South Wales for financial support. Finally, my greatest gratitude is to my wife, Bernadette, and daughters, Madeleine and Julia.

DG

Denise Grannall's critical eye and counsel to make the discussions practical and readable has been much appreciated, as has the patience of Noah, Jared and Anthea in allowing me time away from other things in order to complete this project.

SC

Introduction

Why should business students study ethics? What good might be expected to come from such a study? Although business ethics has been taught at American institutions for many years, the introduction of ethics into Australian business courses was greeted by many with scepticism. There were the customary jokes about the brevity of a course on business ethics and its oxymoronic nature. More seriously, some suggested that ethics courses were unnecessary because it was hardly the case that students were currently being taught unethical practices, that philosophy did not belong in business courses, or that ethics would not make a difference to behaviour in business. There was also some justified scepticism about using morality to make business look good after the failures and excesses of the 1980s. Beyond these reservations, however, there persists what might be called 'social discomfort' about the public discussion of ethical issues. After all, is not ethics a matter of personal belief, preference and values? How could one talk of business ethics when there is so much disagreement about ethics in general, let alone in one particular area? Are there reliable surveys to tell us what most people want from business ethics? Why is it important to bring up children properly if the morality they learn from their family, neighbours, school and peers is not good enough to serve them in life? What will we have next: shopping ethics, sports ethics, disco ethics?

These questions illustrate some of the most common kinds of objections faced by business ethics, but none of them has slowed the development of the subject and its incorporation into the curriculum of business courses. It is worth taking such questions seriously not only because they remain current, but also because the justification for business ethics provides a useful way of introducing the subject.

It is odd for teachers to argue that ethics education makes no difference to behaviour: one might as well argue that teaching organisational behaviour or marketing will make no difference or that any form of education is flawed if it does not turn out pre-formed products. No one would seriously argue that books, films or television programs which portray certain modes of behaviour never affect people or that they do not give them cause to consider their own behaviour. As any student or educator knows, education is more than reading and writing. To avoid explicit discussion of ethical issues in a field of study is to send a message that ethics is dispensable. That message is not one that responsible educators or business would want to risk sending today. People cannot be 'made good' by telling them to do X or to avoid doing Y; but standards of conduct and acceptable values can be entrenched in people and in organisations, and people can be put in a position where they make informed choices in the professions and occupations in which they work. This is the minimum ethical education that a student of any practical course has a right to expect.

In this respect, business has for too long been short-changing itself in Australia. While degrees for the professions have had requirements for ethics to be included in their courses, business degrees have lagged. What has been regarded as standard in medicine, law, social work, nursing, veterinary science, engineering and architecture has, until recently, been seen as a luxury in commerce and industry. If some in business think that this is acceptable, they will quickly find that the public will not tolerate it any longer. More than ever before, business is expected to be accountable, not only to shareholders, but also to society.

The view that ethics is superfluous assumes that people will act as they must and will leave the idealism to the classroom. Perhaps, but that implies that ethics has nothing but idealism to offer. Sometimes, however, it is the case that people of goodwill do not know what the ethical thing to do is in a complicated situation. Particular ethical studies, whether in accounting or medicine, engineering or marketing, should at least offer some clarification and perhaps even some answers. An important point here is that ethics should help a person in making a decision and, further, ethics should help people live with themselves and their society even after a tragic decision. Ethics is not a salve for the bruises of life, but it places in perspective the moral problems, which, after all, affect only those who are already concerned with this aspect of their conduct. Ethics will not make people good by some magic; but what good reason could there be for keeping people in ignorance of the ethical demands society makes of business, or more adventurously, for keeping business professionals from exploring the possibilities and problems that will confront them at a time of great technological and social change? In short, why would business practitioners not wish to advance the professional status of their occupation?

This reference to business as a profession is not casual; the term is not meant as a synonym for occupation. The point about professions is that they serve and are responsive not only to clients but to other interested sections of society, nowadays called 'stakeholders', which is the topic of chapter 3. Professions rely on conceptual thinking and embody their distinctive ways of doing things in what are called 'practices'. It is common to hear talk of architectural practice, psychological practice, legal practice, engineering practice and so on. It is important to note that this is not just a fancy way of describing what these professions do. Take, for example, surgery. We do not say that 'surgery' was practised on prisoners of war who were subject to experiments, even though the operations were performed by surgeons, sometimes with great skill. There is such a strong distinction between treatment and experimentation that it can be difficult even for critically ill patients to be treated with drugs that are still experimental. This distinction between experimentation and treatment is based upon the idea that the respect to which people are entitled forbids their use as a means to some other good. People are goods in and of themselves; they have value as people per se. Treatment is directed to securing that good. To ensure that the paths to this good remain clear and unconfused by ulterior and ignoble objectives, the medical profession has assumed and codified a body of ethics. This code is a shorthand way of indicating a commitment to a morality of practice. If a practice like surgery were simply the knowledge and skills necessary to operate, then there would be little to distinguish the experimenter from the surgeon. In fact, we do not recognise experiments on involuntary subjects, such as prisoners of war, as medical practice because basic human values are attacked and, in this particular case, because there is a failure to respect the value of humans as such. There is a failure to regard the value of individual humans as other than instrumental in the achievement of other values or goals. It is the ethical direction of the accomplishments of a profession (particularly its regard for the individuals who are subject to its activities) that entitles it to a certain status and power, such as self-regulation, and other marks of social recognition. And that is why unprofessional conduct usually refers not merely to competence, but to conduct and decorum in a wider sense — doing the right thing with one's knowledge and skills and using them to serve rather than to take advantage of people.

'Practice', then, is a very useful notion, for at its heart is a conception of human good which directs the application and use of the competencies that it embodies. Central to a practice is an ethical commitment, not just a skilled way of doing a job, and the practice of business is no different from the practice of other professions in this respect.

Like the professions, business is conceptual, intellectual work. It is not simply a matter of routine, repetitive tasks. It cannot be reduced to mere administration. The signs of a successful business are keeping employees, customers and the tax man happy and taking a profit at the end of the day; and making these very different things happen is the real vocation in business. It takes skill, knowledge and practical wisdom to secure the future of a business and make it grow. Successful business does not happen by chance; it is the product of skill and intelligence.

One major implication of this view is that business needs a stock of concepts. This stock embraces concepts from law, accounting, marketing, industrial relations and many other areas, as well as concepts relating to the kind of industry with which the business deals, such as medical supplies or software sales. All of these concern human values. Business is about supplying the needs and desires of human society and is therefore about human goods and the best means to provide them. And this is where ethics comes in. Ethics is concerned with the identification of human goods (ends) and their pursuit (means), including direction and constraints that might be involved in their pursuit.

Whether or not ethics is explicitly considered in its various functions, it is inescapably part of business. In dealing with ends and the means to those ends, business is making ethical decisions, even if such decisions are not perceived by managers and boards in this light. This book provides an ethical perspective on the appraisal of means and ends in business life, and thereby enriches the stock of concepts recognised as necessary to it. If there is no conception that a decision entails ethical considerations, and if there is no adequate conceptual vocabulary to make sense of ethical requirements, then reasonable ethical standards in business become a matter of luck. In this respect, we claim to be contributing to the stock of conceptual tools that are useful in doing business successfully.

People do not have to do a moral philosophy course in order to be ethical. Ethics is expressed in the lives of people who have never heard or uttered a philosophical syllable in their lives. We do not always need to be acquainted with the theories of academics in order to get on with life. This point has been well made by non-academic critics of modernity and the domination of life by theory. One of the most famous paintings of the great surrealist painter René Magritte depicts a tobacco pipe and is titled *Ceci n'est pas une pipe* (this is not a pipe). This title startles with its obviousness: we are so used to a theoretical understanding of the world that we are apt to confuse the representation of things with the things themselves. And so it is with theories of ethics. There is no substitute for the practice of the thing itself. Conversely, just as Magritte's picture has its own value, so does ethical theory.

Of course a strong objection to business ethics might be inferred from this line of reasoning, and that is that most business has got by ethically for a long time without the help of jargon about concepts and, in general, without the analytic input of academics. Why worry about formal business ethics and conceptual thinking? This objection has truth but it is also partly false. It is false in that traditional business virtues and conventional ethical concepts hid a spectrum of injustice. For example, the labour of women and children was, and in some cases still is, unjustly exploited, and the rights of indigenous people were too often simply ignored in the pursuit of mining and pastoral wealth. But the social environment has changed. Traditionally, people were brought up in the family business and learned to be proficient by way of a kind of apprenticeship. Few would find that satisfactory today. Now proficient business requires the ability to deal conceptually with all aspects of the business environment, and one aspect of that environment is ethics. The social context in which business occurs today is one in which concern for ethics is not merely an option.

People may well display high levels of personal integrity but remain unaware of the demands of institutional ethics. How would they deal with questions of social responsibility, equity and accountability? Would they even be able to conceptualise what the issues at stake are? The importance of such questions has been underlined not only by the ethical failures of the 1980s, but also by the demands of the social agenda. While the 1980s were not unique in raising critical ethical issues, they provided a wealth of illustrations of the damage that ethical ignorance as well as unethical behaviour can do. Unless managers are aware of ethical issues, know how to think about them conceptually, and can devise justifiable solutions, they will fail to institutionalise ethics in corporate life. Ignorance can be as pernicious as malice; the dictum that 'greed is good' goes hand in hand with the 'myth of amoral business', as Richard De George calls it.[1] Both slogans are excuses for unacceptable business practices, but only the latter claims the dignity of ignorance.

Bluntly, ethics is not an option. If a company or industry cares nothing for ethical requirements, it may expect from government a policy and legislative response that imposes standards and practices. This is already happening, and some of these pressures are discussed in chapter 10.

Already this suggests a kind of negativity about ethics that can be distorting. Just as fine cooking is not a response to fast food, so business ethics is not only a response to ethical failure. There happens to be great scope for ethical repair work, but if we take seriously the notion that business is conceptual work, there is greater scope for using ethics to promote excellence in business. At its simplest, ethics is a normal part of everyday conduct, a normal part of business. At its best, ethics is about human excellence. An Australian Manufacturing Council study of Best Practice compared high performing firms with less successful manufacturers. The former had strong growth with fewer industrial disputes, greater investment in staff training, better industrial safety records and more modern plants. The managers of the successful firms tended to give greater priority to quality, while managers of the poor performers tended to focus on cost.[2] There is a clear relationship here between excellent management inputs into companies and excellent outcomes. A concern for ethics is part of this drive to excel. It should lead to a pro-active stance by business on ethical issues, and a greater preparedness for the crises that will inevitably emerge in the business community, just as they did in the 1980s. Being well brought up is a fortunate basis on which to build good ethical practice, but it is not the only way and not a sufficient way of achieving this.

About this text

Most business ethics texts begin with a smorgasbord of ethical theories, followed by topics and cases in specific areas. Readers are often invited to choose a theory to apply to a topic in order to resolve an ethical problem. This can suggest a kind of 'off the shelf' approach to ethics, which we eschew. Certainly the philosophers who have developed each of the major positions did not regard them as substitutable by rival theories; they argued for them because they believed they were true or in some other way preferable to other theories. So, while it is important to have some familiarity with the main theories of morality, this is more in the interests of understanding the conceptual language of contemporary ethics than to provide some kind of algorithm for the solution of ethical 'dilemmas'. Indeed, chapter 2 shows that often there are no clean solutions; that no matter how well people try to act, they can still end up with 'dirty hands'.

Hence, in seeking to acquaint readers with widely used ethical vocabularies, we are not suggesting that ethical solutions are simply about making the right choice of theory and applying it to a problem. In order to avoid confusion and a false sense of choice in moral theory, we deal with this matter only in a summary fashion. We do, however, set out a theory of reflective equilibrium, which we believe provides conceptual tools for considering and resolving ethical problems. Further, it will be clear from the Introduction that we believe that people espousing different moral theories and religious views can exhibit the same virtues, can meaningfully and fruitfully discuss ethical problems with each other and, indeed, can often agree on practical solutions to moral problems. In this respect, we suggest in chapter 1 that a commitment to 'moral pluralism' or to 'relativism' does not stand as a barrier to fruitful ethical discussion.

Near the end of chapter 1 we say a word about the benefits of approaching a study of business ethics through case studies. We note there that sometimes our purpose is to call attention to something that has gone wrong (or right) and sometimes it is to call attention to some ethically problematic aspect of behaviour or organisational structure. Given that we are dealing with case studies, often having the nature of vignettes only, we recognise a limitation, a constraint and a danger that it is also important to signal. In 'telling the stories' as illustrative of various themes or problems, we are concerned to present salient features which are relevant to the points we want to make. And, while we certainly do not wish to distort facts, and do believe that we provide reasonable accounts, we do not provide 'full' accounts of all the cases. Further, we would allow the possibility of another side of the story. In this respect we invite the reader to approach the cases as problematic in more ways than one. Perhaps you know of or could imagine additional facts that would be relevant to a moral appraisal of the situation as well as to possible suggested solutions to the ethical difficulties presented. That the context be seen as Australian and the problems recognised as real and serious are important. Beyond that, whether or not an illustrative example is itself factual is relatively unimportant. It is worth repeating, however, that we do attempt to give factually correct accounts of the cases.

What this text is and what it is not

This text is not a catechism or a 'deuteronomy' for business and professions. It is not a handbook of exhaustive questions about, and definitive answers to, moral problems that arise in those contexts. Sometimes issues are clear and sometimes they are not. Sometimes there is a clear solution and sometimes there is not. The most important aspect of the text is the sense that we can think through ethical problems and ethical issues systematically, and that we can arrive at an answer or a response that has integrity. There are conceptual tools to help us do this. A response should be justifiable, and should not shy away from offering justification, even if it is not the only justifiable response. Sometimes for reasons of 'dirty hands' (see chapter 2), and sometimes for other reasons, the response is not something that can simply be 'ticked off' and from which we can move on. Ethical problems sometimes need to be revisited and reconsidered. Ethical decision-making often lacks the certainty we might desire. This does not make it wishy-washy, soft, unimportant or unsystematic. Our aim is to make this clear in the chapters that follow.

An important consideration in a book such as this is to present an appropriate balance between, on the one hand, theory, principles, and conceptual tools, and, on the other, practical examples and case studies. We do, in fact, make a comment about that near the end of chapter one. One response to the first two editions of the book has been that a greatly expanded section on moral principles and moral reasoning would be desirable. We have also found in the Graduate Programs in Professional Ethics, which we direct at the University of New South Wales, that the most popular electives later in the programs are those which allow students to get a better grounding in and to have the opportunity to think more precisely about the area of theory, principles, and conceptual tools. We have taken these as indications not that a chapter in this book should include more about moral theory and moral reasoning, but rather that a different book — concerned only with those things — would be helpful. One of us, Stephen Cohen, has now written such a book (also published by OUP).[3] People who are interested in further exploring ideas about moral theories and, in particular, the structure and process of moral reasoning might be interested in having a look at that book.

Ethical Reasoning in Business

1

Chapter outline

- What is ethics?
- Top-down and bottom-up approaches
- Ethical defeat
- Reflective equilibrium
- Consequentialism
- Nonconsequentialism
- Virtue ethics
- Relativism
- Business
- Moral pluralism
- Case studies and moral theory
- Review questions

Business ethics covers the whole spectrum of interactions between firms, individuals, industries, society and the state. In other words, business ethics is as complex as business itself. It is not an optional accessory to business life or a mere enthusiasm of philosophers and moralists; business ethics is about how we conduct our business affairs, from the basest fraud to the highest levels of excellence. It is about individuals and the institutions with which they deal. And it is about the expectations and requirements — including the social and economic requirements — of society.

Such a scope suggests that individuals might have a limited role in ethical matters. After all, if they have a limited range of business responsibilities, then they will not be in a position to make much of an ethical impact. An important way of looking at the responsibilities of individuals is to examine their roles. Company directors, for instance, have fiduciary responsibilities to act in the best interests of shareholders. Does that entitle them to ignore ethically suspect practices that benefit shareholders? Sometimes people's role in business is itself the problem. Should their occupational role diminish their moral responsibility for actions done in the name of their company or employer? If so, where do individual conscience, character and choice come in?

The same kinds of questions might be asked not only of individuals, but also of firms and industries that operate under socially determined legal and economic constraints. What are the ethical responsibilities of 'non-natural persons' — legal entities that have no character or conscience in the usual sense and are persons only in law? How is ethics to be made part of the fabric of institutions? Should ethical standards be imposed in a market economy?

What is ethics?

If ethics were only a matter of rules, customs and contracts, then such questions would be relatively straightforward. We already have procedures, instruments, conventions, and regulations ranging from law to etiquette in abundance. But to say that ethics does not duplicate these is not to measure its importance or scope by them. Ethical issues are often grey; ethical reasoning is not as concrete (or sometimes as precise) as legal reasoning; people can differ on the subject of ethics as they may not on the laws of physics or the facts of geography. Although these are facts about ethics, they are not reasons for believing that ethics is conceptually soft or trivial. Ethics is not poor reasoning, vague law, indeterminate custom, or an ideological form of social control, but one of the most important sources of motivation and guidance in human conduct. It occupies an important field of knowledge in its own right.

Aristotle gave a view of the matter in a famous passage of his Nicomachean Ethics:

> Our account of this science (ethics) will be adequate if it achieves such clarity as the subject-matter allows; for the same degree of precision is not to be expected in all discussions … Therefore in discussing subjects, and arguing from evidence, conditioned in this way, we must be satisfied with a broad outline of the truth; that is, in arguing about what is for the most part so from premises which are for the most part true we must be content to draw conclusions that are similarly qualified … it is a mark of the trained mind never to expect more precision in the treatment of any subject than the nature of the subject permits; for demanding logical demonstrations from a teacher of rhetoric is clearly about as reasonable as accepting mere plausibility from a mathematician.[1]

Ethical reasoning, according to Aristotle, is not a matter of applying the appropriate algorithm to a situation and mechanically calculating the correct moral result, the correct moral prescription. Ethical reasoning is more subtle, less precise, often more difficult. Not all ethical thinkers have agreed with Aristotle. Some have tried to put a much more precise formulation on moral duties. Nevertheless, given the kinds of debates about ethical problems in Australia, it is clear that lack of precision is not the problem, or at least not the major problem, in solving them.

In order to gain a clearer grasp of what ethics is and is not, consider the film *The Godfather*. At the beginning of the film we are disgusted by the violence and absence of humanity in the Mafia. As the story progresses, however, we come to see the internal rules of 'the Family' at work and realise that, although they are contrary to the rules of normal society, they make their own kind of sense. At the end of the film, the anti-hero, Michael, is attending the baptism of his son in a church while his henchmen systematically kill his rivals for leadership of the Family. This is how life is in the Mafia. This is what we understand to be necessary, to make sense in terms of that kind of culture. The Mafia has its own ethos, its own rules and mores. This is a dark parallel to the ethical values of the wider society, and it is this parallel, rather than the ruthlessness and violence per se, which causes *The Godfather* to be shocking.

The film raises all kinds of ethical questions that apply equally to society and business. Is just any system of binding rules, norms and duties a system of ethics? Is it possible to say that one system is better than another? Does not moral luck determine the circumstances of people's birth and development and therefore the attitudes they bring to life? The importance of these questions is readily apparent. If people born in Australia in the late nineteenth century believed wholeheartedly in the White Australia Policy, how can they be blamed? If a person grew up as a white child in South Africa during the Vorster regime, why is it blameworthy to have white supremacist attitudes? And who is to say that one system of social beliefs and customs, even if racist, is worse than another? These are real questions, requiring thought and careful consideration.

If cultural relativism is the case, then business must adapt to the norms and practices of the cultures in which it operates. What is unethical in Australia might be good manners in one of our trading partners. What would be poor working conditions here might be superior working conditions overseas. Australian sharp practice might well be the norm elsewhere. Surely it is mistaken to try to universalise our standards of right and wrong in our dealings with other countries. Or is it?

Defining ethics

What is ethics? What does it mean to have an ethical point of view or an ethical opinion or to behave ethically? A definition will not solve the problems raised but will go some way towards clarifying what is at stake.

The term 'ethics' owes its origins to ancient Greece, where the word ethikos referred to the authority of custom and tradition. When Cicero sought a similar word in Latin he chose mos, from which we derive the terms 'moral', 'mores' and 'morale'. So it seems that 'ethical relativists' have at least a good historical basis for their views: ethics and mores originally referred to the customs, habits of life or traditions of a people. We shall consider ethical relativism in our discussion of ethical reasoning, but a relativist could say that we have as much right to condemn the customs of the Mafia or apartheid as we do any foreign system of behaviour — that is, none. Or rather, we can condemn them in terms of our moral system, but we should not and cannot insist that others who do not share our values listen to our complaints.

Plainly this will not do. A definition of ethics that dignified any and all customs would not answer to a common-sense understanding of the term. The Mafia and apartheid are objectionable, and not just because most people think so. Here is some further definition.

The nineteenth-century German philosopher Georg Wilhelm Friedrich Hegel distinguished between ethics as the customary norms and ways of behaving in a society, and morality as a reflection on those norms and the deliberate generation and adoption of principles that may well modify them. On this distinction, the ethos or ethics of a particular culture might require reverence for older people or assign special responsibilities to the oldest son. An example of moral thinking would be the growth in recognition of human rights, and the greater sensitivity to suffering in animals. Another example can be seen in the deliberate study of professional and business ethics. In this sense then morality is the missing part of ethics that as modern people rather than villagers regulated by custom and tradition, we often take for granted. In fact, so familiar to us is reflective, conceptual thinking about ethical issues that customs and traditions are often ignored or dismissed as irrelevant. Both custom and reflection are part of ethics. Together they show why just any set of norms cannot be an ethics; why among thieves and racists there can be no honour.

By and large there is no reason to make a distinction in meaning between 'ethical' and 'moral'. There is certainly no difference in meaning that could be attributed to their etymological roots. Sometimes some moral philosophers or 'ethicists' distinguish them from each other, but not all philosophers do; and those who do distinguish them from each other do not all distinguish them in the same way. Some have distinguished 'moral' and 'ethical' in the manner of Hegel, but others have distinguished them in a variety of different ways. It is recommended here that the words be considered as synonymous except in some peculiar usages. We will see later, in discussing codes of ethics, that there is an issue about whether or not the use of 'ethics' in 'code of ethics' is a specialised use, or whether it is even there synonymous with 'morality'. We will suggest that, in that context, 'ethics' is a specialised use and should not be confused with 'morality'. That is the only exception to our use of these words as synonymous.

What is ethics? What kind of thing is a moral reason? What is being considered when one considers the 'moral dimension' of a problem? What makes this different from the non-moral aspects of a situation? Is there anything peculiar about moral reasons? These questions themselves have been debated among moral philosophers. Without entering into the debate or prejudicing a position, it is possible to say something about what ethics is. We can offer a 'minimalist' description that offers only the bare bones of what must be involved in something being a moral concern. It is then arguable whether perhaps something more must also be involved in a consideration being an ethical one. Keep in mind that for now we are not talking about what is involved in the correct moral opinion, but rather about what it is for an opinion to be a moral opinion at all, be it correct, incorrect, or whatever.

- Considering something ethically requires that one go outside, or beyond, one's self-interest alone in reaching a decision. Moral opinions, then, are not opinions based only on the promotion of one's self-interest. Moral opinions are impartial.
- An ethical judgment is one that can be 'universalised'. It is one that is perceived to apply to everyone in similar circumstances, and not only to oneself.
- Ethical opinions must be able to be defended with reasons. This requirement distinguishes ethical opinions from biases and mere preferences, for which one might have no reason at all: 'I don't have a *reason* for liking vanilla ice-cream more than chocolate raisin; I just do. I *prefer* its taste'.

- Ethical opinions are not subject to a 'vote', in the way that political opinions and decisions are. A moral opinion is not just whatever a majority decides it is. An opinion or a position on something does not become moral in virtue of popular support for it. In this respect, moral opinions are non-negotiable.
- Moral opinions are centrally 'action-guiding'. They are not only of theoretical or academic interest. They are centrally concerned with *behaviour*. They are concerned with evaluating behaviour and with prescribing ways in which people should behave. To at least some extent, this requires that one thinks about the consequences of one's actions. Here are some examples of what some philosophers have said that ethics amounts to:

morality is, at the very least, the effort to guide one's conduct by reason — that is to do what there are the best reasons for doing — while giving equal weight to the best interests of each individual who will be affected by one's conduct.[2]

morality amounts to 'guidelines that set the boundaries of acceptable behavior' — concerned with harming others, paying the proper regard for others' well-being, and treating persons with respect.[3]

morality is concerned with 'rules, principles, or ways of thinking that guide actions' ... it refers to 'values, rules, standards, or principles that should guide our decisions about what we ought to do'.[4]

The notion of living according to ethical standards is tied up with the notion of defending the way one is living, of giving a reason for it, of justifying it ... Ethics requires us to go beyond 'I' and 'you' to the universal law, the universalisable judgment, the standpoint of the impartial spectator or ideal observer, or whatever we choose to call it ... In accepting that ethical judgments must be made from a universal point of view, I am accepting that my own interests cannot, simply because they are my interests, count more than the interests of anyone else.[5]

Where do ethical principles come from? Are they matters of religion, society's inculcated beliefs, universal rational truths? Are they principles which are formed as a result of a bargain which individuals reach in order to live together, each having their own welfare as their top priority, but realising that in order to successfully advance their individual self-interests, they must operate according to mutually acceptable principles? These very important questions will not be dealt with here. They are by no means easy, and there is no universal agreement about what their answers are. However, although we should be aware of them, it is possible to proceed without answering them.

Ethical reasoning

There are three central points with which we are concerned in this book:
- that there are moral concerns
- that you should address them
- what it means to address moral concerns.

Very few people would deny that there are moral concerns in their lives. In this respect, then, it takes little or no convincing that there are moral concerns. There might be significant debate over whether a particular concern is, in fact, a moral one, and there is debate over how to respond to some moral issues; there is also debate over what is the morally correct thing to do. But, by and large, there is no debate over whether or not there are moral concerns at all. This being the case, we will not spend much time arguing that there are moral concerns. Rather, we will be presenting some moral concerns to you, indicating what there is about them that make them moral, and then dealing with them in a systematic way. In presenting moral issues we have a few key matters in mind, not all of which can be dealt with in each instance. Sometimes we call attention to something that is clearly a moral impropriety, and then proceed to discuss what exactly is wrong and how it might be rectified or, more importantly, how it might have been avoided. We are equally concerned, however, to call attention to some matters that are problematic and which, for that reason, should generate thought and argument in the context in which those matters occur. Serious, genuine analysis is called for, and people in business or in the professions should not avoid devoting some time to it.

As an individual or as an organisation or as an individual occupying a position (a role) in an organisation, you should address moral issues. Why? There are a number of answers to this question, and the question itself can be addressed at a number of levels, ranging from a theoretical interest in moral philosophy to a purely pragmatic and self-interested concern. At the most theoretical level, the question 'Why should I be moral?' is one to which philosophers have offered an array of answers since the time of Plato, over 2000 years ago. Some theories have urged that rational behaviour and rational thinking themselves require people to be moral. Other theories have referred to morality as empirically compelling, and others have made reference to a feeling people have about what they regard as moral. Many arguments suggest that we should be moral, because that is what we want to be, if we could find the moral thing to do in any particular situation. Suppose, however, that at the theoretical level such answers left you cold. What more could be said? When we discuss codes of ethics specifically, we will urge that, given the amount of public awareness and accountability required these days, coupled with the possibility (or threat) of governmental regulation over many aspects of business conduct, the climate in business is such that it is in people's interest to pay attention to moral, not simply legal, requirements. There is a good deal of truth to the practical dictum 'good ethics is good business'. Perhaps purely self-interested motives for adopting a moral point of view are not noble — or not as noble as compassion or a sense of fairness or other motives which are not themselves based on one's own welfare and concern for advancing one's own interests ahead of those of others. Still, there can be no denying that requirements of public accountability are greater today than they have ever been before, and that public awareness of, interest in, and demands concerning the conduct of businesses and the professions are very great, perhaps enlightened. Clients, customers, shareholders or society at large will not tolerate professional or business conduct that is perceived to be unethical.

There is an important analogue to the question 'Why be moral?' as it arises in this context. Political philosophers and philosophers of law often discuss the question of whether or not people should obey the law. This question, 'Why should I obey the (legal) law?' is, in those discussions, most significantly directed to looking for a moral reason to obey the law. However, at another level, an appropriate answer to the question is a resounding, 'Yes, I should obey the law, because if I don't, I'm going to get into trouble with the law'. This is an answer that cannot be ignored when considering why we should be moral in business as well.

Top-down and bottom-up approaches

If we recognise that there are moral concerns, and we appreciate that we should address them, then what is it to address them? What is the nature of moral reasoning? Consider a couple of possibilities. The first is a top-down approach, according to which the first principles of moral reasoning are general or universal moral principles that can be applied to specific situations. This conception of moral reasoning envisages the reasoner approaching a moral situation armed with general principles, for example, 'tell the truth', 'advance people's welfare', 'keep your promises', 'honour fiduciary relationships', and a number of others, all of which rest on some kind of general foundations. Moral reasoning, then, would amount to applying the appropriate principles to the situation and overlaying those principles onto particular situations as those situations arise. For example, when faced with a moral choice, a committed utilitarian might engage in tallying up and comparing the amounts of welfare that would be produced by the various alternatives. The act likely to produce the most utility would be the one that the utilitarian principle would direct be performed. The principle — in this case the utilitarian principle — drives the reasoning, and its application to the particular situation determines the correct, ethical result. According to the top-down approach, the task for moral reasoning is to bring particular moral judgments or intuitions about particular situations into harmony with overarching general principles.

According to a bottom-up approach, on the other hand, the first principles of moral reasoning are the moral judgments we make personally — perhaps moral intuitions or reactions we have to particular situations. It is these ground-level judgments — perhaps intuitions or feelings — themselves, rather than overarching principles, which are the first principles of moral reasoning. This conception of moral reasoning sees moral encounters as situations in which the reasoner is struck by the nature of the situations themselves, and need look no further to appreciate the moral dimension which is present and arrive at a moral decision. If one were interested in doing so it might be possible to enunciate general principles that are coherent with the intuitions that emerge from the particular situations to which we react. The starting point and the foundation of moral principles in this approach, however, rests with the evaluation of the particular situations.

Ethical defeat

People are reluctant to admit complete 'ethical defeat' — that is, to grant that their acts have no positive ethical justification at all, that their acts are completely immoral, bereft of any positive moral elements. This is an important feature of human nature. It shows that, by and large, people do not dismiss ethics as an unimportant concern. Sometimes they get it wrong — sometimes their acts are immoral — but seldom do the agents themselves dismiss morality altogether. This is important. People do not simply admit to being caught with the smoking gun, with nothing to say for themselves. We are not oblivious of — or impervious to — moral argument about what we do. In this respect, we do not need to be convinced to enter the moral arena for the purpose of evaluating potential courses of action. They are already there, even though their moral perceptions may not be 'correct'. This point was vividly illustrated many years ago in a newspaper report about drug trafficking in New York City: a heroin dealer pointed out to the reporter that he only sold good dope and that he never sold to kids.[6] Even at this level, the dealer is hearkening to the moral defensibility of some aspect of what he is doing. He is not oblivious to the importance of such a concern, even though, in his case, it was particularly misplaced. The moral of this story is simply that the answer to a question such as 'Who cares about ethics anyway?' is 'nearly everyone'. And, if this is the case, then it is unnecessary to spend much time trying to convince people that they should be interested in the moral aspects of what they do. However, there is, of course, much work to do in determining exactly what those aspects are and what course of action one should take, or what courses of action are permissible. But this is an entirely different problem from the question of why we should be concerned about ethics in the first place. The point is that, on a practical level, we really need not address this question at all.

It is not infrequent that invitations — or pleas — to business and the professions to engage in moral reasoning carry with them the suggestion that the reasoners might choose whatever moral principles they want, recognising that they might well be attracted to different and disparate principles. Such invitations allow the possibility of 'moral pluralism', the presence of a number of different, perhaps incompatible, moral principles. The point of such invitations is to get business people and professionals to recognise that there is a moral dimension to the problems they face, and to urge that this dimension not be ignored but dealt with systematically by the various practitioners. The invitation is for people to engage in reflective moral consideration, and to confront the notion of 'principled action', which requires consideration of principles (to which the whole idea of principled action refers).

In routine matters routine ethics can work quite well. In critical situations that are other than routine, however, managers have to fall back on character rather than rules. In this sense, character and the virtues that inform it serve as repositories of moral knowledge and wisdom. It is these — not overarching principles — that lead to individual moral judgments. This might be seen as a feature of the bottom-up approach.

In a similar vein, Jonsen and Toulmin have argued that agreement on ethical issues is more likely to come from the consideration of concrete cases than from a dispute about principles.[7] People might agree about particular matters for different reasons; that people of good faith might differ in their principles need not preclude a workable ethics being shared among them. Argument from cases is more likely to secure this than a battle fought to secure commitment to a philosophical position or overarching principle.

Reflective equilibrium

A third approach regards neither particular judgments nor general principles as first principles. Both are important, and the interplay between them is what drives moral reasoning. In 1970 John Rawls introduced the phrase 'reflective equilibrium'.[8] As he used it, the phrase refers to beliefs about justice. However, the notion has been discussed as having an important role to play in understanding the nature of moral reasoning and moral theorising in general. As such, it refers to the state of a person's beliefs when their moral principles and moral judgments are in harmony. Notice that 'reflective equilibrium' refers to a result, or end state. A reflective equilibrium is something to be achieved. 'Top-down' and 'bottom-up' approaches both clearly refer to processes, aimed at arriving at a result. It would make sense to say that they, too, would be aiming at a result where principles and judgments are in equilibrium. As it is used, however, the phrase 'reflective equilibrium' is also a view about *how* to establish this result – a process – not just the result itself. Roger Ebertz has written:

> I find it helpful to speak also of 'the reflective process' to refer to the activities which lead one to reflective equilibrium. These include carefully considering individual beliefs, comparing them with one another, considering the beliefs of others, drawing out consequences of beliefs, and so forth.[9]

According to this view, neither particular judgments nor general principles are preeminent. Further, it allows us to skirt the question of whether there are any immutable moral facts or whether there are any objectively true moral propositions. Moral reasoning is a matter of bringing into harmony, or consistency, various particular judgments with each other and with the principles that we hold. In this respect, moral reasoning is seen to be centrally neither top-down nor bottom-up. Rather, it works in both directions, with the goal of reaching an equilibrium between the principles to which one subscribes and the particular judgments which one makes. Moral reasoning is also concerned to achieve consistency among one's particular judgments (relative to each other), and among the various principles to which one subscribes (relative to each other).

Reflective equilibrium between principles and judgments:

Principles	$P_1, P_2, P_3 \ldots$
	$\updownarrow$
Judgments	$J_1, J_2, J_3 \ldots$

Reflective equilibrium among principles:

Principles	$P_1 \leftrightarrow P_2 \leftrightarrow P_3 \leftrightarrow \ldots$

Reflective equilibrium among judgments:

Judgments	$J_1 \leftrightarrow J_2 \leftrightarrow J_3 \leftrightarrow \ldots$

Reaching a reflective equilibrium is essentially a dialectical process, which involves a give and take of principles and intuitions. Neither the principles nor the intuitions are immutable; reaching a reflective equilibrium involves 'massaging' both. It is important to us to have a consistent set of beliefs. Notice, for instance, that when we argue with others, our strongest arguments are in terms of allegations that the other party is failing to be consistent.

Suppose that, for whatever reason, I am attracted to some moral principle. For example, I think that I should try to maximise utility. Suppose also that I think that in a particular situation I should keep my promise to drive a friend to the airport, even though it appears that I could produce more utility by doing something else. Here there is an apparent conflict between a principle to which I am attracted and a particular judgment that I feel is correct. I might argue that keeping the promise will maximise utility, or I might argue that my commitment to the utilitarian principle is modified by some other (theoretical) commitments, the result of which is that I am not being inconsistent in believing that I should keep my promise on this occasion. It will be important to me not to be a hypocrite about the situation, however. It will be important to me that my ground-level judgment not conflict with my purported theoretical commitment. It will be important to me to resolve the apparent conflict.

In considering my position on both the practical and theoretical levels, I allow that there can be interplay between them, and that my beliefs, commitments or intuitions about something at either level are subject to review in the light of my beliefs, commitments or intuitions about something at the other level, as well as in the light of my beliefs about something at the same level. That is, it is important to me to strike a reflective equilibrium between the principles to which I subscribe and the judgments that I make. And it is important to me that my judgments are consistent with each other, and that I can consistently maintain a commitment to the various principles to which I subscribe. If I offer apparently inconsistent judgments on some occasions, it is important to me to either correct this inconsistency (and so alter my judgment or some aspect of my theoretical commitment), or 'distinguish' the situations so that the apparent inconsistency is revealed to be only apparent, not actual. For example, on one occasion, I thought it was permissible for me to break my promise, whereas on another I thought that it was not. When pressed (either by myself or by someone else), I might perceive that on one of the occasions the promise was to a workmate, and on the other occasion it was to a business acquaintance and that it would have disastrous consequences for my business if I kept the promise. In view of this, I might try to articulate the principles according to which these individual judgments are not inconsistent with each other, and neither of them is inconsistent with the principles to which I subscribe. The process of moral reasoning allows for modification and revision of the principles to which one subscribes, as well as of the particular judgments that one makes.

Consequentialism

'Consequentialism' refers to a moral outlook that evaluates actions or behaviour according to the consequences of that behaviour. According to this outlook, an act being morally right or wrong is due to it producing some specified type of consequence — for example, happiness, welfare, pleasure or knowledge. Moral appraisal of a mode of conduct, then, is a matter of judging how well that conduct produces the relevant consequences. The most well known form of consequentialism is utilitarianism. The effective founder of utilitarianism was Jeremy Bentham (1748–1832), an English thinker and social reformer. His guiding moral principle was that the ethically right thing to do is that act which produces a greater sum of utilities than any other act could. In Bentham's case, that meant producing in one's acts a greater amount of pleasure than pain, because he believed that pleasure and pain were the two driving forces of human action. Of course, a puzzle immediately arises here: if humans are driven by pleasure and pain, then why do they need a moral theory to tell them to act to maximise pleasure and minimise pain? After all, other animals are not in need of such guidance. A simple answer to this question is that, as a moral requirement, utilitarianism prescribes that people look not merely to their own pleasure. They should be concerned to maximise pleasure wherever that can be achieved. As a moral prescription, utilitarianism requires agents to be concerned not merely with the consequences which impact upon them, but also with a wider view of pleasure and pain effected more generally.

It is because humans do not act merely from instinct (and that humans can choose to act one way rather than another) that moral theory has a place at all. Later utilitarians, notably his protégé John Stuart Mill (1806–73), refined Bentham's theory, and many twentieth-century followers have since modified it. As to the requirement that individuals look outside themselves, Mill commented:

> the happiness which forms the utilitarian standard of what is right in conduct is not the agent's own happiness but that of all concerned. As between his own happiness and that of others, utilitarianism requires him to be as strictly impartial as a disinterested and benevolent spectator.[10]

Bentham's simple notions of pleasure and pain have come to be replaced with other measures of utility, such as intrinsic goodness, satisfactions, preferences, desires and second order desires. Whatever meaning we might ascribe to 'utility', the basic idea is to maximise benefits and to minimise costs.

In Bentham's vision the greatest happiness of the greatest number was a moral and a democratic principle. The happiness of one person ought not to count for more than the happiness of another. This view accords very well with political liberalism and a free market economy: we choose our lawmakers, our consumables, and our pleasures freely. No one is better than another politically, in the market, or morally. There are no intrinsic moral norms except the maximisation of pleasure and the minimisation of pain.

There are difficulties with this formula to solve human ethical problems. It seems to put all kinds of pleasure-seeking and pain-avoidance on the same footing. Bentham was a radical and did not mind challenging conventional ideas about morality and politics, but his view would have destroyed notions of altruism and self-sacrifice, virtues such as courage, and elementary principles of morality such as telling the truth for its own sake. It would also have put minority and individual rights at risk, allowed the ends of any act to justify the means in an unqualified way and, as John Stuart Mill pointed out, it gave no recognition to human dignity or any spiritual quality in humanity. Mill believed that utilitarianism could accord these important human characteristics their proper due, while still defining 'utility' in terms of pleasure. Mill argued that not all pleasures are on the same footing, that some kinds of pleasures — those requiring intellect — are qualitatively better than others.

It is already clear that there is a great deal of utilitarian thinking in the ways in which business justifies itself ethically. Philosophical discussion, as noted earlier, is present in world affairs.

A great deal of utilitarian thinking is present in the ways in which business justifies itself ethically. This is not at all surprising. Human goods are always at stake in any moral practice. A theory that did not take account of them would be grossly deficient. Our actions have consequences and it is part of being morally responsible to include some appraisal of them in our assessment of conduct. If we could not do so we would be at least partially blind to the morality of our acts. Business and any other practical activity must pay attention to results, to remain viable and to remain ethical.

Modern utilitarianism no longer deals in the somewhat crude measures of pleasure and pain or of intrinsic and extrinsic goods. It is more likely to argue that preferences are to be accommodated as fully as possible. This avoids making value judgments about the interests of others as though there were an independent platform for morally appraising the world. If a business met the preferences of most of those likely to be affected by its actions — the stakeholders — without disproportionately thwarting the preferences of others, then it should have a right to call its actions ethical. After all, every day decisions have to be made in business that are not to the advantage of all. To take care of the interests and preferences of most stakeholders would clearly be the mark of an ethical enterprise for utilitarians.

So much of utilitarian theory seems common sense that it can be difficult to see how rival accounts of morality have a place, but deontological ethics is also a familiar moral outlook.

Nonconsequentialism

Consequentialism identifies the moral worth of conduct in terms of how well that conduct produces some effect. In this respect, consequentialist reasons are 'forward-looking'. They look to the future (the expected consequences which would result from the various actions open to an individual to perform) in order to determine what a person ought to do. In contrast to this, a nonconsequentialist moral outlook is either 'backward-looking' or 'present-looking'. Nonconsequentialism is often called 'deontology', from the Greek etymological root, '*deon*', meaning 'duty'. Nonconsequential — deontological — reasons look to the past or to the present. According to a deontological outlook, an act's being morally right or wrong is due to something other than its consequences. Perhaps, for example, the rightness of an action depends on that action being a matter of keeping a promise that one made (backward-looking). Perhaps the rightness depends on the fact that the other party is a personal friend of yours (present-looking). Deontological ethics requires people to do the right thing simply because it is the right thing to do — regardless of the consequences. What makes a thing right is something other than its consequences; for the deontologist, consequences can never be an adequate ethical justification for an act. The most famous deontologist was the great German philosopher Immanuel Kant (1724–1804). Arguments for a deontological outlook (albeit a non-Kantian one) have been advanced strongly by defenders of individual rights and liberties.[11] Kant's view was that morality is a matter of doing one's duty, regardless of consequences, and that duty itself is determined not by reference to consequences, but by reference to consistency and the requirements of rationality.[12] Consistency is certainly one of the things expected from moral behaviour. If we do not lie to our friends and family, are we being inconsistent and hence immoral if we lie to strangers? Is 'lying' the operative notion here (Kant thought it was), in which case it is clearly a case of being inconsistent, or should some moral weight be given to the fact that on one occasion it is a friend who is the target, and on another occasion it is a stranger? If we do not cheat our neighbours, then are we being inconsistent if we cheat people from other cities, states or nations? Kant claimed a very tight connection between morality and rationality and, in particular, logical consistency. He believed there could be a science of morals just as there is a science of the physical world.

How is this possible? And if it is possible, how is it that people disagree about morality in ways they do not disagree about physics or geology? Kant believed he had developed an argument that answered these questions. He believed that a science of morals is possible because humanity has the use of freedom and reason. We can and should choose our own morality — the subjective part of morality — but we have available an independent objective standard against which to measure our subjective choices: the moral law. When we do any act, we act with an intention and our intention includes a maxim, a general principle. For example, if I intend to give to charity there is in my intention an implicit maxim that one ought to give to charity. That maxim may be tested against a standard of morality which Kant called the 'categorical imperative', and which he formulated in a number of ways, the first of which is 'Act only according to that maxim by which you can at the same time will that it should become a universal law'.[13] This test is a thought experiment that involves generalising an action: What would it be like if everyone behaved like this? Would it be possible? Would it be desirable? For example, say it was my intention to lie for a good cause. Could I universalise the maxim that it was justified to lie in a good cause? Kant would say 'no', because my lying involves people believing that I am telling the truth; generalising my intention to lie would undermine the very institution of telling the truth. In other words, the inconsistency involved is destructive of the moral institution on which lying depends. Suppose I am considering not helping someone who is in need. Could I will that the maxim of not helping become a universal law? Kant says I could not: I can imagine a world in which no one helped anyone else. There is no logical inconsistency involved. But I cannot see it as desirable; I could not will it. For one thing, I cannot but believe that occasionally I will need help myself. And, of course, I will want help on those occasions. A universal law of people not helping each other would be inconsistent with this. Kant produced a second formulation of the categorical imperative, which perhaps is more familiar and certainly very important: 'act so that you treat humanity, whether in your own person or in that of another, always as an end and never as a means only'.[14] This is sometimes expressed as respect for persons. This is a meaningful requirement for business relationships, as well as for individual interpersonal relationships. In business, it means that management and owners should not see employees simply as human resources on the analogy of natural resources: they are first and foremost people deserving of respect. The same would hold for customers, suppliers, creditors and others involved in some way with the conduct of business. This should not be seen as pious theory without the experience of real life to bring it back to earth. Kant does not say that we should not use the abilities of others to make profits. He says that in our dealings with others we must never treat them merely as means to our ends. People should not be treated as objects or as mere instruments to be used to achieve our goals. In all dealings with people, they must be treated as persons, and accorded respect for their dignity as such.

Kant's theory of duty is not about following an imposed list of duties (such as might be found in the armed services), but about being autonomous and rational agents who make choices for which they are responsible. Nor is it about achieving certain satisfactory consequences. Kant's theory effectively provides an intellectual justification for the golden rule (treat others as you would wish to be treated). His argument demands universality, consistency and reversibility. Treat all other people justly without discrimination, just as you would have them treat you. The moral law treats all people equally.

Considering only these two formulations of the categorical imperative,[15] it is clear that Kant has offered an important counter-consideration to consequentialist theories of morality. Moreover, it fits in well with current views about rights and unfair discrimination, such as sexism and racism. The notions of respect for persons and the autonomy of moral agents have played prominent roles in moral reasoning and moral theorising, and can illuminate an understanding of business conduct without forcing a particular ethical theory on anyone. A requirement of maintaining respect for persons can be expressed in a number of moral theories, albeit with varying degrees of success.

Both consequentialist and deontological ethical theories are relevant to business. It is necessary for business to make a profit in order to survive, but not at any cost. And it is necessary for business to take into account interests and consequences other than profit. There are necessary restrictions on what can be traded — cigarettes, alcohol, drugs and weapons, for example — and there are necessary occupational health and safety laws governing working conditions. We still call our markets free despite these and other restrictions, such as anti-discrimination legislation, the prohibition of child labour and taxation. Utilitarian considerations are tempered by respect for persons and their rights. It should be remembered that Adam Smith believed that the pursuit of individual gain could occur only in an environment regulated by ethics and social controls.[16] It is arguable that business requires deontological as well as utilitarian principles if it is to operate as more than a ruthless struggle for wealth. There is a more positive way of putting this: business must respect rights and assume its appropriate duties if it is to meet the expectations of society and enjoy the confidence of its stakeholders. Making a profit is not the only criterion by which business is judged.

What duties does business have? It is easy to spell out a list of specific duties — such as not deceiving, being frank and fair with shareholders, treating colleagues and employees justly — which will save people thinking this question through, but perhaps that is not the most desirable way in which to raise ethical awareness. Even a succinct hierarchy of duties, such as that proposed by William Frankena, will give a better idea of the requirement to reason ethically than attempts to produce lists of specific duties in business. Frankena's hierarchy of duties is this: do no evil, prevent evil, remove evil and do good.[17] These duties, of course, are general in nature; they apply to everyone. So how are they to be connected, if at all, with the conduct of business? Within business, which of these four general duties apply, and when?

In one way it is easy to answer these questions and in another way it is very difficult. It is easy to see that certain professions, as part of their practice, are obliged to do things that others are not. If a medical practitioner sees someone knocked down on the road, then she or he should render the kind of assistance that passers-by cannot give and therefore cannot be obliged to give. If a social worker is as sure as possible that a child is at risk in a family, then he or she might report the matter or take personal action; but if inexperienced or self-righteous people took it into their heads to act on their own views about what is good for children, they might do a great deal of harm. There is in this case not only no duty to intervene, but also a duty not to. In this type of situation it is significantly true that 'it is none of their business'. In our kind of society, no one demands that an individual should be a certain kind of professional. But if anyone takes on a particular area of practice expertise, then extra social obligations may follow. This is the easy answer, at least in the sense that there are social expectations to be met. Exactly what sort is required of any particular profession or professional, and whether anything is similarly required of business per se, will have to remain as questions here.

The difficulty in applying this kind of reasoning to business is that the roles of business people are not as obviously directed at social goods in the manner of the professions. And yet this view seems to suggest that the creation of wealth, employment, and a taxation base for the provision of social benefits such as education, health, defence and welfare is not a legitimate social role. This is not the case at all; the problem is that the boundaries of business are not as clearly defined as those of the professions. And, according to classical economic theory, it is by paying attention to the success of its own enterprises that a business furthers the common good. To abandon good business practice in order to satisfy the kinds of obligations that are attached to medicine or social work would, it seems, be self-defeating.

Virtue ethics

Since the 1970s, there has been a revival of 'virtue ethics', a conception of ethics that dates back to Aristotle. Virtue ethics stresses the kind of moral abilities that put us in a position to act morally, whether after weighty deliberation or quick reaction. This view of ethics focuses on the character of the person performing the action and rejects the idea of dealing with moral problems by applying the correct theory, at least in any mechanical or algorithmic way.[18] Rather, it focuses on a person's response to a moral problem as that of a moral person, that is, one with the requisite character. Moral behaviour is seen in this way, rather than as a conscious and conscientious application of moral theory to practical situations. One of the difficulties of the applied theory view of ethics is time. Say there is no time to consider an ethically important question. Is all ethical responsibility removed from people who do not have time to make calculations of a utilitarian kind? Clearly this is not so. This was recognised by John Stuart Mill, who defended utilitarianism from the charge that its calculations were too complex to allow ready responses to moral problems by referring to the many responses, which are, or can become, second nature to us.[19] He might have been talking of virtue ethics.

In discussing moral reasoning, reference was made to a top-down approach. Perhaps this can be seen as an analogue of the applied theory view. The applied theory view is essentially 'outside-in'. The theory is imposed from without — for example, objective rules, duties, rights, and constraints of utility — and applied as appropriate. A virtue-ethics view sees the process more as 'inside-out'. Moral behaviour should be the result of, and flow from, a person's character. This is not to say that moral behaviour is only automatic or spontaneous. It can indeed involve difficult and perplexing thinking and deliberation. But, on a virtue-ethics view, a person's character and the kind of person they are is integral to the way that person will perceive ethical situations and the way they will think about ethical matters. Cultivation of an ethical person, then, is very largely a matter of developing the right character.

It is commonly — and importantly — said that in order for a corporate plan, a mission statement or a code of ethics to work effectively, it must be 'owned' by all the members of the organisation, it must emanate from within, rather than be imposed from without. And it must be part of the organisation's soul, or character, rather than something of an appendage. It is fair to say that the virtue-ethics concept of ethics sees the relation of ethical behaviour to an individual in general in this way: ethics is not just a matter of what people do; it is a matter of what people are.

As such, there are a couple of different ways in which we can conceive of virtue ethics. One is a straightforward way, in which virtue is of value because it is effective at leading to actions that are morally correct in terms of the consequentialist or deontological theory that one accepts. The other way places value in the virtues themselves in terms other than those of being instrumental in doing what is morally correct on consequentialist or deontological grounds. The first sees virtues as valuable in terms of their being aids towards doing that which, on other grounds, is morally desirable. The second sees virtues as valuable at least partly in terms of their determining what is morally desirable.

It is important to see that, on the first conception of virtue ethics, it is only in a limited sense that it is an 'alternative' or in 'opposition to' consequentialism and deontology. Consequentialism and deontology are both views about what makes right acts right. For the most part, virtue ethics is a view not about what makes right acts right, but about how to go about achieving whatever it is that gives something moral worth, whether it be the production of consequences of some kind or a deontological feature of the situation. A virtue-ethics approach focuses on the qualities of the agent (or the organisation) as the target for development because it is the qualities, or character of the agent or the organisation itself that will result in the morally correct behaviour, whether consequential or deontological. Or, simply put, virtues are virtues for some reason, and depending on a person's moral outlook, that reason will be consequential or deontological (or a mixture of them).

The second conception of virtue ethics, which is perhaps more interesting but also more problematic in terms both of theory and of practical application, can be expressed as 'virtue is as virtue does, and virtue does as virtue is'. According to this concept of what determines the rightness or wrongness of an action, a particular act will be the right act precisely because it is the act that a virtuous person will perform. It is that which makes it the right act. It is not (simply) that a virtuous person will perform right acts, which are right on independent (consequential or deontological) grounds; it is rather that what a virtuous person does determines the rightness of that behaviour. The fact that it is what a virtuous person would do is what makes it right.

Consider the suggestion this way: Mary is a virtuous person; honesty and benevolence are two of her virtues. Her character is such that she acts honestly and benevolently. Suppose that, on a particular occasion, if she tells the truth some harm will result to the public, and if she is to provide for public welfare, she will have to lie. On this occasion, it is impossible for her to both tell the truth and provide for the public welfare. The situation is such that not only can she not both provide for the public benefit and tell the truth; it is also the case that either truth telling or provision for the public benefit will have to be sacrificed on this occasion. What should she do? On this account of virtue ethics, the question is whether, given the situation, Mary could lie and still be an honest person; or whether she could avoid providing for the public benefit and still be a benevolent person. It will depend on the particular situation; and, very importantly, it will depend on the perception of the situation by Mary herself. Given that her character really is honest and benevolent, it is she who will determine (not simply discover) what is the morally correct thing to do. The question will be whether, in this situation, she can lie and still be honest; or whether she can fail to provide for the public welfare and still be benevolent. This will be a matter not only of how she perceives the situation, but how she would perceive herself. At least partly, it will be a matter of whether she could fail to provide for the public welfare and still perceive herself as benevolent. It would be incorrect to describe the situation as one in which either honesty or benevolence must be sacrificed. It is, rather, a situation in which the issue is what honesty and benevolence require. After all, for instance, to tell the truth in a situation where catastrophic effects would result would not exemplify honesty, it would be fanaticism. Such a case is an 'exception which proves the rule' (that is what this phrase means).[20] It is not honesty that gives way; rather, lying in this situation is consistent with being an honest person — it is an exception. In this situation, the person is no less honest for failing to tell the truth.

Many problems are resolved using characteristic modes of behaviour, not as conditioned responses but as a kind of shorthand or use of rules of thumb. We see this in everyday tasks all the time. It is true also of morality. Often it is the case that even when we do deliberate over a moral difficulty we still make our decision not according to a moral algorithm, but according to our character. Further, our character goes a long way towards determining even how we perceive the problem.

Some of these points about virtue ethics may be illustrated through the story of the Roman general Regulus. Captured by the Carthaginians, he was sent back to Rome under oath to exchange himself for certain noble prisoners of war held there. If he did not succeed, he was to return to Carthage and face death. Once in Rome, Regulus persuaded the Senate that it would not be in the interests of Rome to return these brave young warriors to their commands in exchange for the life of an ageing general. So, in the face of his love for family and country, Regulus kept his oath and returned to Carthage to face death by torture. For him, keeping his word was an integral part of the character that made him the person he was. If he had broken his oath because of the commonplace, but for him narrow, conception of self-interest, he could not have lived with his shame.[21] He would have sacrificed an integral part of his character: he would have lost his integrity.

Virtue ethics stresses the kind of moral abilities that put us in a position to act morally, whether after weighty deliberation or as a quick reaction. Both kinds of conduct are regarded as meritorious — or not. Both kinds of conduct are behaviour for which we are responsible.

Relativism

As with our discussion of virtue ethics, where it was important to see that for the most part virtue ethics is addressing a question different from that addressed by consequentialism and deontology as moral outlooks, so it is important to appreciate the location of 'relativism' on the moral map. Moral relativism does not stand opposed to any of those moral outlooks. It too is suggested (by those who advocate it) as an answer to a different question. As well, relativism is concerned with a matter different from that with which virtue ethics is concerned.

Moral relativism is a view according to which moral values are relative to a particular environment. Particular moral values are not universal and they are not absolute. For example, 'When in Rome, do as the Romans do', because in Rome and according to Romans, who are the correct moral judges for behaviour in Rome, that is the morally correct thing to do. Moral truths are relative. Perhaps this means that moral values differ from culture to culture, from society to society, from one time to another or, in the extreme, from one person to another. And perhaps it means that any individual ought to behave in the manner seen to be moral within the environment in which they are operating (when doing business in Rome then, …, and when doing business in Japan, then …). Or, when operating as a private individual, there are certain requirements, and those requirements are different from those that are present when a person operates as an official, an employer or an employee.

It is important to see that moral relativism does not stand as an alternative to utilitarianism and deontology. Moral relativism is, rather, a view about the domain over which any moral position (e.g., utilitarianism) ranges. 'In this country, there's a moral duty to tell the truth.' This claim does not invoke a position other than deontology; it identifies the domain relative to which a particular duty is present. Relativism stands in opposition to 'absolutism', a view according to which there is only one universally correct moral position.

Relativism need not stand as a barrier to conversation between various perspectives and environments. A commitment to moral relativism should not prevent a person from being converted from one (relativistic) perspective to another (relativistic) perspective, and adopting it. We can allow the possibility of 'moral pluralism' (more than one moral view, all of which are equally 'correct'), while still insisting that there can be fruitful moral discussion, argument and conversion from one moral view to another.

There is a considerable philosophical literature on moral relativism that we cannot go into here.[22] Nevertheless, it is important to clear up some of the confusions that arise because people quite rightly believe in tolerating cultural difference and imagine that this toleration commits them to a position of indifference on ethical principles. These confusions are descriptive and normative. The descriptive component is this: there is no reason to assume on the basis of present experience that, say, a universal ethics could not exist. For example, before the British settled in Australia, it was assumed in England that all swans were white. Further experience showed this to be false. The normative fallacy is this: ethics is a prescriptive matter, and to assume on the practice of many cultures that what is practised should be practised is a fallacious move from what *is* the case to what *ought* to be the case. The practical effect of this conceptual point may be illustrated by way of women's rights. The fact that women were not given equal career opportunities with men was used to deny them those opportunities; what was the case was used to argue that there should be no change.

However, it does not follow that, because there are a variety of moral rules, there are no fundamental principles. From two different perspectives, Marcus Singer and John Finnis have argued that universal principles and goods can generate a variety of rules.[23] Thus a moral pluralism in the cultural sense could be grounded on commonly shared universal principles. The general argument is that although specific rules might differ from culture to culture, they are nevertheless grounded in the same overarching principles. We cannot take up the philosophical argument here, but it is important to signal that the argument is two-sided, and that simplistic notions of moral relativism derived from cultural difference should not be used as an evasion of ethical reasoning, which requires justification and the other features noted earlier.

Relativism in business is most often discussed in terms of foreign trade or the conduct of operations in foreign states. Usually the argument comes to this: in country X you cannot do business by our rules. You have to realise that they have different expectations, and that the only way to deal satisfactorily with them is to play by their rules. What this kind of justification often amounts to is not respect for a host culture, but excuses for inducements, secret commissions and bribes. If a person respects the religious and cultural conventions of a country that does not permit the consumption of alcohol, then excuses are not necessary. Genuine respect is almost self-explanatory.[24] But the payment of induce-ments is anything but self-explanatory; it requires excuses. What if everyone agrees that bribes are necessary to do deals? This was very much the case in the early European settle-ment of Australia when convicts were unlikely even to unload much-needed food unless they were persuaded with a measure of rum. In the Soviet Union, vodka was a similar kind of currency. Yet in neither case were bribes of alcohol recognised as legitimate. On the contrary, they were signs of a corrupt system generally.

A business is obliged to operate in a manner acceptable to the host country, both legally and morally. To claim the mantle of cultural difference to justify secret commissions is akin to racism. All kinds of threats are made against businesses in Australia in a bid to secure special conditions or unearned benefits. The evidence of the royal commission into the building industry in New South Wales contains many examples of union pressure against builders and vice-versa, but no one thought that this could be made acceptable by refer-ence to cultural or moral relativism.[25] When questionable pressures are placed on firms operating overseas, they must deal with them in the same way that they would handle similar pressures at home. Part, but only part, of what they should ask themselves is whether the person (or firm) putting on the pressure believes that there is no moral impropriety in what they are doing. Other central questions they should ask themselves are these: Would the government and public of the host country countenance this kind of pressure? Would our shareholders welcome disclosure of our conduct and approve of us acceding to this pressure? Would we welcome disclosure to the Australian government and public of secret commissions or other favours?

In other words, if you would not be ashamed to declare your actions to the world, you have probably not done anything that stands in need of an excuse. Cultural and moral rela-tivity do not come into it. In fact, the normal hospitality and gift-giving that is part of busi-ness needs no excuses or appeals to relativism. When the gifts become more substantial — such as trips to Fiji, or computers, or cars — then it is wise for a company to draft policies and procedures which are made known to clients and staff so that there is no room for misunderstanding. Again, this is common sense and does not necessitate reference to, or a special position for, relativism. 'Relativism' is not synonymous with 'ignore your own moral values'. If anything, it is a requirement to recognise the legitimacy of moral views other than the one relative to you. It is not obviously a directive for you to become a moral chameleon.

Testimony to this is the United States *Foreign Corrupt Practices Act* of 1977. This law makes it illegal for any American citizen or resident to bribe or induce any foreign official or candidate for office to act corruptly to further the business interests of that person. This Act was passed into law relatively quickly over the objections of business leaders, who asserted that payments were often extorted by foreign officials rather than offered as bribes, and that the government should not intervene to prevent managers obtaining the best returns for their shareholders.[26] In the light of such objections, it is not surprising that Congress passed the Foreign Corrupt Practices Act into law so promptly.

Business

Business is the world's oldest profession. Since the beginning of organised society the buying and selling of goods and services have been important means of encouraging the production and distribution of social necessities. Because of the importance of individual initiative and competition in these processes, those who confer mythical powers on the market may overlook the social purpose of business. As with the mythical heroes of legend, great honour has been bestowed on entrepreneurs and their deeds, and the vocabulary of battle and chase has dramatised the mundane affairs of exchange. Of course, if business were like war, no society would or could tolerate it. Business exists not because it suits certain individuals, but because it serves society, and meets collective and individual needs.

This is not, of course, how business is usually presented. The traditional view is that the true market system is essentially free. Adam Smith's view that individual preferences combine to produce order from self-interest is no doubt comforting to rampant individualists, but implicit in all legitimate business transactions is a social licence.[27]

Free markets are a matter of choice, and from time to time societies — or, more usually, governments — have chosen to dispense with them and work through command mechanisms. Although command economies might not have been very successful, they retain a strong attraction for many people. Therefore, business in market economies needs to be mindful that it enjoys its position because society believes that the benefits of the system outweigh the costs. This is even more true of modern societies because of the dominant role in them of corporations and the privileges, such as tax concessions and limited liability, which they enjoy.

Imagine that you are the distributor of a leading brand of desktop computers. You are expecting a big fall in price on your new top-line model in the next quarter, but you have a lot of old stock on hand. As news of the lower price on the more powerful model has not become public, you can continue selling its predecessor without discounting the price. If word were to get out, people would defer their purchases until the more powerful and competitively priced model came on the market, so you warn your staff to be very careful with such sensitive commercial information. One of your staff comes to see you to question this policy. He argues that it is taking advantage of people to deny them access to information that will allow them to make a proper purchasing decision. 'What about your moral duty to the community?' he asks. Your sales manager replies that there is a difference between concealing and not revealing. 'I am not at the moment revealing to you the theory of relativity, but I am hardly concealing it from you', she tells him. 'There is no ethical issue here.' Which of them is right?

Take another case. You are selling a house you have come to dislike. When a buyer comes to inspect it you say nothing about its defects. The buyer makes no enquiries and seems perfectly happy to buy it as it is. Your sister cannot believe that the buyer has not found out about the problems of the house and asks how you can sell a house you know to be defective. 'If you did that in your shop you wouldn't have any customers and the Trade Practices Commission would be after you', she says. 'If it's wrong to sell faulty merchandise, why isn't it wrong to sell a faulty house?' Your brother has a different view. '*Caveat emptor*', he says. 'Let the buyer beware. No one can expect the vendor to do the buyer's job as well.' While you have not disclosed the defects of the house, you have not concealed them. It is the buyer's responsibility to make the appropriate investigations before the purchase. Who is more correct here: your sister or your brother?

One response to these questions is that silence *per se* is not concealment. Concealment lies in seeking your profit by keeping from others information in which they have an interest.[28] Unfortunately, such a definition of 'concealment' does not help us resolve the issues in these cases. At an auction buyers conceal the very thing that it is in the interest of other parties to know, namely the figure they are prepared to pay. Similarly, sellers at auction conceal the amount they are prepared to accept. Concealment is a more complex matter than simply calculating who profits from it.

While we have become used to the notion that certain acts are intrinsically wrong, the attempt to catalogue these for easy reference is shown in these cases to be flawed. It is not concealment *per se* which is wrong, but preventing others from making an informed contract. Quite simply, it is dealing with others on terms that are deliberately set up to disadvantage them. The vice of dishonesty is the thing to discern here, not the relatively simple matter of concealment, which in the case of a surprise party may be a necessary means to the realisation of a good. These cases stop one or two steps before fraud, and so are particularly interesting. Falling short of open fraud makes them morally debatable, thus revealing that something more than a simple moral algorithm is required to resolve them.

There would seem to be a *prima facie* case for some social responsibility on the part of business, and it might be assumed that debate would focus on the extent of that responsibility. But this is not how some writers see it. And it is in this disagreement that fundamental problems of business ethics arise. The standard non-interventionist position was once held by Peter Drucker.[29] He put the case with classic simplicity: society sets the ground rules for business, and business has no other duty than to follow those rules in pursuing its interests. It is not for business to usurp the democratic processes of public policy-making by taking decisions on the spurious grounds of social responsibility. Business ethics is a matter of observing the law of the land and acting fairly. It is not a matter of individual managers or boards assuming responsibilities foisted on them by people who believe that business should pick up the tab for schemes of social improvement.

Milton Friedman has argued for an even stronger directive: not only does business not have a duty to have an eye towards social responsibility; business has a positive duty not to have an eye in that direction.[30] Friedman argues that the notion of social responsibility in business is objectionable. Managers and directors owe a fiduciary duty to shareholders, not to society or putative stakeholders. We elect legislators to make policy in democracies: for non-elected officials to do so violates the democratic mandate, and allows the injection of private decisions, values and priorities into public life. A legislator has to consider the reactions of many parts of society, and seldom has the luxury of indulging personal whims, preferences or values. By contrast, people of conscience (those who would include social responsibility as part of their job-descriptions) have no constituency to answer to: they are defending their personal integrity, which, ironically, is responsible not to society but to themselves as individuals. This may be individually satisfying but it is not, according to Friedman, socially justifiable. It is not mandated, and it is not democratic. There are two things here then: the first is the questionable fairness of placing the burden of social responsibility on individuals; the second is the wisdom of placing it on groups or organisations whose continuing benefits are important to society. In any case, the notion of social responsibility is hardly trouble-free. In a liberal society, the question immediately arises, 'Responsible to whom?' While many accept that they belong to a society, this loose sense of belonging is at the very least questionable. Liberal societies are nowadays more legal communities than moral ones, and this makes public accountability in matters of ethics rather tricky.

The work of philosopher Jonathan Dancy suggests an interesting way in which the question of business accountability might be conceived. He distinguishes between values and moral reasons which apply to everyone generally, and those that apply specifically to certain persons or to persons in certain situations. He illustrates the distinction in the following way. Imagine that you install a phone in your home that will give different rings for different members of the family. In addition to the usual phone number and ringing tone for the common family number, members each have their own number that gives a distinctive ring when their numbers are dialled. All the rings are audible to all the family, but unless the general number is dialled, only the person whose distinctive tone rings feels called to answer it. Others may answer it, just as they might answer an absent colleague's phone in the office, but there is not the same 'obligation' or the same 'call' to do so as when a person's own number rings. If someone is able to take a call and a message for another member of the family, well and good, but if that person is busy or resting, they might prefer to let the caller ring back. People do not feel called in quite the same way as if their own ring or the general ring were sounded.[31]

This is how it is in ethics. The fact that there are personal calls directed to us does not mean that ethics is subjective. On the contrary, for much of the time others can hear our number ringing and may wonder why we do not answer it. Should we, in business, answer the call when it is the general number that is ringing? Should we, in business, pick up a call for someone else when they are not answering? In the following chapters we identify some of the distinctive moral calls to which business should respond. We can be sure that, if business ignores these calls directed specifically to it, then others will decide to answer them to stop the phone ringing. And they might well be hostile to business for having to do so. It would at the very least be prudential, then, for business to heed well the call of ethics.

Moral Pluralism

Recently, a number of writers on ethics and ethical theory have seriously discussed and advocated moral pluralism.[32] There are different types of moral pluralism, and different writers have suggested different approaches. The general idea, however, is that there is no one single moral theory or principle which should be accepted as preferable to others. Rather, there are different, diverse and even mutually inconsistent ethical positions that should be recognised, and there is not necessarily any single moral principle or set of principles that everyone should accept, either because they are true or because they are preferable in some other respect. Although similar in a number of respects, moral pluralism is not the same thing as moral relativism, which, as we have been discussing, claims that moral correctness is relative to time, place, and people. Moral pluralism is not making a claim about relativities.

Good ethics is good business

Shortly after the publication of the first edition of this text, an article by Geoffrey Barker appeared in the *Financial Review Magazine* that was partly a review of the book and partly an article on business ethics generally.[33] Barker understood the first edition to be largely neglecting the possibility that self-interested motives could, in fact, produce ethical behaviour, and that often good ethics can simply be a matter of good business sense.[34] In this respect, Barker was accusing us of unnecessarily taking the moral high ground in the analysis of any moral problem, while neglecting that good business sense can often coincide with ethical requirements and that, in many cases, even where the motives would be considerably different, the outcome is the same — namely, ethical business practice. Barker was urging that, in this context, we should not be so critical of self-interested motives. Barker's concern is an important one. There can be no denying that many apparent ethical problems can be viewed as problems of good business management, *sans* ethics. But this is not the case with all ethical problems.

We should consider this a bit further.[35] The phrase 'good ethics is good business' has received much discussion. Some have suggested that there is nothing peculiar about the issue of ethics in business, arguing that good business decisions as business decisions will, as a matter of course, be ethical, and will certainly not be unethical.[36] That is, some have suggested that there is nothing additional to infuse into good business decisions in order to make them ethical — that a concern to do the ethically right thing need not be a constraint upon business decisions. In this respect, they have suggested, good ethics is good for the bottom line. There is nothing special about 'good ethics': ethically sound decisions will be sound business decisions; the two coincide.[37] We can call this 'the Hobbesian view': the basis and sole concern of ethics is self-interest.[38]

At the other extreme, some have suggested that if all we are talking about is good business management, then we are not talking about ethics at all.[39] This group would suggest that it is not possible for good ethics to be good business. Rather, ethical behaviour functions as a limit or a constraint on, or a correction to, what business may do as business. Ethics and business naturally stand in opposition to each other. Further, decisions made for the sake of sound business management are not, properly speaking, ethical, even when they happen to coincide with ethical requirements. Ethical decisions are, properly speaking, ethical only when they are made in the context of their being in conflict with advantageous business decisions. It is this awareness that, in fact, makes the decision an ethical one. Perhaps we can call this 'the Kantian view': to be an ethical decision, it must be made in the awareness of its conflict with self-interest.[40]

It is worth considering further the scope of arguments that good ethics is good business. Much of the discussion of this topic has seen the question too much in terms of polarisation: either good ethics is directly and immediately good business or else good ethics is not good business. Among other things, this view is too simplistic. Ethical behaviour can be related in a number of ways to furthering self-interest. Possible relationships between ethical behaviour and the bottom line are actually more varied than simply the two extremes of being immediately connected or not being connected at all.

At least for a while, we will ignore the suggestion that ethical decisions can occur only in matters of personal conflict, and that ethical decisions must reflect a decision to forego enhancing the bottom line (Kant's position). Consider these five possible connections between ethical behaviour and the promotion of a business's self-interest:

1 *Straightforward or simple coincidence*

In some cases, doing the ethical thing (or avoiding the unethical thing) is actually the best course of action with respect to self-interest. There is a straightforward coincidence between ethical behaviour and the enhancement of one's interest; the two go hand in hand. For example, the stockholders will read about your activity in the newspaper, and your company's share prices will rise or fall accordingly. People do not want to do business with perceived immoral operators. Or, as Paul Simons has suggested, ethical decision-making will coincide with decisions that are straightforwardly good business decisions — decisions that are straightforwardly good in enhancing the bottom line.[41] Sometimes the enhancement is not immediate or short-term, but rather produces long-term benefits that are, all things considered, the best for the business. Here, one need not have an eye on ethical requirements for any reason other than their direct relationship to good business sense. It is not difficult to think of examples here. For instance, think about the business value of one's reputation for qualities like honesty, integrity, and conscientiousness. Here, then, are cases of a straightforward coincidence, a clear and direct connection between good ethics and good business.

2 *Self-preservation via socially created, institutional coincidence*

Sometimes, doing the ethical thing will be the best thing to do for the sake of self-interest, but not because the ethical thing straightforwardly coincides with the best business decision. Rather — given the community's or society's interest in avoiding certain kinds of business conduct (or, more exceptionally, in fostering certain kinds of conduct) — if the business itself does not regulate its behaviour accordingly, then either the business itself or a particular mode of business activity will be made the subject of external regulation or will fall afoul of already existing external regulation. Perhaps the simplest and grossest illustration of such conduct derives from a consideration of laws that do not apply exclusively to a particular area of business conduct. Usually it is in business's self-interest not to engage in fraud — or at least society has tried to enact legislation so that it will be against business's self-interest to behave in this way. The risks to self-interest and the penalties for so behaving are enough to outweigh the potential benefits of fraud. Therefore, it makes straightforwardly good business sense not to be unethical in this regard. A business person does not need to have an eye specifically on ethics here; it is enough to have an eye on what is likely to be good (or bad) for business. Business also recognises that, with respect to some of society's concerns about regulation and ethical behaviour, business itself is presented with two alternatives: either regulate its own conduct in a certain area (that is, make sure that it reaches some standard of ethical acceptability) or else have that conduct regulated from without. And usually, from the perspective of self-interest, business finds it more appealing to behave ethically or to impose ethical requirements on itself than to have such requirements imposed from without. It is better for business's bottom line this way. Notice that the coincidence here is not a straightforward one. Rather, society has engineered this coincidence. Aside from specific laws, think, for instance, of the position of the Independent Commission against Corruption[42], requirements that businesses have codes of ethics and the like, and, in the United States, the existence of the Federal Sentencing Guidelines, which take into account the ethical environment in which a breach was committed. Perhaps it is the case that society in general, although not business in particular, does have its eye on ethical behaviour *per se*, and it is because of this that good business sense in this area will produce ethical conduct. Nevertheless, from the perspective of the business person, situations like this require focus only on self-interest to appreciate that behaving ethically will be beneficial.

3   *A little effort*

In some situations, it can be in a business's self-interest to do the ethical thing, but only if it does more than simply do the ethical thing. For example, if the business publicises having done something with moral merit, it can get some bottom-line mileage out of its action. Chrysler Motors set up a car buyers' bill of rights, articulating the guaranteed quality of its products and the guaranteed performance of the company in certain areas. It also set up a formal consumer protection 'tribunal' to insure that performance was up to scratch; if it was not, the tribunal was empowered to impose sanctions on the company.[43] (This was ethically commendable performance.) By itself, establishing such a tribunal might or might not (and probably would not) have enhanced the company's bottom line. However, Chrysler used this ethical performance as the basis of an advertising campaign explaining why people should do business with them. And this was good for business. It was not the ethical behaviour by itself that accomplished this. It was, rather, the extra effort made by the company in publicising that behaviour. Here, too, it is not difficult to come up with more examples: Saturn motor cars in the USA, with their hassle-free showrooms and non-negotiable car prices, are committed to this as their marketing strategy (not to mention the fact that they publicise their environmentally and employee friendly factory). The Body Shop, and its promotion of its practice of not selling products that have been tested on animals, is a particularly well-known example.[44]

4   *Lateral thinking or augmentation*

Doing the ethical thing can be augmented (or protected) so that it serves the business's self-interest. However, without this augmentation, it is not clear that this would be so; indeed, it would appear not to be so. For example, a building company that had established a reputation for quoting accurately and completing its jobs on time found that its competitors were understating both time and costs — and winning contracts away from this company. The competitors' quotes were initially lower than this company could honestly offer. But then, within legally acceptable parameters, the construction times and costs of the competitors would increase once the jobs were underway. This, of course, had been anticipated by those competitors. To protect its virtues of honesty and integrity (to protect its ethical behaviour) in this atmosphere, the company decided to offer a bond along with its quotes. The company said to its clients, 'If we fail to deliver in terms of time and costs, the bond is forfeit. All we ask is that you ask our competitors to do the same'.[45] The result was that the company successfully protected its moral behaviour and, with the augmentation of that ethical behaviour, turned its virtues into a benefit for the company's bottom line. This differs from position 3 in that something extra is required here in order to prevent the ethical behaviour from actually being detrimental to self-interest. Here it is a matter of engineering protection for the ethical behaviour (creating a situation in which the ethical behaviour will, in fact, be good for business), not merely publicising its existence. In position 3, it is the ethical behaviour itself that can be promoted in such a way that it serves self-interest. In this case, however, it is not only a matter of promotion; it is also a matter of augmentation or protection.

5   *Good for the practice*

Ethical behaviour might be opposed to self-interest in the short-term, while nevertheless enhancing the practice of business. The result is that, eventually, generically, it serves self-interest. Ethical behaviour can help to define or redefine what the practice of business (or a particular business) is about — perhaps by redefining the playing field. This can inform the argument that business should be more professional, for instance. This point is of vital importance in discussing the ethical constraints on, and goals of, business,[46] but it should not be confused with an aspect of position 1 above: that ethical behaviour does not produce an enhanced bottom line in the short term, but does enhance the bottom line in the long term (as in, for instance, short-term and long-term investments). The point here is rather more complex, and contentious: it involves a change in the practice as well as in perceptions of what the practice is about. Simply, changing the character of the practice from one thing to another (for example, changing it to a profession) creates an environment in which business can enjoy the benefits of that new status.

One argument for the creation of 'the profession of business' is that if the practice of business is re-defined, then ethical behaviour must be regarded as benefiting self-interest (at least in certain areas). Ethical behaviour and self-interest will coincide, although not in the simple way suggested in position 1.

Perhaps part of what becomes redefined here is the very notion of 'self-interest', as well as the type of person or business practice that we are. Somewhere in this process, options for unethical behaviour can simply disappear. They do not occur to the practitioners of the practice; they are not consistent with what the practice is (or has become). Consider the following analogy. Angela is honest (perhaps to a fault). When put in a position in which some people might lie, she will not even consider whether she wants to lie (or whether it could be in her interest to lie). Rather, given the type of person she is, lying is not one of the options available to her. Telling the truth (or not) is not seen, or appreciated, by Angela as negotiable. In the same way, becoming a different type of practice — with its attendant outlook and potential benefits — can produce a different ethical environment, a difference in character and greater benefits in terms of self-interest. Just as some people are 'more ethical', it can be argued that some types of practice are inherently 'more ethical'. This point is contentious, and we note it merely for your consideration. Much of what we try to illustrate throughout the book is based on professionalising business conduct.

6   *Not good at all*

This is the polar opposite of position 1: in this type of case, there is no coincidence whatsoever between good business and good ethics. In such cases, doing the ethical thing is contrary to self-interest, no matter what. Some people have denied that this is a genuine possibility (certainly Hobbes did). It is certainly a view that would not be at all popular among those who advocate that good ethics is good business — and more particularly, among those who advocate that the reason *why* businesses would be ethical is *because* that is good for business. Consider the following simple thought experiments, however:

a   *The Ford Pinto case*

Let us assume that no one would ever have discovered this car's tendency to explode on impact. On this assumption, would it be ethically permissible to allow its production to continue? 'No' is the answer. On the same assumption, would it have been a sound business decision — in the sense of enhancing the bottom line — to allow production to continue? Yes, of course.

b   *An Ok Tedi story*

Assume that in the early days, when the water contamination from BHP's Papua New Guinean mine at Ok Tedi was discovered by, and affected, just a few isolated people, it was possible to 'resolve' the entire matter by annihilating a few families — no one else would ever know. Considering only the benefits for business, this would have been the course of action to take. A crass cost–benefit analysis would point in this direction. Would it be ethical to do this? No.

c   *Nestlé's baby formula*

When Nestlé sold its baby milk powder to Third World countries, they had the opportunity to get rid of their surplus and to make some profit. While exploiting such an opportunity could be good for business, there are other reasons why a company should not behave in this way. Although these reasons might not coincide with self-interest, business should nevertheless pay attention to them. This is exactly the point.

The point in all these cases is that sometimes there need not be coincidence between ethical behaviour and the advancement of self-interest. The further point is that, even so, the right thing for business to do in each case is to take the ethical course of action, foregoing self-interest. Why? – because ethics requires it. That is the nature of ethics.

You might be thinking, in each of these cases, that as a matter of fact someone would find out, and so the business would suffer. (Maybe this could be called 'the Aquinas position': even though you should do the ethical thing for ethical reasons, there will nevertheless be a coincidence with self-interest).[47] But that is a different thought experiment. The thought experiment here involves supposing that people *do not* find out — and supposing they do not; then what? It is not ethically permissible in these cases to cover up or disregard the dangers. The ethically required action is simply not good for business.

It might seem as though these points border on the obvious. It is clear, however, that this kind of thinking has escaped many who believe that good ethics will always naturally coincide with good business — in one way or another — and that the task set in discussions of business ethics is to find the coincidence or ways to make them coincide. Further, this kind of thinking appears either to have escaped or to have been regarded as unacceptable by those who demand that the only convincing reason for behaving ethically is that it is good for business. These are two very separate concerns. As for the first — that ethics and good business must coincide — we have nothing more to say. As for the second — that the only acceptable or convincing reason for behaving ethically is that ethical behaviour also enhances self-interest — we will expand on this further.

If we were identifying the criteria for an ethical opinion (not necessarily a correct ethical opinion), as well as nominating features such as universality, justifiability and possibly 'overridingness', we would probably make reference to impartiality and the necessity of taking a broader perspective than self-interest.[48] For reasons such as this, moral philosophers most commonly think that 'ethical egoism' (not to be confused with 'psychological egoism')[49] is an incoherent position; as an ethical position, it is a 'non-starter', precisely because it identifies one's self-interest as the reference point for the moral world and the gauge of what is morally right and morally wrong. When it comes to thinking about individuals – and simply getting along in the world – it is generally accepted that doing the morally right thing will sometimes differ from acting in one's own interest. While serious questions are often asked about why one should adopt a moral perspective, rarely would we question the proposition that a moral perspective has a broader basis than self-interest alone. Given this, why should there be so much concern to say that the situation in business is different — that good ethics must enhance the bottom line (that is, that ethical behaviour must advance self-interest)? It would seem that those who have pushed this line so hard have ignored the situation for individuals — perhaps in their hurry to offer an easy, prudentially acceptable and palatable reason for business to be ethical. For individuals, sometimes doing the morally right thing works in one's interest, but not always. The situation for business is no different. Perhaps an insistence on the coincidence of ethics and self-interest is an attempt or demand to make the difficult ethical questions easier to comprehend and resolve than, in fact, they are. The important and difficult question 'Why should I be moral?' is no more easily answered for business than it is for individuals.

The search for the ethical–prudential coincidence in business could, in fact, lead to a different conclusion. One might take the view that morality is none of business's business. Perhaps we can call this 'the Friedman view', after Milton Friedman's bold claims in the late 1960s and 1970s about the inappropriateness of allowing ethical concerns into the business arena.[50] From this perspective, business is seen as appropriately out of the moral realm altogether; it is a non-moral or an amoral operator in much of what it does and in much of what it should be thinking about and concerning itself with. Notice, however, that this is a significantly different proposition from the one that suggests that the activities of business are within the moral realm and that the carrying out of those activities should, or can be made to, coincide with the business's self-interest. The Friedman view is an important view to take account of, but it is completely different from — and largely irrelevant to — the discussion here, where it is recognised that business can engage in moral or immoral behaviour, and suggests that reasons should be moral. The plot has been lost when this suggestion has been coupled with the expectation or demand that the only important reasons should be those that point to the coincidence of morality and self-interest.

It is perhaps worth comparing the situation regarding business and ethics to the relationship between law and ethics. Here too, we can usefully look at the individual's relationship with the law in order to draw a parallel with business. In matters of individuals' behaviour, we do not think that law covers the entire area of ethical concerns — and we do not think that it is appropriate for it to do so. Some things are morally wrong, even though they are not illegal (for example, common cases of lying or promise-breaking or breaches of trust). The fact that these modes of behaviour are not ones in which the law reinforces moral requirements by no means implies that, therefore, there is no reason to behave ethically in such situations. Indeed, this distinction lies at the very heartland of ethical theorising and discussion. Again, for someone who suggests that business ethics is completely covered by law (or else that there is no reason for behaving ethically), we should seriously ask why the situation for business should be regarded as different from that for individuals. The answer, we think, is that they should not be regarded differently from each other at all.

There is a serious danger present in 'good ethics is good business' talk and in conceptualising the situation so that this is, in fact, an appropriate way to speak about business and ethics, and about reasons for business to behave ethically. Consider what the point is in making the claim that good ethics is good business. The point is to offer an answer to the question, 'why be ethical?' The answer is, 'because it's good for business.' This sounds straightforward enough, but there is a very worrisome implication of thinking of things in this way, namely, that if some bit of ethical behaviour were *not* good for business, then it would be permissible (in whatever important sense that the listener is supposed to be taking account of) to engage in that bit of behaviour. The idea that ethical considerations might counterbalance or act as a constraint on other considerations is simply dismissed. Ethics is considered to be on the same side of the scale as anything (else) that is good for business. There is no counterbalance at all.

The difficulty in seeing the business situation as one in which good ethics is good business is that this way of speaking invites one to place ethical behaviour on a scale – a scale measuring what is good for the business. The idea, then, is to see where the heaviest weight lies. And this is precisely the danger. The implication is that if the heavier weight lay on the scale in opposition to ethical behaviour, then it is that non-ethical behaviour which should 'win', and so be permissible (in whatever relevant sense), despite the fact of its being unethical. This way of conceptualising the situation places ethical behaviour as just one of the many considerations to be taken into account, the focus of all of which is directed solely toward how good they would be for business. 'Good ethics is good business' implies that the reason for behaving ethically is that such behaviour is good for business, and that if it were good (or better) for business for one to behave unethically, then unethical behaviour would be permissible, perhaps even obligatory. The claim that 'good ethics is good business' implies that ethical behaviour is of instrumental value only. If that were so, then on any particular occasion when ethical behaviour was not perceived to be instrumental toward the achievement of whatever *is* of value, there would be no rationale for behaving ethically.

A note on self-interest

It is not uncommon for people to refer all conduct, including apparently altruistic acts, to self-interest. In business, this unexamined assumption has widespread popularity and has almost attained the status of a dogma. For the characters in films like *Wall Street* and *Bonfire of the Vanities*, drive and ambition are indistinguishable from greed and selfishness. Self-interest has become a shorthand term for both vicious and laudable motives in business, but this does nothing but confuse important issues.

First, self-interest is not identical to selfishness. Selfishness is an undue regard for one's own interests at the expense of regard for the reasonable interests of others. Self-interest may be expressed in observing the dress code at work, in eating a balanced diet, or simply in personal hygiene. None of these instances could be called selfish. Selfishness is an excessive preoccupation with one's own interests, possessions and enthusiasms, even to the exclusion of a proper regard for self-interest. Some business people are so selfishly ambitious that they destroy the very thing they value. It was not, for example, in Alan Bond's interest for Bond Corp to collapse. Sometimes selfishness and self-interest coincide, but they are not conceptually identical. On the whole, it is not in a person's interests to behave selfishly or to be perceived as selfish, but some selfish people are heedless of their own best interests. They might, say, lead a wealthier lifestyle, but this is not a good commensurable with other goods, such as friendship, respect, trust and admiration. The absence of these goods cannot be compensated for by money: they are incommensurable. Selfishness is an inability to count another's good as a reason for acting. It is a socially disabling vice. Self-interest is not disabling in this way. It can be excessive, but it also enables us to live our day-to-day lives in a reasonable way. It is not to be devalued. It is, after all, the pursuit of one's own good, and as long as that good does not exclude the good of others, self-interest not only helps us survive but to prosper and to spread that prosperity to others.[51]

Of course, if self-interest did explain all conduct, this would be something we could never know. This is because it is a view that cannot be falsified: there is no possible set of circumstances that could refute it, so we could never know that it underlies everything we do. In the light of this, claims that people are egoistic in all their acts look very weak and we must seek a richer moral vocabulary with which to describe our ethical experiences.

Case studies and moral theory

What is the best way to present materials so that they will help people to think logically about practical matters? At one extreme, this question is answered: 'Go heavy on the theory'. The point here is that to reason well about practical moral matters, one must be well acquainted with moral theory. We might think of moral behaviour as principled behaviour. If this is so, then in order to reason about moral matters, one must be well schooled in moral principles: what they are and their various rationales. One must develop one's own moral position. This extreme view would continue, 'Once you've come to terms with moral theory, which itself can take years, you've done all the preparation that is necessary for getting out into the world and dealing with practical moral problems. Solid grounding in moral theory is, in fact, what is required for dealing with moral problems at any level'. The other extreme advocates elaborate case studies as the way to help people reason about practical moral problems. The Harvard Business School's case studies are in this mould. This position argues that we don't need to deal with moral theory at all; what we need are detailed case studies. The idea here is that this is the way the real world comes to us: detailed cases, not packaged in theory. What we need practice in is ways in which to sort through and sort out the details with the aim of reaching a moral decision.

We do not favour either of these methods. Each has serious flaws. Briefly, although theory is very important, we do not think that, by itself, it is sufficient to help readers connect with practical moral matters. We have tried to indicate this in the previous discussion about what is at work in moral reasoning, which we suggested is not simply a matter of top-down reasoning. On the other hand, case studies, by themselves, do not reveal the proper importance of theory. In dealing with particular cases, one's consideration should be 'informed' by theory. There is another difficulty with elaborate case studies. A detailed case study often presents itself as a complete picture: no loose ends, no missing pieces, and no particular nuances that need further investigation or further interpretation. Very often, however, the moral world does not present itself in this way. There is more left to do, more left to speculate about; many things are unknown. And sometimes the environment in which the decision must be made is one in which such loose ends remain and cannot be tied up before it is incumbent on us to reach a decision. Generally, the moral world we encounter in real life is a good deal less clear and less complete than that of a self-contained case study.

What we present here are short — some are very short — case studies, which we invite you to consider, being mindful that discussions should be informed by theory. We do not expect that the introduction to moral theory that we have provided in this chapter is where your thinking about moral theory will begin and end. We certainly do not think that the purpose of encountering moral theory is merely to enable you to label things properly. Similarly, the case studies are not the 'be all and end all' of the factual situations that you should consider.

Why case studies?

The connections between ethical reasoning and business are best discussed in relation to cases. Case studies exemplify problems and allow for complexity and ambiguity, but above all, they have the virtue of being believable. On the one hand, it is easy to dismiss talk in terms of principles as sermonising or else as having only academic interest. On the other hand, empirical surveys of beliefs and values might be useful in diagnosing a problem, but they do not tell us what to do. If we are content with our present ways of doing things, then surveys can confirm our beliefs. But we cannot find out what to do simply from looking at what we have done. Case studies tell us more than what we have done; they illustrate values, reasoning, reactions, decisions and consequences. They tell us something of the character of a practice. Take for example the issue of whether what is legal is ethical. Very often there is a close alignment between the two, but often it is to the advantage of one party to insist on what is legal to the detriment of what is ethical. In the following short cases that illustrate this, other kinds of questions are raised as well. These do not extinguish ethical questions, nor does ethics exhaust all important issues for consideration.

Case 1.1   Country Estate share offer

In the early 1990s, a Melbourne securities dealer, Country Estate and Agency Company Pty Ltd, approached pensioners and other small shareholders offering to buy their shares below market value. An ethical issue arises because Country Estate targeted people who did not understand the workings of the stock market. Asked about such tactics, David Tweed of Country Estate gave a typical market defence: 'People can accept [the offers] or reject them. If they don't like them they can put them in the rubbish bin'.[52] But to inexperienced shareholders, Tweed's offers had the aspect of a service. He was thus in a position to build a valuable share portfolio at bargain prices. The Australian Securities Commission investigated the matter at the time and decided that it was not illegal and could not be stopped. Subsequent events have changed this picture, which is more fully presented in Case 4.2, but the point to notice here is that Country Estate denied that there was an ethical problem in offering this service because what they were doing was not illegal. 'It's a free country'.[53] Indeed it is, but that does not mean that people may operate on the assumption that if an act is legal, it is also ethical.

The law, however, is not indifferent to protection of the principle of respect, as Case 6.3 *Horne & McIntosh v Press-Clough Joint Venture & MAWU* in Chapter 6 shows.

Review questions

1   Is it clear what the attraction is to the idea that good ethics is good business? Is it also clear what the danger is with this idea?
2   See two questions at end of chapter 2.

Dirty Hands

2

[T]here is such a gap between how one lives and how one ought to live that anyone who abandons what is done for what ought to be done learns his ruin rather than his preservation: for a man who wishes to make a vocation of being good at all times will come to ruin among so many who are not good. Hence it is necessary for a prince who wishes to maintain his position to learn how not to be good, and to use this knowledge or not to use it according to necessity. (Machiavelli, The Prince, ch. 15.)

This quotation illustrates a difficulty in business that may be called the problem of 'dirty hands'. The term is borrowed from political theory and relates to the ethics of role and the doing of what is necessary, even morally necessary, to fulfil that role. The classic expression of dirty hands can be found in the short, powerful and even infamous work, by Machiavelli, *The Prince*:

…the experience of our times shows those princes to have done great things who have little regard for good faith, and have been able by astuteness to confuse men's brains, and who have ultimately overcome those who have made loyalty their foundation … Therefore a prudent ruler ought not to keep faith when doing so is against his interest …

Moralists have thought this line of reasoning repugnant since it was written nearly five hundred years ago. But Machiavelli was articulating an ethics of public not personal life. Everyone wants to be ethical or at least appear to be ethical but, as Machiavelli shows, such an aspiration can be self-indulgent in a bad world. People can be ethical at home in the bosom of their family, with those they can trust. But to be ethical in this private sense while at work is to fail to notice the changed environment. Such private fancies can ruin a state for a ruler, or a corporation for a manager, and cost employees their jobs, stockholders their investments, and customers their supplies. In business, as in politics, ethics seems to be an option that is not always available.

This argument found classic expression in an article by Albert Z. Carr,[1] which, despite echoing the views of Milton Friedman,[2] caused an unparalleled reaction from readers when it was first published in the *Harvard Business Review*. It remains one of the most cited articles from that journal. For Carr, business is a game-like activity. People do not exactly cheat, but they do not express personal virtues either. They perform as circumstances require and expect that others will do likewise. Hence there is no deception, but rather a shared expectation that all parties will exaggerate or bluff. This is not acceptable behaviour at home, but business is not family life and different rules apply. For example, when a fund-raiser comes knocking on your door asking for contributions to a political party you would never vote for, you give because that is the price of doing business. People can lie in business and politics and break promises too because, to quote Carr, 'within the accepted rules of the business game, no moral culpability attaches to it'. This is not a criticism of business activity. Rather, it is an expression of a difference in the moral hierarchy in business. It is an expression of a difference between public morality and private morality.

Do as you would be done by — the golden rule of Confucius, St Paul and Kant — is alien to business on this account. To quote Carr again: 'A good part of the time the businessman is trying to do unto others as he hopes others will not do unto him'. It does not seem to Carr that, if these are the accepted rules of the game of business, the golden rule must apply. For if people are prepared to do to other players what they would not like to have done to themselves, it is only a matter of time before they themselves are excluded from the game or other players behave as they do and the game collapses.

Carr clearly sees business practices as akin to Stephen Potter's 'gamesmanship', a style of play exemplified in coughing just as a snooker opponent is about to hit the ball, disturbing the concentration of a chess player between moves, or sledging in cricket. These illustrations of gamesmanship are legitimate for Carr as long as the laws of the game are not broken; and the same applies in business. Why? Carr and Friedman would reply that business is about winning, about making a profit, and therefore any legal means to this end are fair. 'The major tests of every move in business, as in all games of strategy, are legality and profit', writes Carr. Altruism belongs in people's private life, and there is no inconsistency between managers who are both tough at work and sensitive and caring at home. For Carr and others like him, business is a zero-sum game, and there can only be one winner. How different that is from the models of American corporate excellence Peters and Waterman identify as collaborative, attentive and values-driven.[3]

What Carr misses is that real people conduct business; it is not just a matter of deals but of human relations, involving belief in, and pursuit of, human values. People not only cannot leave their private values at home; they should not, or at least they should not leave ethics to their private life only. There is now a large management literature which would give the lie to Carr's position, but we shall cite from just one well-known source: 'The productivity proposition is not so esoterically Japanese as it is simply human ... loyalty, commitment through effective training, personal identification with the company's success and, most simply, the human relationship between the employee and his supervisor'.[4] In other words, Carr is very successful at building a model, but that model is not one of successful business. It reflects a narrow view of rationality and the belief that hard numbers trump values.

But is this being unjust to Carr? Have we misrepresented his case? Is he amoral? Have his views been unfairly criticised? Carr has faced a similar response to that accorded Machiavelli's *Prince*, a work of political theory that has upset many modern interpreters. Machiavelli tried to show that a ruler must be prepared to take actions that we would never accept in non-political life. A ruler must be prepared to have 'dirty hands' — dirty in the sense of common morality. Whereas common morality would object to lies, torture, deceit, murder, bribery and so on, these strategies are necessary to the defence and survival of a state and the ruler's position within it. These are not personal matters in any sense; a prince who acts from personal motive will jeopardise the state. These are acts of political necessity.

Can't the same case be made for business? After all, there are actions necessary in business quite apart from the personal preferences of managers? Is it not sometimes necessary for a manager to write a report on a friend that is damaging to that friend's career prospects? Is not a manager sometimes forced to sack people?

These examples are perhaps not morally as significant as others suggested by John Ladd.[5] Ladd distinguishes personal actions from 'social' actions. The former serve personal goals, the latter organisational goals. When managers, judges or politicians pursue their personal goals in their official capacity, they are doing the wrong thing. They must take responsibility for the consequences of such actions individually. Only actions related to the goals of the organisation are 'social', and only these are 'owned' by the organisation. Putting personal goals ahead of organisational goals is wrong, even if the personal goal is usually called moral. Private morality is a personal goal, not an organisational or official one, and therefore is not one to be condoned. In this respect business is like a game, and Ladd is in agreement with Carr.

Games occur in contexts. We do not allow people to punch others in the street. This is assault. But we do permit the sport of boxing, hedged by rules which state what counts as a fair punch, and which require other conditions such as medical certificates as well. So too with business, according to Ladd: 'Actions that are wrong by ordinary moral standards are not so for organisations; indeed they may often be required'.[6] Ladd gives examples of what he means as secrecy, espionage and deception, and argues that while a naval officer who grounds his vessel should be court-martialled for defeating the goals of his organisation, an officer who bombed a village and killed innocent people should be praised for achieving the goals of the military. So much for war crimes. As Peter Heckman points out,[7] on Ladd's account organisations can never do the wrong thing. Their goals, by definition, fall outside the realm of private moral appraisal. This would mean that conventional, private morality should be abandoned as a guide to action in the public sphere, where it is appropriate to judge by criteria of public morality — hence the necessity for dirty hands in political and organisational life. Business cannot avoid such moral soiling if it is to succeed.

What Carr said could hardly have been new to his critics, so why all the fuss? One reason might be that business people did not like acknowledging the truth about themselves and their occupations. Perhaps they preferred to believe that they behaved in business as they would in private life. Instead of speculating, let us look at some of their replies to Carr.

Alan Potter, a senior manager with Ciba, holds that 'it is not at all the case that businessmen do not expect the truth to be spoken ... The economic system would collapse without mutual trust on a practically universal scale among business executives'.[8] J. Douglas McConnell of Stanford Research Institute believes that it is impossible to insulate business from broader social judgments. And Harry R. Wrage, manager of MEDINET at General Electric, puts the stakeholder position:

> Business is not a closed society, free to operate by special rules as long as all the players understand them. Nor does business want this status. The responsible businessman recognises a great responsibility to non players in Mr. Carr's 'game' — to employees and suppliers, to customers, and to the general public ... If we do not all meet all of these responsibilities all of the time, that is understandable, but this is not evidence of the existence of, or a need for, special and looser ethical standards for the business community.[9]

And from Mrs Philip D. Ryan of New Jersey: 'Plainly, the true meaning of a man's work escapes Mr Carr. A man's work is not a card game; it is the sum of his self-expression, his life's effort, his mark upon the world ... '.[10]

Carr has done a valuable service in bringing to the surface a widespread scepticism about business ethics, but he is in error in supposing that some kind of business necessity excuses dirty hands. Many situations in life are tragic, and because of the risks of business and the frequency of failure there are bound to be a fair number of business tragedies. But that does not mean that people have to invent a separate ethic to explain the tragic decisions that must be made. It is arguable that, depending on the context, different moral requirements have greater or lesser weight. Thomas Nagel, for instance, has argued that the context of holding political office is such that the officeholder acquires moral obligations that are not present in private life.[11] It is thus a moral requirement that these obligations be taken into account in determining the morally correct course of action to be taken in a person's role as a political officeholder. Further, Nagel suggests, having regard for consequences is morally more important in public, political life than in private life, where other moral concerns and other moral virtues carry greater weight. It is not just that there are different considerations and different moral requirements. It is also the case that there is an important difference in the ordering of those requirements.

Using the metaphor of a game in relation to business makes it acceptable to abandon ethics and normal standards of conduct. To claim that business has its own ethics and then fail to show that anything counts as ethics at all in business except results is precisely to exempt business from ethics, not to show that business is special. Look at the professions. What distinguishes them from each other and from other occupations is their values. But these values do not exempt professionals from normal standards of conduct; on the contrary, professions take on extra personal and social obligations — for example, *pro bono* work in law, or rendering assistance at accidents for medical practitioners.

In his reply to his critics, Carr seems to retreat a little from the force of his article.[12] But plainly he is still muddled. Here is one disturbing defence: 'My point is that, given the prevailing ethical standards of business, an executive who accepts those standards and operates accordingly is guilty of nothing worse than conformity; he is merely playing the game according to the rules and the customs of society'.[13]

The confusion here is that Carr accepts the prevailing standards of business as normative — as representing a standard not only of how businesses do behave, but of how they should behave. If we are playing tennis or Monopoly, of course we are bound by the current rules, but in the activities of life, this is not so. The game analogy misleads Carr into supposing that business people need to look no further than to established business practice and custom in order to discover what is morally required of them.

We do not want to discount altogether a view of morality that gives some weight to the opinions or feelings of a group as a determinant of moral conduct. As indicated in discussing moral reasoning, we do not want to insist that morality must be a matter of discovering a theory and then overlaying that theory onto practical matters of behaviour. Moral reasoning and moral commitment can very much be a matter of relating theory and practical intuition. In this way, having regard for a community's moral commitment to something is not irrelevant in suggesting a 'correct' moral position. The English jurist Lord Patrick Devlin has gone so far as to claim that:

> If the reasonable man believes that a practice is immoral and believes also … that no right-minded member of his society could think otherwise, then for the purpose of the law it is immoral. This … makes immorality a question of fact … with no higher authority than any other doctrine of public policy.[14]

This very important question — about what morality is, and what the law should consider it as being — has received much attention. Lord Devlin advocates that (at least as far as the law is concerned) morality is a matter of anthropology or sociology: to be moral is to be felt as moral by the relevant group. This view has attracted much attention and criticism. First H.L.A. Hart[15] and then Gerald Dworkin[16] (and many others) offered objections to Lord Devlin's characterisation of morality, and in particular what it is to recognise a group as having a morality or a moral view. While not endorsing Lord Devlin's view wholeheartedly, neither do we want to dismiss it altogether as inappropriate or inapplicable in the context of morality in business. However, recognition of the legitimacy of a view like Lord Devlin's, certainly does not require acceptance of the type of *laissez-faire* view advocated by Carr.

And why would we assume that ethical conduct was not itself a legitimate goal of business? Of course, if we are doing business in morally dubious ways it becomes difficult after a while to see the fault. And then, as some of Carr's critics suggest, business becomes degraded. We can see this with accounting, law, psychiatry, and many other professions that sustain standards and prevent such degradation by striking wayward practitioners off the books. Is business to be the last refuge of scoundrels, where bad or unethical practice can survive as a norm? Given the central place of business in the creation of wealth in our society, one would hope for a more positive view of its aspirations.[17]

That compromise is the rule rather than the exception, and that dirty hands are sometimes unavoidable, is no reason to abandon standards of conduct or to pitch them at the lowest level tolerable.

Consider a case offered by Sir Adrian Cadbury, Chairman of Cadbury Schweppes. Sir Adrian's grandfather was a strong opponent of the Boer War. He was so strongly opposed that he bought the only British newspaper that shared his views so that he could reach a wider audience. But Sir Adrian's grandfather was also opposed to gambling, and removed all references to horse racing from his paper. The circulation of the paper fell accordingly and defeated the point of buying it in the first place. An ethical choice had to be made: report on horse-racing and acquire a large audience for moral arguments against the war, or stick to principle, allow no help to gambling, and lose an anti-war voice. Sir Adrian's grandfather decided that opposition to the war was more important than offering some small encouragement to gambling, and the reporting of horse racing was resumed.[18]

The important point to note here is that, even though Cadbury made a decision he considered ethical, it was not ethically cost-free. He had to sacrifice a principle, something that is as difficult for a principled person to do, as the sacrifice of material goods is for one devoted to wealth. There was an inescapable ethical price to pay, whichever way Cadbury chose. Significantly, he chose to compromise on a strongly held personal belief in favour of promoting an ethical principle of greater urgency and with more far-reaching consequences.

Take another case, this time fictional. Suppose that you are chief executive officer (CEO) of the Healthy Life breakfast cereals company. You rose quickly to this position because of your management skills that have positioned Healthy Life products at the top in a health-conscious market. In fact, you have made Healthy Life just the kind of company that might serve the diversification interests of a corporation trying to protect its future in an increasingly difficult environment. And so it is that Healthy Life is taken over by the R. J. Smudge tobacco empire. In the restructuring you are offered control of a languishing tobacco products division with the specific mission of increasing market share, as you had done with cereals.

You now face an ethical dilemma. You do not like smoking and believe it to be harmful to the health of tobacco users and passive smokers. You did not resign when Smudge took over Healthy Life because you remained in the cereals division. If you are now moved sideways into tobacco marketing, you face the choice of resigning or marketing 'unsafe' products. For some people there would be no problem: they would not market a product in which they did not believe or which they found morally objectionable. They would simply resign.

But is this not walking away from a problem, rather than resolving it? After all, somebody will take the job, probably someone who does not have your scruples. If you do not do the morally wrong thing, someone else will. Does this not give you moral permission to do it? Moreover, the product is legal and it is up to people to make the choice of whether to smoke or not. Your primary task would be to increase the wealth of R. J. Smudge and its shareholders, employees and contractors by maximising its share of a market comprised of people who have made a choice that is legitimately theirs: to smoke tobacco products. What if an alcoholic beverage company had taken over Healthy Life? Would you have faced the same kind of problem? How paternalistic is an individual required to be — that is, how far should a manager let his or her private values impinge on a matter of public policy? Is it not a form of self-indulgence to take a principled stand that ignores the consequences of choices made for others?

These questions require reconsideration of the nature of the problem. For it is one thing to see it as a matter of public policy which it would be unreasonable to expect a marketing manager to solve, but quite another to see it as an issue of personal morality which invites a person to compromise morally or to behave inconsistently.

We have seen that the great sixteenth-century Florentine political thinker Machiavelli held that a ruler ruled well who took account of political necessities and did not flinch from the hard tasks of government because these necessities conflicted with conventional morality. We mentioned that Thomas Nagel has held that the moral requirements are different and the moral hierarchy is different in public and private life. Bernard Williams has argued that in public life (particularly in politics) sometimes the 'right' thing to do is something that is not moral, and that sometimes this has the result of allowing that there is a 'morally disagreeable remainder' even after one has done the right thing:[19]

> The possibility of such a remainder is not peculiar to political action, but there are features of politics which make it specially liable to produce it. It particularly arises in cases where the moral justification of the action is of a consequentialist or maximizing kind, while what has gone to the wall is a right: there is a larger moral cost attached to letting a right be overridden by consequences, than to letting one consequence be overridden by another, since it is part of the point of rights that they cannot just be overridden by consequences. In politics the justifying consideration will characteristically be of the consequentialist kind.[20]

While Nagel argues that moral requirements and the moral hierarchy are different in the private and public arenas, Williams argues that it is not that the hierarchy changes, it is rather that in the public arena it is sometimes appropriate that something override the requirements of morality. Either way, this is often called the problem of dirty hands. Dirty hands are inescapable in life. Barristers avoid questioning their clients too closely about their guilt or they will not be able to defend them. Justice is served by remaining ignorant of the guilt of the accused. Priests hear the confessions of child-abusers and know that such people are likely to re-offend. Priests, unlike doctors, nurses or social workers, will not notify the appropriate authorities. Journalists will expose malpractices in corporations, but will not reveal their sources although this would allow people to prosecute for recovery of their money. Generals will send soldiers to capture a position knowing that casualties will be high. In the best of cases, dirty hands are simply soiled; in the worst, they are bloodied.

In the fictional case of R. J. Smudge, the manager is in a similar position to a ruler, barrister, priest, journalist or general. Like them, the manager must make decisions that he or she might not make in private life. It may be that the manager does not use the company's own products — such as tobacco — at home. But at work a different standard applies because the manager has fiduciary duties to the corporation, to shareholders and, arguably, to the employees. The sphere of decision-making is circumscribed by the role of the manager in the corporation, by the corporation's articles of association, and by the law. The manager has an obligation to further the interests of the corporation. The problem for the ethical manager, then, is the reconciliation of private values with the duties of role and position. How can this difficulty be resolved?

At about the time that Machiavelli was writing *The Prince*, the English lawyer, diplomat and intellectual Thomas More was writing an equally famous book called *Utopia*. In the first part of the book the problem of dirty hands is discussed. The main character, Raphael Hythloday, the wise traveller to the isle of Utopia, the best of all known societies, is asked why he does not serve some European rulers and thereby make more widely available the wisdom of the Utopians. His reply is that the rulers of Europe care only for new territories, not for the proper government of those they already have. If a wise counsellor were to advise them against war and to make better laws for their own peoples, he would be useless because rulers brought up on warfare and injustice are hardly likely to listen to a counsellor who advised them against following their inclinations. So the two courses for a virtuous and wise counsellor are either to agree with the evil schemes of kings or else to resign.

To this defeatist line, another important character, Morus, who understands the politics of dirty hands, replies:

> If you cannot pluck up bad ideas by the root, or cure long-standing evils to your heart's content, you must not therefore abandon the commonwealth. Don't give up the ship in a storm because you cannot direct the winds. And don't force strange and untested ideas on people who you know are firmly persuaded the other way. You must strive to influence policy indirectly, urge your case vigorously but tactfully, and thus make as little bad as possible. For it is impossible to make everything good unless all men are good, and that I don't expect to see for a few years yet.[21]

This is a beguiling solution to the problem, but does it hold good for the manager? Earlier, in the context of acceptable limits of non-disclosure, we briefly discussed an issue about concealing the relevant truth and about informed consent. Is Morus's concern similar or analogous to that discussion, or is it simply different? The role of the manager is not quite the same as that of the politician who might have to make a decision to go to war, to raise interest rates or to cut public spending, or a general who knows that he will lose troops in battle. The reason is simple. The ruler is charged with protecting the interests of the whole community, whereas the manager is committed only to the welfare of the corporation.

There is enough in common between the political leader and the business manager, however, to warrant an analysis of the problems of business ethics through the issue of dirty hands. For both business and politics lay a stress on consequences, on getting a result. (As we have seen, both Thomas Nagel and Bernard Williams have regarded this point as particularly important in the context of political decision-making.) Business and politics are both driven by the imperative of success, and if that is the measure of conduct, it is easy to see why they share the problem of dirty hands. The rationales for action are similar: in the case of the politician, the welfare at stake is that of the state; in the case of business, it is the corporation or enterprise. In both cases, the appeal to a higher cause to justify action does not refer immediately to principle but to a good to be achieved. The good of the state or corporation is assumed to be an adequate justification, whereas self-interest usually is not.

Sometimes, however, altruism is cited as a justification for dirty hands. The classic comedy *Arsenic and Old Lace* is a good illustration of the point. Two old ladies kill elderly gentlemen to relieve them of their difficulties with ageing and, measured by the standard they have assumed to represent good, their actions are not murder but kindness. The telling thing about this comedy is its prescience: it captures many of the moral issues facing modern society, such as euthanasia and the international arms trade. Moreover, it exposes the problem of defining right action solely in terms of some particular desired good. This is shown clearly in the case of the kindly old killers. Does the problem arise here because they did not produce good? In their terms they did. They got their hands dirty, and they were a little crazy in killing their gentlemen friends, but their intentions were good and they were concerned about the welfare of others. Raimond Gaita has called this the RSPCA view of human good.[22] It adopts a perspective according to which evil may be done that good may come, because its benevolent attitude assumes that the alleviation of misery is the prime object of human existence. If this is so then what is done to others cannot be anything but good if it does them no physical or psychological harm. Harm is almost a synonym for pain here. The very notion that one is doing evil to produce good is ruled out definitionally. The ends are held to justify the means as long as the latter are in proportion to the former. Good ends make for good means.

In the film *A Few Good Men*, two marines at Guantanamo Naval Base in Cuba are charged with the murder of one of their fellow marines. The death of the marine had occurred during the enforcement of an informal standard called 'Code Red'. Code Red is the internal correction of infractions of rules or good discipline — that is, the punishment of offenders by their peers rather than by superior authority. The dead marine was a victim of a Code Red action that went wrong. The man had a condition that was worsened by the attack on him.

Under cross-examination, the commandant of Guantanamo admitted that he had ordered the Code Red, and the men were acquitted of murder but convicted of conduct unbecoming a member of the armed services and were dishonourably discharged. One marine expressed amazement at this verdict and the punishment: 'We did the right thing', he says to his companion. After all, they followed orders. The other marine knows the true gravity of his offence. The role of the marines was to protect the weak, and they had killed a weak man even under orders. They had corrupted the organisational aims of the marines. Even within the organisation, obedience to commands is only one requirement. And this was a case where that requirement came into conflict with another, with the verdict that the other requirement was such as to overrule this one. As for the commandant, he is arrested. He nonetheless can see nothing wrong in ordering a Code Red, in lying, or in deception and fraud because he sees himself defending lives. His hands must be dirty by the standards of common morality, but he has no time for such niceties. As he puts it, he has breakfast every morning less than 100 metres from the communist enemy. He believes that those who preach common morality do so from the safe cover provided by his protection and that the price of that protection is acknowledgment of a different kind of correct practice, one that involves Code Red disciplines, and loyalty to the unit and the Marine Corps even before God and country. In other words, he exhibits goal perversion.

Yet to regard the moral victory as going to the prosecutors is too simple, whatever the demands of the plot. For the commandant is expressing the values of agent relativity, and this is also what is demanded of marines in general. For people in any occupation, the issue of agent relativity comes with the job. Agent neutrality is the position of the prosecutors and the audience, and that is the position that is affirmed. This is too simple, too black and white, too ready to cleanse dirty hands — or rather, too ready to declare that the hands are nothing but dirty. For, from the agent-relative position of the marines, they do have reasons to place the corps and country ahead of God, shocking though this seems from an agent-neutral position.

The problem of dirty hands is essentially one of whether evil may ever be done, not just in exceptional circumstances — which most people are apt to find excusable — but as an inevitable part of human life. Is the problem of dirty hands simply part of the human condition, an existential difficulty that cannot be resolved by any theory of morality because it is not a matter of simply making the right moves, but inescapably the horror of having to decide between two repugnant choices? In recent times it has been used to justify carpet-bombing of cities, nuclear weapons, abortion, genetic engineering and some very odd business decisions. Of course, in the case of unusual circumstances it is quite common for the act in question to be defended in terms of choice of the lesser evil. The dropping of the atomic bombs on Japan is just such a case. In less dramatic circumstances, the dilemma is presented as almost unresolvable and inevitably tragic whatever decision is made. A poignant and much publicised case was that of a 14-year-old pregnant rape victim in Ireland who, in 1992, wished to travel to England for an abortion. Arguably, whatever choice she made, morally speaking it was not cost-free.

Public and private morality, and dirty hands

There are two issues to deal with here: one, the distinction between public morality and private morality; and two, the possibility of 'dirty hands'. In the senses in which we are using the terms, 'public morality' does not mean something like 'that which you do in public as opposed to that which you do in private'; and 'private morality' does not mean something like 'that which you do in the privacy of your home'. Rather, 'private morality' refers to morality and moral requirements and considerations present in one's personal affairs, whether or not those affairs are private. 'Public morality' refers to morality and moral requirements and considerations present when one has a public persona, role or position. Questions arise about whether there are different moral factors between these two arenas, and whether a hierarchy of moral requirements might be differently organised between them. For example, in the moral scheme of things for individuals acting in their personal conduct, the duty to keep one's promises probably occupies a fairly high position within a hierarchy of moral requirements. Some have argued that in the case of public morality, however, and particularly in the case of the political arena, keeping promises is not as high a moral priority as some other requirements that, placed in a private arena would rank lower. This is not a claim about how politicians act, nor is it a criticism directed at the untrustworthiness of politicians. Rather, it is a suggestion about the correct ordering of priorities, and a difference in the correct moral ordering between the public and the private arenas.

Dirty hands amounts to a situation that is something like, but not quite like, 'damned if you do, and damned if you don't'. It is a situation in which, even if you do the morally right thing, you have also done something that is morally wrong. Morally speaking, it is better that you did what you did; but that does not mean that in doing it you did not also do something immoral at the same time. That is, moral choices do not always amount to win-win situations. Sometimes there is a moral cost to doing the morally right thing. In some instances where moral values come into conflict, the situation is such that opting for one over the other is not only the right thing to do, but it also involves no moral sacrifice. Sometimes, however, it seems that even when we do the right thing, there is still a moral cost. This is not quite a situation of: 'damned if you do, and damned if you don't.' It is more like 'damned if you do, and more damned if you don't.' That is, the moral cost is not such that it then becomes a matter of indifference which choice you make, but it is nevertheless the case that when you do the morally right thing, you are also responsible for something that is morally not good. For people who have seen this as an appropriate characterisation of some moral choices, this is referred to as a matter of 'dirty hands'.[23] A dirty hands situation is one in which doing something that is right (morally good) carries with it something for which you are responsible that is wrong (morally bad), the wrongness of which, itself, does not evaporate simply because of the rightness of your act. Many moral philosophers have either denied that this is actually possible or that it is a good way to characterise the situation. On the other hand, many have considered the notion of dirty hands to be an important notion, and the characterisation to be an important insight into a particularly difficult and gut-wrenching area of moral decision-making. Consider these examples.

Imagine that you are walking through the jungle somewhere in surroundings that look just right for a *Mission Impossible* adventure. You come upon a firing squad. The sergeant in charge looks at you, cigar in his mouth, which has assumed an evil grin, and he says to you: 'OK, either I'm going to shoot these twenty people or else you take the gun and kill one of them. You choose.'[24] What are you going to choose? What is it that you are thinking about when you are trying to decide what to do? And suppose you choose to shoot one. Will there be nothing of substance to the moral complaints of the parents of that person when they say to you that you murdered their child? Suppose that you decide to refuse to accept the option that would involve you in killing anyone at all. And suppose also that you deny that the blood of the twenty is on your hands. Even in thinking that you have done the morally correct thing, do you think there is anything of substance to a claim that might be advanced against you that you are nevertheless responsible for the occurrence of something morally untoward?

Here is another example: some children are in danger. You can save either your child or some other child. Or, you can save your child or two other children, five other children or, indeed, you can save your child or all of the people in Sydney? What are you thinking about when you are considering what you should do in these cases? And do you think that, even when you have made the correct moral decision, you are nevertheless open to legitimate moral criticism?

Is the following perhaps an example both of the distinction between public and private morality and of dirty hands? Legal ethics requires 'legal professional privilege'. This is a privilege on the part of a client, and an obligation on the part of the lawyer. The lawyer has an obligation not to disclose information learned about clients or from clients for the purpose of giving legal advice or in litigation involving the clients, without the approval of the clients themselves.[25] Suppose a client tells the lawyer that he or she did, in fact, commit a murder. The lawyer cannot disclose this. Suppose a client tells the lawyer that he or she plans to go and rob a bank. It is clear that there is a legal duty not to disclose.[26] It is also clear that there is a professional or 'ethical' duty (which in this context amounts basically to the legal duty) inasmuch as it forms part of the code of ethics for lawyers. It is arguable that there is moral duty as well.[27] We might argue that the legal system we use is morally valuable and that it requires that clients can speak absolutely confidentially with their lawyers. Allowing that it is morally permissible for lawyers not to maintain confidentiality with their clients, or even that there are exceptions to this duty, could damage the legal system. Although some moral harm might occasionally result from the maintenance of confidentiality, more moral harm would result from not strictly maintaining it. Therefore it is not up to lawyers to consider each individual case on its merits in order to decide whether, morally speaking, they should maintain confidentiality. Rather, it is that, morally speaking, confidentiality should be maintained without exception.

Suppose that we accept this argument. Let us notice the points that bear on the discussion of public and private morality and dirty hands. The profession presents an obligation that is not present in private life. This obligation is present precisely because of a person's professional, or public, persona; and it is something different from that present in the area of private morality, where the maintenance of confidentiality has some moral significance, but is not the strict duty that applies within or for the profession. Perhaps this is a difference between public and private morality. Even if a lawyer has done the morally required thing in maintaining confidentiality, might there not be some moral (immoral) repercussions in allowing the client to perform some undesirable action because confidentiality was maintained? If the answer is 'yes', then this is to say that the lawyer has dirty hands, even though the lawyer did what should have been done professionally.

If there is a problem of dirty hands, what, theoretically, makes it possible for such a problem to exist? If the rightness of an action were simply judged by the overall happiness or welfare that resulted from that action (i.e., if simple utilitarianism were the only moral consideration), there could be no problem of dirty hands. In this approach, if the overall result is a balance of happiness over unhappiness, then the act was right; if the overall result is a balance of unhappiness, then it was wrong. If, in the course of producing a balance of happiness over unhappiness, some unhappiness also results, that is just a feature of the production of the overall balance of happiness; 'in order to make an omelette, you have to break eggs'. This is one story. Suppose, however, that moral deliberation is not simply a matter of tallying up the consequences and reaching a sum total. Suppose that the moral features of a situation involve other elements as well — for example, respect for rights, performance of obligations, and doing your duty. It is possible that there are conflicting obligations. It is also possible that rights can come into conflict with duties. In such situations, even if one of them outweighs the other (and it is clear what is required by morality), it might also be the case that the heavier one does not altogether eradicate the lighter one — it simply outweighs it. Perhaps it is thus possible that there remains an element of, say, 'moral unpleasantness' because of the failure to satisfy the one obligation. There could remain a 'moral complaint' against you, a moral uneasiness felt by you, even though what you did was morally correct. As mentioned earlier, Bernard Williams has argued not only that it is possible that there is a 'morally disagreeable remainder', a resulting justifiable moral complaint, but also that it is sometimes appropriate for something (non moral) to override moral considerations entirely (a point significantly different from that suggested here as creating the environment where dirty hands is possible).[28] It is exactly this which, according to Williams, creates a situation where there is a 'morally disagreeable remainder' even when the correct act has been performed. What Williams addresses in the context of politics — the justifiability or desirability of putting political concerns ahead of moral ones — is very similar to a problem which occurs right at the centre of business ethics concerns, namely the justifiability or desirability of putting the business's welfare ahead of transparently moral concerns. For example, you might 'know' that you are acting immorally but also that it is legal to do what you are doing. Or you might witness immoral behaviour within your company or, perhaps, immoral behaviour of your company as a whole. Should you be willing to run the business into the ground in order to quell this behaviour? Is this a situation in which something other than moral concerns becomes paramount? Is it one in which different kinds of moral concerns come into conflict? Is this a problem of dirty hands?

The presence of different kinds of moral values — rights, duties, obligations, consequences — creates an environment in which it is possible that some morally important considerations must be forgone for the sake of others. Possibly the result is not dirty hands (i.e., there is no moral remainder), but possibly there is a genuine moral remainder in such an environment. A terrible danger (for the moral theorist, as well as for anyone who comes face to face with moral decision-making) is that there are occasions on which different kinds of moral values are not only different, but also incommensurable — that is, they cannot be compared morally — so that a moral calculation cannot yield a result ('Do this!') in a situation in which two incommensurable values are involved.

You considered the jungle scenario and the other descriptions that might present the impression of a situation of dirty hands. What might make you think that there is a genuine moral remainder in these situations? Perhaps it is that you are unhappy with some of the features of the decision that you regard as the morally correct one. Perhaps you do not feel good about some aspects of the decision. Maybe that is the answer; but possibly it is not the answer at all. Perhaps the feeling of unhappiness (or whatever) is not a matter of recognising the presence of a moral remainder, a moral complaint that persists even when the morally correct decision has been taken. Perhaps it is, rather, a matter of being affected by other dimensions of the situation as well, one effect of which is that you confuse the moral dimensions with other aspects. These may not be situations of dirty hands; perhaps there are no situations of dirty hands. The point here is not to convince you either that dirty hands is a legitimate phenomenon or that it is not. Rather, the point is to call the possibility to your attention, because, as in war, it is used extensively in business to justify conduct that some people find morally objectionable.

Necessity

Sometimes it seems that evil is inescapable. If a business is to survive, some difficult decisions have to be made. People who do not have to face such basic challenges might view these decisions as unethical. If, say, a firm is operating in an environment where secret commissions are standard, how can it be expected to survive, let alone prosper, without doing the same thing? If a company is faced with cost pressures, how can it avoid sacking staff or reducing wages? If a factory has overseas competitors who freely pollute the environment, how can it hope to keep its workforce employed, contribute to national income, and live to fight more cleanly another day if government regulations, levies and other penalties apply? Perhaps these questions appear easy for the detached and disinterested moralist to answer, but for managers and owners they are not black and white problems.

Good ethics is good business — again

As we stated in chapter 1, the slogan 'good ethics is good business' has considerable persuasiveness. We would issue a caution, however, about reading it as 'ethics is only good when it is good for business'. At first sight this is just the kind of incentive that seems to be needed to get business to take ethics seriously. It appeals, or seems to appeal, to the profit motive and therefore is likely to be more convincing to profit-oriented business people than injunctions to do the right thing for its own sake. The public have an interest in ethical behaviour. And shareholders, the public at large, and the government all have a direct interest in the ways that businesses behave. If a business does not behave in what is perceived to be an ethical way, there is a strong likelihood that it will suffer. Share prices will drop, there can be a reaction against the business's products, and there can be government interference in or regulation of the business's activities. In short, there are strong prudential reasons for businesses to be ethical.

Overcoming the ethical reticence of business in this way, however, solves a practical difficulty at the expense of morality. If ethical conduct is held to produce good profits, then being ethical is a matter of prudence. It might be prudent to be ethical on two grounds: first, that the market will ultimately punish unethical behaviour with failure; second, that if unethical practices abound, governments will legislate to protect consumers and to control trading. Both reasons appeal to self-interest. However, self-interest is not an ethical reason for acting. Hence, appearing ethical to enhance the interests of your business is not what ethical business conduct would prescribe. What is done by a corporation might well coincide with ethical practice, and this is not something that those doing business with that corporation would lightly dismiss. But a routine of transactions based merely on self-interest can never produce an ethic.

But more than these considerations is the issue of what end is to be served by ethical conduct. Ethics is not about self-serving; it is about doing the right thing despite the personal costs. So, if good ethics is good business, it cannot be simply in the sense of making sustained profits free of government interference and a tangle of regulations. Ethical considerations and ethical reasons can conflict with consideration of self-interest alone. These can be considerably different kinds of considerations — perhaps not always, but clearly sometimes.

We do not have to take a cynical view of ethics being good for business: ethics is good for everyone, and for too long business has been considered beyond the pale in some sense. This is no doubt due to a common attitude that blames business for many of the ills which beset society — for example, the banks for high interest rates. There is also the idea that markets have nothing to do with morals; that they are free in the sense of requiring no constraints apart from those that participants voluntarily impose on themselves through entering into contracts with others. This seems to set business off from those occupations which have acquired the status of professions.

The professions have core bodies of knowledge, clearly defined practices, and identities that distinguish them. Business is a more generic domain and is more varied in nature. Yet there have always been practices, knowledge and norms in business that have exercised a shaping if diffuse influence. It is these norms and practices that are the object of ethical interest.

The motto of the Harvard School of Business is 'To make business a profession'. Why should this matter to Harvard or anyone else? The notion of professionalism implies standards of excellence, identifiable competences, a shared body of skills and knowledge, a dedication to community service and concomitant public trust. There are side benefits to professional status, but it is doubtful if these would apply to business in the way they apply to law or medicine, two paradigm professions that show, if anything, that they are typical of no others. Business on the Harvard model would operate on the modern principles of established competences and shared values, whether these conferred social status or not. As it stands, this view does not advance us beyond the argument of self-interest. Business practitioners could still subscribe to self-interest with no other concern than succeeding within the established terms of a given environment. If business is to be anything more than self-interest in masquerade then we must reach some other understanding of its nature.

Every activity has a way of proceeding that may be judged proper or flawed regardless of the results it produces. Medicine may be practised with excellence though the patient dies. Law may be practised in exemplary fashion although the defendant is convicted. Architecture might flourish even where methods of construction are poor. Teaching of the highest calibre might yet fail if learning is impeded. And the instances could be multiplied. The point is simple: if the standards of the practice are at a sufficiently high level, and those standards are observed, the practice stands vindicated. Of course a practice that was never able to deliver results would be called into question, but in order to achieve results in ways that are acceptable (to whom?), professions determine the norms of practice. Individuals might breach these norms to secure a desired result, but this is deemed to be unprofessional. Even a good procured unethically is called into doubt. To secure the conviction of a palpably guilty person through fabricated evidence is wrong. To lie to patients about their chances of recovery in order to spare them is wrong. To sell property by misrepresenting the terms of sale is wrong, even if the parties end up satisfied with the deal.

All these wrongs are wrong because they substitute other standards for professional ones. That is, they use inappropriate norms in the context of a professional relationship. Such dealing is inimical to the practice itself. Corrosion of the standards of a profession is a threat not only to its members, but also to the profession itself, and a betrayal of public trust. Doing the wrong thing for the right reason is inconsistent logically and morally, no matter how well intentioned the motive may be.

The notion of an ethos in a profession is akin to that of character in people. Both people and professions have character, and that character is formed by the habitual performance of tasks. A virtuous character in a person has its parallel in the practices and procedures of an organisation or profession. Whether for good or ill, professions acquire an ethos, just as people acquire a good or bad character through the performance of virtuous or vicious actions. And just as people may be brought up well, like Anne of Green Gables or John Boy Walton, or badly, like James Cagney's character, Cody Jarrett, in the film *White Heat*, so organisations will form the occupational characters of those who work within them. The norms and expectations that attach to positions in the organisation familiarise people with the characteristic ways in which practices are performed. They define competence. They set the conditions under which the service may be provided or the transaction completed. In other words, the very notion of a practice involves standards of correctness. A breach of these standards is a departure from the profession, the organisation or societal norms.

Is the following an example of the presence of an ethos? The example concerns the professional expectations of jockeys, even away from the track.

Case 2.1   Jockeys fined

On 29 June 1993 the *Sydney Morning Herald* reported that trainer Graeme Rogerson and jockey Bill Denmark had been fined $5000 and $2000 respectively by Australian Jockey Club stewards. The fines resulted from a remark made by Denmark at a dinner party to the effect that two other jockeys, Olsen and Banks, had exchanged cash in the Jockeys Room at Randwick on 14 June. This story was passed on to Rogerson by employees who were present at the dinner, and Rogerson took the matter up with Banks personally at Canterbury Racecourse. Brian Mayfield-Smith, the trainer to whom Banks is indentured, happened to arrive while Rogerson and Banks were in conversation, and complained to the stewards. The stewards then investigated the matter, finding that the claims against Olsen and Banks were utterly without foundation. Fines were then imposed on Denmark and Rogerson. Meanwhile, Olsen had not been receiving his usual number of mounts and Banks's reputation had been under a cloud.

The Herald's racing reporter, Max Presnell, raised a question which will now hang over gossipy gatherings in the racing world: 'Will dinner conversation, perhaps over the odd glass of something cheering, be taken down and used in evidence?' It was clear that as far as the reputation of the racing industry and those who work in it were concerned, unfounded and damaging gossip would not be tolerated. This, just as its refusal to tolerate apparently improper personal associations, is part of its ethos. It is part of its character. And, for this business, it is important to the integrity of the business itself that it appears to have this ethos. As Chief Steward John Schreck commented dryly, 'Licensed persons have certain responsibilities'.

Ethical lapses in the professional domain can be very wide indeed. There is a sense in which some professionals (for example, clergy) are never off duty. Responsibilities towards colleagues and peers obtain in all professions and are increasingly enforced as part and parcel of the self-regulation of occupations, as the example from the racing world showed.

The idea that business should be a profession, then, implies that business has a future in terms of a distinctive set of practices and modes of behaviour shared by its members.

Membership of the business community could then be controlled by criteria of competence and behaviour. A breach of ethics could be a failure of competence — say, by way of negligence or indifference, or by way of a bad reputation — that most difficult to specify standard which seems to apply to boxers, barristers, jockeys and brokers with much the same purpose: to protect the practice and those who have in their keeping its reputation and the transmission of its integrity. Notice that this concern is consistent with the point that good ethics is good business. Here, the concern with the integrity of the profession can be a concern for the prosperity of the profession.

Hence, the saying that 'good ethics is good business' means more than conformity being good for profits. Its proper meaning in the moral sense is that if business is to be a profession, it must assume the character and practices of a profession. Ethics is not an option in this arrangement: it is integral to the proper performance of business functions and tasks, to the notion of a right and wrong way of going about things — in sum, to the ethos of a business environment. Such an ethos includes the ethical dimension and integrates it with the practices it informs.

There is some point to the view noted earlier that unless business cleans up its own act the regulators will move in. Unfortunately, this view seems to be more sensitive to the implications for profits and costs of operation than to the protection of the standards of practice. The real concern if external regulators move in is not the bother this will cause the entrepreneur, but the potential for damage to the ethos and practices of the enterprise by people who do not understand the importance of these things. Regulators commonly take a legal–rational view of affairs, and tend to be indifferent to matters such as morale, self-esteem, and the nuances of community life. Theirs is the world of rules, formal requirements, and the bureaucracy of the modern state. So there is another way in which mavericks can harm a profession, organisation, or field of endeavour, and that is by exposing it, by their unethical actions, to a clamour for more regulation. It is the practice that stands in jeopardy in such cases, and that is a more fundamental concern than inconvenience to one or even a hundred enterprises.

A case in point is the fall of Alan Bond, which illustrates not only the way a maverick can damage business, but also the way business and society can attribute their woes to a convenient scapegoat — 'the rotten apple' evasion.

Case 2.2   Alan Bond bankrupt

On 14 April 1992 Alan Bond was declared bankrupt. He had fought his creditors through the courts for several months to avoid the inevitable end of his saga as a businessman. Whether he ever believed that it was possible to hold his creditors at bay indefinitely is difficult to say, but during the years of his dealings with them they had given him every reason to be sanguine about his debts.

Bond is a larrikin, the kind of Australian who is a hero when he is up and a scapegoat when he is down. Bond's singular position is due to the fact that he went down with other people's money. He was not alone in this predicament: others, like John Elliott, Christopher Skase and Laurie Connell were eventually felled by debt they could no longer service. Creditors and investors are always angry after a loss, and the easiest course is to blame the borrower in the person of the boss. Bond was ready made for this role. He was larger than life, loud, liked a public profile, and was perceived as ethically dubious.

Bond has often been quoted as saying that if you owe the bank $20,000 you have a problem; but if you owe the bank $20 million *they* have a problem. This saying is often used to show how unscrupulous Bond was; yet it says considerably more about those who lent him money. If you buy beer for an alcoholic, you do not blame him for drinking it. The question arises, why would you buy beer for an alcoholic? Bond was known around Perth. His financial dealings could not have been a secret, and some proper assessment could have been made of the true value of his assets and of the prospects of his development schemes. When this was not done, who was to blame? Surely not Bond, or at least, not only Bond. He might well be to blame for other things — the way he ran his corporation being foremost among them — but his ability to damage others was directly related to the willingness of creditors and investors to back his way of doing business. They made him rich, powerful and ultimately dangerous. As the former chairman of Bond Corporation, Peter Lucas, said of Bond, 'I don't necessarily blame him any more than I would blame anyone else, the bankers, or the Lonrho clique, or whatever'. Lucas thought that being an entrepreneur has its costs: 'I think every time there is a financial collapse in Australia, the regulators and the do-gooders and the conservatives start jumping up and down and seeking to sheet home the blame and, of course, the high fliers and the entrepreneurs who are the ones that generate the activity are the logical target'.[29]

Lucas was not absolving Bond from personal responsibility in the running of Bond Corporation affairs. He was pointing to the systemic elements in the downfall of Bond, elements that also affected other companies such as Bryan Grey's Compass Airlines. A high profile makes it easy to identify the failings of the system with the failings of individuals. The fact that Bond got his hands dirty does not mean that those who collaborated with him kept theirs clean.

Mavericks can certainly harm an enterprise, but they cannot do so on a large scale without failure on the part of the business system itself. The easy course in business ethics is to identify individuals who do not measure up. The more difficult task is to reform the system so that the damage they can do to it is limited.

Review questions

Albert Carr:
'People can lie in business and break promises because within the accepted rules of the business game, no culpability attaches to it.'

Harry Wrage:
'Business is not a closed society, free to operate by special rules as long as all the players understand them.'

1   These are two considerably different views about the position of business. Are you clear about the difference — and what difference it makes?

2. *'A dirty hands situation is one in which doing something that is right (morally good) carries with it something for which you are responsible that is wrong (morally bad), the wrongness of which, itself, does not evaporate simply in virtue of the rightness of your act.' It is a situation in which even when you do the right thing, there is a 'morally disagreeable remainder.'*

    Is it clear how this is a different view from the one which would offer a characterisation, rather, in terms of 'in order to make an omelette, you have to break eggs', so that if you have, in fact, done the right thing, and there was some unpleasant fallout which resulted from it or was attendant with it, that's a shame, but it is nothing for which you should apologise? That is, there is no 'morally disagreeable remainder'; there is only an unfortunate feature that accompanies doing the right thing in this case.

3   Together with chapter 1:

    Is it the case that business requires the kind of ethics that recognises the realities of the marketplace?

4   In what ways — give two or three examples — are the principles of ethics set out in chapters 1 and 2 relevant to business?

Stakeholders

3

Recent attempts to gain purchase on the problems of business ethics, especially to overcome the bias towards self-interest, have appealed to the notion of stakeholders. The term seems to have been coined in the early 1960s as a kind of pun on 'stockholders'[1] and has found its way into common usage both in the business community and beyond it.

'Stakeholder', as it is used in discussions of business ethics, has a meaning different from that which it has in discussions of law, conveyancing and gambling. If a couple of people are shooting pool, they might want a stakeholder to hold the bet, and then pass it along to whoever wins. If someone is buying a house from someone else, the purchaser might want a stakeholder (usually, the estate agent) to hold the deposit for some period of time, until it is safe to pass it along to the vendor. In these contexts, a stakeholder is a disinterested third party, someone with no vested interest in the activity for which they are holding the stake. In another context, stakeholder means something very different from this. Often in discussion of topics in the areas of business ethics, professional ethics and sometimes simply practical ethics, a stakeholder is someone who does have a vested interest in some activity or some situation, someone who is or will be affected by some outcomes.

The reach of the concept is deliberately broad, but there is a spectrum across which arguments about stakeholders are deployed. A widely held view identifies six groups of stakeholders: owners, employees, customers, suppliers, industry and the community. This notion of stakeholders identifies those whose opposition to a company's operations or goals could seriously harm it: 'Stakeholders do hold the power of life and death over an organisation'.[2] By contrast, Edward Freeman's definition places more emphasis on interdependence:

> *Simply put, a stakeholder is any group or individual who can affect, or is affected by, the achievement of a corporation's purpose. Stakeholders include employees, customers, suppliers, stockholders, banks, environmentalists, government and other groups who can help or hurt the corporation. The stakeholder concept provides a new way of thinking about strategic management — that is, how a corporation can and should set and implement direction.[3]*

Stakeholders are the broad constituency served by business. As such they have a deemed interest in what a firm does in order to earn profits. While stockholders have a prima-facie right to consideration in decision-making, it is not sufficient to negate the rights of society to a say in business dealings. As a former American executive put it:

> *Every citizen is a stakeholder in business whether he or she holds a share of stock or not, is employed in business or not, or buys the products and services of business or not. Just to live in American society today makes everyone a stakeholder in business.[4]*

In a word, the move towards a stakeholder approach is most frequently a bid for social responsibility in business.

In engaging in some practice, the interests of the stakeholders should be taken into account. However, it is a topic of some debate whether or not all types of stakeholders should be taken account of. For example, religious zealots may well have a vested interest in some activity that a business is considering undertaking; and it is problematic whether that business should, morally speaking, take account of those interests in reaching a decision. On one view, although anyone with a serious interest is (by definition) a stakeholder, not all their interests must be taken into account, and not all their moral standing warrants consideration by someone proposing to engage in an undertaking. In some contexts it would be important to distinguish genuine stakeholders from people whose interest is officious; and to distinguish genuine stakeholders from those who might have a genuine interest, but who are not affected sufficiently to give them the status of stakeholders. In some cases, for example, merely being offended by the presence of some practice, or merely having a genuine concern for the well-being of others, does not, by itself, render one a stakeholder in relation to the practice. An analogue here would be that of 'standing', or 'standing to sue', in court, where only those who have 'standing' can bring a claim against another party. In the present context this will not be particularly important. The more important point here has to do simply with taking genuine stakeholders' interests into account, regardless of how the notion of stakeholder itself is characterised or restricted.

What is it, then, to take account of the interests of stakeholders? The simple answer is that it is to calculate the impact of an action or a practice on the stakeholders, and to figure into the overall calculation the effect of the practice or action on them. Usually this is seen as a matter of calculating the utility or disutility of a proposed practice for the stakeholders, recognising that various stakeholders (groups of stakeholders) have different stakes in the possible outcomes of some activity. Kenneth Goodpaster has made the important point that merely identifying a group as stakeholders in some activity does not, by itself, point towards a correct or appropriate ethical analysis of the activity.[5] It may be a significant prerequisite to moral reasoning, but it is not more than this. A stakeholder analysis by itself is not 'strategic'. The phrase 'stakeholder analysis' has had some currency in the literature. While it is an important notion, there is also a danger that, as a phrase, 'stakeholder analysis' might simply become synonymous with 'social responsibility', while presenting a misleading impression that there is some methodological substance to it as a particular type of analysis, or that identification of the stakeholders itself implies something about taking others' interests into account and how to do this. This is a danger. Nevertheless, 'stakeholder' is an important notion, and the injection of a consent consideration into a stakeholder analysis amounts to recognition of a very important element in moral reasoning.

Reaching a decision about whether a possible practice would be advantageous or disadvantageous to a particular group need not involve actual consultation with that group. Sometimes the options available and the choices to be made are such that it is not presumptuous for someone other than the stakeholders to decide what is in the stakeholders' interest. If a certain activity would endanger the health of a group of stakeholders, and offer no prospects of advantage to them or to anyone else, it would not be presumptuous to calculate accordingly, without consulting with the stakeholders themselves. In such a case we probably would not consider that the decision not to endanger their health was being paternalistic. It would simply be deciding not to engage in an activity because of its possible harmful effects on some group — effects that are not offset by anything else.

In some cases, however, decisions about whether to engage in an activity might be based on trying to take account of the group's welfare in the context of competing claims about that welfare, or at least in the context of advantages and disadvantages associated with the activity (e.g., fluoridation of a community's water supply or stringing powerlines over the homes of some of its members). Here, to decide to act one way or another because of the benefit to the group could well be to engage in a paternalistic decision: 'We'll do this, because it'll be for their good', or 'we'll allow this risk, because the likely benefits are such as to make it a risk worth taking', or 'we'll do this because the disadvantages or losses are outweighed by the benefits which will accrue'. In such cases, someone decides the matter for those who will be affected by the activity. This differs from the earlier case (where there was nothing but disadvantage), in that there was, in effect, nothing to decide — given that the proposed activity had no benefits to offset its likely disadvantages. And it also differs from a case in which it is decided that the possible disadvantage to one group is outweighed by the possible advantage to another, and where the original calculation was to sacrifice the disadvantaged group's welfare for something else.[6]

As an alternative to paternalistic decision-making by whoever has the power or the authority (governmental body, professional organisation, business entity or individual), it is important to keep in mind the possibility of taking account of the wishes or decision of the potentially affected group itself. It is important to recognise that stakeholders are not only to be taken account of but, when appropriate, given a voice. Sometimes this is so (or should be so) because the stakeholders can give a worthwhile opinion about the cost–benefit of the proposed activity. Sometimes there might be a real question of what that group would consent to. Given that there are some disadvantages or some risks associated with a possible gain for the group concerned, there might be a real question of whether incurring those disadvantages or risks is worth the possibility of that gain — whether it is worth this to them. And here it should be recognised that it is not always the case (perhaps it is hardly ever the case) that only one decision is the rational (or even the reasonable) one. That being so, there is something to be decided, some choice to be made, on grounds other than simply, say, 'the dictates of rationality'. Here, very importantly, is an occasion for taking account of the interests of stakeholders. And an occasion where being informed of the actual view or opinion of the stakeholders themselves is important to properly take account of their interests.

The problem with the notion of stakeholder

As already indicated, the notion of stakeholder is not trouble free. Unreflective use of the notion can be dangerous. It can lead you to believe that you have moral responsibilities to any number of 'interested' parties when, in fact, there is no particular duty to them simply because they have taken an interest in your activities. An interest is not necessarily a stake. Even people who are affected by your activities do not necessarily have a stake in them. It is salutary to be mindful of Milton Friedman's view — mentioned briefly in chapter 1. It is probably not an overstatement to say that the entire literature on stakeholders has been a reaction to Friedman's view about the appropriate responsibility of business. Friedman's view — developed mainly in the 60s and popularised mainly in the 70s — is that the appropriate interest of a business is its stockholders only. Aside from what is required by the law, a business has no business at all taking anyone else's interests into account. A company not only *need not* but *should not*, have an interest in benefiting anyone else at all. To engage in so-called 'socially responsible' behaviour or to have an eye on the interests of any erstwhile 'stakeholders' is, in effect, to steal from the stockholders, who are the only ones with a rightful claim on the company's concern and its profits. We will not go further, with arguments specifically for and against Friedman's view. We simply want to call attention to the view as a counterbalance to the extreme view that because someone or some organisation could benefit from the attention of a business, therefore the business should direct its concerns toward producing that benefit.

The term 'stakeholder' is useful; but you should be careful that you do not find yourself overcommitted simply by having used that word. On the whole, the literature takes the notion of stakeholder as a given. Yet its character is very much that of an asserted rather than a demonstrated proposition. Indeed, in much of the literature the use of the term is question begging: the social responsibilities of business are the thing to be proved, and talk of stakeholders as analogous with stockholders does not offer such proof. On the contrary, given that business starts from the premise that unfettered trade is a social good, the imposition of obligations beyond those of trade might be thought to stand in need of considerable justification.

Even this simple criticism exposes much that is wrong about using 'stakeholder' to formulate a more inclusive definition of the responsibilities of business. As the quotations from Freeman and Leibig show, a concept that is over-inclusive is virtually useless. Why not just refer to all citizens, rather than referring to stakeholders at all? Nor does the notion of stakeholder of itself present a clear ethical claim for consideration among many. Take the building of a paper pulp mill at a time of recession and unemployment. To some people advocating a stakeholder position, the interests of stakeholders mean the interests of environmentalists. To others they are those of the unemployed, of the community in which the mill will be located, and of the nation through exports. All are right, and this means that the notion of stakeholders does not do more than shift the argument to the question of who are the 'real' stakeholders, or the utilitarian question of which of the stakeholders is greatest, can generate most good, and so on. In other words, a broad notion of stakeholder adds nothing to the discussion of business ethics.

'Stakeholder' is used to connote an interest in business, usually in a particular business. The problem with this is that while society's interest in business as a whole is intelligible and can even be the source of ethical principles, it is difficult to extrapolate from this general social interest to specific interests in particular businesses. Identifying the moral claims of stakeholders in IBM or BHP is potentially a confusing, unproductive and inefficient means of judging the merits of claims.

So while the term 'stakeholder' is a striking contrast to stockholder, it is most peculiar conceptually. For if the term means something different from simply anyone with an interest, then how does one acquire a stake? It is clearly quite like a property holding without explicitly being one: it trades on its similarity to and difference from stockholder. In the sense that stakeholding implies a moral footing with serious claims against property-holders, how is such a holding to be justified?

Robert Nozick is quite clear about this. People acquire a holding not through being affected by an activity but by a proper consensual procedure — that is, not by accident.[7] Even in those cases where business is transacted between parties, this must of necessity be limited to the agreed matters if business is to be done at all. For if every dealing were potentially open-ended there could be no clarity about responsibility, liability and other matters pertaining to fairness and justice. Even in consensual matters there is a limit on the deemed involvement of parties to the matters covenanted.

In a very general sort of way, creditors, employees, suppliers, customers, banks and local, state and central governments have an interest in businesses. They stand to gain from their success. They might even stand to lose from their failure. But such losses are properly described as proximate rather than direct. For stockholders invest in a corporation as a risk, while those trading or dealing with it do so as part of more general activity; no one deal is all or nothing, although unpaid bills are an unfair burden on any business activity. In other words, stockholders make a commitment — even risking the whole of their investment — but those who benefit indirectly, like small retailers in a mall whose major tenant is a crowd-pulling retailer, have not put anything directly into the business. Nor have governments, creditors or banks. Stakeholder claims seem, then, to be asymmetrical: they apply only when self-interest is at stake, not when some sacrifice is required. Clearly whatever is due to the associates of a business must be covered by agreements as well as ethical responsibilities; it is not adequately covered by a notional obligation to them as stakeholders.

Can the same point hold true for employees? This is connected with the very old question of the rights of employees. A view which held that employees were no different from other dealers with a corporation would see the sale of labour as no different from the sale of raw materials or services or credit facilities and would give the employees of a firm in difficulty no priority over the employees of creditors who might also be adversely affected by a corporate collapse. That is, the addition of the term 'stakeholder' to the term 'employee' confers no special rights. Employees are entitled to risk their capital in their place of employment by buying its shares, but a corporation's liabilities extend no further than the legal requirements of the land and the contracts it has freely entered into. Nor should employees be especially privileged, for this must be at the expense of other interested parties, principally stockholders.

The case of employees, however, provides a good illustration of what is wrong with a stakeholder view of business: if one party is to benefit, it will often be at the expense of the others. The stakeholder theory does not by itself rank or give different interests their due. It is a misconception of stakeholder theory that it completes the moral analysis of a situation. This disturbs the long-established view that rewards are tied to contributions. Such a conception seems to give a spuriously democratic, egalitarian hue to the world of business, but only at the expense of the rights of all parties.

All this can be obscured by talk of stakeholders. Stockholders who did not know the extent of liability of the firm they were investing in would not be in a position to assess the risk of their investment. On one interpretation, the notion of stakeholder makes business potentially liable to claims against it in an open-ended way, and thereby asks people to risk their capital with even less assurance of a return than the usual vicissitudes of market and nature provide. The notion might allow that any officious interest, anyone affected in any way by an activity, is therefore a stakeholder in the activities of that organisation. In short, the notion of stakeholder might be superfluous or dangerous. The reasonable aspects of stakeholder analysis are generally covered by other requirements anyway. It adds nothing positive; and it provides a hide for an ambush on a company and the assets of its investors. It is odd that in intention the concept is aimed at a fair voice for all players in the market, but can end up by unfairly disadvantaging those whose capital is essential to any business success — by not transparently favouring stockholders over other stakeholders.

This view cuts across the territory of some critics of business, such as welfare theorists. Their concern for equity makes them sensitive to the misuse of public funds, a concern that might lead them to be natural allies of business but for competing agendas in other areas. The welfare theorist most commonly associated with the criticism of public support of business is Richard Titmuss. Titmuss argues that opposition to welfare is blinkered by ideological views that take payments to the needy to be a drain on the public purse, and ignore the often hidden benefits bestowed on the better off. Hence, Titmuss offers a redefinition of welfare to reflect the transfer of payments actually made in society. Besides the social welfare familiar to people in the United Kingdom, Australia, Germany and New Zealand, he identifies fiscal welfare in the tax deductions allowed to wage and salary earners but denied to social welfare recipients; and occupational welfare in the perks offered to certain employees as part of their salary package in order to avoid tax. All of these measures and not just social welfare are part of the welfare system, argues Titmuss.[8] He has a point; opponents of social welfare are usually on unsafe ground when they base their attack on economics. The decision of society to redistribute wealth on the basis of need is no different in principle from the decision to allow certain expenditures as tax deductions. But that does not make the latter welfare. In this respect, Titmuss is guilty of the fallacy of persuasive definition: he defines his terms to suit his case rather than making that case. The fact that welfare is a transfer payment and that tax deductions are transfer payments obviously does not make tax deductions welfare. (This is the fallacy of the undistributed middle.)

If incentives are offered to business to induce it to enter a particular field, this carries with it no implicit obligations. As a partner in a venture the state is no different from any other partner. But if its interest is to induce the development of a particular scheme, then whatever inducements it offers do not cover the risk of those who undertake the development. Usually the incentives simply make the scheme viable against the competition of rival opportunities for investment and, to that extent, a government might see social or economic advantages in supporting one scheme over another. Ultimately, the wisdom of such policies is something that the voters will decide, but such incentives and the provision of infrastructure and other assistance do not of themselves give government or society a stake in particular ventures. They are environmental policies to encourage private equity to flow in a particular direction, not investment opportunities to bring a direct return to the public purse. Again, the stakeholder theory blurs the kind of interest the public has in business.

The usefulness of the concept of stakeholder

Despite these reservations there are virtues in the use of the term 'stakeholder' in business ethics. The point of our criticisms is to show that awareness of and reference to stakeholders is not the instant solution to moral problems that some writers suppose it to be. Freeman, for example, recommended the mapping of stakeholders in business decision-making as an aid to strategic management, and it might have similar value in identifying the ethical dimensions of decisions. But a stakeholder map does not replace moral reasoning; it can only be a convenient starting point. The virtue of the stakeholder concept is to remind managers, investors and others with a large vested interest in business organisations that a market economy is not an unrestricted one; that a free society makes demands on its citizens not only in a personal sense but as members of social institutions. In this sense, the concept of stakeholder reminds us of the principle of business outlined in chapter 2: business operates on behalf of society, and the free market economy is deemed to provide the most successful way of producing public benefits through business. The concept can be used then as a useful corrective to the mentality that sees the market as the solution to all life's problems.

The following cases consider some of the stakeholder groups who are most directly exposed to the ethical failures of business: lessees, shareholders, employees and customers. Also discussed is how a stakeholder group can decide a company's fate. In the first case the moral claims of a group of small business people were ignored by a large conglomerate. In the second, an optimistic prospectus led investors to buy shares in a company with a poor history of profits. In the third, management has taken a stakeholder approach to employees to resolve an immediate threat to the business. In the fourth the employees were treated as expendable, with no financial protection provided for them. In the fifth, employees took a militant and potentially ruinous position with respect to their employer. The rights and obligations of employers and employees are examined through a discussion of occupational health and safety, and random drug and alcohol testing.

Case 3.1   Smaller stakes, fewer rights?

Among the many colourful stories in Paul Barry's book *The Rise and Fall of Alan Bond* there is the sad saga of the dispossessed publicans. In 1985 lessees of pubs tied to the Tooheys brewing firm began receiving 'notices to quit'. Tooheys had recently been taken over by Alan Bond. Over the years the lessees had developed a tacit understanding with Tooheys about the value of the goodwill in their pubs. Bond declined to recognise this understanding, so when he did not renew the leases, he felt no obligation to pay for the goodwill that the publicans had themselves paid for in their purchase of their leases. About 130 publicans were affected. Bond claimed that he was not party to any arrangement about goodwill, and was not legally bound to make compensation. It was a matter for the leaseholders that they had decided to pay so much for the leases of their pubs. It had nothing to do with Tooheys and nothing to do with him. He regarded neither the original value of the goodwill nor the investment in maintaining it as placing any obligations on him.[9]

Tooheys had never evicted publicans, and the lessees had (reasonably) assumed that they were making a sound investment in their pubs, although they were aware that the sale of goodwill was a matter of custom recognised by Tooheys. Bond formed a company called Austotel to buy the hotels, and this insulated Bond Brewing and Bond personally from the hostility that followed the eviction orders. According to Barry, during attempts to negotiate compensation, two representatives of the publicans were told by Bond executive John Booth, 'You want to know what Alan Bond's message is to you blokes? Well, I'll tell you: Alan says burn the bastards'.[10] Bond's view was that the lessees had made a commercial decision to buy into the pubs, that they should have been aware of the basis of their entry into them, and that consequently nothing was owed to them. They were not entitled to compensation because there was no contract to that effect and the law did not require it. If such conduct was not illegal in business, it was not immoral.

This point might be rephrased to reveal more of its meaning: it really seems to mean that whatever is not explicitly forbidden is permitted; whatever is not *legally* forbidden is *ethically* permitted.

Is it possible to sustain the position, 'whatever is not legally forbidden is ethically permitted' in business? What collateral damage to a conglomerate might flow from indifference to the moral claims of particular stakeholders such as the publicans?

Case 3.2 Stockholders as stakeholders

In 1992 Greyhound and Pioneer bus lines were sold to Perth-based Bowra Holdings, owners of Bus Australia, to form Australian Coachlines, or GPA. In 1993 the relaunched bus line incurred a $3.9 million loss instead of the $13.1 million profit predicted in its 1992 prospectus, a prospectus which raised $7 million in capital from the public. Needless to say, the failure to meet projected profits caused the share price to fall and the Australian Securities Commission to conduct a routine inquiry into the disparity between the prospectus forecasts and GPA's performance.

Sir Llew Edwards, a former Queensland treasurer, became executive chairman of GPA in November 1992, on the day the shares were issued. He was not responsible for the prospectus forecasts but, on the advice of Price Waterhouse, believed them to be attainable. In October 1993, however, he stated that he expected GPA to make a profit of $169,000 in the December half, and a $4 million profit for the year to June 1994. Again shareholders in GPA were to be disappointed. Far from a profit turnaround, GPA made a $1.26 million loss, and Sir Llew revised his full year profit expectations down to $330,000. He blamed ineffective accounting systems, poor management practices, and a failure to integrate the bus lines into an effective single operation. Hence, the savings expected by investors from rationalisation and the elimination of duplication were not forthcoming. He believed that, given more time, GPA would justify the confidence of investors. Sir Llew believed that GPA was set to improve its trading position and that the market might look favourably on an issue to raise $10 million to cut the group's debt.[11]

This case illustrates an ethical problem in seeking investment. An intention to overstate GPA's expected earnings would have triggered action by the Australian Securities Commission.

Should GPA have been more cautious in seeking investors' funds in the light of its history of losses and the time needed to restructure three bus lines into one effective unit?

Should a respected public figure like Sir Llew Edwards have endorsed an enterprise with a history of poor profits by assuming the helm at the behest of its financiers?

There are always ethical issues when capital is raised, and cases like this show them to be far from straightforward.

Case 3.3   An employee–management partnership: the rescue of SPC[12]

In December 1990 the full-time employees of SPC voted to give up a package of employment entitlements over the next 12 months in order to save the company $2.5 million. The package affected not only the 300 or so full-time employees but also the 1300 seasonal employees (who were not consulted). The savings in the wages bill were part of a wider cost rationalisation program throughout the company as it was grappling with projected losses of $10 million over the next year. These losses were due to a failed diversification strategy by management, implemented over the late 1980s in an attempt to secure the company's long-term survival in the face of significant over-capacity in the canning industry, growing competition from subsidised imports, and a federal government decision to dismantle the industry's statutory marketing arrangements.

Facing this scenario, the new board called in accountants KPMG Peat Marwick to conduct a corporate review, and many of their recommendations — including redundancies of one-quarter of the permanent workforce, closing two offshoot businesses, and ending joint marketing arrangements — were implemented immediately. However, SPC's bankers, fearful of the high debt structure of the company, wanted more. The chairman, John Corboy, called a meeting with the union shop stewards and made them aware of the financial difficulties facing the company and the need to cut a further $2.5 million in labour costs. They presented the workforce representatives with twenty-six alternatives, all costed annually, to consider and left the details of the package to them. After this meeting, which ended up with an eleven-point pay-pruning plan, each of the shop stewards discussed the issue with their union members. Most also contacted their union bosses at their Melbourne head offices, none of whom seemed particularly interested in the deal. Consequently, at a secret ballot taken the following afternoon, 94 per cent of workers across all unions voted in favour of the plan. Key savings included the cancellation of monthly rostered days off for all employees, agreement to work Saturdays and Sundays at single-time rates, the removal of a $26 a week over-award payment to seasonal workers, the removal of the 17.5 per cent holiday leave loading for SPC's 150 monthly salary earners (non-unionised workforce only), the axing of meal allowances, and the cancellation of some rest breaks. The agreement was to last twelve months, at the end of which the financial situation was to be reviewed. The company had also promised that when SPC returned to profit, a profit share would reward the workers for the year of going without.

When news of the deal broke it was opposed by the secretary of the Victorian Trades Hall Council, John Halfpenny, who asserted that the SPC workers had no right to trade off award conditions, thereby threatening the conditions of other unionists. The Trades Hall threatened that they were prepared to oppose the agreement by stopping all distribution from the company. Talks between the company and the Trades Hall representatives broke down, and SPC filed to have the agreement ratified before the Industrial Relations Commission. However, further talks between company and the unions over the New Year break agreed on a compromise that left award conditions intact but delivered alternative cost savings to the company by reducing non-award entitlements. The key to the new deal was the cutback of over-award arrangements and work practices at SPC, which meant that the substantial cost saving of $2.4 million could be achieved without touching the industry standard award conditions that the unions had been concerned to protect. The workers subsequently ratified the agreement, and SPC's chairman said, 'As far as the company are concerned, we have everything we could wish for. It is a very practical solution which demonstrates that the system has the flexibility to help companies like ourselves'.

Although, as it turned out, this seems like a good-news story, is there a way to balance the interests of employees as stakeholders with the interests of other stakeholders, particularly stockholders? There can certainly be competing interests between these two. Is there any systematic way that they can be legitimately and fairly balanced when they come into conflict?

Case 3.4   Law and ethics: the case of Freddy Gazal[13]

In May 1990 Freddy Gazal's clothing factory in the Sydney suburb of St Peters burnt down. After initial assurances that the factory would reopen, workers were informed that there would be no more work there and they would get back-pay and leave and other entitlements when the insurance company paid the owners. When this did not eventuate, the workers and their union attempted to take action for recovery of their money. They discovered, however, that Freddy Gazal was not, as they assumed, their legal employer. This was Caladen Pty Ltd, a company with virtually no assets, in which Freddy Gazal was the major shareholder. The assets of the clothing factory and, most importantly, the insurance policies, were held in the names of two other Freddy Gazal companies. In other words, there was no way that the employees could get at the money owed to them by simply suing the company which was their legal employer. Freddy Gazal and his other assets were immune from these employees' claims. And it seems that this arrangement is perfectly legal.

By August, Freddy Gazal was back in the clothing business at Unanderra, outside Wollongong. He acquired from the Gazal Corporation, run by his cousin, Michael, a stake in the production of school uniforms (the brand names, building and machines were owned by Gazal Corporation). Again, a legal maze of companies was present and could shield Mr Gazal from liability for employee claims. Despite assurances to the contrary when Freddy Gazal first took over the running of the Unanderra operation, staff retrenchments began in February 1992, and the factory closed in July: 'When the union discovered that, once again Fred Gazal was not planning to pay … workers one red cent of their holiday pay or long service leave — let alone redundancy pay — they staged a sit-in, the beginning of two months of angry confrontation'.

Another member of the Gazal family also sheltered employment liabilities and assets in different companies. Maurice Gazal's employing company was Montclair Pty Ltd, although his workers thought they were employed by Maurice Pyjamas. When Montclair laid off its workers in August 1991, workers were not paid their full entitlements. Within weeks, however, Maurice was back in business on the same premises with a new workforce. The sacked workers were eventually paid holiday and long-service leave entitlements after successful intervention by the union, but got no redundancy pay at all.

Freddy's and Maurice's factories made garments principally for Gazal Corporation, run by cousin Michael Gazal. Apart from its relation or involvement in those other two operations, this company illustrates a separate ethical problem for business. It has progressively moved its manufacturing offshore, where wage rates are cheaper. In Shanghai, where Gazal is involved in a joint venture, workers earn $80 per month for a seven-day week. 'I would much rather employ 400 Australians any day of the week, particularly with the problems this country has, but the Government sees fit to reduce protection, and if them's the rules we'll abide by them ... We've got a responsibility to shareholders', Michael Gazal was reported as saying in the *Sydney Morning Herald*. Mr Gazal's own termination conditions for his laid-off employees appear to differ greatly from those of his cousin; he claimed that he had paid them more than strictly required: 'This company has a fine reputation in the industry and we have always done things very ethically', he said.

Michael Gazal does not endorse his cousin Freddy's treatment of his workforce: 'the fact that they haven't got their money is self-evident that they have been dudded ... That kind of activity is not something that this company would engage in, and I don't condone it at all'.

Who are the stakeholders who have been damaged by Freddy Gazal's actions?

Should the law protect the moral rights of employees?

Do the employees bear moral responsibility for their plight?

The following case raises the question in general of the right to take industrial action. How far should it extend? How far should contracts of employees to employers and vice versa bind?

Case 3.5   Wanting your cake and eating it too? Union v Dollar Sweets[14]

Dollar Sweets manufactures hundreds-and-thousands, cake toppings and other confectionery. Their employees were members of the Federated Confectioners Association of Australia (FCA). FCA's award allowed for automatic six-monthly salary adjustments in accordance with the Consumer Price Index. This award also required a 40-hour week from the employees. By agreement with its employees, Dollar Sweets allowed that workers working a 38-hour week would be covered by the award. However, a national wage decision, 'the accord', was such that a condition of salary increases was that employees not seek a reduction from a 38-hour week. In 1985 FCA began a series of rolling strikes in support of a 36-hour week. Dollar Sweets circulated to each employee a questionnaire asking whether or not they were prepared to abide by the terms of the award, saying that, if not, they would be fired. Twelve of the twenty-seven employees said they did not want to pursue the 36-hour week. Before the deadline for returning the questionnaire, fifteen employees, together with officials from FCA, set up a picket line that, among other things, blocked the laneway to Dollar Sweets' premises. It was a particularly effective picket. It seriously disrupted Dollar Sweets' business, not just because it was a picket, but because of the behaviour of the picketers: intimidation of drivers of delivery vehicles, threats of violence, some actual physical violence, and more. On application from Dollar Sweets, the Australian Conciliation and Arbitration Commission recommended that FCA lift the picket. FCA refused. Dollar Sweets commenced proceedings, alleging that FCA committed inter-ference with Dollar Sweets' contractual relations, intimidation, nuisance and conspiracy to injure Dollar Sweets. Dollar Sweets also sought an interlocutory injunc-tion to restrain the picket pending the hearing. This action was successful:

> the picket has obstructed all persons who have wished to do business with other shops in the said lane, shops unconnected with the plaintiff ...
>
> The apparent success of the picket line in disrupting deliveries to and sales from the plaintiff's premises would appear to be due to the fear which drivers and suppliers have of the consequences should they defy the picket ... the acts of all the defendants which have now been repeatedly performed over many months cannot be considered to be a lawful form of picketing, but amount to a nuisance involving ... obstruction, harassment and besetting.[15]

Occupational health and safety

In March 1993, the National Occupational Health and Safety Commission (Worksafe Australia) published *Industry Occupational Health and Safety Performance Australia*, the first comprehensive study of work-related injuries in Australia. Not surprisingly, the study showed that the mining, construction, manufacturing, transport, agricultural, and fishing industries, and electricity, gas and water production had higher incidences of occupational injury than the national average. Community services and retailing were lower than the average. A particularly interesting aspect of the findings was that most of the injuries in the high-risk categories were preventable. They were caused by over-exertion and physical stress — for example, incorrect lifting or attempting to move too weighty an object.[16]

Case 3.6   Regulating for safety protection

According to Renata Musolino, occupational health and safety coordinator for the ACTU, 1200 workers die each year from cancers caused by exposure to chemicals in the workplace. In March 1993, the National Occupational Health and Safety Commis-sion considered new national regulations for workers in the chemical industry. Employers were strongly opposed to their adoption, citing a Victorian study that opposed the new standards. The new regulations would require employers to inform employees about the effects of chemicals they are handling and to ensure that chemicals are dealt with in accordance with manufacturers' directions. Employers would also have to keep registers of all chemicals used and update them every five years. This national standard would replace less demanding and variable state laws across the country.

Employers claimed that introducing the new standards would cost them between $77 million and $2 billion over twenty years, according to the ACTU.

Are the employers' objections ethically acceptable?

What facts about this case are most relevant to assessing the ethics of requiring higher safety standards of employers?

Does stakeholder analysis help in sorting out the ethical issues?

Random testing of employees

Australia often follows trends in the United States, and this could be the case with respect to workplace testing for consumption of drugs and alcohol. In February 1994 an arbitrator decided that coalminers at Newland Mines in Queensland could be breath-tested at random to ensure the safety of all workers at the mines.[17] The testing of employees for drug or alcohol intoxication at their place of work has long been discussed as an option for employers, especially those in industries and services where safety is paramount. In some industries, such as airlines, there are already stringent restrictions on the consumption of intoxicating substances. Ferry masters and train drivers, it has been argued, should be subject to the same random testing for intoxication as truck and taxi drivers. Opponents of such measures see this as an invasion of privacy that cannot be justified as a preventive measure. If a person is clearly intoxicated at work, then action should be taken; employers should not go looking for drug and alcohol abuse.

The problem for employers is that they are required to ensure that minimum safety measures are met. A failure in this respect could leave them and their companies vulnerable to a successful suit. Random testing could also be seen as being in the interests of employees, for it could protect them from the unsafe work of intoxicated colleagues. This was a view put by Brian Noakes, head of the Australian Chamber of Commerce and Industry.[18]

The other side of the issue is that random drug testing could detect drug use by employees during non-working hours. This is an invasion of privacy that could be used as an excuse for retrenching employees, compiling damaging records on them that have nothing to do with their work efficiency, or setting a precedent for discriminatory employment policies, such as the hiring of non-smokers only. In short, once this type of intrusion begins, it is difficult to know where it should stop or to what use it will be put. When does private behaviour become of concern to employers? Victimisation and discrimination could infect a workplace under the guise of occupational health and safety. Where do you stop? If some employees are tested, should not this apply to all employees from the board of directors down? And should testing just be a company-by-company matter, or should there be a rule for all in order to avoid indirect discrimination?

In any case, it is not clear that testing for substance abuse works. According to Lewis Maltby, vice-president of American manufacturer Drexelbrook, one-third of American companies using drug testing believe it is unhelpful. Maltby believes testing is bad management because it is aimed at drug use rather than poor workplace practice; it is looking at the wrong thing. Moreover, it establishes a climate of distrust between employees and employers.[19]

Consumer protection and product safety

In the United States there are many famous cases of component and product failure that raise legal and ethical questions. The Ford Pinto, Challenger Space Shuttle, Bay Area Rapid Transit System, and Ford Explorer/Firestone Tire are among the most famous cases of manufacturer neglect. Australia has not produced a consumer advocate such as Ralph Nader and we do not have the same level of interest group pressure on behalf of consumers, but similar cases arise here. The question that defenders of the minimally regulated market must answer is this: why would manufacturers with a great deal to lose risk their market by supplying dangerous goods? Undoubtedly they must in some very important respect think it is worth the risk. Still, a product that puts the lives or health of consumers at risk places a great ethical responsibility on all concerned with its manufacture, approval and supply.

The Mistral fan case provides a good example of problems associated with the responsibilities of all the parties concerned, and good material for stakeholder analysis.

Case 3.7   The Mistral fan case[20]

In Melbourne in January 1988 two children were killed in a house fire. The fire started with a Mistral fan and the subsequent coronial inquiry exposed a sorry history of indifference and poor regulatory control.

The Mistral Gyro Aire was introduced in 1968 and soon accumulated a number of design awards. In 1976 the fans caught fire twice during quality control testing at the Mistral factory. The following year the fans caused severe damage to a Singapore Mistral showroom. By 1977–78 the fans were the subject of a product recall notice in New South Wales, Queensland and Asia which did not mention the fire risk; comparatively few fans were returned. In 1977 Royal Melbourne Hospital was supplied with forty fans assembled from parts of obsolete units; two of these fans caught fire. Mistral again won a design award in 1980, and expanded business to the United States. A further fire in the Melbourne factory in 1982 did not prevent the fan winning another award, but in 1984 nineteen fires were reported. In 1984 Mistral's CEO, John Hasker, resigned. In a report to the board quoted by the coroner, he stated:

> The problem at Mistral had developed from poor leadership and bad management ... Evidence of ineffective management style was seen in excessive stocks, debtors out of control, (and) inferior quality of products, both from a design and manufactured aspect.

By 1985 the manufacturer had before it evidence of fifty-two fan-related fires. Mistral's product development manager, Kevin Cummins, sent a memorandum to his superiors and the firm's solicitor in which he stated, 'I strongly believe there is nothing Mistral can do about these units, short of a product recall'.

The deaths in 1988 of two children in a fan-related fire prompted a public warning about the faulty models by the Coroner's Court, and Mistral, which had been acquired by new owners the previous year, began a systematic recall. Mistral has since changed owners again, and the current proprietors have issued public warnings to 'destroy the old fans'. This warning was echoed by the State Electricity Commission of Victoria in a full-page advertisement in *Electricity Supply Magazine*, June 1992.

The coronial inquiry revealed just how extensive were the problems with the fan and its manufacturer. It contained faulty or inappropriately specified electrical components that Mistral's own engineers identified in reports. The manufacturing processes were not of high quality. And the plastic case surrounding the fan was combustible. In short, the Mistral was a time bomb. The coroner put it in these terms:

> The central problem … is that at some point in the life of the fan … failure is likely and the casing is not made of flame-retardant plastic. If the failure results in sparking or over-heating, ignition of the casing is a strong possibility. The fan motor will continue to operate during failure and with the fan blades turning, the fire … is fuelled by oxygen and the plastic body provides the combustible material.

In his report the coroner detailed a series of missed opportunities, irresponsible management decisions and professional failures. Most of the minutes of Mistral management meetings, having gone missing, were unavailable to the coroner, and only one director, who claimed ignorance of the fire risk, gave evidence to the inquiry. Despite these handicaps, the coroner concluded: 'By 1976 it should have been clear to the designers and engineers … that measures aimed at reducing the risk of fire should have been part of the design brief'. He also criticised the manufacturers who, 'once the problem [was] identified, as a matter of expediency [chose] to supply and accept recognised underrated components with an inadequate safety factor'. He found that Mistral tried to protect its corporate image at the expense of public safety and failed to seek assistance from the appropriate authorities. The coroner attributed this 'sheer incompetence' in management to three senior executives whose indifference to public safety in the face of known risk 'contributed … to the deaths of the Stott children'. The only risk considered by management was financial; there was no recall during 1984–85 and 'nothing was done to warn the public'. He concluded:

> Perhaps the financial corporate ethic of the 1980s was an influence in placing public safety lower on the scale of priorities than it should have been, and the Mistral Fan fire saga is only an apparent example of where financial expediency and eventually corporate survival came first.

What of the regulatory authorities and insurance companies? The inquiry found that Mistral was evasive and sometimes outright deceptive. Management gave misleading figures about the number of fans that caught fire although it was aware of the truth. Mistral's insurers were not told the truth for many years about the fire risk of the Gyro Aire fans, but the coroner found that by 1986 they had enough information 'to take action in the public interest', as well as their own.

The State Electricity Commission of Victoria Approvals Board was criticised for failing to collate information on fan fires, and for keeping inadequate records on its dealings with Mistral. One aspect of the commission's oversight of the Mistral affair was the presence on its Approval Board of L. Milton, the inventor of the fan. Although no longer with Mistral, Milton's presence led the coroner to make these comments: 'The position of Milton on the Approvals Board is a matter of considerable concern and it is difficult to escape the conclusion that the decision not to take the matter further may have been affected by his involvement'.

The technical context in which the Mistral incidents took place should have triggered a timely and complete recall. In 1977 Underwriters Laboratories in the United States evaluated the Gyro Aire and found that the plastic housing did not meet American flammability standards. Ironically, only a few years earlier a committee of Standards Australia was established to examine flammability testing for electrical products. A Mistral representative was a member of the committee. An Australian standard was not available until 1978, four years after the review began and six years after the appearance of a standard developed by the International Electrotechnical Commission. Before July 1979 the approval of electrical fans was voluntary. Electric shock was seen as the main danger, not fire risk. The coroner observed that 'There was a considerable delay in the introduction of an obvious safety standard'.

Who were the stakeholders that Mistral noticed? Who were those they ignored?

Which other parties were indifferent to stakeholder interests in this case?

In what ways would stakeholder awareness have changed the ethics of the major parties?

The notion of stakeholder is not conceptually trouble-free, and this has practical limitations. But it does immediately offer a way of calling attention to the interests of others affected by a business decision. And it does enrich the business vocabulary ethically without having the appearance of unwelcome moralising. It provides a way to take into account two very simple but universal assumptions in our society: people should be informed about things done to them and risks presented to them and, where possible, people should be asked for their consent before things are done to them, whether they are directly concerned in a business decision or are third parties.

Review questions

1   Why would it seem important to widen business' appropriate concerns from stockholders to stakeholders?

2   Do you think that business has a duty to take account of stakeholders' interests – interests beyond those of its stockholders? Why?

3   Do you think there is a way to determine whose interests a business should take into account beyond that which is legally required or required by some appropriate regulatory body — i.e., who should be regarded as stakeholders in any particular business's activities?

4   Is it clear what it means to say that a stakeholder analysis is not 'strategic'?

5   Sometimes looking after stakeholder interests is a matter of paternalism, and sometimes it is a matter of other things — e.g., stakeholders' wishes. These are different types of considerations. Can you itemise the different kinds of considerations that can enter into trying to take account of stakeholders' interests?

6   We mentioned that in the United States there are many famous cases of component and product failure which raise legal and ethical questions about appropriate regard for stakeholders: The Ford Pinto, Challenger Space Shuttle, Bay Area Rapid Transit System, and Ford Explorer/Firestone Tire. If you are not familiar with some or all of these, you might want to learn about them. They are easily discoverable through a search on the internet.

Ethics in the Marketplace:
Generosity, Competition and Fairness

4

It is not surprising that some writers, such as Carr and Friedman, should apply the notion of rules and laws to business and exempt it from the moral considerations that apply to natural persons. Most of contemporary business is built upon law. Businesses are commonly what might be called 'enterprise associations', collectivities of people working for the purposes of the business who might not share much beyond those purposes. These enterprise associations can be distinguished from social or community ones, where conviviality or even a loose set of objectives provides the rationale for the association.[1]

The relationships in enterprise organisations serve the purposes of the organisation rather than personal or social ones. We can see, then, why corporate obligations have been cast in legal terms. Corporations are legal creatures, artificial persons. They do not give up their seats in buses to the infirm; they do not argue with parking police; they do not console a colleague who has lost a parent; they do not lose their temper when the supermarket trolley veers to one side. The obligations of corporations appear to be only the things that they have contracted to do or for which they are liable under law. Increasingly, however, this view of obligation has failed to meet either public expectations or legal judgments. The argument that business operates under laws, rules and assumptions peculiar to itself, while ethics regulates the relations of real persons of flesh and blood, does not carry the conviction it once did.

If ethics is about human excellence, it is also about setting minimum standards for any agent, whether natural or artificial. Natural persons are people, human beings. Artificial persons are corporations or collectivities that can exercise powers of agency. When corporations like HIH or Enron or OneTel fail, the ethics of the managers and directors occupy the public spotlight. Figures of the moment, such as Ray Williams, Jeffrey Skilling, Jodee Rich and Brad Keeling, have their lifestyles covered on the evening news. Ethics in such cases means personal morality. Business ethics also refers to minimum standards of organisational conduct. The nature of corporate personality has been debated, with some philosophers claiming that a corporation can have a decision-making capacity that gives it attributes of natural persons, such as a conscience. We shall not enter into that debate here. Indeed, some writers believe that the law has overtaken the philosophers and that the courts now view corporations in similar terms to natural persons.[2] This is particularly the case in the United States, where *Federal Sentencing Guidelines for Organizations* have been in force since 1991.[3] The Guidelines basically penalise companies that come before the courts without having made any effort to take ethics seriously. What the Guidelines seem to require, as a minimum, is the introduction of ethics programs into the workplace. It is hardly surprising that organisational ethics should be given such legal support given the powers that corporations possess and the powers that flow to those who run them. As Lord Denning put it over fifty years ago:

> *A company may in many ways be likened to a human body. It has a brain and nerve centre which controls what it does. It also has hands which hold the tools and act in accordance with directions from the centre. Some of the people in the company are mere servants and agents who are nothing more than hands to do the work and cannot be said to represent the mind or will. Others are directors and managers who represent the directing mind and will of the company, and control what it does. The state of mind of these managers is the state of mind of the company and is treated by the law as such.[4]*

Personal ethics is a matter of virtues and character. Organisational ethics is a matter of systems of compliance, accountability and culture. It is not usually possible to make ethically weak people moral gladiators through organisational means, but it is possible to require all members of an organisation to meet minimum obligations and standards set by their employer. There might not be much personal credit in observing a minimum, but compliance can go a long way in sustaining a corporation's integrity.

Although ethics sets a higher standard than the law, the legal standard is not to be despised. Law sets the publicly promulgated, enforceable minimum standards upon which business can build. Some would say that legal standards are the only ones that should apply and that ethics is a matter for people, not corporations.[5] This is not the position of the law, especially as United States courts look increasingly for institutionalised ethics and corporate integrity in their deliberations and sentencing. Moreover, a reliance on law over ethics in setting standards sends a dangerous message to business. This message comes in two forms: the first states that if conduct is legal, then it is ethical; the second form states that if conduct is not illegal, then it is ethical. In other words, if ethical issues have any real substance to them, then they ought to be covered by law. This message suggests that the only effective controls on business behaviour are external. This suggestion is not only inaccurate, but also risky.[6] Demands for more regulation, increased surveillance and harsher penalties will not produce a more successful business environment. They are reminiscent of the unfortunate fashion of the 1970s, when bars and restaurants, not content with carpet on their floors, ran the stuff up the walls as well. Carpeting business with regulations is no more attractive or functional that this bygone fashion.

Consider this image of the relation of law to ethics. Imagine that you are in the Sistine Chapel. Where is your gaze directed? — to the ceiling. That is the reason you are there. What do you stand upon to observe that ceiling? — the floor. Without the floor, there is no platform from which to view the ceiling. Without the ceiling, there is no point to standing on the floor. Each has its function. So it is with law and ethics. Law is in the floor, along with directives and other limits to discretion. Ethics is in the ceiling. It is what we aspire to above the law. The Sistine Chapel would not be enhanced by having either more ceiling or more floor. So it is with laws, rules and regulations in society. Maybe 'there ought to be a law against it', but maybe the creation of new laws, policing and penalties is the architectural equivalent of driving the floor of the Sistine Chapel up the walls. It is not a matter of reaching for legal measures to shore up ethics. We will return to this point — and, in particular, the error of trying to create ethical behaviour and the exercise of good judgment by the creation of rules and regulations — in chapter 7.

Corporate gifts and benevolence

Although gift giving has long been an accepted part of corporate life, the practice is coming under increasing scrutiny. The rationale for external corporate benevolence is that it builds relationships with clients or that it gives a corporation public profile. Hospitality offered to staff of a corporation is justified as rewarding performance, showing appreciation or boosting morale. Whatever the justification, corporate giving involves the expenditure of funds that was once regarded by many as discretionary. Also discretionary within limits was the receiving of gifts. While in the public sector all but token gifts, such as ball point pens or mugs, have been prohibited by codes of ethics, in the private sector attitudes have been more flexible. That seems to be changing. For example, the Australian Institute of Purchasing and Materials Management has prohibited members from accepting anything more than a token gift on ethical grounds. If a company is involved in tendering, then its members are counselled not to accept even tokens as gifts. The reason for rejecting even minor gifts is to retain a sense of independence and both the appearance and reality of probity. Moreover, there will be no danger of an incremental creep: a small gift one day, a bigger one the next, and so on until the receiver is compromised. Of course, the size of some kinds of gifts may be a disincentive to accepting them. A ride in a jet trainer, for example, can cost over $1,600 for a short flight, and this can place an obligation on the receiver to reciprocate with a favourable business decision.[7]

Gifts that can influence a decision are corrupting and harmful. They are akin to bribes and do the same kind of damage to trust in the market system. If they influence business decisions, then products will not be bought and sold on merit but on grounds that could not be justified in the cold light of day. However, this view is not accepted universally. Nick Reid, former president of the Australian Incentive Association is not concerned with the size of gifts if they come without strings. If the recipient is not involved in a decision about the giver, then a large gift may be accepted. Another exception he would allow is a gift given after a deal had been closed.[8] It is difficult to reconcile these views with ethical appearances. There are no free lunches, let alone laptop computers, extreme adventures, or tropical cruises.

Although corporate gift giving for business purposes has attracted public criticism, benevolence to charities and community projects — the kinds of giving Friedmanites would question — has not. On the contrary, it seems to be expected. This, no doubt, is because corporate persons are often held to the standards that apply to natural persons. In the *1999 Millennium Poll on Corporate Social Responsibility* sponsored by PricewaterhouseCoopers, more than 25,000 consumers were interviewed about the role of business in society. The poll found that 'Two in three citizens want companies to go beyond their historical role of making a profit, paying taxes, employing people and obeying laws; they want companies to contribute to broader societal goals as well.'[9]

As an example, take the celebrated neurosurgeon, Jeffrey Rosenfeld, who has been frustrated about inadequate funds for research and development in Australia. Rosenfeld asks, 'Why can't we encourage our major companies to put major dollars into healthcare? The Government can only do so much. I'm not critical of the Government. I'm critical of the corporations'. Among the corporations that attract his criticism are drug companies that will not devote their resources to diseases that plague the Third World. Profits are difficult to generate in such environments, so remedies for these diseases are not researched. 'They have a responsibility to spend some of their profits on Third World disease,' says Professor Rosenfeld.[10] It would be good for exotic diseases to be fought with medical science, but that science is expensive and investors take a risk with their money in funding it. But that is not the main point. Like so many others, Rosenfeld treats private and corporate wealth as though they were equivalent. And corporate responsibility is taken to equate with the responsibilities assumed by generous individuals like Professor Rosenfeld. The problem with this way of thinking is that it can lead executives to treat the corporation's money as their own as long as they believe a cause is worthy of support, and it can excuse improper uses of executive discretion.

The best-known instance of this in recent times is found in the generosity of HIH founder, Ray Williams.

Case 4.1   HIH – A worthy cause?

Ray Williams, founder of HIH, was a quiet but generous donor to medical research and other worthy causes.[11] Indeed, he added HIH money to his own contributions. He gave the Reverend Dave Smith of Dulwich Hill in Sydney, $15,000 for his work rehabilitating drug addicts, and another $10,000 from HIH, after reading about the difficulties facing Smith's foundation. After the collapse of HIH, Williams received more publicity than he had been accustomed to, and just about all of it was bad. Smith did not forget his friend in such difficult times. His response to criticisms of HIH's donations to charity reveals some of the confusion that surrounds this issue.

> I still find it preposterous to think that the media should have acted so self-righteously, so indignant, about the fact that the poor shareholders were losing potential income because it had gone to the children's hospital. It is just ridiculous. And it is appalling the number of people who have turned their back on Ray.[12]

Another who has praised Williams' generosity is Harold Sharp, chief executive officer of the North Shore Heart Research Foundation. 'If I had to stand up in court and give a character reference under oath, I would have to say he is one of the finest people I have ever met,' said Sharp. The problem, according to those who worked with Williams, is that there was often confusion about whether Williams or HIH was the donor. HIH Royal Commissioner, Justice Owen, found that Williams did not keep his shareholders and directors adequately informed about company donations. While Williams' personal generosity was unquestioned, his largesse with company funds — estimated to have been worth $20 million — earned him criticism. Moreover, Williams sat on the boards of several charities that benefited from HIH donations. This conflict of interest was a point of criticism during the Royal Commission by senior counsel, Wayne Martin, but it is a problem that does not seem to have occurred to Williams.[13]

Williams is not alone in his views and, considering the value of reputation, perhaps corporate benevolence is more justifiable than Friedman and his followers have recognised. This is an area not sufficiently recognised as grey. Indeed, some who subscribe to Friedman's view wish to go further than the master. Elaine Sternberg accuses him of being 'too polite' in describing the use of a corporation's funds for benevolent purposes as 'socialism' and covert 'taxation'. She calls it theft:

> Business managers who use business funds for non-business purposes are guilty not just of the legal crime of theft, but of the logical offence of teleopathy: in diverting funds from strictly business objectives to other purposes, they are pursuing the wrong ends. And teleopathy is a serious offence, the generic form of prostitution. Just as prostitution occurs when sex is proffered for money rather than love, so it exists when business pursues love — or 'social responsibility' — rather than money.[14]

Sternberg is mistaken, of course, in calling teleopathy a logical offence. It might be a moral offence to aim at the wrong goals in corporate life, but it is hardly illogical to be immoral. It would be a nice argument with a prostitute to inform her that her trade defied logic. But Sternberg also makes the mistake of Friedman in taking profit maximising to be the *only* goal of business and the *only* goal of the owners – by which she means shareholders. The activism of shareholders across environmental and ethical investing fronts gives the lie to this.[15] And she also seems to assume that it is possible to draw a clear distinction between business and non-business purposes. This overlooks the importance of reputation and customer perception. If the ethical use of corporate funds amounts to justifying their use in terms of business purposes, then that need not exclude benevolence. It should exclude, however, managers using their discretion unaccountably and without respect for investors. That would really be to substitute stakeholder theory for traditional concepts of ownership.

Fair dealing and care

The requirements of fair dealing and care in business relations are difficult to observe in the face of the competitive nature of business and its regard for self-interest, on the one hand, and the moral and fiduciary requirement to take advantage of opportunities to improve profits for shareholders on the other.

The ethical basis of a market economy is that it places a great deal of emphasis on respect for individual autonomy and choice. This implies strong limitations on the role of government and an anti-paternalistic bias. According to this view, if individuals are to be free to make genuine choices and to create the kind of demand that will sustain an economy, then government should not have too strong a presence. This limitation on government respects the rights of individuals to choose to consume alcohol or smoke or view pornography, as well as to invest, sell and purchase as they choose. This also means that governments should not fund the choices of individuals or be expected to pay for their consequences. Such an emphatically liberal view of the market is held by prominent economists, one thinks again of Friedman,[16] but like any model, it works perfectly only in theory. We do restrict the buying and selling of certain goods such as tobacco and alcohol because we believe that the harm done from an unrestricted market in such goods outweighs the social benefit. In cases of hardship resulting from individual choice, the government either intervenes as the agent of society, or abstains and allows the development of social conditions that make life in that society unpalatable. It is true that government interventions reduce the incentive of people to exercise their own control (as indeed insurance coverage can make people less cautious).[17] Yet it is implausible to suggest that the market could be a perfect instrument for meeting human needs and desires if only it were allowed to operate freely. Markets are social constructions; they do not arise if individuals are left to their own devices, but rely on a social context and, concomitantly, on government to provide order, security and continuity.

Between government regulation and utter licence lies ethical responsibility. That is, it is possible to have a relatively unregulated society when its members preserve core ethical values, hence, the importance of ethics to a market economy and the society that benefits from it. Individuals are worthy of respect. We can take a positive ethical view of market economies and see them as being, if not perfect, at least a good way of accommodating and respecting the autonomy of buyers and sellers.

What are these core ethical values? Here are some important ones: honesty, trustworthiness, compassion, fairness and justice. Honesty is a kind of accountability; it means being accountable for the truth to certain individuals. If a friend asks if you like his new tie, an honest answer will help him decide or perhaps save him from embarrassment. If your host at a dinner party asks you to admire her new painting, it would be insulting, not honest, to tell her she has poor taste. People's relationship to each other dictates the nature of what honesty requires. This is not a value carried around like a pocket calculator to assess situations or find universal answers; it is a way of addressing a variety of situations with very different demands and responsibilities attached to them. While it is care for the truth, not all information belongs to everybody who asks for it. An honest person will find it repellent to deceive, and to deceive those who have placed trust in one — family and friends, or shareholders, employees and customers — especially so. Trustworthiness is the other side of honesty; it is being able to receive a truth or a responsibility and sustain the confidence of others that you will not use it lightly or in an inappropriate way. A person who keeps their word is such an individual. Compassion means that one respects the full humanity of others. It is a spirit of generosity that can soften the rigours of justice. It would give a sucker an even break. Fairness does not mean being unstrategic or stupid in doing business. It means avoiding dirty tricks and underhanded tactics to get your way. Fairness is part of justice, the part which relates to equity: treat everyone with respect, treat equals (or like cases) equally and unequal persons (or dissimilar cases) unequally. Give each and every person their due. Do not let self-interest overwhelm decision-making. Follow procedure. Beyond these prescriptions, fairness is often a matter of law and is determined in the courts. The same is true of justice, but legal justice is not identical to moral justice (what positive law calls justice can only be part of what any society means by the term). Justice takes into account things that many definitions of fairness leave out: need, contributions, merits, social value and risks are seldom present in the same theory.[18] Compassion and caring could also be added to the list, and then justice becomes the inclusive virtue of ethics, the principle that orders all others and is their best expression.

There is another ethical aspect of markets that should incline us to a positive view of them. They should provide the most efficient allocation of scarce resources to meet demand. Without market competition there is no incentive to minimise waste and maximise productivity, and prices will be higher than they should be. The strength of a market economy should be to provide the most efficient allocation of scarce resources to meet demand. Competition is essential to the market, for without it there is no incentive to minimise waste and maximise productivity. Without competition, resources will be allocated inefficiently and prices will be higher than they should be. From this line of thinking, it follows that businesses and customers must be relatively unconstrained. Each seeks to gain from a transaction: the customer wants the lowest price, and the seller wants the maximum profit. They meet at an equilibrium point on price. In a kind of premonition of chaos theory, Adam Smith showed how these free and competitive transactions worked by an 'invisible hand' to bring about the maximum economic benefit to society.

Smith's insight has been used to argue against government intervention in the market and to justify liberties that Smith would never have countenanced. The self-interest that he believed motivated people to be productive was not an unfettered right to pursue profit. Gain should only be sought within the confines of justice and social morality. It is these moral restrictions which are usually forgotten when Smith's theory is mentioned.[19] Business is not, as Carr imagines, run according to its own rules, but must work within the rules and conventions of the social system.

Business, then, should function in a market economy in accordance with, or constrained by, the principles of justice and morality that prevail in society. There is a constant temptation, however, to minimise competition and the access of customers to alternative sources of goods and services. Marx believed that a movement to oligopoly and monopoly was characteristic of late capitalism,[20] but this is a latent tendency of business and can be as strongly supported by labour (in order to preserve jobs) as by management and owners. Although the law attempts to deal stringently with this area of business, the pressures of competition, especially during a recession or when a business is in decline,[21] can be difficult to resist. Hence, there is a common problem in business-to-business relations of dealing fairly not only with one's stakeholders, but also with one's competitors.

The following cases illustrate some of these issues. They give the lie to the belief that market systems are self-rectifying and need no externally imposed ethical and legal constraints. They are cases not only of personal moral failure, but also of the failure of business ethics.

Nowhere is this difficulty more apparent than on the issue of fairness. The first three cases below illustrate the variety of ways in which fairness – which is a fundamental aspect of justice — can be compromised.

Case 4.2   David Tweed and National Exchange

For many years, a licenced share dealer called David Tweed has bought and sold shares through his companies, Country Estate and Agency and National Exchange. Tweed has been called a bottom feeder because he goes through share registers and targets people who hold small parcels of shares, often from demutualisation schemes. It would more apt to describe his activities as long line trawling. He throws enough net into the waters to harvest a good catch, typically from slow moving or unaware investors. This has been going on for some time, but recent changes to traditional businesses have provided him with new opportunities.

In the 1990s, many cooperatives and friendly societies such as the NRMA, AMP and IOOF, de-mutualised and presented their members with shares. Among other changes, this often involved completely new names for the de-mutualised entities. NRMA Insurance, for example, became IAG. The potential for confusion among some shareholders in the new companies was thus considerable. Many had no previous experience with or knowledge about the operations of the share market. Quite a few were ignorant of the value of their stock. They had never held shares or dealt with a broker. Quite a number of them were elderly pensioners. It is not surprising that some were enticed by an official looking letter from National Exchange offering to buy their shares for a price they did not understand was well below market value.

When some companies learnt of approaches to shareholders, they issued cautions. IAG, formerly NRMA Insurance, for example, sent a letter in May 2002 to shareholders warning that National Exchange had been buying shares for $2, although the market price was $3.42.[22]

These offers are not illegal but are they ethical? The answer has been an unequivocal 'no'.[23] Tweed's schemes have caused such an outcry that the *Financial Services Reform Act* was tightened in 2003 and subsequently ASIC has imposed a condition on his licence in order to curb his activities. He, in turn, has found ways to evade such obstacles. That in itself raises an ethical issue: if the activities of a business raise sufficient concern to invite the attentions of regulators, then a business that deliberately reconstructs its activities in order to pursue similar activities without regulatory hindrance must raise doubts about its ethics.

David Tweed was asked about his approaches and replied with a typical market defence: 'People can accept [the offers] or reject them. If they don't like them they can put them in the rubbish bin'.[24] The ethical issue is whether the people who had to decide on the offer were in a position to make an informed decision. Tweed's defence of his practices is hackneyed: 'It's a free country'.[25] Indeed it is, but that does not mean that if conduct is legal, it is therefore ethical. It is indeed the case that a great deal of business has to do with asymmetries in knowledge. A corporation that develops a new drug or a new model of stock market analysis has the advantage over its competitors until that knowledge becomes widely used. We accept that such advantages are legitimate rewards for effort expended and risk taken.

Tweed's activities, however, are of a different kind. Fairness is the issue. Through targeting vulnerable stock holders, Tweed has consolidated a valuable share portfolio at a bargain price at their expense. The position of these vulnerable people was closer to that of fish about to be shot in a barrel than of willing participants in the sport of the market. Recognising this, IOOF executive Tony Hodge expressed the view that ASIC should do something about the morality of Tweed's tactics even if it could not act on them legally, not only because they took advantage of individuals, but also because they undermined trust in markets.

> If we are to have a strong capital market and a better savings environment we need integrity, and this activity does not help us with either. We think the market owes the investor a duty of care that is not just legal but ethical and moral. We would like to think that David Knott (then head of ASIC) is not happy about this and could do something that goes further than the legal test.[26]

As it is not illegal to offer a price for shares that is below their current market value, it is difficult for regulatory agencies to prevent the kind of schemes run by Tweed. Even companies have to act carefully in trying to protect the interests of their shareholders. In 2002, Tweed offered former members of OFM Investment Group between 50 and 62 cents for their newly issued shares ahead of the company's float. The shares were subsequently listed for $1.60. When the board of OFM tried to prevent the registration of shares acquired by Tweed through his offer, he retaliated with successful legal action. Yet the board had simply tried to act with a duty of care to former members (now shareholders). The chairman of OFM explained the board's decision in these terms:

> I felt aggrieved when he wrote to our shareholders because I felt the board still had some trustee or protective role. OFM was started about 20 years ago to encourage older Australians to save. Many of our members, therefore, were unsophisticated in terms of investment skills.[27]

In the light of such experience, AMP and AXA Asia Pacific could do little else but warn their shareholders to check the current value of their shares and to seek independent financial advice before accepting unsolicited offers — $7.50 (market price above $10) for AMP and $1.50 (market price $2.40 and above) for AXA — from National Exchange.[28] IAG issued similar warnings to its shareholders.

Nevertheless, ASIC did act to restrict Tweed's activities. In May 2003, it imposed a condition on the licence of National Exchange that required Tweed to disclose the market price of any shares he was offering to buy. The condition also applies to unlisted shares. It requires any offer 'to set out a fair estimate of the value of the securities and the method by which the estimation was reached'.[29]

When IOOF demutualised, it had around 75,000 shareholders mostly elderly. Tweed's National Exchange Pty Ltd sent out letters to a number of these shareholders offering to buy an option to purchase shares at $2.80. That price gave the option a value of 10 cents a share. The letter did advise the shareholders to obtain independent guidance. On the other side of the letter were printed the terms of the offer. These included an expiry date of 2007, giving Tweed the right to exercise the option over a five-year period for 10 cents a share.[30]

Perhaps in the past more people in business would have excused such conduct on the principle that, if an activity is legal, then it is also ethical. Now, that kind of rationale no longer convinces. Pursuing the shares of old people who might not be in a position to seek independent advice continues the pattern that Tweed has established over the past decade. Talk of free markets, the free exchange of property and the like do not excuse it: it is naked opportunism that violates the core values nominated as essential for the conduct of business – honesty, trustworthiness, compassion, justice and fairness.

Although legal hurdles have not stopped Tweed's ethically dubious practices, the law has not been kind to him recently. National Exchange had taken legal action against vulnerable shareholders who have changed their minds about accepting its offers. One of them, David Vane, was brought to court by National Exchange in a claim for $977. Vane represented himself before a magistrate, who ruled that he had not validly accepted National Exchange's offer. National Exchange appealed and lost, and was then unable to proceed against other shareholders on the grounds used against Vane. Moreover, it was liable for their legal costs.[31]

A classic case of obviously unfair competition was revealed in the legal action taken by Virgin Atlantic against British Airways.[32]

Case 4.3   Virgin Atlantic and British Airways

In December 1991 Richard Branson, founder of Virgin Atlantic airlines, wrote an open letter to non-executive directors of the board of British Airways alleging a dirty tricks campaign by British Airways staff against Virgin Atlantic. British Airways' chairman, Lord King of Wartnaby, alleged in turn that Branson was simply trying to generate publicity for his airline. Branson replied with a libel suit, and British Airways cross-sued over his initial allegations.

In January 1993 the claims were settled in the High Court with Lord King and British Airways agreeing to pay Branson £500,000 and Virgin Atlantic £110,000 (a total of $A1.4 million) and costs of £3 million. Lord King also offered Branson an unreserved apology for the dirty tricks practised against Virgin Atlantic. Counsel for Lord King and British Airways accepted that their employees had been guilty of 'regrettable' conduct, but stated that British Airways directors 'were not party to any concerted campaign against Richard Branson and Virgin Atlantic'.

The man directly responsible for the campaign against Branson's airline, public relations adviser Brian Basham, claimed otherwise. In an affidavit he asserted, 'At no time did I act without the knowledge or approval of the British Airways board'. A letter from Basham's lawyer declared that:

> Lord King, Sir Colin Marshall (British Airways' chief executive) and Robert Ayling (director of marketing and operations) well know they and the company gave full authority to his actions and it was Brian himself who played a major role in exercising restraint in what was allowed to appear in the press about Branson.

The dirty tricks included computer hacking, poaching passengers, impersonation of Virgin staff, document shredding, and press smears.

The Tradestock case is more difficult ethically because it does not involve dirty tricks but the exercise of free choice in the market. What is at stake ethically is whether established transport interests sought to reduce opportunities for competitive pricing through the exclusion of Tradestock Pty Ltd. This is a case for subtle reading. The notion of a market economy is to deliver the lowest possible prices for consumers and the most efficient distribution of resources within the economy. The way the market actually operates, however, could make one sceptical about these claims: free enterprise is great — if you can get a piece of the action.

Case 4.4   Tradestock

Tradestock was founded in 1975 initially as consultants in transport and then as transport brokers using the name TIC Management Consultants. As transport consultants, Tradestock advised clients on competitive quotes, little known or unpublished discounts and rates, and about entering into long-term fixed price agreements. It also offered its negotiating services — for example, to seek competitive quotes or in making representations to transport companies designed to stop rate increases. Fees were charged at either an agreed flat price or an agreed percentage of claimed savings to the client.

Within a year it had become clear that Tradestock would not be able to establish a viable business based on such activities and so decided to commence a more comprehensive transport broking business. The nature of this business was to investigate clients' freight transport needs and prepare reports and proposals for the most efficient ways of meeting them. Then it would negotiate contracts with freight carriers for the best service to its clients. Clients agreed not to deal with freight companies directly for the duration of the brokerage. No fees were charged to the client and Tradestock's profits were made by way of a percentage of the fee charged by the freight companies. While other attempts had been made to set up transport brokerages, none had been successful and Tradestock was the only such broker in business at the time.

Tradestock was at first successful, dealing mainly with small freight companies who agreed to its commission terms. Clients were attracted to Tradestock in the belief that it could negotiate better rates than they could. Tradestock had difficulties in dealing with the major freight companies, however. Some simply refused to respond to Tradestock's approaches at all. Others dealt with Tradestock for a time and later withdrew from contact and made it clear to Tradestock's clients that they would not negotiate with them unless Tradestock was excluded entirely from all relevant communication.

Many of these major freight companies were members of the National Freight Forwarders Association (NFFA). At meetings of NFFA, Tradestock's business approaches were discussed, and at three of these meetings there was unanimity that it was better for the client and freight company to deal directly without the intervention of a broker.[33] There was a general expectation that, with Tradestock as an intermediary, the carriers' charges would rise by the amount of the broker's commission. Tradestock had pointed out, however, that the carriers would require fewer sales staff and thus be able to reduce costs accordingly. Tradestock's business as a transport broker was not successful. For a short time it operated directly as a freight forwarder, but eventually went into liquidation in 1978.

In December 1976 Tradestock commenced proceedings against the major freight companies alleging restraint of trade — that the freight companies had shut them out.[34] Tradestock's allegations were never resolved as it was unable to continue proceedings due to lack of funds. In 1978 the Trade Practices Commission took over the proceedings pursuant to section 77 of the *Trade Practices Act 1974* for the recovery of pecuniary penalties (section 76) and the grant of injunctions (section 80). The Trade Practices Commission alleged that the defendants were parties to one or more of three arrangements or understandings (as evidenced by the minutes of the meetings of the NFFA), each in breach of section 45(2)(b) of the Act.

The court found that, although certain arrangements or understandings were proved, these arrangements or understandings were not in restraint of trade because they did not have the requisite significant effect on competition between major freight forwarders. The court found that the field for the transport of goods in Australia was highly competitive at all relevant times and the freight forwarders competed actively with each other.

What about the situation with Tradestock itself, and its relation to the major freight forwarders?

Is there anything wrong with the major freight transporters not allowing themselves to be brokered through Tradestock?

Two tales of Western Mining

Case 4.5   Lady Bountiful

In June 1987 Consolidated Exploration Ltd (Consex) paid $201 million for a half-share in a Western Australian goldmine called Lady Bountiful. Only three years earlier, Lady Bountiful had been valued at about $1 million. Consex bought the stake from Western Mining Corporation Ltd after receiving advice from Sydney stockbroker Ord Minnett that the price of $201 million was 'fair and reasonable'. The mine did not live up to production estimates, and by the time it closed in 1991 Consex had lost millions. It then sought damages of $175 million plus interest and costs from Minnett for misleading advice. The basis of this figure is the estimate of N. H. Cole and Associates, who argued as an independent expert that $201 million had not been a fair price for the mine and that the true figure was closer to $30 million.

Others had been optimistic about Consex. The stockbrokers Jacksons Ltd had described the stock as 'good value': 'The company's two major assets, the Lady Bountiful and Davyhurst mines, will have a combined production of approximately 75,000 ounces a year'. But according to Consex's lawyers, Mallesons Stephen Jaques, Minnett should have known better. Mallesons held that Minnett 'appeared to have adopted a comparative valuation technique, based on gold mining share price relativity'. They held that the open market value of the mine was the standard of valuation that should have been used. Mallesons claimed that Minnett should have taken specified steps to protect their client.

In reply to this claim, Ord Minnett's lawyers, Ebsworth and Ebsworth, argued that Consex's directors should, among other things, have done their own valuation and produced a report on ore reserves. In other words, the directors should have checked more carefully before the purchase as part of their normal responsibilities.

The case is complicated because the information for Minnett's independent valuation was derived from financial statements and geological reports from Consex itself. Both Western Mining and former Consex directors were joined as third-party defendants. Consex claimed that both had provided information for Minnett's valuation. The valuers who signed the valuation were quoted as saying, 'We have relied upon directors of Consex to provide us with details of the various transactions being proposed'. The valuers did not actually inspect the mine in preparing their report.

In June 1987 Consex shareholders had the Minnett valuation before them and agreed to the purchase from Western Mining. This was made with $100 million in cash and $101 million in Consex shares. Western Mining has not emerged happily from its dealings with Consex.[35]

Does the hire of expert advice relieve an obligation on the buyer to beware?

Should Consex's directors have been more cautious?

Is any special ethical issue involved in this case?

Case 4.6 Ernest Henry

In October 1991 Savage Resources Ltd sold an option over six mining leases near the northwest Queensland town of Cloncurry to Western Mining Corporation Ltd and its junior venture partner, Hunter Resources Ltd, for $1000 a year. A matter of weeks later, in December 1991, Western Mining announced the discovery of a world-class gold–copper ore deposit on one of the leases, known as the Ernest Henry deposit. The deposit was described as being capable of supporting a life-long mine with the capacity to produce more than 100,000 ounces of gold and 100,000 tonnes of copper concentrate in a year. The potential value of this deposit was speculated at $2 billion. Under the option agreement, Savage was due to transfer the leases to Western Mining and Hunter by 20 October 1992.

The executives of Savage Resources, however, were suspicious of the speed with which Western Mining had found such a large and valuable deposit so soon after signing the option agreement. As Western Mining held most of the ground adjacent to the crucial lease, the Savage Resources executives believed that Western Mining's geologists might have conducted exploration on the lease (the Savage Resources site) before the option agreement. Savage Resources decided not to transfer the leases. Lengthy negotiations with Western Mining failed to reach a settlement. So, in October 1992, Savage Resources began court action against Western Mining, alleging trespass, misrepresentations and fraud. In the meantime, Hunter Resources executives had become concerned that Western Mining's actions might have put at risk their very valuable interests in the Ernest Henry deposit, and made it clear to Western Mining that they would sue for damages should Savage Resources' allegations prove correct.

Western Mining's first reaction was to go to court to challenge Savage Resources' title to the lease. This action was settled out of court, and the parties moved on to the main litigation in July 1993.

In court, Western Mining was forced to admit that their geologists had trespassed and conducted magnetic surveys on the lease and had even taken samples in a drilling program. Those explorations had discovered early indications of the size of the Ernest Henry deposit, but the Western Mining executives said nothing about the encouraging exploration results to Savage Resources when negotiating the option deal. Indeed, a letter sent by the Western Mining legal department to Savage Resources said that no 'significant [exploration work]' was carried out on or in the immediate vicinity of the Savage Resources lease prior to 16 October 1991' (the date of the option agreement). On hearing this evidence, the judge ordered an adjournment of the case and advised

Western Mining to consider its position 'at the highest level'. A few days later Western Mining and Savage Resources announced a settlement according to which Western Mining surrendered all claims to the Ernest Henry deposit. Additionally, Western Mining had to pay Hunter Resources $17.5 million for its share in the now defunct joint venture and the substantial court costs of Savage Resources and the Queensland Government (which was at one stage involved in the dispute), and provide Savage Resources with all the technical information gathered on the orebody. Altogether, the costs of the litigation amounted to an abnormal loss of almost $20 million. Over the final week of the court hearing leading up to the settlement, Western Mining's shares had fallen 43 cents whereas Savage Resources' shares had more than doubled.

The directors of Western Mining immediately ordered a review of internal procedures. In a statement they said:

> The board of WMC Holdings considers it a very serious matter that such a situation could have arisen. The procedures within the company which allowed it to happen will be subjected to an immediate investigation — with participation of appropriate people from outside the company — and corrected.[36]

A three-man inquiry team, headed by recently appointed director, Ian Burgess, former managing director of CSR Ltd and self-styled corporate troubleshooter, reported back to the board at the end of August. Burgess described the Ernest Henry affair as 'something of a misadventure', involving 'no conscious dishonesty on the part of WMC staff'. 'It isn't a very bad breaking of the law, if I could put it at that', he said. The inquiry said that assignment of the blame was complex, but that there 'may be some shortcomings in the Western Mining organisation and internal procedures that need attention'. However, dismissal of company officers was not warranted. Instead, senior executives involved, including managing director Hugh Morgan, who had accepted responsibility for the affair, were to be denied participation in the senior officers' share plan for the next two years, and the exploration manager directly involved was to be transferred to a non-managerial position within the exploration department. Additionally, Morgan's workload was to be reduced and his personal and political activities curtailed, so that he could concentrate on implementing the board's reforms of management procedures, including a code of conduct for all company officers. A new executive committee, consisting of the chairman of the board and two independent directors, 'would be available to the managing director for advice and consultation between board meetings, in particular to review unusual developments and discuss progress in any problem areas'. Although Morgan would not be required to consult the committee before taking decisions, commentators believe that the establishment of the executive committee represents a severe curtailment of his ultimate authority as chief executive.[37] The trespass on Ernest Henry seems to have been an innocent mistake. The ethical issues arise subsequently.

What should WMC have done when the mistake was discovered?

What should they not have done?

In considering these questions, what weight should be given to fair dealing with Savage?

In November the board adopted a code of conduct 'as a statement of values', believing that 'WMC's reputation for integrity is a competitive advantage that it is essential to maintain'. The 10-page booklet had been written by employees and outlines a five-point plan of business ethics for its workforce. A selection of senior executives would be surveyed annually about the implementation of the code, and an advisory committee of senior management had been set up to review ethical issues. The code states: 'We conduct ourselves with integrity, are fair and honest in our dealings and treat others with dignity'.[38]

In chapter 10 codes are discussed at some length, but suffice it to say here that WMC responded appropriately to a series of chastening experiences by reviewing its values and stating its commitment to ethical business. This contrasts with other enterprises whose only clear values are competitive advantage and the profits this brings. Though often obscured by the demands of competition, fairness and justice remain integral to the practice of business. Sometimes business is reminded of this only by the emergence of a crisis.

Review questions

1   'We do restrict the buying and selling of certain goods … because we believe that the harm done from an unrestricted market in such goods outweighs the social benefit.' What are the competing interests alluded to here?

2   Explain: 'Between government regulation and utter licence lies ethical responsibility.'

Marketing and Advertising Ethics

5

Chapter outline

- Formal regulation in Australia
- The story of advertising
- The moral problem in advertising
- Advertising placements and endorsements
- Bait advertising, and the bait-and-switch
- Morals and marketing
- Tobacco marketing
- Review questions

More than $6 billion is spent on advertising in Australia each year. Advertising is very big business. In introducing a discussion of advertising ethics, two questions come to mind at the outset. First, what scope is there for ethical concern, apart from a legal concern about the practice of advertising and the particular content of individual advertisements? (E.g., fraud is illegal; what additional room is there for ethical concerns? If it is legal to sell some product, then should it not be legal to advertise that product?) Second, is there anything morally peculiar to the situation of advertising, and are there any special considerations that should be taken into account here that might be absent from the moral arena in other situations? The short answer to both these questions is that there is plenty of room for moral concern, and that because of the nature of advertising and its audience, legal concern itself is not (and should not be) limited to fraud and the like (i.e., there is an expanded set of legal interests when it comes to advertising — beyond the range of those present in other public arenas).

Moral concerns about advertising are present on three levels. At the macro level we could discuss the moral justification of the practice of advertising *per se* and about its place or overall justification within society. At the micro level we could consider particular advertisements and evaluate them morally. Some writers have suggested that in order to consider the micro level, reference must be made to the macro level, because it is only by considering the social justification for advertising as a practice that criteria for the evaluation of particular advertisements can emerge.[1] Between these two perspectives there is another not related to the entire practice of advertising or to individual advertisements, but rather to concerns about advertising different types of products. The Trade Practices Commission and the (now defunct) Advertising Standards Council, for instance, both recognised that special considerations should apply to advertisements pertaining to alcoholic beverages, cigarettes, slimming products and therapeutic products.

Advertisements can be 'objectionable' in different ways and according to different criteria. It is possible that an advertisement offends you or that you find it objectionable, but that, nevertheless, you do not believe that it is morally objectionable or that it should be subject to legal sanctions. You may believe that it is ugly; you may find the product itself or the depiction of it unappealing; you may also find the advertisement to be in bad taste. Maybe the old Rita-for-Eta-margarine advertisements fall into one or more of these categories, or maybe the advertisement for Stayfree Maxipads (the blood of the murder victim is mopped up with the pad), or Ajax multipurpose cleanser (worshipped by the housewife in the bathroom), or WILD-FM (featuring amputees who cannot dance to the great music played by the radio station).

In thinking about the ways in which advertisements, and advertising in general, can go wrong, it can be helpful to try to distinguish types of objections into three groups: moral, legal and other. In using 'legal' here, we are not referring to present laws, but suggesting that legal sanctions should be present: 'there ought to be law'. Surely it is possible that some advertisement is objectionable in some sense, but nevertheless should be morally and legally tolerated — i.e., there should be no legal or moral sanctions against it or legal or moral criticism of it. There is a significant question as to whether (and to what extent) it is possible to believe that an advertisement is morally objectionable and yet, at the same time, there should be no legal sanctions against it.

Advertisements can deceive by means other than simply lying. They can deceive by means of half-truths, and by implying something that is not the truth, without actually lying. Esso once advertised its petrol with the claim that cars run better on an additive present in Esso. The advertisement did not mention that all brands of petrol — not merely Esso — had the additive. Duracell advertised that its batteries outperform Eveready batteries. The television ads showed the Duracell bunny powering ahead of Eveready in a race. In 2001, Energizer took legal action over these ads, pointing out that the ads actually compared Duracell's alkaline (top-end) battery with Energizer's second-tier, Eveready carbon zinc battery, rather than with Energizer's alkaline battery, and that this was misleading to consumers. Initially, Energizer won their claim, basically on the grounds that Duracell had neglected to mention that Energizer also stocked a comparable alkaline battery, and so it appeared that the advertisement's claim was simply that Duracell's batteries outperform Energizer's comparable batteries, when, in fact, the advertisement was not comparing like with like. On appeal, however, the judges ruled in Duracell's favour, but required modification to the script so as to make clear that it was alkaline batteries that were being compared with carbon zinc-batteries. The advertisement was allowed to be aired with the script, 'Duracell alkaline beats Eveready Super Heavy Duty'. It would seem, however, that a normal viewer would still believe that they were hearing a claim about a comparison of apples and apples, rather than apples and oranges. There is something of a technicality here, which makes the story more interesting — and perhaps more difficult. Energizer batteries used to be *Eveready* Energizer. A company restructure in 2000 and a difference of branding resulted in dropping 'Eveready' from the name. So, 'Energizer' is now the name of the top-tier alkaline batteries made by this company, the Eveready Battery Company. 'Eveready' now refers primarily to a group of batteries which are not alkaline batteries, one type of which are 'super heavy duty', which have, in fact, been around for a long time, and also to 'Eveready Gold', a lesser quality alkaline battery. So, strictly speaking, it is true to say that Duracell alkaline batteries outperform Eveready batteries – because, these days, 'Eveready' refers only to non-alkaline and admittedly lower quality alkaline batteries. It is nevertheless the case that the *meaningful* comparison would be between Duracell alkaline batteries and Energizer (alkaline) batteries. The context of the advertisements — including the history of the ad-campaigns about these batteries, our out-of-date 'knowledge' about 'Eveready Energizer', which, in fact, no longer exists, and our expectation that the advertisement really is comparing apples with apples — leads us to believe that the claim is about two comparable (alkaline) batteries, which, of course, it is not. It is not the actual claim that would lead us to buy Duracell over Energizer or over Eveready, but our reasonable understanding (which is actually a misunderstanding) of the claim being made. Despite the fact that Duracell states the 'facts' correctly, this is a readily predictable misunderstanding, which, one might well believe, is being counted on in making the claim about Duracell's out-performing Eveready. After all, how effective an ad would it be if it said, 'Duracell alkaline batteries outperform all non-alkaline, carbon zinc, lower quality, less expensive batteries, including Eveready — and, by the way, we're not talking about Energizer here'?

Advertisements can coerce and manipulate. The extreme of manipulation is subliminal advertising. The message need not be subliminal in order for it to be manipulative, however. Related to this point is the fact that it is possible for advertisements to fail to treat people as persons, and fail to respect their autonomy, their role as decision-makers. They can fail to allow people to enter the transaction as autonomous agents making their own decisions through informed choice.[2] The extent to which an advertisement is coercive or manipulative depends not only on the construction of the advertisement itself (as in the case of subliminal advertising or blatant lying), but also on the audience for the advertisement. For example, advertisements aimed at children, slotted into children's television time-slots, or which have other particularly vulnerable target audiences are well positioned to manipulate either intentionally or unintentionally.

There is another side to concern for autonomy. On the one hand, a concern for respecting people's autonomy is a reason to consider the imposition of formal, legal limits on advertising. On the other hand, however, a concern for people's autonomy can offer reasons for refraining from imposing limits. The imposition of legal limits amounts to taking a paternalistic role with regard to the people who are exposed to advertising. It amounts to formally, legally, assuming the role of looking after their welfare, and making decisions about what they should and what they should not be exposed to, and what they should and what they should not be allowed to expose themselves to. The other side of the concern to protect people from entering into unfair, manipulative transactions is the possibility of not allowing people to enter into transactions into which they would otherwise choose to enter. This question about how paternalistic it is desirable to be in this area has been briefly considered by Richard De George, who suggests that this is a political question rather than a particularly moral one. That is, in this area, 'the proper paternal role of government should be decided by the people through their representatives, and with a majority rule, limited by the rights of individuals and minority groups'.[3] According to this view there is nothing morally compelling about paternalistic concern in the area of advertising, but neither is there anything morally repugnant about it. Like a number of other important matters within society, this one is properly left to society's preference about what it would like to do — whether it wishes to be more or less paternal in its conduct in this area, whether it wishes to have more or less paternalistically oriented legislation about advertising. This is a very important point. Not every significant decision that we make about what to do or what kind of society or person to be must be a moral decision. Many very important decisions are rightly matters of preference or 'political' decisions, that is, decisions about which it is appropriate to take a vote.

In appraising whether or not an advertisement or an advertising practice should have moral and, in particular, legal sanctions imposed on it, we must consider not merely whether the advertisement or practice is morally offensive or is in some other respect morally objectionable. Having decided that it is objectionable should not settle the question of whether the advertisement should have sanctions imposed on it or whether those who judge it to be objectionable should tolerate it. Toleration is recognised as an important principle in other areas of interpersonal activity, and the principle should carry some currency in this area as well. Having said that, however, we offer no suggestion about exactly how much weight should be accorded to this principle.

Some things that we might want to consider as unethical advertising are actually scams, and not advertising at all. Sometimes there are no products at all on the other end of these 'advertisements', but just someone to take your money. The Internet has certainly given rise to lots of these, and also provided lots of examples of unethical advertising (probably, in fact, far more unethical and/or illegal advertising than legal).[4]

Here is an interesting type of misleading advertisement. Different people react to this in different ways: some are outraged and completely misled by it, while others seem not to be misled at all.

Case 5.1   Free sunglasses

An email arrives, with the subject line, 'Free sunglasses for j.brown [the name of the email addressee] – pick them up today!' The body of the email then says 'Overstock sunglasses. Sunglasses for free'. And then,

'WHAT'S THE GIMMICK? How are you giving away sunglasses for free?'

The answer, we are told, is this: 'Sunglass Manufacturers produce millions of dollars in excess inventory each year. Overstocked Sunglasses has built a relationship with select, leading manufacturers, and retailers to move this inventory and make room for new merchandise. *While these manufacturers will accept a loss on these products, they would rather give them away and opt for a Tax Write-off than sell them for near cost and reap no benefit.

click here to view entire selection of Free Sunglasses or to order [hotlink]

The Sunglasses featured here are First Quality Sunglasses you will find in the store that sell for anywhere between $19.95 & $49.95 and compare to designers like Armani, Maui, RayBan, and Killer Loops!

click here to view entire selection of Free Sunglasses or to order [hotlink]

The only catch is that most of our products come in limited quantities – so if you see something you like, choose it now, because when they're gone, they're gone!

click here to view entire selection of Free Sunglasses or to order [hotlink]

If we go to the website, we see a list of brands of sunglasses. We can click on any of them and we get a better look at and description of those glasses — and all the rest are shown under them. We then discover that the particular ones we are interested in cost either $1 or are free, and the postage and handling to anywhere in the U.S.A. is, roughly, U.S.$5. This still seems like a tremendous deal for quality sunglasses. If we look carefully, we might notice that above the list of brands of sunglasses, the heading is 'Inspired Styles'. Then, we might also happen to scroll clear to the bottom of the screen and happen to notice this, in very small print:

'Disclaimer: *We have no association or relationship with the above named sunglass companies, stores, products, or trademarks whatsoever. The reference is to simply compare our prices and products to the above. Our products are unique and different than the above-mentioned products. We do not represent our sunglasses to be the originals nor are they copies of the above.'

So, an 'inspired style' might be Christian Dior, Nike, or Bollé, but those are 'inspired styles' only. And while it is true that the disclaimer does appear on the website, it would be very difficult to argue that the website is not designed to appear to provide sunglasses which are the real McCoy; particularly when one goes to it by means of the direction that is included in the personalised email. If we re-read the second paragraph of the email, after having noticed the disclaimer on the website, then *maybe* we can get an inkling that the sunglasses are not really name brands at all. But even here, it is still *maybe*; and it is a certainty that the enticement for the sunglasses is a claim that the sunglasses on offer are the real thing.

Formal regulation in Australia

In Australia, advertising is scrutinised and subject to formal regulation from a number of sources, particularly the Commonwealth's *Broadcasting Act 1942* and the *Trade Practices Act 1974*. From 1974 to 1996 an Advertising Code of Ethics and four product-specific codes were in place, and were administered by the Advertising Standards Council (ASC).[5] The ASC was established by the (now defunct) Media Council of Australia, which was the advertising industry's accreditation authority. The codes were the advertising industry's self-regulating codes of conduct, in that they applied to all member bodies of the Media Council.[6] The codes and other formal regulations divided the media into the categories of print, television, radio, cinema and outdoors. Additionally, there were — and still are — separate clearance bodies for each of the various media organisations. Each medium has its own organisation to which advertisements must be submitted for clearance — for example, the Commercial Acceptance Division of the Federation of Australian Commercial Television Stations (FACTS), and the equivalent division of the Federation of Australian Radio Broadcasters (FARB). These organisations preview advertisements, checking for content that is specified as unacceptable by the Australian Broadcasting Tribunal, as established by the *Broadcasting Act 1942* (Cwlth), and they can also receive complaints. For example, both FACTS and FARB prohibit, among other categories, advertising that is misleading, subliminal, or inciting of hatred on grounds of race. The ASC did not preview, or function as a clearance body for advertisements. Its role was to respond to complaints from the public concerning advertising that they had seen or heard. In order to impose any sanction on an advertisement (such as requiring that the advertisement be altered or that it be removed altogether), the ASC would have to find that the advertisement breached one or more clauses in the general advertising code of ethics or in one of the specific product codes. By far the most significant and widely invoked clause in the general code was clause 6[7]: 'Advertisements shall not contain anything which in the light of generally prevailing community standards is likely to cause serious offence to the community or a significant section of the community'. Surprisingly, a particularly contentious and troublesome clause was clause 7: 'Advertisements shall be truthful and shall not be misleading or deceptive'.

The ASC's treatment of these two clauses probably played a major part in its downfall. On a number of occasions, the ASC was accused of paying too much attention to the letter of clause 7 and not enough attention to the spirit of that clause. For example, according to the ASC's case report for November and December 1998, it received five complaints regarding a lamb roast advertisement in which a young girl asks her mother if she can have dinner at a friend's house. Her mother agrees, but when the girl realises that her mother is cooking a lamb roast, she tells her friend that her mother has refused permission. She told a lie. The ASC wrote to the advertiser, cautioning them about using such 'fib' devices in future advertisements. In this respect, the ASC was seen by a number of advertisers as being draconian and out of touch with the community.

Clause 6 was very important, and by its nature required that the sanctioning body be in tune with community feelings. The ASC itself trumpeted the fact that the code was to be 'a living code' — that is, changing as the community's mores change. However, the ASC was often criticised for being out of touch with how the community at large would react to particular depictions in advertisements. The presence of a directive such as clause 6 also raised serious questions about the limits of what should be tolerated, even if it is objectionable. We noted this consideration earlier.

There were probably two or three major factors that contributed to the demise of the ASC. As just discussed, one factor was that a significant portion of the advertising industry thought that it had become out of touch with the community, as well as too authoritarian, rule-bound and perhaps capricious in its judgments. A separate — but not unrelated — factor was strong dissatisfaction within some parts of the industry with the operation of the Media Council and a certain amount of unhappiness with the presence of such a body at all. As mentioned above, the Media Council was the umbrella organisation governing the ASC, as well as being its funding body. The industry decided to do away with the Media Council as its self-regulatory and accreditation body. Among other things, this involved the disestablishment of the ASC. In this respect, the demise of the ASC was an effect of the disestablishment of the Media Council, which was the central target. Inasmuch as the Media Council was the industry's accreditation body, disestablishment of this body amounted to deregulating the advertising industry in other ways as well. It also seems that a significant group of advertisers wanted a new regime because they wanted more freedom in advertising; they did not want to be responsible to an organisation that had real clout in its decision-making and sanctioning functions. All these factors seem to have been at work. The noteworthy outcome was the end of a relatively long-standing regime, a hiatus, and then the institution of a new regime.[8]

The new regime

In 1998, under the umbrella of the Australian Association of National Advertisers (AANA), the Advertising Standards Bureau, the Advertising Standards Board (ASB) and the Advertising Claims Board (ACB) were established, as was the AANA Advertiser Code of Ethics. Like the former ASC, subscription to the Advertising Standards Bureau by advertisers is voluntary. Unlike the ASC, the ASB does not have legal clout in sanctioning advertisements. Instead, it relies on the prominence of the board members themselves and the publicity emanating from the board to furnish incentive for advertisers to comply with the board's decisions. The ACB deals basically with matters of truth in advertising. Its principal role involves dispute resolution among competitors. The ASB's principal role is to judge matters of taste and decency in advertising, responding to consumer complaints. Using the Advertiser Code of Ethics as its terms of reference, the ASB 'considers advertisements which people find offensive on the basis of discrimination (race, nationality, sex, age, sexual preference, religion, disability, political belief), violence, language, portrayal of sex, sexuality or nudity, health and safety, alarm or distress to children.'[9] The Code is set out in Appendix 2.

The story of advertising

Here is how advertising advertises itself:

> WITHOUT ADVERTISING, THE PRICE OF A JAR OF HONEY COULD REALLY STING YOU
>
> *It's basic economics. The more people who know about a product, the more people are likely to buy it. Advertising is the medium that brings the message to millions. It helps increase the volume of sales and decrease the cost. So whether it's a jar of honey or a jar of pickles, advertising helps keep a lid on the price.*[10]

The basic function of advertising is to inform buyers about what is available in the market. It allows sellers to attract customers by praising the virtues of their goods and services. Advertising, then, may reasonably be seen as a fundamental part of the operation of markets. It informs, allows comparisons of products and prices, and is essential to competition. As these basic functions also support newspapers and other media outlets, advertising thus performs a public service beyond its role in marketing.

These basic functions, however, have become more complicated in the world of modern technology. Advertising is more than just the transmission of essential information. True, most advertising is still placed in the classified columns, but most of the national advertising budget is spent on mass campaigns through direct mail, glossy magazines, posters, radio, television and film. Most of the services and products advertised are consumer goods that depend on volume sales for their success. So advertising must persuade as well as inform. This is where modern technology comes in and where most ethical objections arise.

Persuasion has always been a part of selling. Socrates had a good deal of sport at the expense of the universal persuaders of ancient Athens, the Sophists. In turn, the Roman satirist Lucian made fun of the extravagant claims of philosophers to give instruction in what today we would call lifestyles. But modern techniques of persuasion, and the ability of modern media with their information on demographics, allows for more pervasive, intrusive and subtle forms of persuasion than were previously available. The excessive boosting of products, the use of subliminal and other psychoactive techniques, product placements and endorsements, and the use of sexual or violent images all give rise to ethical concerns about advertising. The question is whether such concerns are justified.

Perhaps the central ethical issue in advertising is deception in a variety of hues. It is questionable, however, how far this issue extends. Medieval philosophers distinguished between officious, jocose and mischievous lies. The last kind, outright lying, say for the sake of fraud, is not ethically contentious: it is just plain wrong. Real questions arise, however, about the first two cases in which the truth is distorted or exaggerated. St Thomas Aquinas was prepared to countenance the first two types — lies that have a good purpose — as not seriously wrong. The law, as well, tolerates a fair amount of 'puffery', untruths or exaggerations that are assumed to be recognised as such by people who are exposed to them.

Take the ultimate case of deceptive advertising: the promotion of a product that does not exist. As part of research on the effectiveness of billboard advertising, Chris Tyquin of General Outdoor Advertising put up a large poster for Haka bitter, a non-existent beer. The poster carried the slogan 'Naturally booed in Australia' (the first choice, 'Haka bitter — for those sheepless nights', was abandoned after being rated unacceptable by the Outdoor Advertising Association). Demand for the beer eventually saw the hoaxers make a licensing arrangement with a small brewer to produce the beer in limited quantities, with the agency's profits being donated to the Prevent Blindness campaign.[11] This is the kind of story more associated with improbable fiction than fact. It is amusing, at least to Australians; our cousins across the Tasman have not been favourably impressed. The point about the case is that it illustrates the enormous power of advertising in the creation of a market, and the opportunities to deceive consumers with that power.

It is generally accepted that advertising does exaggerate but it is not always clear that this is wrong, for if everyone is in on the act it hardly becomes a matter of deception.[12] For quite some time, the law has recognised 'puffery' as acceptable, for exactly this reason.

In the film *Crazy People,* Dudley Moore plays an advertising man who is tired of lying. He suggests to his employer that it would be novel to tell the truth about the products he is promoting: Volvo is boxy but good; Metamucil keeps you regular and lessens the risk of death from colonic cancer; 'Sony — because Caucasians are too tall' (to work accurately on integrated circuits). The humour only works because these are precisely the concealed messages of conventional hyperbolic advertising. The low-voltage irony of this film is that the only people capable of telling the truth are psychiatric patients; when the Madison Avenue executives realise that truth works, they try to write truthful campaigns themselves — and fail. They have become so used to lying that they can no longer talk straight, no matter how hard they try. This irony is underlined by a role reversal in which the patients become more like the men on Madison Avenue the more advertisement writing they do.

The point is that most of the time exaggerated advertising is obvious. Is this a moral problem? To insist that it is allies one with a venerable but mistaken line of moral theorising. Tertullian, a father of the Christian Church, wrote against stage plays because the players took the parts of various characters. Tertullian held that such pretence was a species of lying and therefore forbidden to Christians. What he seems to have ignored is that such impersonations were not designed to deceive the audience into believing that dramatic roles were anything but roles. Therefore no deception was intended and indeed could only arise for a few exceptional people not familiar with the conventions of the theatre.

The same is true of advertising. Anyone unfamiliar with its idioms is likely to make poor judgments about the moral problems involved. This is not to deny that product boosting often crosses the line between praising real or imputed virtues and making claims that are insupportable. Just as dubious is what is left unsaid, or merely suggested. Lying and deception take their character from the contexts in which they are practised and are difficult to define in simple generalisations.

It might be thought that saying something false is lying, but people can often mislead others by saying something that they believe to be true but that is nonetheless false. A resident of Alaska, for example, might reply to his daughter's question about the capital of Australia that it is Sydney. Or we might honestly but falsely believe that Auckland is in the south island of New Zealand. On the other hand, we might tell an ailing relative that they will get better soon, believing death is inevitable when in fact a diagnosis has been made and indeed the relative will recover. The fact that we believed that death would come makes well-intended words a lie even though they turned out to be true. So we can lie even if we are not telling a falsehood. Even a relatively straightforward definition of lying, then, turns out to be difficult to construct. If it were simply about intention to mislead, then fairy stories told to children would be lies, and so would many a compliment around a barbecue and dinner table. If it were simply about deception for personal gain, then do untruths designed to protect other people cease to be lies?

Not only is the definition of lying difficult, then, but also more importantly its significance is also context-dependent — that is, it depends on what the liar is trying to do in a particular context. A person who intentionally and deliberately misleads you so that your surprise party will not be spoiled should be judged after the party, not at the point of telling the lie.

Advertising which makes false statements that the public is expected to take at face value is patently wrong and that is the end of the story. The real issues reside in advertising which does not make false claims, but which may nonetheless be misleading. The important point has to do with misleading, not with lying. People can mislead by telling the truth. Remember the example of Esso noted earlier. The line between what is permissible boosting of a product's merits and misleading exaggeration is a matter of pitch, context and the assumptions of the reader.

Should advertisers and marketers avoid exaggerated, offensive or tasteless campaigns altogether?

Should there be legal prohibitions on them?

It is clear that many vocal groups in society would answer 'yes' to both these questions. Not long ago, Hahn beer advertised itself in a poster featuring a smiling African man with an elongated neck adorned with rings and the caption 'Didn't even touch the sides'. A number of people found this advertisement racist. Similar complaints of tastelessness and sexism have been made in graffiti on posters advertising women's underwear. In 1993 Magistrate Pat O'Shane dismissed charges against two women who defaced a billboard for Berlei underwear because they found its depiction of a woman being sawn in half sexist. Sometimes it is the slogans that seriously offend. An advertisement for Thermos hot and cold containers proclaimed 'It takes more than big chests and nice jugs to attract customers'. Many years ago, an advertisement for Speedo women's swimwear featured an attractive woman in a brief (for then) swimsuit, with the caption, 'Gentlemen, start your engines'.

One of the most controversial advertising campaigns of recent times was run by Benetton with eye-catching posters of a burning car, poverty, an AIDS sufferer, and a naked Signor Benetton himself. These advertisements attracted much comment and some outrage from people who thought they exploited human suffering for commercial advantage. Perhaps the most controversial advertisement of 1993 was a one-day newspaper poster by Saatchi and Saatchi for the Toyota wide-body Camry, as follows.

Case 5.2 The Toyota case

The advertisement for the Toyota wide-body Camry attracted a great deal of public attention, for it featured not a picture of a car but the naked torso of a pregnant woman together with the caption 'There's Nowhere More Comfortable Than Inside a Wide Body'. The advertisement parodied a Ford campaign that featured a man jumping into his Falcon and travelling at high speed in wet conditions. At the end of that advertisement, we see that he has been driving his very pregnant wife to hospital. The advertisement also suggested the controversial cover of Vanity Fair featuring a pregnant Demi Moore posing naked. The Toyota advertisement certainly attracted much public attention and created debate about whether it demeaned or exploited women. Many feminists found it offensive and exploitative. Women parliamentarians supported this view, Senator Margaret Reynolds declaring the advertisement 'Insulting and dehumanising, firstly because it ridiculed pregnancy, and secondly because the picture showed a headless woman'.[13] And, at least as far as the media reported the reaction, only a few women commended the advertisement or were neutral towards it. As those who found the use of the pregnant woman objectionable had not been asked about the cover of *Vanity Fair*, it is not possible to state whether they also found that objectionable. What is clearer is that the controversy surrounding the Moore photograph was of a different kind, more about seeing a celebrity disclosing her pregnant nakedness than appearing naked *per se*. Yet this act was no less commercial: Moore was selling *Vanity Fair*, and selling herself too.

A few months after the Toyota advertisement appeared, a very large billboard appeared in Melbourne displaying the naked body of a 17-year-old youth, Vadim Dale, advertising boxer shorts. It read, 'Every day every man should drop his pants, look down and smile'. No complaints were received by the Advertising Standards Council according to then executive director Colin Harcourt, who said, 'Although the number are increasing, the percentage of complaints we receive about the depiction [of men] is still minuscule'. The advertisement was the work of Style Counsel, whose spokesperson, Laura Kininmonth, reported a favourable response to the poster, saying: 'It is a flagrant flaunting of young flesh. More and more you are seeing it happen, men dropping their pants in television commercials and movies. It is something to be flaunted and it is an indication of how much men have evolved.'[14]

The questions that arise in the Toyota case are many.

Why is it objectionable to use a naked pregnant woman in an advertisement to sell cars, but less controversial to use one to sell magazines, or for that matter, Demi Moore herself?

What precisely is objectionable in the Toyota advertisement: the use of a torso without a head, the use of pregnancy to sell cars, the caption across the photograph, the calculated and dramatic use of an ordinary but very precious human condition to capture public attention, or the sexist nature of the advertisement (using naked women yet again as objects to sell other objects)?

These questions apply to many advertisements today and are perplexing in a liberal society. The same kinds of displays can be acceptable or objectionable depending on who is publishing them, the purpose for which they are being published, and who is viewing them. The feminist journal *Refractory Girl* published a photograph of a naked pregnant woman holding a melon in front of her head in its August 1993 issue. Fairfax and Roberts jewellers ran advertisements for Paul Picot watches in the *Australian* and *Sydney Morning Herald*. The first advertisement featured a Helmut Newton photograph of a woman sitting on a chair with one hand on her lap and the other holding a book, which she is reading. She is wearing a satin evening gown, one strap falling off her shoulder. Standing behind her chair is a man … with his hand down the front of her dress, holding on to her breast. Two quotes from the copy are: 'If you're searching for satisfactions …' and 'When you see this model in the flesh, you'll express your desire for it on sight. After all we never told you to look but not touch'.[15] As with the Toyota advertisement, the Advertising Standards Council received a great number of complaints. Typical of the complaints were: '[The advertisement] conveys the dangerously misleading message that women condone and enjoy being molested by men and that this behaviour is completely normal. It objectifies women, demeans women and advocates sexual harassment and abuse, which is absolutely unacceptable.' 'I am amazed that an advertisement which is blatant soft pornography is tolerated in what I would consider a family newspaper.'[16] As with the Toyota advertisement, this advertisement was judged to be in breach of clauses 5 and 6 of the Advertising Code of Ethics, with the result that the advertisements were withdrawn from publication. Notwithstanding this sanction, and perhaps owing in some measure precisely to the storm of protest that they generated, the advertisements were surely effective as one-shot exposures.

The line between sexy and sexist may not be clear. The term 'sexist' implies that women are being demeaned or dominated for the purposes of men. The use of women in sexual advertising is held by some feminists to be objectifying. Suppose this is true: why is it unethical? Other feminists, however, believe that there is a puritanical strain in feminism that wants to deny that the sexual element in women is as strong as it is in men. If this were so, it would explain the tendency to blur the distinction between sexual and sexist.[17] The innuendo in 'Sleep wonderfully warm with Linda' has been played up to the point of inanity. So has a suggestive series of posters on buses and elsewhere of rugged males sprawled between sheets adorned with slogans like 'Supreme in bed'.

A market-oriented view would take the position that if these advertisements are sexist, offensive or inane they will not work and will be killed off by others in a kind of Darwinian struggle to survive. This libertarian view could be applied to all the ethical questions about advertising. It would hold that if a product or service is legally available, then its advertising should not be restricted.[18] The market will decide what kinds of advertisements will work. Obviously that which offends most people will be ineffective, as will misleading or exaggerated or deceptive advertising. But is this so?

The moral problem in advertising

According to one of Australia's most successful advertising men, John Singleton, the only kind of advertising that is objectionable is that which does not work. Responding to the controversy created by the Benetton campaign, Singleton asserted: 'There are no wrongs involved. The ad campaigns really deserving of debate are all those you cannot remember'. If an advertisement shocks people, creates controversy, or even outrages, so much the better. 'The tactics are not new, nor are the hysterical outbursts that multiply their effect', wrote Singleton. His rationale is that: 'It doesn't matter to Benetton what percentage of the market they alienate because it's only the ones they win that are important. It doesn't matter if you lose 90 per cent if you win the other 10 per cent as market share.'[19]

On Singleton's reasoning, Toyota's wide body advertisement might not be as successful as they had hoped. When selling to a mass market it seems sensible to be aware of consumer values. Still, this is a liberal pluralist society, and if firms with services and products to sell wish to use unorthodox, even outrageous, means to do so, should they not be permitted the liberty to fail or succeed?

This is an ethical question. So too is the issue of stereotyping women, people with disabilities or ethnic groups. It is simply incorrect to say that the market will exclude bad advertising, unless 'bad' is used in the sense of 'unsuccessful', in which case it is trivially true that bad advertising will be excluded. Advertisements that sell may still be offensive, as Singleton acknowledges.

The Toyota advertisement ran for one day, but provoked a record ninety-five complaints to the Advertising Standards Council. The ASC had been subject to strong lobbying from women's groups to act on sexism in advertising. Before the Toyota advertisement, John Singleton had run a highly controversial campaign for Eagle Bitter in South Australia around a scene in which a dog pulls a woman's jeans off. This caused a storm of protest to the ASC, though curiously, not as much as Saatchi and Saatchi's use of a pregnant woman to sell a car.

Although a member of the National Women's Consultative Council had a seat on the Advertising Standards Council, the latter had been holding meetings with women's groups in order to keep its views in line with those of the public. Eventually, the ASC ruled that the Toyota advertisement contravened two articles of its code and censured Saatchi and Saatchi.

Kate Henley, former executive director of the Australian Association of National Advertisers, expressed the view that the industry has lost touch with some shifts in social attitudes and beliefs:

> We can no longer ignore marginalised attitudes … The traditional response to attacks has been that this is a fringe and ratbag element. But I think we have to accept that these women's groups have pinpointed the trend. Advertisers need to accept that a change has taken place — that views held by women are less radical but also widespread. They have not come up to speed on that shift.[20]

If Henley is right, then free speech will ensure that advertisers are self-regulating; they will not run advertisements that alienate customers. But to opt for political correctness, to deny free expression even of offensive views is contrary to the kind of democracy which the West has long stood for. It may seem a small cost initially to ban advertising that offends any one, but the long-term costs — political and social rather than economic — will be much greater. Balancing the important democratic principle of toleration with, say, provisions 1 and 6 of the Advertising Code of Ethics was very difficult indeed.

Advertising placements and endorsements

There has been concern expressed in the United States about the ethics of product placement, and we see the same trend in Australia. Product placement involves buying a place for a product in a film or television show. Clearly identifiable products, such as cars, will be commonplace fixtures of film and video entertainments, but product placement can enhance the prominence of, say, a soft drink or evade restrictions on tobacco advertising. Some years ago, Paramount Pictures produced a television series called *Viper* after the name of its central 'character', a Dodge Viper sports car. A New York Times report, reprinted in the *Sydney Morning Herald*, commented on the marketing–entertainment symbiosis:

> Not only would Viper double as a program-length commercial for the Chrysler model but plans call for merchandising the series with tie-in products such as toy cars and apparel. That, of course, offers the potential to deliver still more advertising messages, over and above those that the viewers of Viper would watch in the form of commercials appearing in each episode.[21]

Similar concerns would apply to some game shows in Australia. Some companies are virtually acting as sponsors for game shows by donating prizes in return for publicity. But one game show, *Supermarket Sweep*, was nothing else but a competition built around supermarket lines. Is this not product placement? And what if it is? What is wrong with product placement?

Product placement is an ethical problem because consumers are exposed to a form of subliminal advertising. The placing of subliminal messages in films was banned in the 1950s, but product placement is a camouflaged variation on the practice. The camouflage used is in a sense obvious: the Coke signs are obvious when Sally Field walks into James Garner's drugstore in *Murphy's Romance*. And that is the whole point. Depending on the context, the reference to a product might or might not be an endorsement. In the film *Rain Man* two large corporations are mentioned favourably and unfavourably. In the most famous piece of (apparently) free advertising it has ever received, Qantas is endorsed by Raymond, the autistic prodigy, who refuses to travel by any other airline because they have had crashes. However, K-Mart does not fare so well. Originally an exclusive K-Mart shopper, Raymond changes during the course of the film and says at its conclusion 'K-Mart sucks!'. Of course, if this is product placement, not endorsement, then John Singleton's point holds: mere mention of a retailer is more important than endorsement, and K-Mart's unfavourable mention counts for as much as the implicit endorsement of Qantas.

Clearly the fortunes of K-Mart or Qantas will not stand or fall by these few remarks, but it is also clear that it would be unethical to pay for such lines to be inserted into a script. Why? Is it important that we know that an advertisement is an advertisement? Is this an element in the objectionability of product placement? Brand names are part of our lives and our culture (some, like Biro, Hoover and Kleenex, become generic names) and it would be artificial, and silly, for cinema and video to refrain from mentioning them. (Was Andy Warhol's painting of Campbell's soup tins an endorsement, a subtle product placement?) But this is precisely why it would be unethical to seek favourable treatment or to belittle a competitor by paying for product placement or displacement. Like subliminal advertising, it would be an abuse of freedom of speech and artistic licence. When endorsements are made by prominent people or organisations it should be clear that the endorsement is not posing as something else — say, information, entertainment or even news.

Endorsements

It is not always necessary or desirable that endorsements be paid for. Some public interest organisations make recommendations for the public good. The National Heart Foundation counsels about diet in terms that are not helpful to the dairy industry. The Australian Conservation Foundation has for the first time made an endorsement, giving approval to a low energy, long-life tube to replace the conventional incandescent light globe. It sees this product as furthering its interests in energy conservation, pollution savings and so on. The danger with paid and unpaid endorsements is that the credibility of the public figures and public interest organisations can be brought into question. From the advertiser's viewpoint, high-profile figures can become exclusively associated with a product, something that can have ramifications beyond the conduct of their personal lives. If they were, say, to advertise a competitor's product, there would be implicit comparative advertising.

In a case before Justice Davies of the Federal Court, Raid insecticide was restrained for a time from using the radio announcer John Laws to promote their product because of

Laws's long association with rival brand Mortein. Although Laws had not uttered the Mortein slogan ('When you're on a good thing stick to it') for eleven years, Justice Davies reasoned that Raid had recruited him 'precisely because of that association'. The judge ruled that Laws could mistakenly be taken to be endorsing another Mortein product, but an even more likely inference to be taken here is that Raid is engaging in masked comparative advertising. After a sufficient elapse of time, Laws advertised a rival product using a parody of the Mortein campaign: in his newer ad, Laws said (for Raid), 'When you find a better product, switch to it'.

Bait advertising, and the bait-and-switch

Bait advertising is the use of selected items to attract customer interest when the advertiser knows full well that there is sufficient stock for only a few customers. The practice is for sellers to then harness the interest of the potential buyer in the unavailable item and use it to sell another product. In other words, it falls under the head of false pretences. The 'bait-and-switch' is even worse. The ploy here is to advertise something which you plan not to sell: either, you do not have it, and you then try to convince the prospective buyer that something else (more expensive or with a higher mark-up) is available, or you have it but have planned to try to convince the prospective buyer that it is not the thing to buy, whereas something else which you stock is. The idea is that you use something that sounds very attractive as bait, planning all the while to switch the prospective buyer's interest to something else. Here is an interesting example of bait (perhaps bait-and-switch).[22]

Case 5.3   Le Winter's Radio Stores

In New York in 1938, Le Winter's Radio Stores displayed a refrigerator, attached to which was a sign. In large letters on the sign was printed '1938 Norge $119.50'. In smaller letters, the word 'from' was placed in front of the price. Le Winter's was taken to court over this matter. In *People v Le Winter's Radio Stores, Inc.*, it was argued that Le Winter's was not ready to sell the refrigerator at the price printed on the sign, but rather was ready to sell only a smaller refrigerator.[23]

Apart from the legality of the matter, the sign was clearly misleading. Still, it is worth asking: Given that a prospective buyer does not have to buy, what is so terrible about bait advertising?

What about bait-and-switch advertising?

Some situations are not so clear-cut.

Case 5.4   Grace Brothers

It is common practice for department stores to hold post-Christmas sales. In 1992 the Grace Brothers Sydney store had advertised remarkable bargains on selected white-goods, typically refrigerators. The store stated in its advertisements that only a certain number of such items would be available. Crowds gathered in such numbers for the bargains that people were hurt in the crush to reach the few heavily discounted items first. People knew that bargains on household appliances were few, so this form of merchandising does not seem at face value to be bait advertising. Yet the offer, even of a few items at extraordinary discounts, raises an interesting ethical question. The fact that people have been hurt in the rush for such discounts indicates that they are substantial crowd-pullers. And, the selected whitegoods themselves would surely not have been regarded by Grace Brothers as warranting such massive advertising.

A change of heart ensued in the face of poor publicity. Grace Brothers no longer massively discounts a few whitegoods, and security procedures have been improved for the post-Christmas sales. Moreover, the store has also improved the atmosphere among the bargain-hunters who gather outside its doors in the early morning. Both the publicity for the sale and Grace Brothers' image has improved.

Is this a form of bait advertising?

Grace Brothers' initial response was to deny responsibility for the harm caused to customers by this 'first-come, first-served' form of marketing. Was this defensible?

Morals and marketing

Beginning in July 1993, telephone customers were asked to vote for the long-distance carrier of their choice — Optus or Telecom (now Telstra). If customers did not vote, the default option was Telecom, so Optus had a large stake in just persuading people to vote, especially as surveys showed that most people were averse to the idea of a ballot.[24] In order to provide an incentive to vote, Optus wanted to offer prizes such as cars and holidays. Not surprisingly, Telecom, which had an interest in people not voting, but was shown in a Time–Morgan poll to have a substantial lead over Optus,[25] was opposed to such incentives.

Would Optus have been acting ethically in offering incentives to vote?

Was Telecom acting ethically in opposing incentives?

Case 5.5   Telstra v Optus

On 3 June 1993 Telecom ran two full-page advertisements in the *Sydney Morning Herald* labelled 'Corrective Advertisement'. They began: 'The Trade Practices Commission has directed Telecom to issue this corrective advertisement'. Both advertisements admitted that previous advertising might have been misleading. The second stated in part:

> The advertisement may have misled readers to believe that the cost of a five minute call from metropolitan Sydney to metropolitan Brisbane is cheaper using the Telecom Business Circle Flexi-Plan as compared with the Optus standard rule. In fact, at no time

would the cost of such a call be cheaper under the Flexi-Plan, in comparison with the Optus standard rate, when the $1 per month Flexi-Plan access fee and the Optus advantage discount are taken into account.[26]

If the Trade Practices Commission had not directed Telecom to publish these corrections, it seems that consumers might have been none the wiser. Pressure for government regulation of advertising is increased by cases like this. Of course, Optus might also have complained to the Advertising Standards Council, under provision 7 of the Advertising Code of Ethics. If they had been successful, then 'self-regulation' (i.e., industry self-regulation) would have been effective against the Telecom advertisement. Without the intervention of a regulatory body, misleading or incomplete information might be provided to customers. As Lemke and Schminke have argued, the incentives to mislead are greater when business is under stress, as Telecom clearly was by the entry of a competitor into the long-distance telephone market. Marketing under conditions of stress may produce inflated claims and ethically suspect strategies. The presence in the marketplace of an adjudicator can make a difference to the confidence of all stakeholders and other interested parties when such claims and strategies are challenged.

It will not always be possible to monitor the ethics of marketing, but this does not relieve marketers of their responsibilities to have regard for core ethical principles. Sometimes they do not even seem to perceive the presence of an ethical question. The following case illustrates this situation.

Case 5.6   School Sample Bag Company

In June 1993 a school-based marketing scheme was the subject of some controversy. Children in New South Wales state primary schools were given sample bags to take home by the School Sample Bag Company, and the schools received cash payments of up to $500. The practice attracted the ire of Carl Vagg, a parent at Faulconbridge Primary, whose 6-year-old daughter brought home a bag labelled 'dedicated to learning' and containing product samples and a survey with a Gold Coast holiday as an incentive to return it. Also in the bag to which Vagg objected was a copy of *Who Weekly*, which contained a photograph of a woman showing scars from the removal of breast implants.

The Department of School Education's policy is to let individual principals decide whether to distribute the bags. Vagg, however, found the practice objectionable: 'It is a deceptive Trojan horse invasion into the home posing itself as an educational product, whereas it's really a slick marketing exercise'. Of course, there is nothing intrinsically wrong with slick marketing, but the president of the NSW Federation of Parents' and Citizens' Associations, Dr Graham Aplin, said he was 'dumbfounded' at this use of children.[27]

Can an arrangement that benefits schools, parents, marketers and producers be unethical? Why?

If the contents of the bags were uncontroversial, would the ethical difficulties disappear?

The moral issues in marketing are an extension of those in advertising.

Is it wrong to market foundation and skin-nourishing creams to women knowing that claims about skin rejuvenation are false? Cosmetics manufacturers say that they are making women feel better about themselves. Marketers know that some kinds of packaging are more appealing than others.

Is it wrong to sell products in large-volume containers which suggest a larger product or which give a better image or a higher profile to perfume or breakfast cereal?

Is the problem one of deception or of wastage in packaging or both?

Some of these questions are clearer if we take as a case a range of children's bath-time products from Johnson & Johnson.

Case 5.7   Johnson & Johnson

Johnson & Johnson's children's bath time products come in the shape of animal characters from A. A. Milne's stories of Winnie the Pooh. The first question that arises then is the marketing of such products in packaging that will appeal to children (and perhaps their parents) because they have the appearance of toys. These products could be harmful to children if their contents were consumed from the container or came into contact with their eyes. Hence there is a warning on the label, in rather small type, 'This is not a toy'. Might such a warning not be rather beside the point when the product presents as a toy, is modelled on a storybook character, is cast in soft plastic, and belongs to a range of similar items that distinguish themselves from other shampoos and bubble-bath soaps by their shape and colour. Such denials are known in philosophy are pragmatic contradictions, and Johnson & Johnson would do well either to acknowledge that their product differentiator is in fact a toy and take appropriate safety measures, or to repackage their products and find some other marketing strategy for selling children's bath soaps.

A second question arises in relation to these products, however, from a report made public by the ABC television program *The Investigators*.[28] The program found that Johnson & Johnson had imported bottles of bubble bath from the United States in the shape of the Pooh character Tigger the tiger. The American label with a warning about safety had been covered by an Australian one with no warning at all. Australian labelling laws are less strict than their American counterparts, and do not require the safety warning that the soap could sting a child's eyes. Johnson & Johnson's new (Australian) label covered this warning on Tigger, the only one of the five characters whose contents are not 'no more tears'. This action was legal. But was it ethical? This behaviour might seem all the more peculiar, given the particular position of Johnson & Johnson, which apparently has taken to heart and seriously tried to put into practice its Credo, which includes the following:

We believe our first responsibility is to the doctors, nurses, and patients, to mothers and all others who use our products and services. In meeting their needs everything we do must be of high quality …

We are responsible to our employees …

We are responsible to the communities in which we live and work and to the world community as well. We must be good citizens …

In a series of 'Credo Challenge Meetings', the company's CEO held frank and open discussions with employees around the world about how to implement the philosophy and provisions of the Credo, allowing that the document could be changed. Commitment to the Credo was truly put to the test in the late 1980s. Over a short period there were instances of intentional contamination of some containers of Tylenol, one of the company's products. A very expensive decision was made (not even by the top management, so well was the Credo instilled throughout the company) to remove all Tylenol from the retail shelves in the interest of customer safety. In the company's view this was the right decision. The public's welfare was seen to be paramount, and this ethos was evident throughout the company. Of course, the possible damage that could be caused by the Tigger bubble bath cannot be compared with the damage that could have been caused by a terrorist's spiking of Tylenol. There is, nevertheless, a generic question about looking out for the welfare of the consumers of the product.

Consider the marketing of the Saturn motor car in the United States, compared with the marketing of other new lines of motor car.

Case 5.8   Saturn cars

Honda marketed the Acura in separate showrooms and under a separate badge from the rest of its range of motor cars. Honda distanced (not to say, 'concealed') its association with the Acura. Mazda did the same thing with the Eunos. Toyota has the Lexus. In each case, the manufacturer was trying to enter a market with which it had not been associated, and it believed it could best move up in class by, as it were, introducing a new player, rather than by introducing a new product by an old player with a reputation in a lower-class market. On one level, the situation in the United States with Saturn motor cars could be regarded as analogous. The Saturn is a General Motors car, marketed, manufactured, and sold under its own badge. It is, in fact, produced by the Saturn Corporation. In this case, however, the car itself is quite mediocre. Unlike the story of the Acura, the Eunos, and the Lexus, the story here is not one of moving into a more expensive market, where the quality of the car is higher. Its new class is one of ethics and customer care. The Saturn distances itself from General Motors by breaking new ground in these areas. There are basically two fundamental tenets underlying the marketing of the Saturn that mark its move to a higher class:

1 Absolutely hassle-free car buying

Saturn's prices are transparent and non-negotiable. They even have a Web site, where you can click on the various options (there are not many) and the model and colour you are interested in (there are not many) and see the price. And it shows you what you will pay. Salespeople are not pushy. They have escaped the mould of 'car salesman'. Apparently, the car has become particularly popular with women car-buyers, who statistically are more put off or intimidated by the typical car sales techniques.

2 Fair, above-board dealing in selling cars, and an ethical approach to manufacturing them

Throughout the company, the employees are recognised as part of the management team. Throughout the organisation, the notion of 'team' figures prominently. The Saturn 'Shared Values' statement promises that 'We, at Saturn, are committed to being one of the world's most successful car companies by adhering to the following values: commitment to customer enthusiasm, commitment to excel, teamwork, trust and respect for the individual, continuous improvement'. Saturn boasts that, at its factory in Spring Hill, Tennessee, 'the air leaving the plant is cleaner than the air going in, and when we built the plant, two hundred trees were moved to a nursery and later replanted on site, rather than being killed'.

The company's approach is very much as stated in its 'Shared Values': it is out to do the right thing by its customers. It is this, rather than any particular qualities of the cars themselves, that Saturn is trading on. And it is apparently doing so with considerable success. Saturn reports, Saturn leads the automotive industry in customer and sales satisfaction. Recently, Saturn captured the No. 1 position in the J.D. Power and Associates Customer Service Index and Sales Satisfaction Index — the first non-luxury brand to capture the top position for both in the same year.[29]

Tobacco marketing

Take another case of questionable marketing practice, that of Peter Jackson cigarettes.

Case 5.9 Peter Jackson cigarettes

In January 1993 Peter Jackson cigarettes were being marketed in a twin pack with an audio cassette tape of the band *Noiseworks* sandwiched between the cigarettes. Purchase of the cigarettes provided a musical bonus at a negligible cost, and the tapes of other bands available from the tobacco company were advertised at a discount. This form of marketing casts doubt on claims by the Tobacco Institute that cigarette advertising is not aimed at the young. What else is going on here but an enticement to young people to purchase a twin pack of Peter Jackson to get the tape? Association of a dangerous substance with popular music is probably not much different from tobacco sponsorship of sport, but in the former, both the inducement to smoke and the message that smoking is a normal leisure activity are more direct. The fact that selling tobacco to those under eighteen is illegal makes no difference: the cassette tape invited teenagers to smoke, reinforced the smoking habit, and legitimated smoking for young teens.

The lie here is not patent, but the suggested message is no less potent. The dangers of smoking are all but completely drowned out by the other messages on the pack: its association with music, youth culture and leisure. Packaging, promotion and pitch are important in interpreting the warnings on products like cigarettes. If a product is promoted as safe or user friendly, a purchaser can be misled into believing that it is risk-free or requires no skill in operation — despite warnings! Chain saws and power tools commonly have safety devices to provide a 'safe exit' for the unwary or the beguiled. Manufacturers of electrical products place warning stickers on the access covers of electrical products, and better designs for commonplace items like lamp-holders are now proof against people who do not switch off the power before changing a globe.

Of course there is no safe exit in cigarette smoking. But the tobacco industry suggests low-tar cigarettes are a less risky option. Apparently these cigarettes contain a ring of ventilation holes near the filter tip, just about where most smokers would place their fingers. If fingers do obstruct these ventilation holes, the tar content of the cigarettes is about the same as in the unmodified variety. As most smokers do not even realise that these holes exist and that their presence is the sole warrant for the claim of less tar, some warning might reasonably be provided to make good the claim. Otherwise consumers might be misled into believing that they have minimised the risk of contracting a disease.[30] In *Crazy People*, one of the inmates of the mental hospital offers this slogan for a tobacco company: 'If you're going to risk cancer, shouldn't your cigarette deliver real flavour?'. This is at least more honest than pretending the problem does not exist or that it can be minimised. In pointing to the legality of the product and claiming that advertising is only to sustain or expand market share, the tobacco marketers are being disingenuous. The whole of the tobacco advertising industry is geared to glamorising a lethal product, one legalised before its dangers were known and which health authorities are progressively making less acceptable. Experience indicates that making tobacco illegal would have much the same effect as prohibition did on alcohol in the United States. So pointing to the legality of tobacco products is no argument at all; we are stuck with this legality. We are not, however, stuck with tobacco advertising, and the force of moral argument has driven changes to the advertising laws for the electronic and print media.

So it seems that there are moral obligations deriving from the public interest requiring advertisers and marketers to sell products in certain ways, for example, by explaining risks or by being informative in more than a perfunctory way.

Review questions

1   Do you think there is anything ethically objectionable about the advertisement for sunglasses that was described in the chapter?

2   We quoted John Singleton as stating that the only kind of objectionable advertising is that which doesn't work. What do you think about this point of view?

3   Not everything that is objectionable — even morally objectionable — should be sanctioned. Toleration is the appropriate regard for some such things. Could you give an account of what makes any particular objectionable advertisement sanctionable rather than tolerable? What role, if any, does 'awareness of community standards' play in your thinking?

4   Do you think there are 'special' moral considerations about advertising of some types of products, such as: alcohol, tobacco, firearms, prescription drugs, breakfast cereals, toys, health food, or anything else? If you do, why?

5   Do you think that, legitimately, there is anything left to 'let the buyer beware', when it comes to listening to an advertisement?

Equal Opportunity, Discrimination and Affirmative Action

6

Perhaps one of the earliest lessons in life is that outcomes are not equal. This is clear from games, school and business. The very existence of difference seems to breed inequality. Yet one of the most familiar democratic ideals is equality. As a society we identify injustices and set policy agendas in its name. The notions of 'one vote one value', of 'the equality of franchise', and of 'equality before the law' are the normal expectations of citizens in a democracy.

For all that, there is constant confusion between the political and moral senses of equality on the one hand, and people's physical, psychological qualities and abilities on the other. Most people do not believe that we are all equally endowed with talents or that the talents of each person are merely different in kind rather than in degree. Some people are very gifted and some are relatively deprived. This confusion becomes more clearly an issue when the moral ideal of equality is transposed into corporate life. How can business be expected to compensate for the missed life chances of individuals, and why is it the responsibility of business to do so?

Identifying the responsibilities of business in these respects is first a matter of looking at the law. Equal opportunity, anti-discrimination legislation and affirmative action programs all regulate business to some degree. Beyond these requirements, the old questions about equality arise.

A voiced concern is that disadvantaged groups lack the power to rectify the legacy of discrimination, and that injustices will be remedied much too slowly if radical measures are not employed. If a lack of power has prevented some members of society from enjoying equality of opportunity, then power should be used to redress this. While this view may have had some sway with governments and the requirements they impose on business, what moral obligations are there on business itself to pay regard to equality?

If people differ in ability, what is it that business should pay attention to? When we talk of people being equal, it is obvious that we do not mean that they are the same height or weight. Nor do we mean that they have the same talents or the same potentials. What we mean is that their differences should not be used as a reason for treating them less fairly than others. For example, in the past, women were paid less for doing the same work as men. Such distinctions are unfair and inappropriate, inasmuch as they have nothing to do with criteria of reward, such as merit and contribution.

But what if a person has a disability or even just becomes pregnant? Why should they not be less well favoured than a person able to fit more easily into a company's system? A caution is necessary here: we should not assume that a disability or even pregnancy is a barrier to high performance. It is easy to give examples like Stephen Hawking, who is a first-rate mathematical physicist despite suffering motor-neurone disease for virtually all of his adult life. One of Australia's leading judges gained the medal of one of its top law schools while pregnant. Too much can be made of disability or pregnancy and not enough of a person's abilities.

Still, there is a legitimate question here. A company might not be set up to employ people who use wheelchairs. Most do not have child-care facilities. Over the past two decades there have been changes to the law to require more of business, and doubtless more changes in the name of equality will follow. But what is the moral basis of this?

The idea of equality behind anti-discrimination, equal opportunity and affirmative action is that of fairness. If people are worthy of equal respect then there is an obligation to place them in a position to give their best, just as the state provides public education to allow all people to develop their abilities and potential. Hence, those who have suffered some disadvantage must be treated 'unequally' in some circumstances in order to satisfy the demands of fairness. Those in need or denied opportunity might receive more resources than people without disadvantages in order to allow them to attain some social norm, such as a certain level of education or employment. Likewise, appropriate arrangements must be made for those with disabilities. In March 1993 the Equal Opportunity Tribunal found that Gwenda Woods, who suffers paraplegia, had been discriminated against by the builders of a shopping complex in Wollongong. The builders had not provided facilities for people with disabilities comparable to those enjoyed by people without them.[1] This amounts to forgetting that a certain number of customers will require access. Once, this kind of attitude would not have caused a second thought. Today, it is a form of negligence. The courts will decide the legalities, but the central ethical idea behind such decisions is fairness.

Employment discrimination

Employment is considered almost to be a right in advanced industrial societies. People depend on employment, unemployment is regarded as a personal and social problem, and governments institute programs to enable people to find work. The denial of work on irrelevant grounds to those who are capable of performing it is unfair. It can cause personal harm in the denial of a host of life opportunities — independence, personal development, family, education, a full social life — as well as various social and economic losses — lost wealth generation, welfare dependency, health expenditures, and taxes foregone. So employment is an area that is subject to criteria of individual and social justice. The same is true of the work environment. Issues such as wages and conditions have long been subject to regulation, but stronger measures to protect the health and safety of workers and others in the workplace have increased the regulated responsibilities of employers. So have anti-discrimination measures. To adapt a theme that runs through this book, if the responsibilities of employers are restricted to observing the letter of the law they will not achieve fair hiring and promotion policies, a safe workplace or a confident and fully productive workforce.

Discrimination can be direct or indirect. It can be overt or concealed. It can be intended or unconscious. It can be singular or systematic. It can be an effect of history or result from a current prejudice. In each case it is an example of unfairness and injustice, and that means that it requires rectification. That rectification is not always in the form of compensation for individuals. When people are discriminated against because they are members of a group or class, then provision for that class might be necessary. The following discussion deals with these issues.

Discrimination does not result only from an intention to discriminate. Discrimination can be the result of some activity without being the aim of that activity. Sometimes this is referred to as 'indirect discrimination', in contrast to 'direct discrimination', which is the intention to discriminate. Suppose a business advertises for 'men to load trucks', and then hires accordingly. This is direct discrimination against women. Suppose that a business, concerned that its employees be strong enough and that they can negotiate over tailgates, stacked-up cartons, and so on, advertises for 'truck-loaders, must be at least 175 cm tall'. Hiring according to this criterion would result in a (statistically) disproportionate number of male employees as a much higher percentage of men than women would meet the height requirement. As such, this amounts to indirect discrimination against women. It is, of course, direct 'discrimination' against everyone shorter than 175 cm. Of course, any conditions or criteria of employment — for example, the ability to type at least 55 words per minute — would, strictly speaking, amount to direct discrimination against the group who do not satisfy the conditions. But not just any employment criteria are fair, relevant or appropriate. A height requirement for truck loaders may or may not be irrelevant. Thus, ethically speaking, notions of 'fairness', 'relevance' and 'appropriateness' make all the difference in an analysis of justified or permissible discrimination, and impermissible discrimination. Equality is a remedy against unjustifiable discrimination. It remains a relevant principle in measuring injustice, and for that reason it is an important concept, not only in political ethics, but in business as well. The importance of the effect of discrimination is illustrated in the cases that follow.

Case 6.1   BHP and employment opportunities for women

On 23 February 1994, 743 women won compensation from BHP for their exclusion from the workforce in the early 1980s. BHP had maintained two waiting lists for employment at its Port Kembla steel works: one for men and one for women. The women's list had more than 2000 names and up to seven years' waiting time for employment. Those on the men's list usually had work within a month. Women constituted only a small part of BHP's workforce. After complaints to the Anti-Discrimination Board in the late 1970s, women were hired at Port Kembla, but within three years most of these women had been retrenched in line with the company's 'last-on, first-off policy'. Thirty-five of the women alleging discriminatory employment practices took the case to the New South Wales Equal Opportunity Tribunal, which awarded them more than $1 million. This determination was overturned by the New South Wales Court of Appeal, and the women then took their case to the High Court. In 1989 the court made a finding that followed Canadian and American precedents that eight of the women had been indirectly discriminated against, and confirmed a $1.4 million compensatory damages payment.[2] Then 709 women, mainly of non-English-speaking backgrounds, took legal action on the same grounds, and this matter was settled out of court in February 1994. The compensation agreed to by BHP is confidential, but is believed to have been about $9 million.

Michael Hogan, director of Sydney's Public Interest Advocacy Centre, which assisted in the women's case, said:

This historic case has resulted in jobs being available to women in a host of areas, not just the steelworks, based on merit and capacity rather than on stereotypes and prejudice…The case drew attention to the unfairness of and inefficiency of traditional approaches to the employment of women.

According to Dr Chloe Mason, an occupational health and safety expert, the women's case has had positive results in other areas. Old safety procedures and regulations have been reformed, and improved codes of practice have been adopted. 'It has brought about fundamental changes in practices and attitudes to the employment of women, the implementation of anti-discrimination and affirmative action,' she said.[3]

Case 6.2   Telecom and equality in recruitment practice

In 1991 three women engineering students complained to the Human Rights and Equal Opportunity Commission about the employment practices of Telecom. They had each applied for engineering cadetships with Telecom after completing a substantial part of their degrees at Royal Melbourne Institute of Technology. The specifics of their complaints differed, but the common theme was the discriminatory way in which the interviews were conducted.

C. told the commission that she was asked how she felt about working in a male-dominated area and noted 'conspiratorial' glances between the interviewers. She was repeatedly asked the same question on technical details, even when she answered that she did not know. In the end she gave any answers just to stop the interviewers badgering her. She alleged that she received no positive feedback during the interview and was made to feel stupid.

M. reported a similar badgering style of questioning on technical matters, the interviewers again being unsatisfied with an 'I don't know'. M. also alleged that the interviewers asked inappropriate questions such as, 'You're from the western suburbs, aren't you?', 'What do your parents do?', 'What do you think about Bob Hawke?' and 'Do you have a problem working in a male-dominated area?'. One interviewer wrote the word management on a whiteboard and said, 'There are things you have to take into consideration when managing a project. Write down about ten words beginning with 'm' that a manager would have to take into consideration when managing a project.' When M. replied that she could give things a manager would have to consider, but had trouble getting the actual 'm' words, one of the interviewers replied, 'All right, but we don't think you will be able to get the first one'. He then wrote the word 'men', saying, 'A manager needs to get men to work on the project'. M. alleged that at this point the interviewers gave her a quick look to check her reaction.

S. reported that her questioning ran along the following lines: 'How many staff members in Telecom?', 'How many engineers in Telecom?', 'How much profit did Telecom make in the last financial year?', 'What type of company is Telecom?', and 'Can you buy shares in Telecom?'. To this last question S. replied, 'I don't think you can, can you?', whereupon the interviewer yelled at her, 'Answer the question, don't ask us'. Other questions included: 'Where in Italy is your father from?', 'What do your parents do?', 'Have you been to Italy?', and 'What were your favourite cities?'. S. answered the last question by naming Venice, Florence and Milan, to which one interviewer responded, 'You like Milan, that dirty, smoggy, smelly city?'

In its defence, Telecom called two men and two women who had been interviewed by the same panel and had gained places in Telecom's cadetship scheme. The men said that they did not find the interviews tough but, on the contrary, friendly and encouraging. There was no badgering. The women, however, said the interviews were aggressive.

In April, 1983 Telecom had issued guidelines for interviewing women.[3] One interviewer said he had a general knowledge of these guidelines; the other said he had none. Telecom, it seems, had not ensured that its own guidelines were known in the engineering division of the organisation.

The commission found that the complainants by reason of their sex were treated less favourably in their interviews than males in circumstances that were not materially different. The intimidatory and hectoring conduct of interviews with women, the introduction of questions of arguable relevance, and the failure of Telecom to implement its own guidelines were grounds for the commission's decision.[4]

This case illustrates that care has to be taken in ensuring fair treatment in employment practices. Yet the matter might not be as straightforward as it seems.

What if the questions asked were designed by the interviewers to see whether the women would be able to work effectively in a setting where such questions might arise?

What if the interview was used as a stronger test of the women because, equal opportunity notwithstanding, women still have to deal with sexism in the workplace?

Consider these objections. Think of some more of your own. Do they stand up ethically? Would they provide justification for treating women and men differently in the employment interview? Was it possible to show equal respect in treating the women differently? Imagine that you are a person with a disability, and check your own reaction to being treated differently.

Workplace discrimination

In April 1994 Heather Horne and Gail McIntosh were awarded compensation of $92,000 for sexual harassment by the Western Australian Equal Opportunity Tribunal. In a path-breaking decision, the tribunal ruled that the compensation was to be paid by the employer and the women's union.

Case 6.3   Horne & McIntosh v Press-Clough Joint Venture & MAWU

Between 1990 and 1992 two women, Heather Horne and Gail McIntosh, who worked as cleaners, were subjected to verbal abuse, graffiti, and the display of soft- and hard-core pornography in their place of work, the Goodwyn A gas platform being constructed near Fremantle. Complaints to their union organiser and male workers about offensive displays in the workplace were met with hostility; the men, who dominated the workforce by six hundred to two, insisted that the environment was male and the women 'would just have to cop it'. Horne and McIntosh accepted this to the extent of tolerating semi-naked pin-ups, but drew the line at grossly offensive and degrading hard-core porn. Male workers, however, threatened to strike if the pornography was removed. The union took their side against the women and convinced the employer that the problem had been resolved. After more than a year of such conduct, Horne and McIntosh found the work environment so stressful that they resigned. No one concerned with the matter disputed that the material displayed was pornographic, but after Horne and McIntosh complained to the Equal Opportunity Commission, the offending material was removed and an equal opportunity training program was instituted.

In deciding for the women, the tribunal criticised their employer, the Press-Clough Joint Venture, and their union, the Metals and Engineering Workers Union, for treating complaints of harassment with contempt:

We do not say it was easy; but we are positive in our view that the issue had to be confronted. Anything less is capitulation, and that is what happened here. The short

answer to the question posed is quite simply that we must do what we know to be right,
to stop what we know to be wrong.[5]

Jennie George, then assistant secretary Australian Council of Trade Unions (ACTU) agreed: 'The boys have got to understand there are legal penalties and moral responsibilities', she said.[6] While most people would agree with the decision of the tribunal, some would find it politically correct, paternalistic and even undemocratic. They would ask:

Why should two women be able to dictate to six hundred men what they put on their walls? Why should the union take a special interest in the moral and gender position of two members against the wishes of the overwhelming majority of its members?

Why should the employer support two women who have a choice to work under prevailing conditions or resign?

Why should minorities be able to arrange things as they please and have their private choices backed up by public authorities?

These questions are not uncommon, and in answering them we can provide a model for case analysis in business ethics.

First, what is the nature of the offence? This case offers a clear example of the violation of the ethical principle of respect for persons. The two women were respected neither by their fellow workers and union nor by their employer. This is ethical failure at the personal, group and institutional levels. Where a dispute affecting individuals and their access to work cannot be resolved by employers, unions and employees, it becomes a matter for independent arbitration. As the charges of harassment affect legally protected rights, the Equal Opportunity Tribunal had a proper role in this case. The legal protection of rights is hardly undemocratic because it safeguards a minority from the majority.

To suggest that two women wished to dictate to six hundred men misrepresents the situation; the display of offensive pornography was anything but innocent. The two workers were bullied because they were different. This difference happened to be one of sex. It might as easily have been one of religion: how would a Muslim have greeted such a display? The fact that the harassed employees were women is in one sense not significant, for bullying tactics against anyone is morally reprehensible. In another sense, the harassment is a particularly nasty display of sexism; the women were attacked as women. There was a clear assumption that women did not qualify for equal esteem with men (let alone equal employment opportunity and conditions), that they were powerless and that they could be degraded through ridicule of their sex. None of this is acceptable in society at large, and has been proscribed in the workplace. Yet the union turned a blind eye to the plight of the women, whom it seemed to regard as insignificant and expendable in the face of a hostile majority and their threat to strike. This reveals moral cowardice in an organisation one would expect to defend the powerless against the arbitrary exercise of power. To suggest that the victims of harassment should accept such treatment or resign is to abandon the notion of justice in the workplace.

It is the employer's responsibility to ensure that the workplace is a safe and suitable environment for employees. This means that an employer should know if overt harassment is being practised and should treat complaints from employees seriously. The failure of the employer in this case illustrates the dangers of ignoring this. Quite apart from considerations of justice, the penalties attached to discrimination and negligence in protecting employee rights can be heavy. Many Australian laws give protection to moral rights, not only to the benefit of the individuals directly concerned, but also to the community of stakeholders with an indirect interest in such exemplary cases.

A modification of the facts in this case could give rise to some other serious questions. For example:

Is it significant that the display of pornography was directed at the two women employees and that they were subjected to harassment, or should the mere presence of hard-core pornography be prohibited? The transmission of pornographic images in the workplace via email has met with increasingly tougher penalties from employers.[7]

What if there were no objections raised by the women or all the workers were male? Some types of objectionable behaviour should be tolerated. As a matter of fact, commitment to a principle of toleration is itself an important moral commitment.

At what point, in the matter of morally objectionable conduct, does toleration become less important than some other moral value?

This issue was the focal point in the following cases.

Case 6.4 *Catherine Nowland v TNT*

On 8 June 1993 the New South Wales Equal Opportunity Tribunal awarded Catherine Nowland $20,000 compensation against her former employer, TNT. The tribunal found that her supervisor, John Archer, had through his remarks and attitudes caused Nowland 'a considerable loss of self-esteem and dignity as well as … humiliation and embarrassment. Indeed, on any objective view, his conduct was highly offensive, sexist and demeaning and can only have been intended to promote the subordination of women'. Although Nowland had won various awards as a national sales executive, the tribunal found that she was treated less favourably than male peers 'on the ground of sex'. It rejected her claims that she had suffered discrimination by being denied an office, company car, and business-class airline tickets to a conference in London. Archer was reported as saying to Nowland, 'Don't get me wrong Cathy, I'm not as you see me. I think women have a place in the workforce and that is to provide a second opinion'. The tribunal also accepted that Archer said to her, 'If you want to work in a man's world, you have to behave accordingly'. To another woman he is reported to have said, 'I don't pay you to think, you're only a female sales exec so just do as you're told'. In front of twenty witnesses he also said, 'I don't employ women in my sales team, I can't believe you're talking about women doing well'. Because of such sexist attitudes in her work environment, Nowland resigned from TNT and complained to the tribunal.[8]

Case 6.5   SPC share issue

In 1993 the fruit canning company SPC floated a share issue that attracted too many applications to be met. The underwriters, ANZ McCaughan, therefore decided to limit subscriptions to one per household. They did this by allocating shares to the men in the households, an admission made to a woman who complained that her husband's application, lodged at the same time as hers, was successful while hers was not. SPC was clearly embarrassed by the behaviour of their underwriters, and wrote to women denied shares in this way offering them the difference between the issue price and the current value of the shares.

Pregnancy discrimination

Case 6.6   Lesley Mutsch v Beaurepaires Tyres

In June 1991 Lesley Mutsch was dismissed from her position as a record keeper at Beaurepaires Tyres in Wodonga, Victoria. Beaurepaires claimed that the dismissal was part of a retrenchment scheme following the introduction of a computerised accounting system. Commissioner Kevin O'Connor of the Human Rights and Equal Opportunity Commission found, however, that Mutsch's pregnancy was a factor in her dismissal, and awarded her $12,000 compensation. [9]

Mutsch's case is not unusual, according to the New South Wales Anti-Discrimination Board. It found persistent widespread discrimination against pregnant women and women of child-bearing age. It also found that instances of discrimination were often not reported, and that law reform in the area was necessary. While complaints of sex discrimination fell from 424 in 1988–89 to 367 in 1991–92, complaints about discrimination on the grounds of pregnancy rose from forty-seven to 101 in 1990–91 and then fell to eighty-one in 1991–92. Complaints to the Human Rights and Equal Opportunity Commission between 1988 and 1991 rose from 575 to 803 for sex discrimination, and from fifty-two to 156 for pregnancy discrimination. [10]

According to the Anti-Discrimination Board, there is still a widely held view among employers that women are 'temporary' participants in the labour market who do not want a career and will leave the workforce after having children. [11] 'Some employers still refuse to employ women of childbearing age and include questions on plans for children and contraceptives in application forms and interviews', the report said. Other forms of discrimination identified include dismissal, demotion, and denial of promotion, loss of employment benefits and training, and workplace harassment.

The report specifically mentioned that pregnant women were being denied access to sick leave related to their pregnancies, and that confusion about entitlements to annual and long-service leave during pregnancy and maternity was widespread. 'In some instances, clear information about entitlements is withheld from women', it stated.

Discrimination against pregnant women has been worst in areas of employment that have been traditionally male, and in small business. No employer has ever been prosecuted for dismissing an employee on the grounds of pregnancy under the New South Wales *Industrial Relations Act 1991* despite evidence that such dismissals occur.[12]

Maternity leave

The Anti-Discrimination Board states that Australia is out of step with its major trading partners in not providing for paid maternity leave.[13] Women and 'their families bear the loss of income and the increased financial costs of maternity', states the board. Is this fair? What would be fairer?

At present, employers can compel a woman to take maternity leave at any time in the last six weeks of her pregnancy. The employer is not bound to take into account the woman's competence or her wish to continue working, or her financial position.[14] Is this fair? What would be fairer?

The board argues that the New South Wales *Industrial Relations Act 1991* does not adequately protect a woman's right to employment after taking maternity leave. Many women are retrenched shortly after returning to work or find their positions abolished. The Act only guarantees the right of return to a position if it still exists or to one of comparable status and pay if it does not, and if the woman is able to perform the new duties. But such reassignment may involve reclassification, loss of status, changed work hours, a changed location, or different work altogether. Is this fair? Is there a fairer arrangement?

Glass ceilings, glass walls

When Patsy Peacock, partner and director at McCarthy Watson and Spencer, resigned from the advertising agency she reflected on the difficulties of a woman making it to the top. She had become frustrated over the years with the struggles faced by women in reaching senior-level management positions in the advertising industry. At the time of her resignation she was one of the last female executives left in advertising. Peacock believes that agencies have not adequately recognised the merit and contributions of women:

> *Definitely the talent is there, all you have to do is look in middle management in agencies. [Women] seem to be held at that level ... Advertising is a combination of a lot of commonsense and emotion and traits that women generally have a greater percentage of than men. In my almost 19 years in the business I've only ever had one client that had a problem working with a female in the agency side.[15]*

Patsy Peacock had hit her head on the 'glass ceiling'.

The glass ceiling is the term used to describe this sudden halt in progress to the top. It refers to an invisible barrier that prevents qualified people from rising beyond a certain level of rank or salary in business organisations. The term has become increasingly common in Australia, but has received official recognition in the United States, where a Glass Ceiling Commission was established in 1991. Although the glass ceiling is most commonly associated with discrimination against women, it also applies to minorities such as particular ethnic and religious groups and to people with disabilities.

The glass ceiling may be defined as an institutionalised form of bias that prevents the promotion of qualified individuals to higher levels of management on the basis of characteristics such as sex, religion or ethnicity. This is different from discrimination in employment; equal opportunity and affirmative action programs are aimed at minimum requirements, but strategies to remove transparent barriers to executive positions demand a lot more of a company.[16]

How is the presence of a glass ceiling to be detected? The conduct of a self-administered audit is one way in which a company can find out about artificial limitations imposed on some groups of employees. Statistical analysis of the composition of the workforce compared with composition of management will provide a good starting point. How many women, for example, were hired or left in the period under review? At what levels did these women leave? These questions bear on equal employment opportunity (EEO) in an organisation and have implications for hiring as well as promotion practices.

Next it is useful to ask:

What does it take to become an executive in this company?

Are women and people from minority groups included in the grooming of successors to present management? If not, why not?

Talent is presumably distributed evenly over all groups represented in the workforce, so what barriers are preventing diversity being reflected in senior levels of the company?

Once these barriers are identified, steps to overcome them may be taken. A mentor scheme, experience-broadening assignments, or special training are ways in which obstacles to advancement can be overcome.[17]

In the United States the Department of Labor did not require companies to abandon their corporate culture in order to deal with glass-ceiling problems. It was not seeking to advance women and minorities in some token way, but to remove 'artificial' barriers to fair competition on merit. The promotion of women, say, because of gender does neither the women nor the organisation any good. It can breed hostility from men who are evaluated on merit, and from women who have to try harder to prove that they hold their positions because of their abilities. And, of course, it raises ethical problems: is it fair to advance individuals from under-represented groups at the expense of individuals from over-represented groups in order to correct systematic biases? For the Department of Labor the crucial aspect was not necessarily to change corporate culture but to change corporate behaviour so that women and minorities are included rather than excluded from career development on demonstrated merit.[18]

In a case similar to Patsy Peacock's, Roseanna Donovan was unable to secure promotion to creative director in a large multinational agency despite having twenty-five years of industry experience. She too resigned and started Australia's only all-female advertising agency.[19]

This experience is not unique to Australia. Advertising Women of New York surveyed 800 men and women in the advertising industry. The survey found that 35 per cent of women believed that sex discrimination had held back their careers. Earnings figures lent support to this: the median salary for men was $73,400, but for women was only $34,900

— a gap of $38,500 (amounting to 110 per cent of the median salary for women). And while 68 per cent of male respondents were in senior management, only 28 per cent of women occupied such positions.

American men were less likely than women to acknowledge the existence of a glass ceiling. One respondent said, 'I don't think most men are wicked and mean and are intentionally holding women back, but there's something in the system that lets that happen'. Marsha Coupe echoed the Australian experience in starting her own agency: 'I was one of the top people, and there were men who were substantially below me in title and responsibility who were paid more than me. When I discovered that, I felt very betrayed, and I was naive enough to be surprised. But that's what motivated me to strike out on my own'.[20]

Ingrid Hestlow began work as an ambitious architect in a medium-sized firm in the early 1980s. Nine years later, after doing everything she could to be promoted to director, she resigned. She could see no future in her male-dominated firm. 'They kept moving the goalposts to the point where I got completely disheartened. At the time I didn't know that I had hit the glass ceiling. I just knew I had hit something', she said.[21]

One female manager of human resources at a manufacturing company believed she had hit a glass wall. Although her firm was paying her way through a management school, she felt she had few future prospects because she headed a service, not an operational division. 'I'm seen as the soft option', she said. 'I am often excluded from general manager meetings because they don't think I have anything to offer. A lot of stuff gets done on the golf course and I don't play golf.'

This view encapsulates the subtlety of the glass ceiling. It allows a clear view to the top, and it has transparent promotion and performance evaluations. Thus the bias is not apparent, and because the culture of organisations can be invisible, males are quite likely to be unaware of it. They would deny overt prejudice, but if business culture is organised around male interests, gatherings and social occasions such as golf, then some adjustments beyond the more obvious structures are required for women to be accepted at the top. The glass ceiling can be a nasty shock for women. It can also confirm the secret beliefs of some men that women cannot really succeed at the highest levels of business.

It is also the case that women are often only able to make it to elevated positions in certain parts of an organisation: the 'soft' support or staff sections, rather than the line-management or strategic sections. It is much more likely that a woman will get to the top in an organisation's human resources department than in the area of strategic management. If you looked at an organisational chart, these branches might well appear on the same level. The fact is, of course, that there are significant differences in status, authority, and remuneration between the 'soft' areas and the engine-room ones. This is not a case of a glass ceiling but what we might call a 'glass wall', standing in the way of lateral movement into the more operational areas of the organisation. The point, however, is that it is not just a wall; the bar is not merely to lateral movement. These other areas — the 'hard' areas — are more significant and do, in a very important sense, stand above the soft areas. The organisational chart implies that it is only a wall, but in reality it is also another instance of a bar to vertical movement — another ceiling. (Maybe, then, it is neither a ceiling nor a wall, but rather a 'dormer window'.)

Not all women, however, accept that the glass ceiling is a barrier of this kind. Some say that the very concept is disempowering for those it is supposed to help. Linda Bardo

Nicholls believes that women in executive positions have to be more flexible to secure advancement. That is, they have to pursue career paths across the globe if need be — just as men do. If women wait until corporate life changes, then they will lose out. Bardo Nicholls puts a view often criticised by those who stress the structural barriers to women's advancement: 'This will not make me very popular among the sisterhood [but] I hear a lot of people who haven't made it whining about the glass ceiling. But I don't hear people complaining about it who have managed to crash through it'.[22]

There may be truth in this view (Leonie Still points out that some barriers attributed to the glass ceiling have been erected by women themselves[23]) but it cannot go far in explaining the kind of pattern that betrays the existence of the glass ceiling. While statistics do not tell the whole story, they can reveal patterns that cannot be explained simply by the particular circumstances of individuals. Women who should have every prospect of advancing to the highest levels of organisations stop well short of the goal in sight, resign, and typically go off to work in smaller ventures, often ones they start themselves. Still suggests a reason why: 'The culture of the current business organisation is not comfortable for women'.[24]

Michelle Murphy was just such a case. She worked for fifteen years in a multinational accountancy firm, managing a high-income-producing division. 'Every six months, when my review came up, I would always ask about the chance of becoming a partner', she said. She was continually knocked back. None of the company's Australian partners were women, and only 5 per cent of partners internationally were women. 'I was definitely a victim of the glass ceiling and I think a lot of my friends have also experienced it', said Murphy. She resigned to found her own accounting firm with her husband as the only way forward in her career.[25]

The trend for women to respond to corporate frustrations by setting up in small business repeats a pattern reported in the mid-1980s in the United States by Carol Hymowitz and Timothy Shellhardt.[26] The Business Council of Australia's Equal Opportunity Council has reported a 'disturbing trend' among highly skilled women leaving the ranks of middle management to set up their own businesses.[27] This was despite a decade of anti-discrimination laws and affirmative action programs running for almost as long.

Moreover, latent discrimination could be said to pursue women into small business. According to a study by the Small Business Research Unit of the Victoria University of Technology, *Issues Affecting Women in Small Business*, about half of Australia's 757,000 small businesses were expected to be owned by women by the year 2000. The main issue for women has been the availability of finance, and hence their businesses tended to be smaller than those of men. In the 1990s, only 41 per cent of women starting small businesses applied to a lending institution for finance. Most used personal assets or sought support from family and friends because they believed they would be rejected by banks and lending institutions.[28] This kind of figure illustrates that, while formal types of discrimination have been removed, there remain areas where a more positive attitude to female participation in commerce is needed.

The glass ceiling has not disappeared, but cracks are beginning to show. Only two decades ago, measures like EEO were considered radical and a threat to business, family and society. We have learned to look at the situation not only from the perspective of justice for women, but of social and economic benefits for the community. Now that same transformation is gradually being extended to other groups who have historically been excluded from participation, such as those with disabilities discussed later.

Sexual harassment

Sexual harassment has been mainly, but not exclusively, an issue of discrimination against women. It is surprising that it should still be considered acceptable in some quarters. Sexual harassment is like any other form of bullying or abuse of power. Its distinctive element is the making of sexual comments, suggestions, jokes, remarks or gestures that are objectionable to the person to whom they are directed. Showing an interest in someone is not sexual harassment. Pestering them with sexual innuendo or touches is.

Although there has been a great deal of publicity given to the problem of workplace sexual harassment, it still occurs. Here is a case that illustrates the problem well.

Case 6.7 Effective Cleaning Services & K-Mart

In 1989 a woman cleaner employed by Effective Cleaning Services to clean the K-Mart store at Garden City in Brisbane was told by Brian Drysdale, a manager, that she was a 'naughty little girl and needed [her] bare bum smacked'. The woman had been made to kneel by Drysdale, ostensibly to clean under cooking equipment. Drysdale had then placed a hand on her head, lifted her T-shirt, and pulled down her pants and panties, exposing her bottom. On other occasions he had lifted her up, chased her around the tea room, made comments about her legs and bottom, and had referred to her as a naughty girl. When she complained about this behaviour to management, Drysdale's denial of any impropriety was accepted. The woman, who had been sexually abused as a child and had later suffered physical abuse, felt humiliated and took her case to the Human Rights and Equal Opportunity Commission. Commissioner Kevin O'Connor found that the woman had been sexually harassed by Drysdale and that the employer was also at fault. The commission awarded the woman $11,000.[29]

The award was one of the largest made for this kind of offence. It constitutes a tangible sign that behaviour such as Drysdale's and laxity on the part of employers with respect to discrimination will not be tolerated. That sexual harassment is not a trivial matter ethically is made clear by exemplary operations of the law.

Disability

It is common now to talk of 'people with disabilities' rather than talk of 'handicapped' or 'disabled' people. This is not just pedantic language. The idea is to stop the identification of the whole person with the particular disability she or he has. Some disabilities, of course, make it difficult for a person to participate fully in the workforce, but according to Mark Bagshaw, international marketing manager at IBM Australia, too much is made of this. He argues that if the community provides people with disabilities with the assistance necessary for them to lead their lives, then such people should be able to make their contribution in the workplace just as any other citizen would. He notes that only 34 per cent of working-age people with severe disabilities participate in the labour market. This costs the community $2.2 billion in welfare assistance and a good deal more in lost productivity and taxation.[30]

Two obstacles to fuller participation in the workforce for those with disabilities have been the lack of access to community services — for example, transport, attendant care, and appropriate education — and sympathy. Bagshaw recognised that he is fortunate: although quadriplegic, his condition has not prevented him from doing the things that most people are able to do: driving a car, getting married or being ambitious in employment. But sympathy for people with disabilities has restricted their employment opportunities because disability is what Bagshaw calls 'a benign issue — it's difficult to generate heated debate about it'. AIDS has probably changed this, but even AIDS makes Bagshaw's point: sympathy for AIDS sufferers seems markedly less than for those with disabilities such as quadriplegia.

What are the rights and responsibilities of business with respect to people with disabilities? Employers have a right to expect that a person appointed to a position will be able to assume its duties fully and productively. This means that employers 'have a responsibility to match a job to a person's ability rather than their disability'. This in turn means that companies have to know something about disability and should not have preconceptions about it that diminish equal employment opportunity. Says Bagshaw: 'When I was first seeking employment I deliberately did not inform my prospective employers of my disability before the first interview. I wanted an opportunity to influence the interviewer's perceptions of my disability'.

Beyond the responsibilities of dealing with employees, Bagshaw identifies four social responsibilities of business with respect to disability: first, companies should have a policy on employing people with disabilities; second, they should identify suitable positions in their organisations to be filled by people with disabilities, and seek the assistance of disabilities organisations if necessary; third, companies should take advantage of government assistance, and fourth, companies should advertise their disability employment policies to relevant recruitment and disabilities organisations.

These social responsibilities are supported by legislation. In 1992, the Disability Reform Package was important in giving impetus for reforms to employment of people with disabilities. The *Disability Discrimination Act* gives force to the principles outlined by Bagshaw. It requires employers to modify the workplace in order to allow a person with a disability to perform a job properly if they are the best person for that job, for example, by building ramps or providing a large computer screen or by giving mentoring support. Employers can gain advice on these matters either from the employee or from a qualified agency or expert. The Act does contain an unjustifiable hardship provision that exempts an employer from making these modifications if they will cause unreasonable costs. This does not let employers off the hook. A claim of hardship has to be backed up with evidence. The Commonwealth Department of Family and Community Services has introduced a range of measures to protect the employment rights of people with disabilities, and to encourage their participation in the labour market.[31] In 2004, a National Disability Recruitment Coordinator began providing comprehensive employment services to industry and people with disabilities through a new organisation called Disability WORKS Australia.[32] None of this government sponsored support can address the demands of fairness by itself: it is necessary but not sufficient. It is important that employers should not see the hiring of staff as a private matter for which they might not be held accountable by an external body. On the contrary, it would be in the best interests of all stakeholders for employers to be proactive in the cause of fairness, if not for ethical reasons, then for prudential ones.

Case 6.8 The HIV positive employee[33]

In October 1990 Harry Beecher was working as an area manager in Queensland for The Complete Table when he learned he was HIV positive. He informed his employers about his status. There was no immediate adverse reaction to his disclosure, and Complete Table told Harry that his conditions of employment would not be affected by his HIV status. But later, in conversation with senior management, there was some discussion about all staff being informed of his condition, and mention was made of using polystyrene cups for hygiene. Neither of these suggestions was put into effect. About eighteen months after informing Complete Table of his status, Harry told his boss that he wished to move to Melbourne to be closer to his doctor and specialised medical treatment. Complete Table agreed to a transfer, but to a shop assistant's position at $25,000, not to a comparable management position at $52,000.

Harry felt the company's actions were demeaning and discriminatory and took his complaint to the Victorian Equal Opportunity Board. He told the board that Complete Table had an obligation to counsel him, to make plans for his short-term and long-term future with the firm, and to ensure that he did not suffer financially due to his disability.

What was the ethical responsibility of Complete Table in this case?[34]

Was Harry being discriminated against?

What are the ethical issues relevant to this case?

Perhaps the most obvious aspect of equal opportunity programs to business is their cost. Such a focus ignores their benefits not only to individuals but also to commerce, industry and the community. Equal employment and anti-discrimination programs might also be viewed as prejudice-removal programs. When prejudice obscures respect for persons and the capacity to make a fair assessment of their abilities, then all parties lose. Business needs the best people. Prejudice against women, people with disabilities, or any other group is not only morally objectionable, it is bad business.

Review questions

1 Much of the concern about anti-discrimination concerns the provision of 'equal treatment'. Yet much of the concern seems to require 'special allowances'. Do you think these two notions can be reconciled?

2   We noted some apparently rather objectionable interviews that were held with some female applicants to engineering positions within Telecom in the early 1980s. At the end of that discussion, we posed some questions. Perhaps you didn't pause to think about them: What if the questions asked were designed by the interviewers to see whether the women would be able to work effectively in a setting where such questions might arise? What if the interview was used as a stronger test of the women because, equal opportunity notwithstanding, women still have to deal with sexism in the workplace? If your answer to these questions is on the order of 'that shouldn't make any difference; the interviewers were still out of line in the way they interviewed the women', then why is that so? What do you think is inadequate about the possible responses that we have presented?

The Ethics of Accounting:
The Case of a Profession in Business

7

Professional ethics is sometimes thought to involve no more than observing the norms and regulations of the professions. Nothing could be further from the truth. Good professional practice calls for judgment because the principles of a profession need to be interpreted and applied in ways that are just and compassionate. This is true whether the practitioner is self-employed or works in an organisation. While being a salaried professional — a lawyer, architect, engineer, or accountant, for instance — does not exempt one from judgments and ethical responsibilities, it can put a twist on common problems. This is well illustrated in the decisions facing accountants and auditors. Many of these problems relate to the issue of autonomy. The ethics of being a loyal servant of the organisation while at the same time exercising professional judgment gives rise to a host of potential ethical conflicts. On the one hand, organisations have a right to expect that directions will be followed. On the other, professional status is often defined in terms of independence. Professionals take on ethical responsibilities additional to those that apply to people generally. Richard De George makes this point in a characteristically direct way: 'Any profession

... is appropriately given respect and autonomy only if it lives up to a higher moral code than is applicable to all'.[1]

Overview of the accounting profession

The practice of accounting is centuries old, but the profession of accounting grew out of the industrial revolution and the use of the limited liability company as the engine of economic growth. The need to give a clear accounting of the performance of companies necessitated the development of management accountants to advise senior management of the options open to them in decision-making, and of financial accountants to prepare accurate reports on the financial health of companies. External auditors were needed to assess the fairness and accuracy of financial statements, and accountants in public practice progressively grew in importance, offering a range of financial services from personal taxation to superannuation.

In a series of Morgan surveys over a number of years, *Time Magazine* consistently rated accountants as being regarded as reasonably trustworthy. Their professional ethics and honesty rating has, however, gently declined in recent years. In 1984 they scored 48 per cent; in 1994 they scored only 42 per cent. Doctors, by comparison, went from 64 per cent up to 66 per cent, school teachers from 55 per cent to 65 per cent, and the police from 53 per cent to 56 per cent.[2] Accountants themselves have misgivings about the standards of their colleagues and the ethical standing of their profession.

One survey found that over 37 per cent believed that ethical standards had declined in the preceding decade, and a further 18.5 per cent were uncertain.[3] The family was rated the strongest source of values (94.2 per cent), then the conduct of peers (88.2 per cent), accounting practices (87.5 per cent), prevailing societal norms (76.9 per cent), then the professional code of ethics (68.1 per cent) and religious formation (61.5 per cent). This relative weighting can mask the still high impact of the profession on members' ethical perceptions; it would seem unusual for members of any profession to rate a code above religious formation on this score. Yet only 49 per cent of members believed that their colleagues had any degree of familiarity with the professional code.[4]

The ethical issues identified by accountants as most important were:

1   client proposals for tax evasion (83.3 per cent)
2   client proposals to manipulate financial statements (80.2 per cent)
3   conflicts of interest (79.3 per cent)
4   presenting financial information so as not to deceive users (76.3 per cent)
5   failure to maintain technical competence in professional practice (71.3 per cent)
6   coping with instructions from a superior to behave unethically (70.7 per cent)
7   integrity in admitting one's mistakes (66.7 per cent)
8   using insider information for personal gain (63.8 per cent)
9   maintaining confidentiality (63.6 per cent).

The respondents also ranked favours and gifts, and the solicitation of work as significant ethical issues.[5]

Some of these items apply to accountants in public practice, some to salaried accountants, and some to both. The strongest theme running through these results is professional independence and the proper exercise of professional judgment. Of the most important ethical issues identified by respondents, the first, second, third, sixth, and ninth all relate to independence and pressure applied by clients or employers to achieve a certain result.

A strong sense of independence is characteristic of most professions. Some writers make it a necessary condition of professional status: 'so long as the individual is looked upon as an employee rather than a free artisan, to that extent there is no professional status'.[6] According to this view, only accountants in public practice would be true professionals. The concern informing this view is that employees will be unable to make serious commitments to ethics and the public good on the basis of their own independent assessment because an employer can issue contrary directives that must be obeyed, even if an individual disagrees with them. Even if such directives are not made, the professional judgment of the employee is circumscribed in a way that does not apply to a self-employed practitioner. This view, extreme though it is, stems from a very commonly held belief that professional status derives at least partly from the fact that those practising within a profession must regard the public interest as their first priority.

A contrasting view holds that it is precisely in serving their clients and employers that professionals attain their status. According to this view, 'it is essential that professionals should serve' those employing their services rather than 'filtering their everyday work through a sieve of ethical sensitivity'. Personal judgments are alien to this concept of professionalism: the professional is not an expert on the public good and should not be called upon to make judgments about it. Regulation and law, not personal morality, are the appropriate constraints upon what a professional may do for a client.[7]

The view that internal accountants are restricted in their professional judgment by the power and authority of the employer will be correct in certain cases (though it must be remembered that their role is not that of a 'watchdog' in the manner of an external auditor). But even external accountants in the best accounting firms can have difficulties. Consider the following case based on an actual incident.

Case 7.1 Bruce's dilemma

Bruce was twenty-six years old when he joined a large accounting firm after graduating with a good degree in commerce. He was assigned to a team of auditors at Transition Technologies, which had just been acquired by Paradox Corp. Bruce's firm had been the auditors at Transition before the takeover and had offered to continue at around half the going rate. Shortcuts in auditing resulted. Proper auditing procedures were not adhered to, and Bruce was frequently left to make decisions by himself, although he was not experienced. Bruce was aware that he was in a competitive environment and that he was, in a sense, on trial. He did not agree with the shortcuts and felt that it was unfair to Transition and himself that he was sometimes left to deal with matters beyond his experience. But he also remembered being asked at his job interview if he was a team player who could carry other members of the team when circumstances required. What should Bruce do?

Whatever you decide in the case of Bruce, there is one aspect to note: it is not the fact that he is a salaried professional per se that limits Bruce's professional judgment. It is that his firm is not behaving ethically, that he is a new and junior member of the audit team, and that he should have been under close supervision until he had developed the expertise — including independent judgment — that comes with experience. None of these conditions need exist for a salaried accountant.

According to the second view of professionalism, Bruce is in the clear until he breaks a law. This view, however, is far too restrictive of the role that professionals play in organisations as diverse as schools and hospitals. The notion that true professionals should serve their employers as far as the law extends confuses servility with service. The old maxim that it is stupid to buy a dog and bark yourself applies here: when a salaried professional is hired, that person is expected to exercise independent judgment within the limits of her or his expertise. Working to direction is part of working in an organisation, and having to do so in some areas does not imply a lack of independence in all of them.

In any case, independence, for all its importance, must take its place beside other values in professional settings. According to the British Statement on the Ethical Responsibilities of Members in Business, 'the concept of independence … has no direct relevance to the employed member … Even for the practising accountant independence is not an end in itself: it is essentially a means of securing a more important end, namely an objective approach to work'.[8] This objective is also secured by other key professional values: honesty, trust and good faith, fidelity and loyalty, justice and fairness, care and compassion; responsibility and accountability, and the pursuit of professional excellence all contribute to the ethics of a professional. So too does regard for the public good, but this value usually differs significantly from the global suggestion that a professional accountant, lawyer, or teacher should act in the public interest as the first principle of practice. It means something more important: taking a principled position on issues of public importance that come within the area of one's professional expertise.

Independence is important to accountants in two ways. The first might be peculiar to their technical expertise, and the second is generic to professions in general. First, independence is especially important to accountants providing external certification of a company's financial position. It goes to the heart of the profession's role that the declarations that an accountant makes in, say, a financial report are not prejudiced by the power and influence of those who stand to gain by a particular result. It is equally important that the accountant have no interest at all in the company and should not stand to gain or lose by any outcome of financial scrutiny. This aspect of independence is at the very basis of the profession of accounting, for upon it rests the trust of the public in the most inclusive sense. Threats to this independence typically come in the following forms:

- undue dependence on an audit client
- loans to or from a client, guarantees, or overdue fees
- hospitality or other benefits
- actual or threatened litigation
- mutual business interests
- beneficial interests in shares or other investments
- trusteeships

- voting on audit appointments
- provision of other services — such as valuations — to audit clients
- acting for a client over a prolonged period of time.[9]

The central importance of independence to accountants is clear from even a cursory look at the profession's code of ethics, but independence clearly serves a professional purpose and harmonises with the other values enshrined in the codes. This brings us to the second sense of independence. Many of the classic injunctions of professional practice have a strong personal direction. 'Do no harm' is a principle directed not so much at a profession (though it might be) as to its practitioners. The same applies to other precepts and principles about competence, confidentiality, trustworthiness and honesty. In turn, each of these principles assumes a high degree of professional autonomy and occupational discretion on the part of individual practitioners. These are often the very qualities that organisations try to restrict. Organisations are not peculiar in this: individuals often compromise their ethics when it suits them. Professional people who act with integrity will retain sufficient independence to allow them to act ethically, but accountants must do this in a very special way in order to do their job at all. One of the issues raised by the collapse of Enron and other US corporations was whether the auditor was too enmeshed in their affairs. Consider the case of Arthur Andersen and Enron.

Case 7.2   The fall of Andersens

In June 2002, after ten days deliberating and a difficult time sifting the evidence, a federal jury in Houston convicted Arthur Andersen of obstruction of justice in the Enron case. Andersens then announced that they would cease auditing publicly listed companies from the end of August. Thus fell one of the giants of modern accounting. With revenues in 2001 of over nine billion dollars and 85,000 employees in 84 countries, the fall of Andersen's caused shock waves around the world. Founded in 1913 by Arthur Andersen, the firm had become a byword for integrity until its pursuit of profits led to its entanglement in the adventurism of the 'new economy'. Enron was not the only dubious client for whom Andersens provided services. Others included WorldCom, Sunbeam and, in Australia, HIH. The fallout from such clients cost Andersen's reputation and money. The SEC fined the firm $7 million for overstating the earnings of Waste Management corporation by $1.4 billion. Shareholders sued Andersens when Sunbeam admitted inflating its earnings, and Andersens settled out of court for $US110 million.[10]

What could have led a firm founded on integrity to abandon its basic values? Barbara Toffler describes Andersens as rotting from within, a victim of its own demand for conformity from employees.[11] According to Toffler, it lost its independence when it placed its lucrative consulting services before its auditing role and became less inclined to anger clients. That might account for its failure to caution Enron and other clients like WorldCom about their revenue statements. The fundamental value of accounting, independence, had been compromised. Andersens were Enron's auditors for sixteen years. In 2002 alone, Enron paid them US$25 million in audit fees and $27 million for consulting services.

Enron's accounts were notoriously difficult to understand and for a very good reason. Its chief financial officer, Andrew Fastow, had created a number of 'off the books' partnerships, that is, related but separate entities in which Enron could place debt or assets that it did not wish to appear on its balance sheets. Such partnerships are not of themselves improper, but the uses to which Enron and its executives put them were. Fastow, for example, made millions of dollars in secret transactions at the expense of Enron.[12] And investments in the partnerships were reported by Enron as revenue.

There was an issue here for Andersens because the Generally Accepted Accounting Principles (GAAP) required partnerships with more than a three per cent investment from Enron to appear with the consolidated accounts. Enron's investments in its partnerships exceeded this minimum. Andersens should have presented balance sheets that accounted for the partnerships, but according to its CEO, Joe Berardino, it did so only in 2001. Andersen's alleged departure from GAAP standards has been investigated by the Securities and Exchange Commission.[13] Beyond the requirements of the law, there was the propriety of using related entities as Enron did. The wisdom on this is well established. Clarke and Dean note that similar arrangements have served improper purposes in the Australian context, where

> ...the corporate group emerges as a corporate oddity. Parent companies and the entities they control are selectively considered to comprise a single entity, more or less according to how the circumstances suit. Selectively, because changed circumstances usually dictate whether manage- ment regards it financially beneficial to present the companies comprising a group as separate companies, or lumps some or all of them together and treats them as a composite unit.[14]

Clarke and Dean identify typical signs of stressed corporations in Australia and, perhaps not surprisingly, they are similar to those at Enron and WorldCom in the USA and Polly Peck and Canary Wharf in the United Kingdom. Complex corporate structures with many related party transactions, overvalued assets, understated liabilities and bad debts, reckless borrowing, and the use of accounting 'fictions', such as Future Income Tax Benefits, can camouflage the precarious position of corporations at risk.[15]

Andersen's problems compounded when it was disclosed that Houston partner, David Duncan, had ordered the deletion of emails and the shredding of Enron documents relating to Enron after the SEC had commenced its investigation. Andersen's informed the authorities of Duncan's actions, but the firm was indicted and found guilty of obstruction of justice.

A clutch of Enron executives have been indicted. In January 2004, Andrew Fastow, CFO at Enron, pleaded guilty to charges of fraud in a bargain that will save him years in jail in exchange for assisting in the investigation of other Enron executives. The indictment of Enron accounting and financial services executive, Richard Causey, quickly followed. The Securities and Exchange Commission, alleged that Causey, Fastow and others manipulated 'expenses, revenue, debt levels, cash flow and asset values ... through means including fraudulent valuations, misuse of off-the-books partnerships ... and intentional mistreatment of accounting reserves.'[16] It has emerged that Enron exploited California's deregulated energy market to hike prices and 'extort' $US30 billion from that state.[17]

Enron's operations were riddled with deception and sharp practice. There are questions of law about this and questions of ethics. While the law takes its course, the ethical questions hang in the air.

What should have been the role of the auditor with clients like this? Andersens seemed content to take the view that the data they were given could be interpreted according to prevailing accounting standards.

Should Andersens have noted that the thicket of Enron accounts was a classic indicator of corporate risk? (The chair of Enron's audit committee was a former dean of Stanford professor of accounting and he claimed he didn't understand the corporation's audits.) Enron could not have gotten into a mess without its auditors having some idea of what was going on.

Did Andersen's duty of confidentiality to the client override their obligation to the SEC and various stakeholders from investors to taxpayers?

Did not Andersens have a duty to investors to prepare reports that more accurately reflected Enron's level of risk?

Should Andersens have warned that it would not continue to act as Enron's auditor unless the conglomerate changed its conduct?

Did Andersens compromise professional independence by becoming too dependent on contracts with Enron?

Should they have been internal auditor, external auditor and provider of management consulting services to Enron simultaneously?

How could shredding Enron documents be called a normal part of document retention policy when Andersens knew that their client was under investigation by the SEC?

There is a bigger question to be answered as well:

Would a closer adherence to Accounting Standards have prevented the Enron debacle? Would more rigorous standards and policing of them have prevented the rash of corporate collapses that occurred at the same time?

One answer to this has already been delivered by American legislators. Another quite different answer is given by Australian academics, Clarke and Dean.

The huge losses of Enron, WorldCom and other corporations proved too much for Congress and the American public. The response was the typical one of tightening regulations, although the SEC's powers were already considerable. Nonetheless, Congress passed the *Sarbanes-Oxley Corporate Reform Act* of 2002. That Act and the SEC regulations under it, seek to strengthen the independence of external auditors. Auditors may no longer be appointed by senior management but only by the audit committee of the board, and auditors must report to that committee, not to management. All members of the audit committee be independent directors. The reforms prescribe the structure of boards and specify the duties of directors and some employees. The same firm cannot offer auditing and consulting services. Transparency is enhanced and off balance sheet transactions must be disclosed. Audit records must be retained. Companies must disclose whether they have a code of ethics for their CEOs, CFOs and senior accountants.[18] This is the kind of reaction to large-scale ethical failure that enshrines ethical basics in law and, as we noted above in chapter 4, that will not be sufficient to do the job. The profession itself has been sensitive to issues of independence and professional integrity. The International Federation of Accountants (IFAC) has proposed amendments to its code because of the risk that auditors might be captured by their clients. The amendments for auditors require the leading partner on the contract to be rotated at least every seven years, and prohibit that partner from participating in assurance for a further period, normally two years.[19]

The Sarbanes-Oxley Act has been much criticised in the US, but there are similar criticisms to ever more regulations and their effect on professional judgment. The argument of Clarke and Dean has been that 'shackling' auditors' independence to Accounting Standards will do no more good in the future than it has in the past.[20] In other words, it might not matter where the shackles are anchored — whether to corporations and their fees or to regulations and standards — if the independence of auditors to draw upon their experience and practice wisdom is curbed. Moreover, they argue that standardisation of input has obscured the importance of the usefulness of output in financial statements. If the notion of 'true and fair' is equivalent to 'meeting the defined standards' then, despite the best of intentions, the published financial statements of a firm might not meet the criterion of serviceability. They conclude that 'Unquestionably, compulsory compliance by accountants and auditors with prescribed Accounting and Auditing Standards provides them with a safe harbour'.[21]

Accounting practices referred to as 'aggressive' at Enron challenged the spirit of the law and of professional probity. Individuals intended to evade ethical obligations by concocting schemes that boosted the price of Enron stock, and hid debt and poor performance. Eventually the courts will decide the legality of Enron's schemes and the culpability of those who devised them, but the jury on the ethics of Enron's corporate governance, financial reporting and deceptive practices has delivered its verdict and gone home. This is hardly surprising when similar practices are found in other corporations and they share the same auditing firm. The legal verdict delivered on Andersens in Houston in 2002 was enough to bring down the whole enterprise. This was a case, if ever there was one, where the higher standard of ethics was also the prudential one.

Professional codes of practice

The Institute of Chartered Accountants prefaced the 1997 version of its Code with the following statements:

> This Code of Professional Conduct is designed to provide members with authoritative guidance on minimum acceptable standards of professional conduct. The Code focuses on essential matters of principle and is not to be taken as a definitive statement on all matters. Members should be

guided not merely by the terms but also by the spirit of the Code. The fact that particular conduct does not receive a mention does not prevent it from being unacceptable or discreditable conduct thus making the member liable to disciplinary action.[22]

Codes will not make people honest or responsible, but they do support a culture of honesty and responsibility and declare to all who will take notice that a profession stands for these things even when its practitioners do not.

The central professional values expressed in the successive codes of Australian accountants are similar to those that apply internationally.[23] They basically address the relations of practitioners to various stakeholders and the standards of professional and personal integrity expected of accountants. There is a high degree of linkage and overlap between the principles, and their number varies from code to code, but they can be summed up under five headings. Firstly, the Public Interest: Accountants are expected to act in the best interests of clients except when those interests conflict with obligations to society, the law and social and political institutions. The Australian Institute of Chartered Accountants' Code specifically acknowledges that the profession serves the collective welfare of society. This is linked with the second basic value, integrity, which means that accountants should be honest and sincere in their work. They should do nothing to bring their profession into disrepute. Thirdly, accountants must display objectivity, that is, they must act fairly and free from conflicts of interest. Fourthly, independence is fundamental to accountants and should be apparent as well as real. It also means that accountants should not do anything that could suggest that their independence might be compromised. Fifthly, accountants should exercise diligence and due care in the performance of their duties. They should exhibit competence and ensure that they are competent to perform the work assigned by clients, and they should maintain their competence through appropriate measures. They should adhere to accounting and auditing standards, and to standards issued by their professional association. Finally, accountants must maintain confidentiality, which means not only that they may not disclose information provided by clients to unauthorised third parties, but that they should not use information gained in the course of their duties for personal or third party gain.

There is much in these principles that applies generally to the professions. In this respect, accountancy represents an example as much as it represents a special instance, but the responsibilities of accountants in the business world, and hence in society at large, mean that ethical failure can have huge ramifications.

Recognising conflicts of interest is very important. It is also important that the professional not even appear to be in a position in which there could be a conflict of interest. This is important in all professions, but it is especially important in accountancy, which frequently identifies independence as the cornerstone of the profession. Consider, for instance, what the purpose of an audit is, and what it is that an auditor attests to. The requirement of independence is closely related to what the profession has come to recognise as a central ethical issue in accountancy: whistleblowing (see chapter 9).

Professions almost always recognise both a duty to the public interest and a duty to the maintenance of the profession itself. These duties are often expressed in terms of, on the one hand, making the public interest a first priority and, on the other, doing nothing that brings the profession into disrepute. These are very important duties, but they can sit uneasily next to each other. For example, it might be in the public interest to criticise some aspect of the profession. Such situations — and they are not uncommon — can easily bring these two duties into conflict with each other.

As with other professions, issues accompanying the position of the professional as salaried employee are prevalent and often difficult to resolve. Professionals carry the ethical responsibilities of the profession with them into their positions as paid employees — positions that have their own ethical requirements. Put simply, you owe something to your employer (call it 'loyalty' to a greater or lesser degree) and you also owe something to your profession as a professional. You carry this obligation with you into your employment.

Constitutive and regulative rules

Accounting is one of the most regulated of professions. It seems that when any major infraction hits the headlines, a new rule is introduced to prevent its recurrence, or there are calls for new rules and tighter standards. The rules of accounting are not primarily regulative, however, but 'constitutive'.[24] That is, most of the rules in accounting are about the practice itself, not the regulation of practitioners. These rules determine what the practice amounts to — that is, what constitutes it. They exist to promote the practice of accounting, not to restrict practitioners or catch out frauds. The whole purpose of accounting is to give an accurate and reliable — or, according to the classic phrase, 'a true and fair'[25] — account of a company's business affairs, but that does not stop some practitioners from committing crimes and many more from deviating from the spirit of accounting standards. Introducing tighter regulations or new standards might not be the way to counter such deviations. Rather, ethical controls related to the personal principles of the practitioner might be a better way of assuring fairness and honesty in the duties accountants perform than imposed external regulations — rules whose aim is not constitutive but regulative. F. L. Clarke, G. W. Dean and K. G. Oliver argue that the ethos of the accounting profession — its commonly understood and shared principles and norms — has been replaced by regulations and standards: 'Contrary to the popular view, it is our proposition that compliance with the so-called spirit of many conventional practices and endorsed Standards produces grossly misleading data, without necessarily any intention to deceive on anybody's part'.[26] The situation is very much compounded when a wobbly professional ethos is required to stand up to deceptive and legally risky conduct, as the case of Arthur Andersen shows.

Accounting is not the only profession or activity to suffer from the misconception that the way to rectify ethical difficulties is by the introduction of more and more regulation. It is, in fact, quite a common call to arms in the face of ethical (or other) difficulties: 'we need more regulation'. However, not only is increased regulation not always an effective remedy; it sometimes exacerbates the difficulty. It can exacerbate the problem by shifting attention from the real difficulty, which is usually a matter of the exercise of bad judgment and a systemic problem with the organisational culture onto the regulation and its technicalities.[27] There is an attractiveness about regulation as a solution to problems, in that it is simple and neat, whereas doing what is necessary to improve individuals' and corporate judgment, ethical decision-making skills, and organisation culture is a much more difficult task.

This is only a slight exaggeration, and it is easy to give lots of examples, including many from accounting failures: Something has gone wrong; there has been basically an ethical failure. The profession and the community at large want to remedy the failure — they do not want it to happen again. So, from whatever external controlling body or bodies comes the pronouncement, 'Clean up your act, or else!' The 'or else', as a threat, usually amounts to the possibility of dramatic legislation or regulation from an external body. Under this threat, the profession knows what is being targeted, and knows what needs to be improved — and it is almost always ethical failure of one kind or another. Its focus is on that. It wants to fix it. Now, suppose the situation progresses, and regulation is introduced. The stimulus for the new regulation was the failure, in virtue of which there was the threat. Now that there is regulation, however, the focus of the practitioners — and maybe even of the profession itself — is directed onto that specifically, rather than onto the stimulus and the real problem. So, the practitioners' concern now becomes doing exactly what the regulation requires, or, better, doing whatever can be done to get around the new requirements.[28] Any concern for the real problem — and the concern to 'clean up their act' — becomes lost in technicalities, procedures, and repairs. 'It's simpler that way!'

In accounting education, ethics is sometimes discussed separately from skills and knowledge. We suggest that this view is mistaken. Rather, ethical performance is integral to the practice of accounting *per se*. The internal ethical requirements of a profession — standards, norms, expectations, competences, commitments, and procedures — both enable and govern its effective practice. If a doctor refuses to treat patients with chronic illnesses, that doctor is hardly practising medicine. If a lawyer takes only cases that can be confidently won, this is hardly the competent practice of law. If an engineer takes shortcuts that endanger lives, that person is a substandard engineer. If an accountant does whatever an employer instructs, even if the accountant believes it to be unprofessional, then that accountant is behaving not only unethically but also incompetently. In all these instances, the practitioners behave unethically because they behaved in a manner contrary to the standards of their professions. These standards create the internal obligations of a profession. They do more than regulate; they constitute the competent practice of the profession. Professions have a tradition of service to the public and, in return, the public confers upon them certain rights of practice. Betrayal of this trust through shoddy, careless, negligent or hasty professional practice is unethical. It is not only the nakedly corrupt professional who has abandoned ethics; it is the uncaring, 'unprofessional' and incompetent practitioner as well. A wilfully underskilled, ignorant, or negligent practitioner is unethical. In this internal sense, ethics is integral to professional practice, not an add-on component to the knowledge-plus-skills model.

Consider this case:

You have been an accountant in public practice for ten years. One day at a family picnic, an old friend and colleague asks what arrangements you have made for your clients in case you suddenly die or become incapacitated. Does this strike you as an odd question? Is it your responsibility to provide for your clients? You have provided for your family because they are your responsibility. But is not the responsibility of the professional accountant more limited? These seem to be ethical questions, but they are also professional because they impact on your clients. What would your immediate response to them be?

Litigation and auditing

There are penalties for not retaining sufficient professional independence in auditing. The two cases below illustrate just some of the litigation brought against auditors in recent years.

Case 7.3   Bankers Trust

In 1992, Bankers Trust and eight individual shareholders brought an action for $60 million against the former auditors of Westmex Ltd for negligence and for misleading and deceptive conduct. The unusual action under section 52 of the *Trade Practices Act 1974* was filed in the Federal Court against Richard Moffitt, Westmex's former auditor, and his partners. Westmex, Russell Goward's vehicle for buying and selling companies, went into provisional liquidation in February 1990. Just five months earlier it had received an unqualified auditor's report from Thompson Douglass & Co., of which Moffitt was then a partner. Bankers Trust's action is directed against the firm and all of its partners.

Proceedings in the matter commenced in 1992 but received fresh impetus in January 1996, when the Companies Auditors and Liquidators Disciplinary Board (CALDB) suspended Moffitt from registration as a company auditor for five years. The suspension followed an application by the Australian Securities Commission. CALDB found that Moffitt had not adequately and properly performed the duties of an auditor during the course of the Westmex audits in 1988 and 1989.[29]

The second case involves issues related to an 'independent' report that turned out to be not so independent.

Case 7.4   An 'independent' report?

Angus Pilmer, partner in the leading Perth audit firm of Nelson Wheeler, completed an 'independent' report on a takeover by Kia Ora Gold of the merchant bank Western United in September 1987. Pilmer valued Western United at between $101 and $113 million. Following the disastrous October stock market crash, its value had fallen to $3 million, but Kia Ora had proceeded with the takeover. It later emerged that Western United and Kia Ora had common directors who were the main beneficiaries of the takeover. Even before the crash, however, Pilmer's valuation was a long way from the figure put on it by Jeff Hall of Grant Samuel: a mere $10 million. In what was to become the world's longest trial, Pilmer and his firm were sued over his report.[30]

All professions must now consider the possibility of litigation, and accountants and auditors are no different. The pursuit of remedies in suits against auditors will not solve the basic problem of greed. Moreover, litigation could have unintended and undesirable side effects. According to one commentator, 'Men and women of means and competence may well decide that being an auditor or company director is just too difficult. It is a reasonable observation that ever increasing professional indemnity cover is likely to increase legal suits rather than decrease them'.[31] In other words, the distinction between culpable and accidental error is in danger of being blurred, and particularly so if competency is reduced.

George Sutton suggests some strategies to protect the auditor. First, he recommends a cap on professional liability, which would reduce the incentive for litigation and subsequently the costs of insurance premiums. (The South Australian government, for instance, commenced a suit against Price Waterhouse for A$1.1 billion over its audit of Beneficial Finance). Second, he seeks a return to the old-fashioned notion that the auditor's real clients are the shareholders, by whom they should be thoughtfully elected and to whom they should be accountable by being required to present a company's accounts. The corporation that employs an auditor is, in effect, identified merely with its officers and employees:[32] 'The good auditor understands that transparency sometimes requires going beyond the scope of strict legislative disclosure requirements and after intensive discussion with the board, he must be secure enough to push for his view for the benefit of the shareholders. The auditors should read aloud their audit report as part of the formal proceedings at the annual meeting'.[33]

If ethical decisions are inescapable in professional life, they are almost an occupational hazard in accounting and auditing. Clarke, Dean and Oliver lament that 'there are no good explanations within the framework of accounting and auditing rules with which accountants have to comply', so that exposure to litigation and loss of professional status are persistent occupational risks.[34] If this is true of formal standards and rules, then most of the general points about ethics will be less helpful than practitioners might expect because rules in accounting are not transparently grounded in ethical principles. An ethical accountant might well claim to know what honesty requires, but that is of little help when confronted with a case in which adhering to the letter of a set of accounting standards involves departing from their spirit. Everyday practice decisions do have ethical implications. In a sample of 108 financial reports in the first half of the 1992–93 financial year, sixty-five prompted inquiries about apparent departures from accounting standards or the *Corporations Law 1990*.[35] That is, 60 per cent of the sample raised questions about accounting practices and compliance with standards and the law. If this is so, then such practices also raise ethical questions, but this would not seem to be acknowledged, perhaps because the survey was not concerned with imputing improper conduct. If this is so, then an excessively narrow view of ethics is at work, for, as stressed above, ethics deals also with matters of competence, discretion, responsibility and excellence. It should be noted that, of the sixty-five inquiries about departures from standards and regulations, thirty-six were regarded as matters for the professional discretion of auditors and most of the rest received satisfactory explanations. Practitioners need to be able to justify their decisions, and most can. This too is a matter of ethics. So when most of the auditors surveyed 'accepted the need for improved presentation and disclosure and undertook to persuade their clients to make improvements in the following year's financial report',[36] they were facing up to professional responsibilities that were both technical and ethical. Whether they recognised the ethical element of their position is another matter.

In recent years the accounting profession in Australia has adopted a number of strategies to raise the ethical awareness of its members and to reinforce the importance of ethics in accounting education.[37] Most of these initiatives are aimed at individuals, rather than at the systemic problems of the profession identified by Clarke, Dean and Oliver. Given the immensity of that task, it is more a matter for public policy than a matter for the action of professional associations.

Consider the following fictional case, which raises some of the kinds of problems that confront accountants working in organisations.

Case 7.5   Zanicum Metals

Zanicum Metals is a rapidly expanding producer of non-ferrous metal castings. Demand for its product is strong, and it is negotiating a large bank loan in order to increase production. As part of its regular maintenance cycle, Zanicum must decommission some of its furnaces so that they can be overhauled. This is an expensive process, and it is important to minimise the impact on the company's total operations. Management accountant Richard Ng and a team of engineers have been assigned to prepare costings and recommend one of three potential contractors for the furnace overhaul. The kinds of factors they have to consider include the time the furnaces will be out of commission, the likely effect on production, and the cost and quality of the overhaul. Richard's team recommends Thermatic, but the managing director of Zanicum, Sally Richfield, is unimpressed. She seems to regard it as a matter of course that the contract will go to Fusion Furnaces, an enterprise in which her family company, MTSC, has an interest. Sally questions some of the assumptions upon which Richard's team made its recommendation. She requests Richard to reconsider his assumptions and to make appropriate changes to the costings. Richard agrees that some assumptions are open to different interpretations, but asks her whether there might not be a conflict of interest in her position. Sally laughs and tells him that she has more shares and options in Zanicum than in Fusion, and that her success is bound up in leading Zanicum to successful expansion. There is no conflict of interest, she declares. Richard is directed to revise his costings and his recommendation of a furnace maintenance contractor.

Gloria Vineman, the newly appointed finance director with Zanicum, is preparing the company's annual financial statements. She knows from the previous year's audited accounts that cumulative provision of $1.5 million had been made for furnace maintenance, and that costings had been prepared in the current year for the work to proceed. She asks Richard Ng for details of the costings, but he merely gives her his recommendation and refers her to Sally Richfield. Sally is evasive and eventually does not present the costings. She informs Gloria that the costing exercise put a figure of $1.5 million on the overhaul of furnaces, but Gloria is unhappy about this verbal advice. She has heard engineers in the firm mention a figure twice as large. Sally firmly states that if Gloria has any concerns based on such hearsay, she should keep them to herself and not upset the auditors — especially during the negotiation of a large loan from the bank.

John Ryan is the senior partner in Ryan McGrath, auditors for MTSC, Fusion and other metal working companies including Zanicum. Almost all of Ryan McGrath's business comes from the metals industry. John reviews the financial statements of Zanicum prepared by Gloria and notes a significant audit risk against the refurbishment of furnaces. Despite direct requests to Gloria, John has been unable to obtain the costings documents from Zanicum. Sally will not discuss the matter beyond saying that the growth of the company and sustained demand for its products are the best evidence of the financial health of Zanicum. She also makes an indirect but clear suggestion that if Ryan McGrath cannot provide a trouble-free audit before she meets with the bank to finalise the loan, then there are other auditors who are more familiar with the operations and needs of the metals industry.

John and Sally eventually reach an agreement that Zanicum should make provision of $1.75 million for furnace maintenance, and Ryan McGrath signs Zanicum's statements as presenting a true and fair view. The bank loan goes through, and the furnaces are serviced by Fusion at a cost of $2.7 million.

This case raises a number of ethical problems, but the central one concerns professional independence.

What would you have done in Richard's and Gloria's positions?

To whom are Richard and Gloria accountable? Is it Sally? Does she have the right to exercise her position as she has with Richard and Gloria?

To whom should the accountant be responsible in these cases?

What of the responsibilities of Ryan McGrath? John Ryan has placed a large part of his company's business in a narrow field: the metals industry. Has he not put himself under avoidable pressure by auditing companies with business connections and sometimes overlapping directorships?

Is Ryan properly cognisant of his statutory and ethical responsibilities? Sally Richfield made it clear that Ryan McGrath would be jeopardising its own business if an unfavourable audit went forward. Is this a credible threat? What, for an auditor, constitutes a proper distance from a client?

There are also other issues here that draw upon the problem of dirty hands (see chapter 2). If one is implicated in covering up sharp practice, then later one can be caught in all kinds of difficulties, which seem to result in disaster no matter what one does. This might well apply to John Ryan, but consider also the position of Richard Ng. Say he changes his costings at the behest of Sally Richfield. He considers this a small thing. Then when he is approached by Gloria Vineman for details of these costings, he must evade the difficulty and refer her to Sally. If he told what he knows to John Ryan, the loan with the bank might be jeopardised, and the future of the company and the benefits to its employees and other stakeholders might be adversely affected. If he conceals what he knows, he is acting against his professional integrity. This is a situation he has got himself into by initially acceding to Sally's request — that is, by an initial compromise of independent professional judgment. Of course, not all cases of professional failure give rise to dire consequences or produce dirty hands later. But ethical consistency can at least reduce the chances of being confronted with such problems down the track. In this case, consistency would involve saying 'no' to Sally initially and sticking with that decision. This view says nothing about personal costs, but these are often entailed in principled action in any case, and there is always the possibility that one unethical act will create the conditions for much more costly ethical failures later.

The significance of professional independence is clear in the light of these reflections. Note that similar ethical issues regarding independence, responsibility and accountability arise in connection with the roles of other kinds of salaried professionals working in organisations. One has only to think of the engineers who advised against the launch of the space shuttle Challenger. These issues are about the nature of the professional role, and of what can reasonably be demanded of people whose profession entails a good measure of autonomy.

Review questions

1   We note the results of a survey about where accountants identify the source of their values: family, conduct of peers, accounting practices, prevailing societal norms, processional code of ethics, and religious formation. Such surveys are not uncommon. If such places are where people believe their values come from, is there any place for critical reflection or critical evaluation – making up one's own mind – or independent thought about values?

2   We discuss two senses of 'independence' as the notion applies to accountants. Are you clear about what these are? Do you agree that these are different senses?

3   What do you think of the suggestion that increased regulation can exacerbate a problem, rather than solve it?

The Environment | 8

There is no question about whether business has some responsibility for the environment. Laws require employers to provide safe work places and businesses to offer goods and services that are safe to consumers and the public. Industries must comply with waste and pollution regulations. There are issues that arise for business in connection with the environment. The first is whether businesses that ignore environmental factors in their operations are sustainable. This is a prudential issue rather than a moral one, but ethical questions are not far behind. Does business have ethical responsibilities to the environment in addition to legal ones? And if so, what is the extent of the responsibility of business in this area?

Recall Milton Friedman's objections to business engaging in socially responsible activity: First, such activity diverts profits from shareholders. It is up to them to spend their money on worthy causes, not for the directors of their corporations to do this for them. Secondly, businesses should not trespass on the role of governments. Governments have the role of setting social policy agendas and they have the mandate of voters to do so. Business has neither. It is for governments to set the legal frameworks in which business operates and for business to generate wealth within the laws and regulations established by government. Social responsibility is not a part of the obligations of business.

We repeat these arguments because they have figured and continue to figure in the positions of corporations that wish to reject a role in environmental protection. They are, as it happens, out of date. The rise of the *No Logo*[1] attitude, a scepticism about corporate citizenship and genuine concern for social responsibility, along with shareholder activism and the greater spread of share ownership, especially in Australia, mean that directors have a more complex duty to the owners of listed companies than forty years ago. Many activities once thought extraneous to business purposes are now an ordinary part of commercial enterprises.

Even Friedman would have to allow as exceptions socially responsible actions which support the reputation of a corporation and hence its capacity to earn profits. If environmentally responsible conduct can enhance a company's reputation, then it has added value to the shareholders' investments. Levi's, Saturn cars, Dick Smith electronics, Proctor and Gamble, Johnson & Johnson, and The Body Shop have all benefited from good reputations. Then there are cases of damaged reputations because brand names came to be associated with socially irresponsible practices: Nestlé, Shell, Nike, Union Carbide, Exxon, and Alcoa are a few examples. In 1990, McDonald's had to protect its reputation by replacing its polystyrene hamburger boxes with paper packaging. There was no clear scientific evidence that paper was more environmentally friendly than plastic, but consumer sentiment was against polystyrene, and McDonald's took a precautionary strategy and changed its packaging. Because reputation is valuable, it is both a strength and a weakness. It can be a mark of trust in the market place, but it also exposes a company to activism as well as customers' attitudes and beliefs. In 2003, for example, an activist group called 'People for the Ethical Treatment of Animals' (PETA), organised a boycott of KFC outlets. By placing pressure on the point of sale, the group hoped to improve the conditions in which chickens were held by KFC suppliers. The Kentucky Fried Chicken (KFC) brand, like other fast food chains, was under pressure from law suits brought by litigants claiming that fast food had contributed to their obesity. In other words, PETA took advantage of the public mood about fast food to leverage better conditions for chickens, and the KFC brand name was the lever.[2]

So, far from being a diversion of shareholders' money into causes unrelated to the purposes of the business, socially responsible action may enhance the bottom line. And neglect of such action might well weaken the performance of the business, especially if competitors have taken a pro-active position.

As for Friedman's objection about business intruding into the domain of governments, it is clear that there is no clear boundary to be crossed here.[3] Social concerns – including environmental issues – are now very much within the responsibilities of business. The example of the potential effects on reputation is an indication of this.

The Australian public feels strongly about environmental issues, whether from dissatisfaction with the nation's environmental record or from a concern for the future.

However, the strength of that feeling does not make the matter an ethical issue or an issue for business. Henry Bosch, former chairman of the National Companies and Securities Commission, has put the position that not 'all matters of public policy, or even "national social justice" are matters of ethics'. He illustrates the distinction by referring to the case of an MBA student who was disturbed that a paper on corporate conduct contained no standards on equal opportunity or the environment:

> The student seemed quite certain that because such questions as the preservation of forests are matters of vital concern to him they must be ethical issues … Of course such a position leads to absurdity … Ethics must be based on a value system and, while the business community would be wise to pay attention to what is going on in society at large and remain open to persuasion, it must set its own ethical standards based on its own values.[4]

In a different context altogether (in talking about imposing requirements and sanctions on advertising and marketing), Richard De George suggests that some very important matters are for political, rather than moral, decision-making.[5] We touched on De George's point in chapter 5. In some areas, although regulation would not be morally objectionable, neither is it morally necessary. Some matters can be matters of general preference without being matters of morality and, De George suggests, sometimes it is permissible to legislate because of preference. It can be a matter of politics rather than ethics. This is an important point: not all preferences – even strongly felt ones — are matters of morality, and some things which are not matters of morality should not therefore necessarily be considered as beyond governmental interference or regulation. The enthusiasms and passions of individuals do not make their concerns ethical issues. Conversely, however, just because business groups are uninterested in environmental issues or are immersed in their own values does not mean that the environment is not an ethical issue.

Business hostility to the environment is difficult to understand in the light of the history of industrialism. Among the great number of articles and books on the fate of the environment under industrial capitalism, one of the most interesting discussions has been over the 'tragedy of the commons' — the fate of commonly held property or resources. Where things belong to everybody it is often the case that they belong to nobody, and nobody expends sufficient time on their care and upkeep. Or, worse still, they are regarded as 'free' resources to be used at will, as in the case of manufacturers who pollute the air and water because there is no 'owner' to harm in the process. This is, of course, free-loading on a huge scale, and it is puzzling that some cannot recognise this as a moral problem. Ultimately such individual opportunism is harmful to all. As Garrett Hardin observed nearly two generations ago, its cumulative effects end up destroying us all.[6]

This has long been foreseeable. In 1833 W. F. Lloyd observed that cattle grazing on common land in England were leaner than those grazed on private property. The feed on the commons was poorer because of over-grazing. Over time, each farmer had increased his herd by only one or two cows — not much for each individual and not enough in each case to make a difference to the commons. But the combined effect of such increases in individual herds meant the destruction of the commons. The message here is clear: the earth's resources are finite, and the demands already made on them by human populations have produced changes in the atmosphere, the oceans and the soils.

The exercise of even small economic liberties can have devastating social and environmental effects. DuPont, for example, used to dump 10,000 tons of chemical waste each month into the Gulf of Mexico from its West Virginia plant because it was cost free. Even with this level of dumping, the contribution to the pollution of the gulf would be negligible. But if every plant along the gulf acted in this way, the gulf would suffer the same fate as the commons.[7]

The environment is not a source of 'found' resources. While the environment does not 'belong' to anyone, this does not mean that people's rights are not violated by excessive exploitation and abuse. Our ethical obligations are not confined to privately owned property. Someone in the present or in a future generation will have to bear the cost of exhausted soils, depleted energy resources, or pollution. When old coal-fired power stations generated electricity, not all the costs were included in the bills consumers paid. There was no charge for the atmosphere, for the greenhouse gases, for the fallout on neighbours.[8] With nuclear energy, will the same attitudes prevail? Will the costs of safe disposal of radioactive waste be reflected in the cost of electricity? There are no free lunches: someone has to pick up the bill, and it really should be the 'user'. The true costs, including the environmental costs, of doing business should be reflected in the price of the goods and services produced. Prices should include a component for social costs and not just the private costs — wages, raw materials, taxes, interest charges and rents — of production. Then we could make informed economic choices about whether we could really afford some products and whether we would be prepared to live well at the expense of others in the present and perhaps in the future. If it is not to be the user who pays, we must recognise that someone must. Where and upon whom those costs fall is a question of justice.

The care of the environment, then, is a matter of ethics, even if not all environmental issues raise ethical questions. Still, we need to be clear about the nature of environmental ethics. To whom is business ethically accountable for environmental decisions? To nature or to humanity? To future generations? Answers to these questions divide into two broad groups, the humanistic and the naturalistic.

The humanistic argument

The first kind of answer is that the environment is an ethical matter because without a clean environment, human health will be harmed; and without a natural world with a diversity of species, human life will be diminished. Similarly, without a stock of non-renewable resources for future generations, their life will have less quality than our own. This is the anthropocentric or humanistic argument. It is clear that chemical companies that pollute streams and bays with mercury have a direct influence on the food chain, which can lead to ill-health in humans. Factories that pollute the air can cause respiratory problems in young children and elderly people. When business pollutes, there is a cost to be paid, whether it be financial, in health or in amenity. This payment is a subsidy from the person who pays it to the business, and such an imposition is unfair. Such instances of environmental free riding have been relatively common, and illustrate the anthropocentric argument about environmental ethics.

William Blackstone argues that everyone has a right to a livable environment and that therefore others have an obligation to allow the free enjoyment of this right.[9] A person cannot flourish or develop potentials without an environment that provides clean air and water, natural beauty, and so on. The right to these overrides considerations of property and economic development. This argument is an extension of Immanuel Kant's requirement to treat people with respect. If respect for persons entails respect for those things that are necessary for their well-being, then we must respect nature.

The difficulty with Blackstone's position is that it does not tell us how we are to live and still respect nature. If we do not use the resources of the earth, then we might also be showing a lack of respect to persons who, as a result, will live a diminished life. There has to be a compromise.

The problem with effecting a compromise is that the environmental debate has become polarised, with the green movement in effect occupying all the pro-environmental territory, and business and industry often looking like defenders of the indefensible. Ultimately, economics bites, but if compromise means waiting until either the environment is degraded or industry shuts down, then the outcome is more in the nature of an accident than a decision.

The naturalistic argument

The second kind of answer is that nature has intrinsic value. As but one part of nature, humans have no dominion over it, no unqualified right to harm or extinguish the lives of plants and animals or to destroy the ecosystems that support them. The right to exploit the resources of the planet is qualified by the gravity of reasons that support the inherent right of nature to our respect. With the world's population growing alarmingly and placing demands on non-renewable resources as all nations seek a share of the developed world's lifestyle, the problems of resource and pollution management increase. But environmental ethicists want more than protection for economically valuable and life-sustaining resources. They want respect for the natural world, an ecological or naturalistic ethic.

Michael Hoffman, for example, believes that placing a humanistic value on the environment provides no protection in the long run. If business is convinced of the slogan that 'good environmental ethics is good business', then protection of the environment comes to depend on the profitability of responsible practices. It is the same potentially misleading promise of the parallel slogan that 'good ethics is good business': there is the suggestion that an ethical position is just one more way to make a profit. It would follow that if environmental irresponsibility were better business, then one ought to take that position, good business being the relevant standard for all policy. But neither ethics nor environmental care is cost free. According to Hoffman, it is important that the natural world is valued for the right reason, and that involves according the environment the kind of intrinsic respect we give to human beings.[10]

A number of writers, led by Peter Singer, have argued that as sentient beings animals have interests that deserve consideration by humans. To disregard those interests is 'speciesism', an analogy with racism. Speciesism 'is a prejudice or attitude of bias in favour of the interests of one's own species and against those of members of other species'.[11] Of course, the problem here is that racism is unjust discrimination within a species, whereas speciesism is one species making use of another. It is a genuine question whether the term 'discrimination' can be used in relation to the way that humans treat animals. To deny equal consideration to people on the grounds of irrelevant differences such as ethnicity or skin colour is discrimination precisely because we all belong to the same species. To deny equal consideration to animals on the grounds that they are not human is not so obviously unjust. Singer argues that because animals can suffer and feel pleasure, it is unwarranted to give consideration to humans at the expense of the pain (and pleasure?) of animals. He does not require that animals be treated equally with humans, just that their interests should receive equal consideration. How one gives equal consideration without giving equal treatment is not clear. Singer nonetheless makes an important point about the intrinsic value of animals: if they are the kind of beings which can suffer and feel pleasure, then our attitudes to them are not the only things which count morally. Cruelty is reprehensible whether inflicted on humans or animals. Almost five hundred years ago, Thomas More condemned the widely accepted sport of hunting:

> … if you want to see a living creature torn apart under your eyes, then the whole thing is wrong. You ought to feel nothing but pity when you see the hare fleeing from the hound, the weak creature tormented by the stronger … Taking such relish in the sight of death, even if only of beasts, reveals … a cruel disposition.[12]

The case for respecting animals and their habitats is easier to make than that for inanimate nature. Humanity is enriched by animals.[13] Domestic pets and animals in the wild are loved and valued, even by meat eaters, graziers and poultry farmers, just as forests and gardens are loved by wheat farmers and rice growers. The world is a lesser place when it loses a species of plant or animal. But do we weep for such losses? And what of inanimate nature? What intrinsic rights does nature have? Most of the universe is cold, dark, and lifeless. Should these desolate places count ethically?

Imagine that we could conduct an experiment that would reveal some fundamental facts about the universe. This experiment would be very dramatic but completely safe to humans. It would involve crashing one of the moons of Jupiter into the surface of the planet. What reasons could there be against such an experiment? Would it matter that Jupiter had one less moon? Would we even need to justify this experiment in terms of the value of the knowledge to be gained? In what possible ways could this experiment be unjustifiable? Imagine another scenario much closer to home. Say we have devised a way to produce electricity that is a cheap and safe replacement for fossil fuel generators. It will save hugely on carbon dioxide emissions, but alas will produce a large quantity of nuclear waste if it is widely adopted. Thankfully, we can solve the waste problem through using the latest generation of space vehicles to ferry the waste to the moon. This should not be a problem because the waste dumps will be on the dark side of the moon, and not visible to Earth. What possible objection could there be to such a plan? We could dispose of our waste on an uninhabitable space object and forget all about it. As it is, tonnes of debris fall every year on the moon, so adding a bit more from Earth will not matter.

An appeal to intrinsic value might cause us to pause before destroying Jupiter's moon or dumping on ours. But how can we justify such a valuation? Is it just an appeal to the strength of our preferences that makes us claim intrinsic value? Is it not rather that what is valuable is what we value. If we were dealing with animals, we might appeal to Singer's argument and the extension of regard for animal life to the protection of the habitat on which animals depend. In short, appealing to the intrinsic worth of inanimate nature only seems to work with people who share one's appreciation of nature. Or does it? If a person defaced a work by Rembrandt or Picasso, would we not be shocked and saddened? When the Taliban destroyed Buddhist statues with dynamite in Afghanistan, were not all decent people horrified? One does not have to be an art lover or a Buddhist to be appalled by vandalism and wanton destruction, just as one does not have to be an animal rights campaigner to react to cruelty to animals. We can understand barbarity and appreciate that a good is being destroyed even if we do not participate in the full meaning of that good. That is how it is with the moons of Jupiter and with our moon. We do not destroy the environment wantonly and should not cause major disturbances without the strongest reasons for doing so. There is a good even in the things we do not see, and the life of humans is diminished when species, habitats and even cold and lifeless rocks in space are the victims of rapacity. We should not deface our heritage, but enhance it for transmission to future generations.

Growth

An ethically responsible policy towards the environment must deal with the problem of growth. There are strong arguments that the earth cannot sustain present growth patterns, let alone extend them to cover more of the world's growing population. Affluence is the problem.[14] Yet, in times of recession, growth is the watchword of those seeking employment and profits. Whether we must have economic growth or can develop a sustainable steady-state economy are questions that cannot be answered by an ethicist. One can simply take note of the increasing demand on fossil fuels and the polluting effects these will continue to have unless curbed; and of the increasing demands of expanding economies in China and South-East Asia and the pressure these will place on known energy reserves and arable land. It hardly makes sense to talk of globalisation in business and restrict this to profits and growth. Collateral effects such as rising expectations, limited resources and pollution must also be considered. Moreover, we should not take the solutions of conventional economists at face value. Growth statistics do not tell us much except the size of the economy. Although Australia increased its gross national product by about 30 per cent in the 1980s, poverty doubled, unemployment trebled, and real wages fell. Public infrastructure declined as railway services were cut back, hospital waiting lists increased, and the gap between rich and poor widened. Growth benefited relatively few. The same is true of the United States, which on one index of economic well-being that takes account of social and environmental factors has become worse off despite years of economic growth. [15]

Intergenerational issues

No generation has an unfettered right to use the world's resources for its own advantage without regard for the fate of future generations. Because this possibility exists, it is something that must concern business, not only in a strategic sense but ethically.

But why should we assume responsibilities that no other generation has had to assume? Why is there a moral obligation here? John Rawls argues that we should adopt a 'just savings principle' or 'an understanding between generations to carry their fair share of the burden of realizing and preserving a just society'.[16] Each generation should preserve the social and economic gains it has received, and put aside for the next generations what it would consider fair to have received from its predecessor.[17] We should leave the world in no worse a state than we found it. After all, that is what we should be grateful for from our parents. This has implications for the use of non-renewable resources and energy, the production of waste and pollution, and the release of potentially harmful substances into the environment.[18]

The following case illustrates some of these issues.

Case 8.1   Carson & DDT

Rachel Carson achieved enduring fame for her classic study of the effects of the miracle pesticide, DDT, on the environment. That work, *Silent Spring,* was published in 1962, and had such an impact that DDT was progressively banned around the world. One of Carson's main allegations against DDT was that when it entered the human food chain it was carcinogenic. These claims gained wide currency, and many scientists backed the banning of DDT. The problem is that the claims were not supported by evidence, and there has been in consequence a backlash against Carson. The main charge of the critics is that the banning of DDT allowed mosquitos bearing the malaria parasite to spread unchecked. Had DDT been available, the health and lives of millions of people could have been spared.[19]

Michael Crichton, author of *Jurassic Park*, is one of Carson's critics. He has attacked the environmental movement for being quasi-religious (working from faith, ideology and passion) rather than empirical (getting the data and interpreting them scientifically). According to Crichton, only genuine scientists are in a position to make sound judgments about environmental policy. Proper policy debates are not possible with people who will not accept facts. You cannot talk somebody out of a religious position, asserts Crichton, and that is exactly the position knowledgeable people find themselves in when confronted with the unshakeable beliefs of ideological environmentalists.

> I can tell you that DDT is not a carcinogen and did not cause birds to die and should never have been banned. I can tell you that the people who banned it knew that it wasn't carcinogenic and banned it anyway. I can tell you that the DDT ban has caused the deaths of tens of millions of poor people, mostly children, whose deaths are directly attributable to a callous, technologically advanced western society that promoted the new cause of environmentalism by pushing a fantasy about a pesticide, and thus irrevocably harmed the third world. Banning DDT is one of the most disgraceful episodes in the twentieth century history of America.
>
> ... I can tell you that second hand smoke is not a health hazard to anyone and never was, and the EPA has always known it. I can tell you that the evidence for global warming is far weaker than its proponents would ever admit. I can tell you the percentage the US land area that is taken by urbanization, including cities and roads, is 5%. I can tell you

that the Sahara desert is shrinking, and the total ice of Antarctica is increasing. I can tell
you that a blue-ribbon panel in Science magazine concluded that there is no known tech-
nology that will enable us to halt the rise of carbon dioxide in the 21st century.[20]

Criticisms like these point to a difficulty for business:

Should environmental responsibility take the form of specific responses to problems or should it be a commitment to a belief system or ideology?

Does business have to subscribe to a package of environmental beliefs in order, say, to reduce waste or to ensure a safe workplace?

It is clear that some environmental groups want nothing less than fundamental social and economic change, and that is a difficult proposition for business to support. This concern is not misplaced. Even reputable green groups make mistakes, and sometimes those mistakes arise from zealotry. The following case shows what can happen.

Case 8.2   Shell & Greenpeace

Greenpeace and other environmental groups organised a campaign against Shell over the disposal of its obsolete Brent Spar oil rig. The campaign included boycotts of Shell petrol, demonstrations and publicity offensives. The problem was that Greenpeace was wrong. They mistakenly believed that Brent Spar contained 5000 gallons of waste oil and protested against its disposal in the North Sea. In the face of sustained public opposition generated by the environmentalists, Shell decided to move the rig to Norway for break up and disposal. This proved to be not only a more expensive, but also a more environmentally hazardous option.

This incident could be instanced as an example of the dangers of knee-jerk responses made on the basis of ideology rather than facts – the kind of reaction that Crichton warns against. It could be seen as an opportunity for a corporation with less than satisfactory systems to change them. Shell did so by changing to triple bottom line reporting, aligning its business principles with social and environmental objectives[21], and thereby projecting a strong image as an ethical and responsible corporation. In 2001, Shell was joint winner of the British Social Reporting Award for its 1999 Report.[22]

While the demand for better scientific evidence in environmental decisions, standards and policies is reasonable in theory, in practice it can take a very long time to produce and interpret such evidence. In cases like the Brent Spar, a less emotional atmosphere in discussing the issues might have produced a more satisfactory environmental outcome. The evidence should have prevailed. Not all environmental issues, however, are like this. In some — the impact of mining on an environment, the planting of genetically modified crops or the effect of farming on atmospheric conditions — the evidence takes a long time to accumulate and analyse, and by then irreversible damage might have been done. Herein lies the lasting value of Carson's warnings.

The precautionary principle

In 1992, the United Nations held a Conference on Environment and Development in Rio. One of the resolutions contained in the Rio Declaration stated that:

> *In order to protect the environment, the precautionary approach shall be widely applied by States according to their capabilities. Where there are threats of serious or irreversible damage, lack of full scientific certainty shall not be used as a reason for postponing cost-effective measures to prevent environmental degradation.*[23]

What is the precautionary principle? The widely quoted 'Wingspread Statement', drafted in 1998, puts it like this:

> *Where an activity raises threats of harm to the environment or human health, precautionary measures should be taken even if some cause and effect relationships are not fully established scientifically.*[24]

The precautionary principle asks business to scan the horizon, and even to look over it for the unintended harms that might come from its activities. The absence of clearly established scientific proof has often prevented environmental concerns from being taken seriously, and the precautionary principle reverses the burden so that it falls on those who wish to engage in potentially harmful activities.

> *In essence, the precautionary principle provides a rationale for taking action against a practice or substance in the absence of scientific certainty rather than continuing the suspect practice while it is under study, or without study.*[25]

This is a higher standard than the law in environmental matters. The precautionary principle should be a check on rashness, but reversing the onus of responsibility is not a universal remedy in environmental controversies. Think of the example of DDT: It might have seemed precautionary to ban it, but it was simply wrong to continue that ban when the evidence did not show that it caused cancer and suggested that it might be used without wholesale environmental damage.

The precautionary principle operates in areas where such evidence is absent, but there are real concerns about harm. It is meant to serve as a restraint where concern, but no causation exists. An activity might not be known to damage health, but one might reconsider it or restrict it until concerns are allayed. This kind of thinking is really common sense, but it has been elevated to the status of a principle because those who oppose it ask for scientific proof. Such proof cannot always be produced, so the precautionary principle is now invoked to change the onus of responsibility, and sometimes provocatively: prove that the activity is not dangerous! The principle could, however, be usefully extended. It could prompt corporations to ask the following questions. What could go wrong? What systems do we need to ensure that the risk of things going wrong is minimised? What would we do if something did go wrong? What back-up facilities and safe exits should we build into this project? Space engineers have learnt about safe exits from incidents like the Challenger and Columbia shuttle disasters, but business needs to think of exit strategies for the public and the environment — not for managers and directors — should a system fail.

The precautionary principle is not cost free and can bring about its own unintended consequences. One critical supporter argues that its widespread introduction would have costs beginning with the introduction and implementation of regulations, then impact on productivity, wages and prices, and end up diverting money available for other public health priorities.[26] In other words, application of the precautionary principle might end up harming health more than protecting it. That is what might have happened had the precautionary principle been applied to the banning of DDT. As it was, that pesticide was banned on the basis of scientific evidence, but the case illustrates that one cost of applying the precautionary principle could be the loss of a health-protecting chemical. Just as some toxins reveal themselves only in cumulative effects, so the removal of a useful substance as a precautionary measure can have long-term deleterious effects.

The precautionary principle changes the default position. Instead of requiring a business to determine an acceptable level of risk, it asks whether risky action can be avoided. It encourages the asking of questions from a broader social perspective. While a development such as genetic modification of foods might present a business opportunity, application of the precautionary principle would pose the question of whether there might not be other ways of making a profit in the food industry. The precautionary principle is an amber light to technology. It warns of a stoppage, whereas a risk assessment weighs the odds of getting through an intersection before the red. Risk assessment can sometimes resemble a green light rather than an amber – proceed with caution. If a new technology has the potential to harm, it is better to re-examine its use rather than to wait and see if the harm eventuates. Genetically modified crops and animals are obvious candidates for the application of the precautionary principle.

Waste or fertiliser

What happens to the waste material of steel mills, power stations, aluminium smelters and concrete kilns? Some of it is sold to farmers as fertiliser. It finds a ready market because it sells for much less than traditional fertilisers. The problem is that these products of industrial waste are not tested by agricultural authorities. Their benefits might be short term, and they might even be potentially harmful. The slag from steel mills, for example, contains heavy metals such as chromium, lead and arsenic. There are few laws in Australia against labelling such wastes as fertiliser and they can even be legally labelled as organic. Even where regulation prevents the sale of waste as fertiliser it can still be sold as soil conditioner.[27] This discovery was shocking to Australians, but the disposal of industrial waste as fertiliser has been occurring in the even less-regulated markets of the US for years. According to the president of one waste 'recycler', 'When it goes into our silo, it's a hazardous waste. When it comes out of the silo, it's no longer regulated. The exact same material. Don't ask me why. That's the wisdom of the EPA'.[28]

Clearly the precautionary principle indicates that this is an area that should be more extensively regulated, but if the precautionary principle were applied by the suppliers, they would do their own testing. The question is complicated in this case because producers, like BHP, are not the suppliers. BHP has professed ignorance of the fate of their slag, which is marketed by Australian Steel Mill Services. The latter dispose of the material to farmers and there is no deception about its source. Does this absolve BHP of any responsibility to ensure the safe disposal of its waste? Considering the potential costs to BHP Billiton's reputation (Australian Steel Mill Services does not enjoy the same profile) if toxins were to enter the food chain, the precautionary principle could work to the advantage both of producer and the public here.

The following cases illustrate these issues.

Case 8.3   Woolworth's Super petrol

When Woolworths began to sell petrol, it imported gasoline containing MTBE (methyl tertiary butyl ether), an additive not used by Australian refiners. MTBE is toxic and has been banned in Western Australia and Queensland. The Federal Government will follow suit in 2004. Australian refiners do not use MTBE, but according to Woolworths, this additive has 'many properties that make it useful in petrol for technical and environmental reasons'.

Conservationists have criticised the use of MTBE, alleging that it poses a threat to ground water. Let us say that the scientific verdict on the risks of small levels of MTBE is not in. Would not a cautious approach have indicated that it was unwise to import petrol with this additive? After all, MTBE was going to be discontinued in any case. Woolworths had to argue after the event that an additive banned by governments was a risk worth taking. And, because neither Woolworths nor Coles, Australia's two leading supermarket chains, has initiated environmental policies to match those of United Kingdom and French retailers, there was no record of public concern to which Woolworths might have appealed.

If the scientific evidence eventually supports the conservationist case, then Woolworths has stored up a problem for itself in the future.[29]

Case 8.4   Alcoa emissions

In 1996, Alcoa commissioned a refining incinerator, called a liquor burner, at its plant at Wagerup in Western Australia in order to improve productivity and cut costs. This device burnt impurities from aluminium ore but emitted a cocktail of obnoxious fumes containing benzine, xylene, toluene and napthalene.[30] Workers and local residents began to complain about the stink and then about sudden illnesses, unprecedented allergies, increased sensitivity to chemicals and pitted enamel on cars. Animals began developing unusual diseases. When Alcoa's new publicist, recruited to improve the company's image, complained about the fumes, she was issued with a respirator — to wear in her office.[31]

Alcoa has since bought properties around its plant and had to face inquiries and audits. A precautionary approach would have obviated much of this. Alcoa always knew that there would be some negative reaction to the liquor burner, but it was too sanguine about its own measures. A useful device in this situation would have been to have an environmental 'devil's advocate' to put the case against the liquor burner and to challenge the responses of the firm to potential complaints. Alcoa did bring in its chief medical officer from the US, Professor Mark Cullen of Yale University. Cullen found minimal risk of illness due to the plant. 'If I had any other view I would recommend the immediate closure of the facility — in line with Alcoa values,' he is reported as saying.[32] Fine, but it is not unknown for corporations to bring in their own experts to counter public concerns by creating uncertainty. In this case the uncertainty was rapidly dispelled and precaution was overtaken by prevention. In the wake of complaints, the state minister for the environment required Alcoa to install modifications to its plant, including special gas-fired burners, and higher stacks to disperse pollutants. She also required an independent audit of Alcoa's environmental management systems, and the upper house of the Western Australian parliament instituted its own inquiry in 2001.[33]

Even before extensive investigations and modifications became necessary Alcoa could have taken a precautionary posture. Andrew Harper, Fellow of the Faculty of Occupational Medicine, told the Western Australian parliamentary inquiry that 'The level of a given chemical may well be below the safety level defined by government standards, but when the chemical is mixed with others in the body it can be toxic'.[34] Given the nature of the toxins emitted — even in small doses — from the Alcoa plant, there was a reason for the corporation to be cautious. At the very least, the company should have been conscious that in seeking to cut the costs of aluminium production, it was imposing social costs on the residents of Wagerup, many of whom were also its employees. Why did not the social costs of installing the liquor burner rank as highly as the economic ones? A more prudent and environmentally pro-active course of action might have satisfied the demand to make a profit and the obligation to do so without harming the welfare of the town or its environment.

Voluntary action

Ethics is quite often the realm of the voluntary. Ethics sets higher standards than the law. The perennial problem for responsible businesses that meet ethical requirements is that less responsible competitors will take the opportunity to enlarge their market share. Christine Parker has argued that deterrence alone cannot explain corporate adoption of environmentally responsible policies. Usually such policies emerge from the context of crisis and the threat or actuality of harm to the corporation. But beyond enforcement and deterrence, Parker shows that management engages with environmental policy for a variety of reasons. An example of such engagement is the Green Challenge.[35]

Facing moves to recommend a carbon tax at the 1995 Berlin conference on climate change, corporations and industry associations devised the Green Challenge.[36] The Australian Government agreed to the Challenge as an alternative to the tax and began a partnership program to lower greenhouse gas emissions in 1996. Membership of the Challenge is entirely voluntary, but the performance of members is audited. Action that could potentially harm the interests of any one business becomes viable if it is collaborative. Collaboration can forestall government action and exert pressure on other businesses to self-regulate.

Another example of Australian business voluntarily taking on environmental responsibilities is found in subscription to the International Organization for Standardization's 14,001 environmental management systems standards. By January 2002, 1173 Australian companies had signed up.[37] Japan ranked first, with 8169 signatories, then Germany, the UK, Sweden and Spain. The US is just ahead of Australia, which occupies seventh position. This indicates that, at least by international standards, Australian business is well disposed to adopt environmental standards.

A further indication of this is the rate of voluntary compliance with what has become the global standard in environmental reporting. In the late 1990s, John Elkington coined the term 'triple bottom line reporting' to indicate that the social and environmental aspects of a corporation's operations were as important as the economic ones.[38] The idea joins corporate social responsibility with profits. One of the ways in which this reporting has been promoted is through the Global Reporting Initiative (GRI) begun in 1997 by the Coalition for Environmentally Responsible Economies (CERES), but now a separate organisation. The object of the GRI is to promote the Sustainability Reporting Guidelines on the economic, environmental, and social dimensions of business activities, which it does in collaboration with the United Nations. By 2002, the GRI had 46 American reporters (signatories), 51 United Kingdom reporters, and 22 Australian reporters.[39] None of this should suggest that regulation is now superfluous, but as Parker suggests, compliance is more complicated than threatening corporations with penalties.

The CERES Principles

Business attitudes have changed over the past few decades and it would be incorrect to characterise them as hostile to the environment or even as defensive. These changes, however, have generally come as a result of crises. One of the best-known examples of a pro-active stand on environmental protection by business is the CERES Principles (formerly called the Valdez Principles), which were a response to the environmental disaster that took place when the Exxon Valdez ran aground in King William Sound, Alaska in 1989.[40, 41]

The CERES Principles attempt to extend environmentally responsible business practices across the globe and across all kinds and sizes of business. Although the Principles seem to add to an ever-increasing list of standards, experience has shown that if business is unprepared to regulate its own operations, government agencies are not reluctant to regulate for them. So, for all the difficulties of adopting a code like the Valdez Principles, there are incentives for large corporations at least to support it and give it credibility.

There are ten principles:

1 *Protection of the biosphere*: provides for the elimination of pollution, protection of habitats and the ozone layer, and the minimisation of smog, acid rain and greenhouse gases.
2 *Sustainable use of natural resources*: commits signatories to conservation of non-renewable resources, the responsible use of renewable resources, and the protection of wilderness and biodiversity.
3 *Reduction and disposal of waste*: obliges signatories to minimise waste, to dispose of it responsibly, and to recycle wherever possible.

4   *Energy conservation*: commits signatories to conserve energy and use it more efficiently.

5   *Risk reduction*: provides for minimising health and safety risks to employees and the public by using safe practices and being prepared for emergencies.

6   *Safe products and services*: seeks protection of consumers and the environment by making products safe and providing information about their impact on the environment.

7   *Environmental restoration*: accepts responsibility for repair of environmental damage and compensation to those affected.

8   *Informing the public*: obliges management to disclose to employees and the public information about environmentally harmful incidents. It also protects employees who blow the whistle about environmental or health hazards in their employment.

9   *Management commitment*: commits signatories to provide resources to implement and monitor the Principles. This also means that the CEO and the company's board will be kept abreast of environmental aspects of the company's operations. The selection of directors will give consideration to commitment to the environment.

10 *Audits and reports*: commits signatories to an annual assessment of compliance with the principles that it will make public.

Australian standards and principles

The Australian government is committed to the development of policies of ecologically sustainable development,[42] as set out in the report of the World Commission on Environment and Development (the Brundtland Report).[43] The report argues that economic development and ecological responsibility are complementary rather than contrary.

The Australian approach to developing policy has been sectoral, with working groups producing reports on agriculture, energy, fisheries, forests, manufacturing, mining, tourism and transport. Each sector of industry has its own needs and appropriate methods of enhancing environmental protection. The *Intersectoral Issues Report* stated that 'Ecologically sustainable development can in many respects only provide a starting point ... what constitutes sustainable development in a specific context can often only be determined in that context'.[44] Ecologically sustainable development, then, is difficult to define closely, and not readily specified in terms of pre-cast criteria.

The Brundtland Report defines ecologically sustainable development as 'development that meets the needs of the present without compromising the ability of future generations to meet their own needs'. Ecologically sustainable development attempts to integrate economic, social and ecological criteria, and to balance present economic and social goals and the just-savings principle. In other words, ecologically sustainable development tries to get some perspective on the just requirements of future generations while paying regard to the demands of equity in the present. Of course, the issue facing our heirs might not be the degree of comfort available to them on a planet with depleted resources, but survival itself. In resolving the inevitable clashes which will occur in distributing equitably for the present and saving adequately for the future, the issue of survival should indeed be kept in mind.

Despite the Business Council of Australia's endorsement of ecologically sustainable development, implementation faces obstacles. People are unwilling to begin paying for the environmental subsidies they are accustomed to receiving.[45] As already noted, someone, even if not the ostensible user, is paying these costs. An example might be the use of lead in petrol. When the government put a surcharge on leaded petrol there was an outcry from the welfare lobby in particular. They argued that less well-off people had older cars and so would be paying more than those people who were better off. This violated equity, they said. But someone was already subsidising those using leaded petrol, and that someone was not just the environment polluted with lead; it was children with high lead concentrations in their bodies.

Resistance to measures for intergenerational equity, such as an economic rent on petroleum, could also be anticipated. Proceeds from rents for non-renewable resources could be invested to provide 'a continuous stream of income … and this is equivalent to holding the stock of that capital constant'.[46] Obtaining public and business support for such a measure is another matter.

Policies of recycling at all cost can ultimately lead to the exporting of rubbish, and in the face of low demand this means paying for rubbish to go offshore — an increasing practice condemned by green activists. In Australia, Williams writes, the requirement to recycle rather than incinerate 'can only result in the pressure on landfill being maintained'. A week after this warning, Recyclers Australia sacked twenty workers and refused further waste paper after continuing international price collapses. American and European waste had flooded the market and driven the price down. At Australian Paper Mills, recycling manager, John Davis, said that successful recycling campaigns had resulted in an oversupply of old newspapers. Although the collection, baling, and shipment overseas of old newsprint cost $75 a tonne, Australian Paper Mills can only get $20 a tonne for it. 'We can't continue to recycle unless we have a market for the product or someone is willing to pay for it', said Davis.[47]

Case 8.5   BHP & Ok Tedi

BHP (now BHP Billiton) is one of the world's largest mining companies. With its partners, the Papua New Guinea (PNG) government and the Canadian Inmet Mining Corporation, it formed Ok Tedi Mining Limited (OTML), in which it remains the majority shareholder. The development of the Ok Tedi mine, which sits on a huge copper and gold lode, has been fraught with problems from the beginning of construction in the early 1980s. These have ranged from difficulties with venture partners to strikes to droughts and landslides. The ore deposits are situated on Mount Fuliban in the Star Mountains near the border with Irian Jaya. This area is geologically unstable and subject to powerful erosion. It is drenched by 10 metres of rainfall a year, and the run-off carries sediment from slippage and erosion into the Ok Tedi River. The Ok Tedi flows into the Fly River, which empties into the Gulf of Papua.

Processing at such a mine involves crushing rock to release the valuable minerals and discarding the residue, or tailings, usually in a specially constructed dam. During construction of a tailings dam for the Ok Tedi mine in 1983–84, slippage caused the foundations to collapse and an investment of $70 million to be washed into the river system. This set the scene for all the ensuing problems for BHP and the Ok Tedi peoples. In brief, the mine was developed without a tailings dam, and tailings were thenceforth released into the Ok Tedi River. The result was that the Ok Tedi and Fly rivers were seriously contaminated and that much of the Ok Tedi became dangerously unusable. People who had relied on the river for water and fishing — some for their livelihoods — could do so no longer.

According to the company, construction of a tailings retention dam had not been possible:

> Since [1984], some 120 independent studies on waste retention schemes have been undertaken to find a way to store waste material. With high rainfall and communities living alongside the river, we are primarily concerned about a structure which could eventually collapse causing catastrophic damage and endangering people's lives, not only during the life of the mine but for many years afterwards.[48]

While a safe tailings dam could not be constructed then, BHP insisted that it would continue searching for a way to manage the problem — including construction of a dam. Still, of course, BHP did not cease its mining operations in light of this. In short, its investment was too great. The PNG government has set limits on the amounts of discharge. About forty environmental research and monitoring officers are employed by OTML. Their reports are filed with the PNG government and are audited by independent scientists.

Despite these measures, local landowners, with the support of Australian groups such as Community Aid Abroad, have called the OTML operations at Ok Tedi 'a disaster' and have lobbied for the Australian government to introduce a code of conduct for Australian mining companies operating abroad.[49]

In May 1994, the local landowners launched a $4 billion action against BHP in the Victorian Supreme Court. Two billion dollars were sought for exemplary damages and the building of a tailings dam, and another $2 billion in compensation. An injunction against further mining until a dam was constructed was also sought. The reaction of the PNG government was immediately hostile. In repeated statements, Prime Minister Wingti warned of the damage that such actions could do to overseas investment confidence in his country. He stressed the importance of dealing with such legal issues inside PNG, not through foreign courts. 'The Ok Tedi matter is a matter taking place in PNG and we are going to make it so we handle this within our own country under our own laws', he said shortly after the action was launched.[50] This determination to deal with such actions within his own country led Wingti to consult with BHP over the preparation of legislation to secure a favourable outcome. By the time the legislation was introduced into parliament in December 1995, it had caused a public relations nightmare for BHP and produced its own legal difficulties.

The combined BHP/PNG government case

In order to make any judgment about the issues involved here, it is necessary to place OTML's mining in context. Each year (drought years excluded) rainfall washes over 90 million tonnes of sediment into the Fly River. Mining has added another 40 million tonnes to this, which is mainly deposited over a 20-kilometre stretch of the 1000 kilometre Fly River. The company, however, projects that, when mining is completed, this build-up of sediment will be washed to the sea by the large volumes of water from the catchment. BHP claims that the main problem is the amount of sediment, not the toxicity of mine tailings, and has produced evidence to show that the copper levels of fish in the Fly River are lower than in metropolitan Sydney.

The Ok Tedi mine is the largest enterprise in PNG, contributes about 20 per cent of the country's export income and has provided employment for thousands of local people. Since it commenced operations, benefits from the Ok Tedi mine have included the investment of $300 million in infrastructure, including roads, power, water, communications, schools and medical facilities; the education and training of over 1500 workers; a decline in infant mortality rates from around 33 per cent to less than 3 per cent; generally improved health, with a dramatic decline in malaria infections and an increase in the average life span from 30 to 50 years; and greatly expanded educational opportunities for children. Apart from voluntary compensation initiated by BHP for the Western Province peoples for disturbance to their traditional ways of life, a trust fund has been established for community development in areas such as school buildings and small business assistance. By the time mining has concluded, this trust fund is expected to total $80 million.

BHP summed up its position in these terms:

> BHP is proud of what has been achieved at Ok Tedi but recognises the difficulties the mine has created due to its environmental impact and its effects on the lifestyles of some of the people living along the river. The Company would very much like to find a better solution to the problem it confronts. Closing the mine is not an option — it is too important to the economic and social welfare of Papua New Guinea and is not advocated by any but a small number of people in the region.[51]

The company has declared that 'BHP is committed to carrying out all aspects of its operations in a responsible manner and adopts the same high standards in all countries and communities in which it operates'. It believes that 'the issues relating to the environmental effects of the (Ok Tedi) mine should be addressed within the cultural and political institutions of Papua New Guinea'.[52]

Subsequently, BHP offered a $110 million supplementary package to those affected by the mining. The terms of this offer excluded other general claims upon OTML, but still allowed specific claims, such as damage to gardens. The package had to be ratified by legislation in the PNG parliament, but its effect would have been to prevent the class action then under way in the Victorian Supreme Court. As BHP lawyers were involved in the drafting of the legislation, the Supreme Court found that BHP was in contempt in that the company was attempting to prevent the action before the court. That finding was overturned by the appeal court on a technicality.

What is the ethical issue here? This is an important question. Is it the despoilation of the environment?

Why is mining in PNG an ethical issue when mining in Australia is not?

Are tailings in the Fly River the main issue? If so, how should this ethical obstacle be explained? Under what circumstances could the obstacle be overcome, or is it absolute? Does the issue arise because local residents have had their lifestyle changed or destroyed? Why is this a problem if the nation as a whole benefits from the mining? Is it because these particular stakeholders were insufficiently compensated?

Simon Longstaff of the St James Ethics Centre has suggested that the ethical question is one of a foreign firm driving the government of a developing nation along the path to profits. In other words, there is a power inequality between BHP and the government of PNG, and this power differential raises an ethical difficulty. Do you agree?[53]

Geoffrey Barker of the *Australian Financial Review*, a journalist who takes an interest in ethics, identifies three ethical questions related to the Ok Tedi affair:

1   *Should companies be able to do abroad what they cannot do at home? Should there be universal standards for environmental protection? Should global consistency be demanded of firms like BHP?*
2   *What is the proper relationship between multinational firms and the governments of poor countries desperate for development and foreign exchange? More precisely, how closely should firms be involved in drafting the regulatory frameworks in which they are to operate?*
3   *If local villagers are to suffer losses for wider national gains, should they be consulted by incoming firms? This raises fundamental issues of autonomy and justice: how much notice should firms take of villagers' desires to preserve traditional lifestyles if national governments are eager for development? On what basis should compensation be paid for environmental and other losses?[54]*

In June 1996, BHP agreed to a $400 million out-of-court settlement for the land-holders, that included $110 million in compensation, $40 million to relocate ten villages, and $7.6 million in legal expenses. BHP also agreed to sell 10 per cent of OTML to the PNG government for the benefit of local communities. BHP did not undertake to build a tailings dam, but did promise to look at all feasible options for tailings containment.

If BHP had offered such a package before they commenced mining, would the ethical issues identified by Barker have been avoided?

Consider the second and third of Barker's questions.

Say the PNG Government and BHP were at arm's length during all negotiations about the mine. And suppose that BHP had consulted local villagers and obtained their consent to mining on terms identical to those that apply now. Would the Ok Tedi operation then be ethically trouble-free? If you believe not, then consider this: what amount of compensation would remove ethical obstacles to the mine?

BHP and the PNG government were not at arm's length. They were partners, and one of the partners (the government) was, among other things, responsible for regulation of the other.

Is there an issue here of conflict of interest? Are there other ethical concerns that arise in virtue of the partnership?

A government has responsibilities to its people as a whole, but also to each of its people individually. It has responsibilities to sustain the economy and attract productive invest-ment, but it also must protect its environmental heritage. As a partner in OTML, the PNG government was in a position that made it difficult to discharge its responsibilities. Consider the ethics of the situation in PNG.

These questions pursue only two of the questions asked by Barker. Let us move to his question about standards of environmental protection. Is the more important issue here whether the standards of BHP in PNG differ from those in Australia, or is it the impact of mining on the Ok Tedi ecosystem? Both issues are important, of course, but the question of standards would not arise unless there was a major impact of mining there.

How is it possible to legislate regarding practices from one setting to another?

Would not any acceptable code require interpretation that might permit another Ok Tedi?

In the years following the settlement with traditional landholders, things seem to have gone more smoothly for BHP. A tailings dam has been considered by OTML in the years following settlement, but a pipeline carrying waste or dredging, or a combination of the two, seemed more promising. In May 1997, BHP and its partners signed an agreement with landholders on the east bank of the lower Ok Tedi River. This area will be used to store tailings during a two-year trial of river dredging. Part of the annual payments to the owners will be held in trust until the Ok Tedi mine closes next century. Dredging is the speediest option to implement, but the trial will tell whether it is an effective measure in dealing with the tailings problem.[55]

As Shell learnt from Brent Spar, so BHP learnt from Ok Tedi. It now subscribes to triple bottom line reporting and BHP Billiton has taken a positive attitude to sustainable devel-opment.[56] This does not mean that the corporation does not raise environmental ques-tions, such as the fate of its blast furnace waste. But it is unfair on the one hand to demand change from corporations, and on the other to claim that their efforts to be environmen-tally responsible amount to 'greenwashing'.

All of this suggests that the place to begin discussions of environmental ethics is not with Friedman's objections, but with the reasonable expectations of business in a sustain-able future. While environmental ethics needs the support of enforceable regulations, these will not be effective without the willing collaboration of business.

Review questions

1   We asked, 'Is it not just an appeal to the strength of our preferences that makes us claim intrinsic value for the environment?' What else could it be?

2   Could there be a systematic statement of, and then enforcement of, the precautionary principle?

3   Could there be such a statement that would do justice to all stakeholders in a proposal?

4   What are the practical limits of the precautionary principle?

Whistleblowing

9

Remember Frankena's four basic requirements of ethics: avoid evil, prevent evil, remove evil, do good. Concern for others seems to extend our minimum ethical obligations beyond not participating in evil to preventing harm. Bowie and Duska argue that the level of this responsibility is commensurate with: (a) the extent of the need, (b) one's proximity to the person(s) in need, and (c) the availability of others likely to render assistance.[1] These grounds for acting are relevant to the evaluation and justification of whistleblowing. Consider the following cases from this point of view.

Case 9.1 Dan Applegate & Convair

In 1972 Dan Applegate, a senior engineer with Convair, wrote to his vice-president detailing design faults in the fuselage of the DC-10. Convair were subcontractors on the project for McDonnell-Douglas, and Applegate was director of the project. Applegate's concerns focused on the design of the cargo doors, which he believed could open during flight. This would depressurise the cargo bay, causing the floor of the passenger cabin above to buckle. As the floor housed the plane's control lines, the risk of a crash was very high unless design modifications were made to doors and floor.

Convair's response was a financial rather than a technical one. Management argued that informing McDonnell-Douglas of the problems would place Convair at a competitive disadvantage because the costs of delays and rectifications would be very high. In 1974 a fully loaded DC-10 crashed on the outskirts of Paris; 346 people lost their lives.[2]

Case 9.2   Murder unseen?

Some years ago a woman was murdered in full view of thirty-eight people in New York. Although she called for help as she was being stabbed, and although the attack lasted some time, the innocent bystanders declined to help her, to call the police, or to get involved in any way. At the subsequent investigation their conduct was condemned as morally inexcusable.[3]

Whistleblowing is reporting on misconduct or potential harm or failure from within an organisation or after separation from it. Investigative reporting is not whistleblowing, nor is the work of private investigators. Dissent is not in itself whistleblowing, but public dissent in order to prevent harm or injustice may be. Whistleblowers are insiders in the organisations where the reported misconduct occurs, and therefore in some sense party to the responsibility of the organisation for causing harm. Usually it is moral revulsion that leads them to speak out. Typically this is at some cost to themselves. In this they are somewhat like civilly disobedient protesters: although they do not challenge the law, they do challenge established practices. And, like civil disobedient protesters, whistleblowers are usually prepared to take the consequences of their acts.

Common mythology notwithstanding, an ethical stand does not confer 'good guy' protection from the adverse consequences of whistleblowing. In Australia at present there are no explicit protections for whistleblowers in the private sector. Going to the media might invite an injunction against publication (as happened in the Westpac letters case) or even a defamation suit. The wise course is to see a lawyer before a reporter.

Whistleblowers commonly suffer for their actions. Most lose their jobs or are demoted. Many are subjected to psychological testing by their companies. Some are prosecuted. Many of them face lives marred by marriage failure, alcohol abuse and bankruptcy.[4] Such costs should not be necessary for the conscientious and honest employee. John McMillan has put the principle succinctly:

> *Telling the truth should be neither difficult nor costly. Employment in an organisation should not require that a person accept complicity in all activities which the employer has decided to pursue or to conceal. To accept that employees can be persecuted for honesty, loyalty, or upholding the public trust undermines some of the legal and moral principles on which a society is necessarily based.*[5]

While McMillan is undoubtedly correct from a moral point of view, in practice we live in an imperfect world, and organisations develop lives of their own which defy the rational expectations of justice. Whistleblowing tells an organisation that something is gravely wrong with it, and the organisation reacts to this threat.

Internal and external

Whistleblowing usually begins internally — that is, information on the conduct is reported to superiors in the organisation — as happened, for example, in the cases of the DC-10 and the space shuttle Challenger, which was launched despite clear indications of a significantly high probability of a disaster.[6] If reporting to one's superiors through the established channels of authority fails, one might pursue the matter internally, but outside the normal channels of authority. Here, one would report to someone else (usually higher up) within the organisation. If neither sort of internal reporting succeeds in preventing potential harms from becoming actual ones, then the next stage is often the riskier option of seeking external intervention to overcome the problem. This might mean informing a senior public authority or seeking to elicit public interest through the media. Such actions are examples of whistleblowing.

Although some writers distinguish between internal and external whistleblowing, we believe that only the latter is genuine whistleblowing. Take as an example *Time* magazine's nomination of its 'Persons of the Year' for 2002, Cynthia Cooper, Coleen Rowley and Sherron Watkins.[7] There is no doubt that these are unusually courageous and principled women, but should their actions properly be called whistleblowing? If a matter can be dealt with by an organisation's internal procedures, then reporting it internally hardly fits the category.

Case 9.3   Is this 'whistleblowing'?

Cynthia Cooper, vice-president of internal audit at WorldCom, discovered inaccurate accounting and pursued it. Hunting down a $400 million anomaly, she found that WorldCom's auditors, Arthur Andersen, seemed not to have noticed. So Cooper brought it to their attention — without success. Then she informed the CFO, Scott Sullivan, who told her to mind her own business. Cooper used her internal audit team to review Andersen's audit and discovered the extent of misreporting — a $662 million loss had been accounted as a $2.4 billion profit by calling operating expenses capital expenditures. Cooper informed Sullivan, the audit committee of WorldCom's board, and the corporation's comptroller, David Myers, of her findings. The audit committee fired Sullivan and told Myers to resign. Unusually, Cooper kept her job. At no stage did Cooper resort to publicity. Her pivotal part in the exposure of sharp practice was made known to the press by a Congressman who released her audit memos to the press. She and Coleen Rowley reject the term 'whistleblower'.[8]

   Coleen Rowley's 'whistleblowing' was to testify at Congressional hearings into FBI shortcomings after the September 11 tragedy. Rowley believed that the agency had information — if not the systems — that would have enabled it to track the terrorists who committed the atrocity, but she sent her concerns in memo to FBI chief, Robert

Mueller, and members of the Senate Intelligence Committee. She did not solicit media attention and came to the notice of the press only after her memo was leaked.

Sherron Watkins' whistleblowing was to write in response to an invitation to employees from Enron chairman, Kenneth Lay, to voice any concerns they had about the company. Watkins' reply was an anonymous memo expressing concern that Enron might collapse because of the accounting scandals she had lately uncovered. She had been unable to make sense of accounts that basically hid debt in off-the-books partnerships. When her memo had no effect, Watkins arranged a time to see Lay in person, and she laid out before him the crooked deals that had brought Enron to the brink. Lay told her he would get the firm's lawyers to look into her allegations, but shortly after Enron filed for bankruptcy. Watkins did not go to the media and only became known to the public after the bankruptcy action.

In each of these cases, the term 'whistleblower' is appropriate in the context of the gravity of the issue and the courage needed to bring it to the attention of appropriate authorities. Nevertheless, it is better to reserve the term for last-resort measures to rectify grave injustices. Internal reporting should be part of the normal feedback channels of an organisation, and if they work there is no need to go outside. Even if these normal feedback channels do not work, internal whistleblowing — for example, going straight to the CEO — does not violate the authority of the organisation *per se*, nor does testifying before a parliamentary or congressional hearing.

Whistleblowers are not ranged against pettifogging superiors or incompetent colleagues, but against corporate closure — the mutual protection that can seize members of an organisation and cause it to intimidate, scapegoat, or expel dissidents who disturb its unspoken rules of survival. Whistleblowers have in a sense already moved outside an organisation when they take it on, so only external whistleblowing will be treated as the definition of the term in our discussion.

'Whistleblowing' appears to be a term denoting accomplishment. That is, it is not the mere communication of information to a superior, but the achievement of some exposure through doing so. Whistleblowers often have to persist in the face of substantial obstacles in order to achieve an effect. Although persistence is not necessarily part of whistleblowing, it is one of the difficulties that whistleblowers often have to overcome in order to act effectively. One can think of cases in which important information has been communicated without result. Whistleblowing is not mere communication of the nature of the wrong; it is the pursuit of changes that avert a public harm in the face of indifference or opposition. Imagine that the mysterious 'Deep Throat' in the Watergate affair had told Woodward and Bernstein about Nixon's 'plumbers' resorting to dirty tricks to have the President re-elected, and that these journalists had thought the story too far-fetched to print. That would not have been whistleblowing. It was the persuasiveness of the information that marked 'Deep Throat' as a source, and the publication of a story that made him or her a whistleblower. The view that whistleblowing is an accomplishment restricts the concept in a useful way, but also seems to suggest that the focus of the discussion should be on the heroes who perform this public service. Most studies of whistleblowing have this focus, not unreasonably considering the human drama involved and the fact that case studies of whistleblowing are also the case histories of brave individuals. As Quentin Dempster remarks, 'Without the courage of the whistleblowers we would not be informed about what really goes on in our sometimes very uncivilised world'[9]. The danger with this focus, however, is that it can mistake the conscientious dissenter for the whistleblower, and genuine organisational disciplining of the dissenter for intimidation and retribution.[10] The key question is whether there are adequate systems of reporting, accountability and control within the organisation, rather than whether individual rights to dissent are recognised. As we note below, not all wrongs call for a principled disclosure. A person who took an officious interest in smoking in the toilets or in colleagues who conducted an extra-marital affair out of working hours might be a principled nuisance rather than a whistleblower. We regard this point as important: it is one of the reasons we advocate a restricted definition of whistleblowing.

What counts as genuine and morally justifiable cases of whistleblowing? First, the matter has to be serious and the informant should have good evidence of the alleged misconduct. Sissela Bok suggests that the threat from the misconduct should be imminent and specific: grapeshot disclosures with no immediate effect might make good gossip, but they are not whistleblowing.[11] Second, the information has to be of public benefit, and the public must have a right to know (the public might benefit from many things which it does not have a right to know, such as the secret recipe of Coca-Cola). The information should not be mischievous or malicious. This would exclude from public disclosure personal details of a political, religious or sexual kind. Third, less damaging ways of rectifying the problem, such as internal procedures, must not be available to the whistleblower. Fourth, if other avenues for rectifying the problem were available they should have been tried. Fifth, blowing the whistle is likely to remedy the problem.

There are two considerations running through these criteria. The first is that the public interest is threatened by some policy or procedure of the organisation, and the second is that employees of the organisation have tried to rectify matters through normal lines of responsibility and management. Where the first is present and the second fails, whistleblowing is a legitimate option.

Richard De George goes further and says that if these conditions are met and the whistleblower has documented evidence that would convince an impartial person of an organisation's potential to harm the public interest, and if the probability is good that going public will bring about change for the better, then the employee not only has a right to blow the whistle, but an obligation to do so.[12] Others have argued that, at most, an employee can have a right to blow the whistle, but because of the real possibility of resultant hardship to oneself, one never (or only in exceptional circumstances) has a duty to blow the whistle.[13] Whether one looks to the right or the duty, it is important to stress that the means used should be proportional to the end to be achieved or, more simply, do not use a sledge-hammer to crack a walnut.

Whistleblowing is, on the whole, a grey area. It is important to be aware of the conditions of its justification, but it is equally important not to be beguiled into believing that the term names a clear, identifiable type of conduct which can be used as a template for resolving moral conflicts in the workplace. Whistleblowing is simply a shorthand way of referring to classes of information disclosure.

Ross Webber echoes some cautions about whistleblowing first made by Alan Westin:

1 Verify your evidence. Is it sufficient?
2 Are you objecting to illegal or immoral conduct? If the conduct is morally objection-able but legal, you might not have a future in your industry. Illegal conduct is not as likely to damage your career.
3 Discuss your proposed action with close stakeholders, namely, your family. They will be affected by what you do.
4 Exhaust organisational procedures for dealing with complaints and objections.
5 Consider whether it is better to act publicly or anonymously.
6 Document every action you take.
7 Don't spread your heat: keep the objection confined to those who need to deal with it, and be civil to those handling it.
8 If you are fired you may resort to publicity, but recognise that your right of free public discussion might be limited.
9 Consider a lawsuit.
10 Appreciate that your hands will get dirty whatever you do about unethical conduct.[14]

This last point is worth emphasising. Whistleblowing exemplifies the problem of dirty hands. It does seem to involve betrayal of friends, stress on one's family, hurt to the good as well as to the bad. Apart from the personal risks involved, it amounts to placing an individual judgment above that of the organisation, and forsaking the duty (sometimes a fiduciary duty) that an employee owes to the organisation. Consider the following objections to whistleblowing. First, it is informing, perhaps on peers or mates. Informing was character-istic of the worst excesses of Nazi Germany and the Soviet system. It is sneaky, underhanded and destroys trust in the workplace. Second, it involves disclosure of information that is owned by the organisation, not by individuals. It is theft to disclose that information without authorisation. This might lead competitors to gain an advantage and destroy an organisation as effectively as leaking damaging information. Hence, the third objection: taking on the responsibility of looking after the public interest is arrogant and might destroy the organisa-tion and the jobs of colleagues. How can this kind of conduct be distinguished from leaking? Fourth, a person does not necessarily have the full picture in going public with potentially damaging information and hence might not be in a good position to judge if the public interest will be served by disclosure. In this respect (like the arrogance to which the third objection calls attention), whistleblowers place their own judgment above that of the organ-isation. Fifth, the act breaks an employee's contract with the employer. Sixth, an employee has a duty only to report concerns to superiors, not to rectify the problem personally.

These objections will vary in strength depending on the particular circumstances a potential whistleblower is facing. A whistleblower might be a hero, someone who is not a sneak but puts his or her neck on the line for honesty, probity and the public interest. If other avenues existed for bringing harms to public notice or correcting the harms in some in-house way, who but an idiot or a misdirected hero would risk discovery, loss of job and career opportunity, and perhaps professional censure?

It is also conceivable that a whistleblower might be a sneak, or someone with an ille-gitimate interest, a grudge or a cockeyed perspective on an organisation's activities. We disagree with Bowie and Duska[15] that whistleblowers necessarily act from an 'appropriate moral motive'. A whistleblower might act in the public interest because he or she seeks revenge after being sacked. It is still whistleblowing. Awareness of a whistleblower's ignoble motives might affect his or her credibility (as a practical matter), but it does not mean that they have not blown the whistle.

As for loyalty, moral obligations to colleagues or to an organisation cannot bind someone to immoral conduct — at least not to seriously immoral conduct. Given the damage usually done to them, the question is not whether whistleblowers are morally justified, but whether the silence of others can be excused. This may seem unrealistic or heartless, but perhaps it is better to talk of loyalty in emotional rather than moral terms in relation to major issues. When the DC-10 went ahead, there were people in a position to know but who did nothing. The same is true of other disasters, such as the Challenger: people who knew of the unacceptably high risks did nothing.

What could excuse such inaction? Usually it is a dislike of reporting colleagues or a fear of retribution. The reporting excuse really does not hold water any more. In a random survey of 2000 public sector employees in New South Wales, 94 per cent believed that dismissal of a staff member who blows the whistle on fraud is corrupt.[16] This may, however, be too simple. Research suggests that organisations with cultures which encourage consultation and participation in decision-making view loyalty in terms of people voicing their views. Conversely, silence is likely to be taken as disloyalty. On the other hand, organisations with strong hierarchical cultures are likely to perceive loyalty in terms of silent compliance, and disloyalty in terms of overt criticism.[17] Such organisations are more likely to encourage internal critics to leave than to voice their criticisms. They are also more likely to create the conditions which give rise to whistleblowing.

In all of this there is an important distinction to be made between petty informing and bringing matters of public interest to the public's attention. A criterion of proportionality should help in deciding on borderline cases, but we hold that there is no duty to inform on others where the matter is not serious or the damage caused by informing is not justified by the benefits to be secured. This qualification should not be seen as minimising the issue of rights; we are not arguing that one person's rights may be sacrificed for the good of an organisation and its stakeholders, but that the good to be achieved by whistleblowing should be in proportion to the gravity of the act.

Retribution is a large issue and is likely to remain so, even where whistleblower protection is present. Until recently there were no such protections for whistleblowers in the public or private sectors anywhere in Australia, and whistleblowers have had to take heroic measures to bring matters of urgency to public attention. Ideally there should be procedures and mechanisms for dealing with genuine concerns inside an organisation, so as to minimise the need for heroism with its attendant risks and disincentives. Criticism should be taken seriously, and the reporting of transgressions could be made mandatory, thus removing the discretion from the individual and avoiding the opprobrium that can sour relations between a whistleblower and even colleagues of goodwill.[18] Such measures would need to be internally enforceable, but could be complemented with external safeguards in law.[19] Yet even with better organisational procedures and protective legislation in place, there will still be some instances where whistleblowing is appropriate as the only means of rectifying a serious problem or danger. It will remain an extremely courageous act.

The Institution of Engineers Australia trading as Engineers Australia (IEAust) has recognised that there are situations where there can be a conflict of responsibility for the professional, and where the professional's chief responsibility is not to the organisation but to the public. The first tenet of the IEAust Code of Ethics says: 'The responsibility of engineers for the welfare, health and safety of the community shall at all times come before their responsibility to the profession, to sectional or private interests, or to other engineers'. This tenet amounts to a declaration of commitment on behalf of the professional organisation; and it amounts to a requirement that professionals take responsibility for acting in the public interest, specifically when that comes into conflict with other responsibilities that they have by virtue of being professionals and employees. This would seem to be a commitment to blowing the whistle when that would best serve the public interest. This tenet of the code appears to do significantly more than affirm and inspire institutional ethics among engineers. It is a deterring and disciplining statement: the IEAust can suspend or expel members for breaches. In practice, however, the IEAust has been more likely to censure those who take a public interest voice than those who remain silent.[20]

A great deal of work has been done to take the heroism out of whistleblowing, indeed, to make the act unnecessary by instituting procedures to deal with ethical difficulties and to make it unnecessary to go outside the normal chain of authority. Nevertheless, the fact remains that there will always be some circumstances which procedures will not remedy. And personal courage will always be necessary for ethical decisions. Procedures cannot be a substitute for integrity.

The Australian situation

There are many cases of whistleblowing in Australia,[21] and whistleblower protection legislation has been actively discussed at state and national levels. Whistleblower protection legislation now exists in Queensland, New South Wales, the ACT and South Australia for employees in the public sector. Applying the law to the problem of whistleblowing in the private sector is more difficult, and other kinds of legal remedies, such as claims of unfair dismissal, might have to satisfy this need.

The following case of Alwyn Johnson and the banks illustrates this issue.

Case 9.4   Alwyn Johnson & the banks

There were no laws to protect Alwyn Johnson, an anonymous whistleblower. In July 1990 he was called into the office of Paul Kemp, CEO of Trust Bank in Tasmania, told his services were no longer required, and escorted from the building by a security guard. Johnson had broken the eleventh commandment: he had been found out. But Johnson was no criminal. Quite the opposite; he was a whistleblower whose prompt action had probably saved a bank, and with it millions of the taxpayers' dollars.

Johnson had a strong background in traditional banking. He had been underwriting manager in the treasury department of the National Australia Bank (NAB) in Melbourne before moving to the state-owned Tasmania Bank as a chief manager. At the NAB, Johnson had been marked for rapid promotion, as attested in a letter to him by John Astbury, treasury general manager: 'Your high levels of performance and demonstrated application have again confirmed your forward potential ... we are pleased your efforts warrant our ongoing commitment towards your career progression'.

Shortly after arriving in Tasmania, Johnson became concerned about his bank's exposure to non-performing loans to property developers in its wholesale banking division. His warnings to superiors were ignored, so in June 1990 he wrote anonymously to the premier, Michael Field, warning that 'The bank is in serious financial trouble and immediate, decisive action is required to rescue it from the present disastrous course'. Johnson wrote again in August predicting a run on the bank unless Field intervened. The premier had already brought in the auditors. At a board meeting in November 1990 the auditor's findings were tabled, the bank's managing director resigned, and the board passed a vote of thanks to the writer of the anonymous letter. Premier Field revealed a $150 million exposure due to 'serious management weaknesses'. Preventive action had been taken just in time.

In March 1990 Tasmania Bank merged with the SBT Bank to create the Trust Bank. Johnson wrote to the new CEO of Trust Bank, Paul Kemp, asking for an executive position and revealing that he was the author of the anonymous letter to Field. Johnson claims that from that day he was cold-shouldered by the bank.

The Trust Bank was unique in Australia in having no shareholders. And it was no longer owned by the Tasmanian government. When Johnson became concerned about the loans operations of the merged bank he felt he had nowhere to go except the Reserve Bank. On 1 July he wrote to the governor of the Reserve Bank, Bernie Fraser, stating his concerns and offering to elaborate on them personally by flying to Sydney. He also asked that the confidentiality of the communication be respected: 'Kindly do not contact management of SBT/Tasmania Bank until you are fully acquainted with the facts, by meeting with me personally'.[22] Fraser rang Kemp at the Trust Bank the next day. This has been revealed in a Freedom of Information search, but it is not known if Fraser mentioned Johnson's name to Kemp. Neither Kemp nor Fraser will comment on the conversation, and Freedom of Information access has been denied to the notes made of it. On 3 July Johnson was sacked. Although Johnson was told that there was no place for him in the restructured organisation, he was sent a letter on the day of his dismissal which gave a different impression of Kemp's reasons for firing him:

> The Bank has been advised that you have made contact with various individuals and bodies in order to provide what can only be described as scurrilous misinformation regarding the Bank's affairs. At least some of the recipients of this most improper communication have expressed their concern not only as to the content, which was properly recognised for what it was, but also regarding the fact that a senior employee would see fit to embark upon an exercise which reflected so poorly upon himself.[23]

After Johnson had declared himself to be a whistleblower it would have been no great feat of inference to conclude that he was the person who had approached the Reserve Bank, even if Fraser did not disclose his name. Still, there is an unresolved problem here. When public authorities hold inquiries into institutional failures they often comment on the bravery of those who speak out and lament that others do nothing or cover for their mates. For example, Commissioner Samuel Jacobs of the Royal Commission into the failed State Bank of South Australia asked why no bank officers alerted the government or public to the bank's problems. Ironically, the Reserve Bank has been unable to help Johnson. In January 1993, he wrote to Fraser about possible Reserve Bank action 'to protect people like myself who act in the public interest, from being summarily dismissed from the bank they seek to protect'. Johnson made the point that:

> No bank officer will ever follow my lead and act in the public interest and advise the Reserve Bank of Australia of problems within a bank if the Governor of the Reserve Bank of Australia is going to immediately ring the bank concerned and divulge the identity of that bank officer. If bank officers have nowhere to turn in confidence when they identify problems within their bank, then taxpayers will be destined to continue to pay out billions of dollars as banks fail or are badly managed in the future.[24]

This is a fair point, although it must be stressed that there is no evidence that Fraser informed Kemp that Johnson had written to him. If high standards of public responsibility are to be demanded of people in private positions there should be public protections for them. But in this case there is the added complication that Fraser, as well, had a clear public responsibility. Whatever he said to Kemp on the day after he received Johnson's fax, Fraser had a clear fiduciary and moral responsibility to ensure that the Trust Bank was not in danger. It might have been difficult to do that without indirectly disclosing that Johnson was the source of the Reserve Bank's alert. Moreover, Johnson's request for confidentiality and a delay in response until a personal interview could be arranged could not bind Fraser in any way. As governor of the Reserve Bank, he is akin to a banking police officer, and while attempting to ascertain the facts, he cannot allow the public interest to be jeopardised.[25]

Johnson's case illustrates that protections for whistleblowers are inherently difficult to devise, so that changes in public policy will never remove the need for personal courage, sometimes of a high order, in bringing to light institutional failures which prejudice the public interest. The report of the Martin Committee into banking did not believe that whistleblower legislation was 'necessary at this stage', but did recommend that 'banks establish internal processes that allow staff to report instances of suspected fraud to senior management without fear of retribution'.[26]

After the abrupt end of Johnson's career, Field was unsupportive, Kemp claimed that he 'had been over promoted within the Tasmania Bank', and Fraser denied involvement in his dismissal. Kemp's claim is at variance with Johnson's previous record, but it fits the classic pattern for whistleblowers both in Australia and the United States. Kemp claimed that Johnson had been administered a series of personality tests by consultants Chandler and Macleod, which found him 'unsuited' to a position in the new bank. In the light of Kemp's letter to Johnson, doubt is certainly cast on any claim that this personality test played much of a part in Johnson's dismissal or the appraisal of his performance (it would be odd to check a manager's performance against a battery of tests), but subjection to psychological testing is a standard way of dealing with 'troublemakers', as whistleblowers are traditionally called in Australia.[27]

Johnson's case fits the typical profile of whistleblowers in most respects. In general, publicity can offer some protection because it increases the whistleblower's visibility. It also lends credibility to the whistleblower's claims and puts a face to them. In Johnson's case, his mistake was to reveal his action in the belief that it would make him more acceptable to the bank he saved. But this also made him 'unsafe' in any future incidents of whistleblowing, such as his in-confidence fax to the Reserve Bank.

What should Johnson have done? Should he have disclosed his identity at the time of writing to the premier?

Would you base your view about his conduct on a consideration of Johnson's responsibilities as an executive of the bank or on the fate that befell him?

'Aberrant behaviour' has long been used to explain away whistleblowing in Australia. In one of the most famous cases of whistleblowing in recent decades, Sergeant Phillip Arantz revealed that the Police Department had deliberately published false crime clear-up statistics in New South Wales. With the approval of the police commissioner, Norman Allen, and Premier Robert Askin, Arantz was promptly transported to the psychiatric unit of a major hospital where he was held for some days.

The psychiatric solution to public interest issues is still common. According to Queensland researcher Tony Keys:

> … psychiatry is part of the general strategy organisations adopt in response to whistleblowing because it takes the spotlight off the problem and puts it on the whistleblower. It is a way to avoid dealing with the problem and at the same time make the whistleblower into the problem.[28]

Of course, if a psychologist or psychiatrist assesses the whistleblower as 'personality disordered', then it is possible not only to discredit the complaint and the person making it, but also to shake the person's self-confidence and perhaps control damage. In the former Soviet Union, the detention of dissidents in psychiatric hospitals was most successful when the 'patients' recanted altogether. Consider the case of Jack King.[29]

Case 9.5 Jack King's environmental protection reports

Jack King is a chemical engineer whose efforts to do his job properly made him a whistleblower. King had for many years worked in petrochemicals before joining the South Australian Department of Environment and Planning. His problems began when he submitted environmental protection reports for legislation to protect coastal waters.

His submission to Cabinet was returned with instructions to delete references to pollu-tion from the Port Pirie lead smelter. The CSIRO had found heavy-metal contamination of Spencer Gulf from the smelter and widespread effects on the organisms that lived there. King tried again to get his proposals to Cabinet but was refused. He was told the levels of pollution did not warrant protecting legislation. After fruitless protests to his minister and the public employment commissioner, and the lodgement of grievance appeals, a frus-trated King went to the media. His exposés achieved the desired change in policy.

Unfortunately King's job became redundant in a reorganisation of his department. He was reinstated in the Department of State Development after persistent appeals. His difficulties, however, were not behind him. After resisting approval of a modern piggery, King was pressured to see a management consultant who turned out to be a psychologist. The consultant wanted to administer the Minnesota Multiphasic Person-ality Inventory to King, but he refused. The psychologist wrote a report anyway. It said that 'It is likely that he [King] has a severe personality problem … His personality traits are such as to produce grandiose and obsessive behaviour, paranoid reactions and regular grievance procedures [sic] for insufficient cause'.

King lost his job in mid-1989, but he did not accept the psychologist's report and sought psychiatric evaluation by a doctor of his choice. Dr Keith Le Page found King was not a victim of personality problems but simply a dedicated scientist trying to do his job honestly. After reading the psychologist's report he said, 'I have not found any evidence … that he is grandiose, obsessive, paranoid'.

Without doubt the stress caused to whistleblowers can damage their health. Furthermore, the sheer struggle to have the truth recognised and accepted in the face of official denials can make them obsessive or appear to be so. Nevertheless, it is disturbing that the first reaction of those accused or who stand to lose is to call in psychiatrists and psychologists in an attempt to discredit the accuser. The matter raises ethical questions for these professions, as well as for those who turn to them in cases like these.

The case of Vince Neary and the State Rail Authority also illustrates this issue.

Case 9.6   Vince Neary & the State Rail Authority

In 1986 Vince Neary, a signals engineer with the State Rail Authority of New South Wales (SRA), reported concerns about the safety of signalling. Repeated complaints to his superiors were ignored so, in 1989, Neary went to the head of the SRA, Ross Sayers, with his concerns, not only about safety but also about alleged schemes involving spurious consultants in the organisation. Sayers set up an investigative task-force. After repeated efforts to obtain the results of this inquiry, Neary was told that it had found no evidence of impropriety. There was no mention of signals safety.[30] After failing to obtain satisfaction from his local member (who was also premier) and the minister for transport, Neary took his complaints to the ombudsman.

Neary claimed that since making his original complaints he had first been ignored, then harassed and victimised, and finally denied work in his career choice of signals. He was sent to three psychiatrists on four occasions for assessment. One day he was presented with a directive from his superior to attend a medical examination without being told the reason it was required. Neary claimed that half an hour's notice was unreasonable for such a consultation: having attended four psychiatric consultations before, he wished to take the advice of his lawyer and union before consenting to another. Neary's superior immediately ushered him from his place of work. A few weeks later Neary consented to the examination that, not surprisingly, turned out to be a psychiatric one.[31]

Many of Neary's complaints were taken seriously by the ombudsman's report, which recommended a public inquiry to address the issues he had raised. Of Neary himself, the ombudsman stated:

> the way in which the investigation by this Office was regarded by officers of the SRA, was influenced by the view that Mr Neary was a 'troublemaker' … There is much in the material available to this Office relating to the Authority's treatment of Mr Neary to lead to the conclusion that Mr Neary's complaints are regarded by the Authority as an unwelcome intrusion and a hindrance to its business.

The ombudsman lamented that the whistleblower protection legislation being contemplated for New South Wales would not allow him to investigate complaints of victimisation against whistleblowers such as alleged by Neary, but only threats to those who complain of maladministration.[32] Vince Neary was sacked from the SRA in May 1993.

Although we have argued that external protections will never make whistleblowing safe, we believe that they should go some way towards changing a culture that has countenanced the use of labelling by psychologists and psychiatrists. Whistleblowers may always be necessary, and they should cease to be seen as deviant.

Because of the courage typically involved in whistleblowing and the damage that it usually does to career, family and social life, whistleblowers are rightly viewed as noble and self-sacrificing. They are defenders of the public interest. We do not usually see them as public nuisances. But there is another side to all this. Because of its special status, there is the potential to abuse whistleblowing.

Consider the case of Orlando Helicopter Airways as related by its founder, Fred P. Clark.

Case 9.7 Orlando Helicopter Airways

In 1986 Orlando Helicopter Airways (OHA) won a contract with United States Army Missile Command to produce special helicopters — basically imitations of the Soviet Hind attack helicopter — for training purposes. It supplied fifteen aircraft over a three-year period for around US$7 million. Large defence contractors had quoted $20 million and a much longer completion time. The army commended the OHA aircraft and support service as 'outstanding'. In November 1989, however, an office employee of six months' standing at OHA wrote a memo to the Defense Criminal Investigation Service (DCIS) alleging engineering safety breaches in the construction of the helicopters. This person was not a pilot, an aeronautical engineer, or even a mechanic. He did, however, owe $500,000 in back taxes, and in the United States whistleblowers are promised up to 30 per cent of the money the government recovers from successful prosecutions resulting from their evidence. The army's own investigation found no fraud or other wrongdoing at OHA. An ambitious investigator at the DCIS, however, was determined to make a case against OHA, and encouraged past and present employees to remove company documents. Although nine separate investigations had found no evidence of any corruption at Orlando, this investigator pursued his quarry by digging into OHA's certification compliance procedures back to the 1960s. Some people in the DCIS were determined to prosecute OHA.

During the two years of investigations, the company was the victim of slander and innuendo, its reputation suffered, business fell off as contracts went elsewhere, and it eventually closed its doors, throwing forty employees out of work. No findings were made against OHA.[33] It was the victim of zealotry and officiousness and perhaps defence industry politics.

So, while whistleblowing is usually depicted as the heroic stand of a principled individual against some system, this is not the only aspect that should be considered. The fate of organisations and those who depend on them, and the dangers of encouraging malicious reporting should be kept in mind when protection and support for whistleblowing are being determined.

Some writers are concerned about danger from a different quarter: namely ethical support itself.[34] The argument is that ethical support for whistleblowing will actually harm whistleblowers. It holds that once an organisation adopts ethics strategies, it will claim that evil has been eliminated from the workplace. If this occurs, then the whistleblower will, by definition, be excluded. By thus excluding the dissenter, the supposedly ethical organisation is able to use ethics strategically to protect itself. This is an argument reminiscent of Marxist analyses of reform in capitalist economies: the union movement, welfare, state sponsorship of sport and the arts all contribute to keeping 'the revolution' at bay. Popular discontent is abated by such measures, so any view that governments under capitalism can act in the interests of justice is naive: governments act to protect their capitalist masters. On the other hand, if governments do not redistribute wealth or support social activities, then this is proof that capitalism controls the state in the interests of the ruling class. In brief, the Marxist can never be satisfied: governments in market economies are damned if they support social institutions and damned if they do not. The negative analysis of whistleblower support described above comes off the same template as the Marxist analysis of the state. An organisation that acts to minimise the necessity for the practice is enhancing social control in the workplace; an organisation that does not address the problem colludes in exposing the whistleblower to all the penalties of acting according to conscience.

People have to be cautious about informing on illegal, harmful or unethical conduct, not only because they will have to bear the consequences, but also because others will have to live with them too; and there is in any case no easy way of dealing with dissent in the public interest. The best of protective procedures and policies will be limited and can probably be used for corrupt purposes. This is not an argument for doing nothing, but a caution against believing that laws and procedures can accomplish everything we should desire for whistleblower protection.

Review questions

1   Do you think that there is good reason for limiting the term 'whistleblowing' to cases of 'external whistleblowing'?

2   Do you think it is ever the case that a person 'ought' to blow the whistle – that if they fail to blow the whistle, then they will have done something wrong? Or, do you believe that any case of justifiable whistleblowing will be a case of heroic action – that is, action above and beyond what is morally required?

Codes of Ethics and Institutional Ethics

10

An employee shall not conduct himself or herself in a manner which directly or indirectly would be detrimental to the best interests of the Company or in a manner which would bring to the employee financial gain separately derived as a direct consequence of his or her employment with the Company. Moral as well as legal obligations will be fulfilled openly, promptly, and in a manner which will reflect pride on the Company's name. (Enron Code of Ethics, p. 13)

Enron's Code was 65 pages long and had high-sounding phrases about values, human rights and compliance. However, when it conflicted with the goals of corporate executives, it was put in the bin. That is the handy thing about codes. Even the long ones can be dumped quickly in time of need.

Yet codes in one form or another have been used to regulate behaviour since antiquity. The Code of Hammurabi is one such and the Ten Commandments another. We are most familiar, of course, with legal codes and expect that codified principles will be clear-cut and not open to dispute and personal interpretation. Codes have various forms: there may be codes of ethics, conduct or practice, each species being framed to meet the specific needs of the organisation that produced it.[1] Their common purpose is self-regulation through peer enforcement.

Codes have long been used to establish standards in the professions. Medicine came first in the early nineteenth century when physicians wished to establish their respectable credentials by distinguishing themselves from quacks. Pharmacists soon followed, and gradually, over the next hundred years, other professions set boundaries around their tasks and professional identities and established regulatory mechanisms to go with them. Codes came to be accepted not only as important in the ethical sense, but as necessary to a professional status. In this sense they not only serve the public by regulating standards and behaviour, but restrict trade, keeping certain professional territory the exclusive preserve of those approved by the profession. In this way professional bodies serve as 'credential-frankers' for practitioners under the conditions set out in their codes. A certain degree of scepticism about the self-serving nature of professional codes is justified, but a profession without one would be impossible these days.

In business there is altogether more scepticism. For a start, some would not like to see business called a profession because that would seem to restrict entrepreneurship. Professional constraints would limit business opportunities and the participation of people whose qualifications were enthusiasm, ideas and a willingness to take risks rather than a business degree. The ability to develop markets, innovate and sell is not the preserve of professional elites and those with specifiable credentials, and attempts to introduce business codes modelled on the codes of professions would be inappropriate.

The most common form of scepticism, however, is that business codes, values statements and proclamations of this kind are simply so much hot air. One does not have to be unduly cynical to see that codes and statements making grandiose claims are unlikely to be realised in practice. If practice can conform to the code only with great difficulty, then the code is effectively impractical. Such self-defeating statements breed cynicism and reinforce the view that they are useless in all cases.

Another form of scepticism lies in the observation that codes can discourage excellence or even encourage unethical behaviour by stipulating what must or must not be done: where unethical conduct is not prohibited it may be assumed that it is permitted. Similarly, by setting out the minimum requirements of ethical performance, expectations might be pitched too low and thereby discourage higher achievement. As codes can never be comprehensive and are usually general, these objections have some force.

The reply to this scepticism is simple. Some codes and values statements are ineffective and unrealistic, while others are vital parts of more extensive programs to promote corporate ethics. Codes can be used to escape ethical requirements as well as to enforce them. Codes are not magical, but they are indispensable to the development of an ethical culture in a modern organisation.

Because corporations are not natural persons, formal rules are important in establishing their moral status. Although they have their own cultures, organisations do not possess emotions, a conscience, intellect or will. They are composed of individuals who have these things but, as Machiavelli showed so well in *The Prince*, private judgments can bring calamity on a society or organisation. We do not expect individuals to act in a private capacity in performing their employment duties. The closest analogue in a corporate organisation to the virtues embodied in the characters of persons is an ethos. This is where rules come in, and clear ethical rules are no less important than other formal regulations and informal habits of conduct. Ethical rules are ways of ensuring minimum standards, of offering guidance for conduct, and of stating in a shorthand way the main values of the culture of the organisation. They are no more dispensable for organisations than virtues are for individuals.

The motivation for a company or a business to institute a code of ethics need not come from a commitment to morality or from, say, an altruistic concern for the public at large. No doubt a number of business and professional organisations do have such a concern, but it is clear that the history of business is not about these things. Having an altruistic concern or being interested in moral behaviour for its own sake is not the only adequate motivation for a business or a profession finding a code of ethics desirable. Self-interest can (quite properly) furnish the stimulus for a code. Put simply, good business requires the presence of a code of ethics. Perhaps the strongest motivation for creating a code of ethics is that the present climate of accountability, fair-dealing, public awareness and govern-mental regulation is such that it is a situation of 'do it, or else'. In many cases it is precisely a situation of 'you set particular standards for yourself, or we'll do it for you', where the 'we' is some external, perhaps governmental body. Given those alternatives, any organisation would prefer to play a major or perhaps exclusive role in setting its own ethical standards and enforcing them. An organisation will be more sensitive to its own structure, aims, limits and operating costs and benefits than will an external standard-setter.

Avoiding the imposition of external regulation is only one prudential reason for busi-ness to take the initiative. If an organisation does not have a code of ethics, it can suffer from a number of undesirable effects in the market place. Public trust and confidence are clearly commodities which can have a dollar value attached to them. They are good for business. It is interesting to note that the presence of a code of ethics itself has been used by some businesses as a form of competitive advertising, a way of promoting that business above others. For example, the NRMA and Nissan have both dedicated entire advertise-ments to their codes of ethics, and a common sight on the windows of real estate agents is a transfer sticker which states: 'Deal only with a … Member of Real Estate Institute of NSW / Bound by a Code of Ethics'.

Consumers can simply turn their backs on products and services with a poor ethical reputation. The market can be as effective on ethical matters as a regulatory body, as the damage to Nestlé over third-world infant milk-formula sales in the 1970s showed. Its competitor, Abbott Laboratories, developed a code of marketing practice in response to public reaction to selling infant milk-formula into societies where its use might be inap-propriate, but Nestlé persisted with its marketing practices and lost public support.[2] As protection against increased external regulation, it is desirable for the organisation itself to institute its own code of ethics. Shareholders, as well as the public at large, now react adversely to perceived unethical conduct, and information about such conduct is readily available and highly visible in newspapers and popular magazines. In the USA Chrysler has made a different kind of move in this direction. It has established a 'car buyers' bill of rights' and a mechanism to enforce it. Chrysler now claims that it judges the success of dealerships by levels of customer service and satisfaction rather than volume of sales. It is, of course, possible (and likely) that this is itself an indirect gauge of volume. Nevertheless, it is the service and not the volume that is targeted. Chrysler is not unique in valuing honour as a badge to place on a business. Headhunter Egon Zehnder believes that demonstrated integrity is as basic to the appointment of an executive as demonstrated management skills. According to Zehnder: 'If we are to select the man for a key job, select above all, the man with high integrity. Such an integrity-based selection will permeate through management making a strong management team'.[3]

This is not to say that prudential, self-interested reasons for having a code should be allowed to prejudice its content or its implementation; many things in life are done for prudential reasons and are still done well. The same is true of compulsion: although attendance at school is compulsory and it is prudent to conform to this legal requirement, children nonetheless benefit, even if they would rather be elsewhere. The same is true with compulsory voting in Australian democracy. Business, like a reluctant pupil or voter, can read a bottom line: if trust and confidence and the profits attached to them are at stake, it pays to take ethics as seriously as other matters of competitive service. Nevertheless, attempts to extract greater public accountability from some Australian industries, such as banking, have not met with an altogether positive response.

Not all businesses and professions are unconcerned about morality except insofar as moral behaviour is good for business. If we can indicate that even for the extreme case the business itself should see the presence of a code of ethics as desirable, then there can be no question of its general desirability. Devising a code can be part of a review process. The drafting and adoption of a code is an opportunity for a firm to think through and articulate its values and objectives. The process can be as important as the result. It can reveal accepted practices which the organisation would not affirm publicly and which, on reflection, it would wish to change. Once a firm has done an audit on its ethical practices it will be in a better position to develop its organisational culture in more productive and responsible ways. So devising a code of ethics could be seen not as an end in itself but more as the beginning of a monitoring and reform process. The resultant code is a good platform for measuring the success of change and developing the strengths of an organisation to meet emerging ethical challenges. The process that produces it can be refined and modified to update the code. The production process is thus both the first stage in the renewal of an organisation and the object of continuing review.

Every organisation has rules about behaviour, even if these rules are not made explicit in written or oral form. Some organisations have a written code of practice and some do not. Sometimes the written code of practice of an organisation is at variance with its unwritten operational code. When the two are in conflict the unwritten code is usually the more effective. This can be very sobering. An executive of a large corporation once spoke about being the student of a famous professor of accounting. 'He was a wonderful teacher,' said the executive, 'he had wonderful ideals, we learned a great deal from him, and he enjoyed great professional respect. But when I joined my firm I was told, "The first thing you have to do is forget everything professor X taught you. We do things differently here".' The executive was referring not just to skills, but also to values. Organisations may profess one thing and practise the opposite. All have *de facto* codes of practice, though not all have *de jure* (or formal) codes of ethics.

If an organisational culture fosters sharp practice and rewards unethical behaviour, the superimposition of a formal code of ethics will merely be window dressing. A code of ethics prominently displayed can be misleading; far worse than no code at all. Yet contemporary social pressures on business almost compel the adoption of formal codes. Good intentions notwithstanding, this might at best be useless and at worst a trap for the unwary. It is also paradoxical; at the heart of written codes is self-regulation, yet implicit in the social demand is the threat that if a written code is not adopted, then government will do the regulating. This demand seems almost to see regulation, or rather codification, as an end in itself. The essential questions should be: What are codes of ethics for, and what benefits should be expected from their adoption?

The first answer must be that a formal code of ethics states where people in an organisation stand in relation to each other and to the organisation itself. It will also state where the organisation itself or members of the organisation stand in relation to entities outside the organisation (most typically, members of the public, stakeholders or other organisations). The effect of this should be to bring the *de facto* and *de jure* value systems of the organisation into alignment. Then the ethical culture, or ethos, of the organisation will be transparent: every stakeholder group will know where it stands.

The model for this view is the principle of the 'rule of law' in the legal system. Rule of law is an important notion in legal theory and in the philosophy of law. It encompasses a number of aspects, one of which in particular is very important in the context of codes of ethics. An environment of rule of law, and a code of ethics, allows the subjects, or clients, as well as the practitioners to know where they stand in relation to the practice. It allows people to know (and so allows them to expect and to plan accordingly) how they will be treated in certain situations. If the prices of products are announced, then people can choose either to buy them or not, and can expect to pay that amount if they decide to buy. People can plan accordingly. Similarly, if people know that certain behaviour is prescribed in certain situations for practitioners, then they know what to expect and can plan accordingly. This element of consistently knowing what to expect and of being able to plan is itself valuable. To some degree it may not matter what is prescribed (although there are important limits and whole areas where this is not true); predictability and consistency are valuable in their own right.

The model of the rule of law is useful in another way. Just as the law should apply to all people equally, so a business code should apply to all people in an organisation, from the CEO down. A set of rules for employees that excludes management, even implicitly, is sending a false message to the organisation and to the public at large. A positive example is ICI's Code of Ethics, which is clearly identified as being from the managing director, and is sent to employees in an internal mail envelope with a letter addressed 'Dear Fellow Employee', thus deliberately placing the managing director on the same moral footing as other staff. When staff know where they stand in relation to each other and the organisation, and are furnished with a clear statement of moral equality, an organisation has placed a barrier between individuals and unethical conduct. If a manager were to request a junior staff member to do something unethical, the junior employee could point to provisions in the code forbidding this. In other words, unethical conduct cannot be disguised as legitimate direction. This barrier should discourage managers from making unethical demands, protect individuals from being placed in difficult or compromising situations, and safeguard the integrity of the organisation. It should lessen resort to whistleblowing and allow ethical employees to act with the assurance that they enjoy the support of the organisation as a whole in adhering to the spirit and letter of the code.

Codes of ethics and codes of conduct

It is important to distinguish between a code of ethics and a code of conduct. Not everyone uses the phrases in this way, but the distinction itself is important, whether or not one uses the mechanics of a code of ethics and a code of conduct to do it. A number of organisations' codes are actually an amalgamation of these two. We think, however, that it is a good idea to keep them separate.

Code of ethics	Code of conduct
• general	• specific
• values / principles	• prescriptions / directives
• judgment	• uniformity
• 'empowering'	• enforceable statements of specific
• 'aspirational'	behaviours

A code of ethics speaks in general terms. It articulates ethical values and principles that are important to the organisation. As a simple example, let's say 'honesty' is one of the organisation's values. Stating it and saying something about what it amounts to — in general terms — for the organisation is appropriate to the organisation's code of ethics. For those people operating under this code of ethics, 'honesty' is a requirement, then. Now, exactly what honesty amounts to in any particular situation will require judgment. This is the situation for any value or principle listed in a code of ethics. Let's take honesty as the example again. This is, in fact, the hardest example for this point; so, if we convince you that judgment is required in order to determine what is required to exemplify this value, then you will certainly believe that judgment is required for any other value that might have a place in a code of ethics. Honesty is not the same thing as 'always telling the truth'. What is required by honesty is itself a matter for judgment. We spoke about this earlier in talking about virtue ethics. Let us suppose that you are an honest person. Let us also suppose that one evening, a friend, Benjamin, appears at your door, absolutely distraught and scared. He tells you that someone is trying to harm him. You invite him in, take him to the kitchen, make him some coffee; and he is beginning to tell you what has happened — it has something to do with someone going into a rage about what parking spot he had pulled into. This is interrupted by a knock at the door. An evil-looking fellow is standing there, fists clenched and holding some kind of nasty club. 'Have you seen Benjamin Loris?' he asks. Now, honesty does not require that you tell this person, 'Sure, you'll find Ben in the kitchen.' 'Honesty' is different from, say, a fanatical devotion to telling the truth. Although extreme, this situation makes the point that (even) honesty requires judgment in particular situations. Usually the correct judgment will be to tell the truth, but judgment is necessary in order to appreciate a situation for what it is and for what honesty requires. So much for honesty. We could make the same points – and it would be much easier – with any other value or principle that finds a place in a code of ethics. To recognise that judgment is required is to recognise that different responses might be justified. This in itself can be 'empowering' for people operating under the code. They are 'empowered' to behave ethically. They have to make decisions, and they have to be prepared to offer justifications for those decisions. They are responsible for behaviour exhibiting the values and principles articulated in the code. And their actions with respect to each of those values or principles are to be judged by the justifications that they as individuals can offer. That's what the code requires.

'Aspirational' is a word that is often used in talking about codes of ethics. To appreciate the sense of 'aspirational' in this context, it is helpful to indicate what it does *not* mean here. Again using the example of 'honesty' as the value, saying that the code of ethics is aspirational does not mean something like this: 'Right now we're not an honest organisation — actually we're quite the dishonest organisation. However, we aspire to behave honestly — one day.' Rather, to say that a code of ethics is aspirational is to say that although we don't always exhibit the values in the best way, and sometimes we might fall short, we aspire to get it exactly right every time. We realise that these things involve judgment calls, and we aspire to always exhibit excellent judgment. To say that the code of ethics is aspirational is to admit that there is room for improvement in our judgment and behaviour with respect to the values that the code articulates.

We can contrast these features of a code of ethics with those of a code of conduct. A code of conduct does not introduce additional values or principles. Rather, it spells out more specifically what is involved adhering to what the code of ethics requires. It removes the element of judgment, or empowerment, from some situations. Suppose, for example, that we work for an organisation that sells insurance. Our code of ethics might proclaim 'honesty' as one of our values. The code of conduct might say something on the order of this, 'in explaining a policy to a potential customer, we will make certain to inform the customer of all the costs involved to them, and we will make certain to do this in language that the customer understands'. This is, in effect, spelling out what is involved in behaving honestly in a particular situation. This is removing any place for the exercise of judgment about exactly what should be told or presented to the potential customer in the name of behaving honestly. Maybe there have been difficulties with the company in the past. Maybe there are other reasons why it is seen to be desirable to spell out this situation where the issue is precisely one over what honesty requires. Unlike what appears in a code of ethics, where a commitment to values is declared, this requirement is a specific prescription. We have suggested one reason why it might be desirable for the organisation to have a specific prescription in this area: maybe it has had trouble in this area before, and it wants to remove the element of individual judgment. Specific prescriptions can also do something that statements of values cannot do. To the extent that they are complied with, they can guarantee both uniformity of behaviour and uniformity of response to specified situations. Because it requires an exercise of judgment, the statement of values in a code of ethics cannot do this. So, if it is ever desirable to have such uniformity of behaviour, a code of conduct is necessary.

To say that a code of conduct consists of enforceable statements of specific behaviours does not mean that codes of ethics are not enforceable. It means, rather, that codes of conduct, unlike codes of ethics, require specific behaviours. It also means that the gauge according to which one's behaviour is to be judged — and the statements are enforceable – is the quality of the judgment that any member of the organisation has employed.

If an organisation believes that it is important to 'empower' people to behave ethically, and so to encourage sound ethical judgments and ethical decision-making, then the organisation must recognise that each specific prescription in a code of conduct amounts to a diminution of ethical empowerment. As we have indicated, there can, of course, be good reasons for specifying particular behaviours, but the organisation should realise that these requirements come with the attendant cost to ethical empowerment.

Before going further with this account of codes, let us say a bit more about the idea of 'ethical empowerment' in general.

Ethical empowerment is a top-down notion. It involves delegation of authority for ethical decision-making. It authorises, or empowers, members of the organisation to exercise judgment in decision-making. Increasingly, organisations have recognised that they simply cannot afford to be 'risk averse'. They cannot afford for their people in managerial or supervisory roles to avoid making decisions in ethically charged situations. The organisation recognises that the alternatives to ethical empowerment that gives the employee the authority to engage in ethical decision-making, are simply not good because:

- to pass all ethically-charged decisions up the line is a recipe for inefficiency
- to simply avoid making decisions in ethically charged situations is a recipe for stagnation
- to go ahead and do something, whatever you want, is cavalier. It is *very* dangerous to an organisation not to invest in systems (e.g., training) that equip managers to systematically exercise good judgment in such situations. To simply trust to common sense (or something like this), rather than realising that the matter of ethical decision-making can be approached specifically and dealt with seriously is a common error.

Rather, charging managers with responsibility to make ethically defensible decisions is a matter of authorisation, or empowerment. Appropriate responsibility, decision-making discretion is delegated downward through the organisation. Those receiving the responsibility are to recognise that they must make decisions and that they must exercise demonstrably good judgment in making them. Trust goes downward. From top downward, those authorising people below them must trust that those receiving the delegation are up to the task. Of course, this should not be simply a matter of luck — the person who receives the delegation must have the ability and skills to exercise it. It can be a matter of the right person for the job, providing the necessary resources, training, installing appropriate systems, etc. Whatever provisions are made, it is a matter of trusting that the person who is empowered can do the task. Now — and this is at least as important — it is necessary that those who receive the delegation actually trust that the people who gave it to them actually meant what they said. We all know people who, when they say 'exercise your discretion' actually mean something like, 'you had better do this exactly as I would if I were in your position. Otherwise, I'm going to come down on you like a ton of bricks'. This is not trust. This is not delegation. This is not a recipe for authorising ethical decision-making in ethically charged situations. It is, rather, a recipe for second-guessing and looking over one's shoulder. It is not empowerment at all. It is, rather, instilling fear and distrust. So, in an environment of ethical empowerment, responsibility is delegated downward, and trust must go in both directions. By and large this is an important notion for an organisation that is concerned to promote ethical performance. Codes of ethics can themselves be an important tool in this mechanism.

There can be reasons for not empowering, and the reasons why the specificity and particular prescriptions of a code of conduct can be desirable are that specific prescriptions can produce uniformity. Two other possible benefits of codes of conduct are these:

- A specific requirement can sometimes take the heat off an employee. Suppose the code of ethics mentions integrity and also some appropriate reference to handling conflicts of interest. Perhaps the code of conduct goes further — removing judgment in this particular situation — and prohibits employees from accepting any gift with a value greater than $20. Now, imagine this scenario, where a contractor is offering a Christmas gift of Johnny Walker Black Label scotch. The employee wants to decline the gift. The contractor might say, 'What do you think, Mate, I'm trying to bribe you? It's a Christmas gift. That's all'. Here the employee might simply point out that the code of conduct prohibits taking the gift. That's all there is to it. 'It's not that I think you're trying to bribe me. It's just that I'm not permitted to accept gifts.'

- A specific requirement can help the organisation with respect to public trust: it can make a clear, public statement about the types of organisational values that are important to the organisation. It can be a statement about what the organisation allows or tolerates, or, more likely, what it does not tolerate, that is, what behaviour simply cannot be done. Such a statement can be very important. It can be important throughout the organisation, in an organisation's interface with its stakeholders, and with the public at large. It can be a clear statement that 'this is what we stand for' or, 'No, no, no; we will not tolerate *that*'. This is more than a public relations matter; but it can also be that as well. We mentioned that in a setup for ethical empowerment, trust must run in two directions. In what we are now discussing, an organisation recognises that trust runs in only one direction: the organisation needs the public's trust. Sometimes the device of a clear statement, a specific prescription, can help toward that.

The following points are also important to think about in an organisation's creating its codes. First, what are our values? What are the moral values which have particular relevance to and resonance in the activities we engage in? For example, suppose that 'respect for human life' is an important moral value. If we are a firm of chartered accountants, then, although this remains an important moral value for us personally, it is not relevant in our practice, and hence has no place in our statement of values or in our code of ethics. However, if we were a firm of armed security guards it could be a good idea to express this value because it would be relevant to what we do in our business, and show our awareness of our responsibilities and commitments.

Beginning from the values and principles expressed in the code of ethics, the organisation might then consider whether there is need to spell out some of these further and more prescriptively. This, we believe, is the best way to approach the design of a code of conduct. Remember the above example of the insurance company deciding that it is desirable to spell out in this way a particular situation involving honesty.

Professional and business codes

There are structural differences between professions and businesses that distinguish a professional from a business code of ethics.[4] A professional code operates throughout a whole profession and sets the standard for its practitioners. In this respect it operates on a monopoly. Furthermore, it also operates on an area of expertise that is known better by the profession itself than by those outside it. Some distinguishing features of what it is to be a profession are related to the area of expertise exercised by those people within it. This point is significant in that it furnishes a justification for the profession to police itself (at least partially). As itself the repository of the requisite expertise, who is in a better position to know what the profession should do? And who could be in a better position to police its activities?

A business code, however, can operate at the level of individual businesses. One business can have one code, and another a different code, or no code at all. And businesses with vastly different codes of ethics might even be in competition with each other. By the nature of what it is, however, a professional code takes in everyone who is going to perform a specified activity.[5] The same is true of industry codes.

Professional and business codes express a moral dimension to the activities of professions and businesses. However, codes are not the whole moral story, even for the individuals who work within them. As already indicated, codes of ethics do not replace or embody all of morality, even for those activities for which they are written. A code of ethics is not a formal apparatus for rendering an individual's conscience unnecessary; it is not a codified conscience. It is a matter of some argument about how much of morality *per se* is appropriate in a code of ethics.

Content of codes of ethics

Beyond having the proper regard for morality *per se*, and beyond giving due recognition to creating an environment of predictability and consistency in the behaviour of its members, what else should an organisation consider in determining the content of its code of ethics? Each organisation will have particular requirements, but codes typically contain provisions about the following:

1   a general statement of the values of the organisation and its guiding principles
2   definitions of what constitutes both ethical and corrupt conduct
3   competence requirements and professional standards
4   directives on personal and professional behaviour
5   affirmations of fairness, equity, equal opportunity and affirmative action
6   stipulations on gifts and conflicts of interest
7   restrictions on use of the company's facilities for private purposes
8   guidelines on confidentiality, public comment, whistleblowing, and post-separation use of company information
9   identification of different stakeholders and other interested parties, and their rights
10 a commitment to occupational health and safety
11 a commitment to the environment and social responsibility (a broader concern than stakeholders alone)
12 a mechanism for enforcing the code, including sanctions for violations
13 advice on interpreting and implementing the code.

These provisions can be combined or expanded in various ways depending on need. Not all of them are necessary for every business organisation, but the list covers the most common concerns. We shall comment only on some of them.

General statement of values and guiding principles

A general statement of values and guiding principles should commit the organisation to ethical principles as foundations for the conduct of its operations and the basis for the other provisions of the code. Levi Strauss and Co. begin their Aspirations Statement thus:

> We all want a company that our people are proud of and committed to, where all employees have an opportunity to contribute, learn, grow, and advance on merit, not politics or background. We want our people to feel respected, [be] treated fairly, listened to, and involved. Above all, we want satisfaction from accomplishments and friendships, balanced personal and professional lives, and to have fun in our endeavours.

This style of values statement is unusual in a code, but it is clearly consonant with the reputation for ethical business that Levi's has built up over almost 150 years.[6] Values statements, vision statements or codes express the common values of an organisation, so that everybody not only knows where they stand, but knows what everybody else stands for. According to management consultant, Lee Edelstein, 'a good values statement constitutes the ultimate control system: When everyone agrees on values, you don't need a lot of managers'.[7] This sentiment is echoed by John Oertel, president of ME International of Minneapolis:

When you've got people sharing the same values, you've got what amounts to a built-in quality inspector. It used to be our workers picked up ME's values at the company picnic or on the bowling team. Not now. We're growing. Half our people are new. Society itself is becoming scattered.[8]

Oertel's point is that corporations operating in a morally pluralist society need a code of ethics to act as a unifying device. A code permits the declaration and dissemination of a common set of values and demands behaviour in accordance with them.

The ICI Code of Ethics is transmitted to employees as part of a package that includes a statement of the company's Vision and Values. This vision of success and excellence is explicitly founded on stakeholder satisfaction. Shareholders, customers, employees and communities are the stakeholders identified in the vision. The values mirror this vision of excellence. They include the objective to 'operate to the highest standards of ethical behaviour and honesty and with full regard for the safety and health of employees, customers and the environment'. It is clear that ICI (now called Orica) wants to establish a strong corporate personality, and that it wants its staff to identify with that personality and the values that sustain it.

Definitions of ethical and corrupt conduct

The practical definition of ethical and corrupt conduct is really the task of the whole code, but it is appropriate to refer to legal or industry definitions. The ICI code begins with a definition and a statement of purpose:

Ethical behaviour relates to standards of conduct, characterised not only by complying with laws and regulations but also by qualities of truthfulness, openness and freedom from deception and fraud … The purpose of this Code … is to describe the Company's policy in the area of business ethics and values and to provide guidance to all employees in the specific areas on the Company's requirements in fulfilling these values.

Corruption is less frequently defined, but one example, the code of the New South Wales Tourism Commission (a public-sector organisation which operates in the private-sector environment), begins with a preamble explaining what is meant by corrupt conduct according to the New South Wales *Independent Commission Against Corruption Act 1988*. This is appropriate (and probably mandatory) for a public-sector business, but it might well be adapted for use in the private sector.[9]

Competence and professional standards

Matters of standards, competence and quality require reference to the kind of role — or better, the social rationale or justification — of an activity or business in the society as a whole. As a very rough example, suppose we are constructing a code of ethics for civil engineers as a profession. We should ask what the social rationale is for that profession. Let us suppose that the answer is to build safe bridges. The answer is not simply 'to build bridges'. Bridges are no good to society unless they can be crossed safely. If this is so, then something like 'provision of public safety' (where this can be spelled out in enforceable terms) belongs in a code of ethics for civil engineers. The general point is that significant elements of a code of ethics do not come after the fact of the activity; they are inherent in it. A code of ethics does not come simply as a result of considering what would be good ways for the profession or the professional to behave. It does not come from asking in the abstract about what the particular profession, as a profession, should demand from its practitioners. Rather, the question can come about by consideration of the basis of the profession as an enterprise that is socially justified.

Personal and professional behaviour

Codes of ethics provide guidance especially in cases that present themselves as morally uncertain. A code of ethics can give a clear directive about how to behave. However, there is both a good and a not so good aspect to this point. The not so good aspect is that a code may assume for people the air of an *ersatz* conscience or may come to be viewed as dictates of morality requiring no further consideration. Another aspect of this is that a code may be seen as covering everything of moral significance that could occur in the behaviour of the organisation and its members or staff. This danger, then, is that the code could be taken to replace conscience, to speak with the authority of morality, and to cover all areas of moral difficulty for the people involved. The good aspect of a code providing guidance in morally unclear situations is related, again, to the desirability of the rule of law. Situations that are recognised as morally unclear are those where responses by individual practitioners could be expected to vary. This could result in a departure from uniform standards of conduct. However, the important point here is that it creates a lack of predictability for those served by the organisation. They would not know what to expect in certain circumstances; and knowing what to expect is itself of considerable value.

For all their affinities with the law, codes differ because they are internally generated and self-regulating in the corporate and the personal sense. In stating organisational values explicitly, a code does not displace a conscience, but it does mean that the individual does not have to rely on conscience alone. An effective code is part of a culture that supports individuals ethically. The code itself can be conscientiously reflected on, further developed, and modified at the organisational level. As it stands in relation to the conduct of individuals who are members of the organisation, it by no means has the status of stone tablets. In this sense, also, it does not replace an individual's conscience, and it does not replace morality or encompass all of morality.

Social responsibility and the environment

A code of ethics can specify the social responsibilities of the business, that is, the responsibilities that are assumed towards society in general, not only the business's stakeholders and customers. To a great extent, business can set the parameters of those responsibilities. An organisation can present a formal statement concerning its responsibility to society, and can give formal recognition to the fact that it cannot do everything itself. A business has a limited amount of resources and, through a code of ethics can make a statement about what areas it is prepared to take social responsibility in. For example, the organisation might make a formal commitment to reducing pollution, while not making any other commitment to the environment. To a point, this is a perfectly acceptable way of operating. The existence of a formal statement gives it direction, and can also act as a shield against potential claims that the organisation is not doing anything in other areas of social concern.

Interpretation, enforcement and sanctions

A professional code is not merely a claim about an ethical commitment of the organisation. It must have substance in two ways:

1 It must actually prescribe or proscribe something that is identifiable. Perhaps this does not sound like much of a requirement on a code, yet it is surprising how many codes fail to meet this requirement. A code cannot merely be a claim that 'We're good people, and we'll treat you right'. It must say what this kind of treatment amounts to.

2 There must be some sanctions attached to the code. A structure is required so that breaches of a code can be identified and penalties can be imposed. This requires, in addition, that there is a body that has the authority and capability of enforcing sanctions. A code cannot be merely a paper tiger.[10]

It is worth articulating these two requirements further. A code that is too general or vague has virtually no value. A code must say something, and it must operate in an environment in which there is the real possibility of inflicting sanctions on offenders. As not all cases will be black or white, a body to interpret and apply the code is necessary. In this respect, the situation is analogous to a law court. The Tourism Commission and ICI codes are typical in referring employees, in the first instance, to supervisors when difficulties of interpretation occur. The provisions of a code must be capable both of being observed and of being policed. It must require something more than what would be illegal anyway: a code is not simply a statement that 'the law has our wholehearted support'. Whatever the purpose of a code of ethics is, it is not simply to affirm the law. Norman Bowie (among others) has suggested that a code introduces a 'higher standard' than the law.[11] Whether or not the standard is higher, it is not simply the same as the law.

Also, a code of ethics must not be like fire regulations pinned to the back of a door — unread, unintelligible and unserviceable in time of need. The idea of a code of ethics should be to prevent fires. It should not be consigned to the desk drawer after cursory perusal, but a document that is useful in guiding the actions of staff because it embodies the objectives of the business and its considered ways of reaching them. It should be of the same importance as a business or corporate plan, and part of a vision statement or company credo. In order for a code of ethics to function effectively, its relation to the overall structure and policy of the organisation cannot have the character of an appendage. It must be integrated into the organisational structure and mode of operating throughout the organisation. The presence of a code of ethics and the central features of its content must be part of the ethos of the organisation. The Credo of Johnson & Johnson (discussed in chapter 5) illustrates this point. So too do the codes of Levi Strauss and ICI in integrating employee feedback. The ICI Code invites staff 'to comment and contribute to this Code by bringing their ideas to their manager's … attention'.

We have suggested that for 'rule of law' reasons (among others) a code of ethics is desirable. Those reasons are closely related to another feature of a code of ethics, namely that it fosters trust and confidence. The presence of a code of ethics need not foster this atmosphere merely by implying the goodwill or altruism of the profession or business it governs. A strong code of ethics, operating in the environment in which it can flourish, should have more substance than that accorded to it merely by the goodwill of the business or profession. A code of ethics can become integral to the business's infrastructure itself.

Two brief stories of industry codes

Codes have grown in importance in recent years. Australia has followed the United States in this, although Australian corporate culture is still some way behind its American counterpart.[12] In the United States there are legislated incentives to develop ethics programs, including codes, in the revised *Federal Sentencing Guidelines for Organizations*, which have applied since 1991. The Guidelines give parity to Federal Court sentencing across the United States. In the case of transgressions by organisations and their employees, they allow for lighter sentences, including drastically reduced fines, for corporations that have made concerted efforts to introduce ethics programs to the workplace. They are a 'carrot and stick' approach to self-regulation by corporations. More recently, primarily in response to amazing accounting and financial failures (Enron, etc.), there have been other formal reactions, in particular, The American *Competitiveness and Corporate Accountability Act 2002* (the Sarbanes-Oxley Act) which requires the corporations to which it applies to develop codes of ethics. Similar external persuasions have been necessary to convince Australian companies of the advantages of codes. The Australian Stock Exchange (ASX) has had a serious voice in this. The ASX Corporate Governance Council released its Principles of Good Corporate Governance and Best Practice Recommendations at the end of March 2003. Principle 10 of 'the essential corporate governance principles' recommends that listed companies 'establish and disclose a code of conduct to guide compliance with legal and other obligations to legitimate stakeholders'. As already indicated, codes which are embraced by those they regulate will be more effective than those imposed by public pressure or governmental direction.[13] The ASX has put ethics on the agenda. And, it seems clear that these recommendations will acquire more bite, and come to have more the character of requirements than recommendations.

The Banking Industry Code of Practice

Consider the Banking Industry Code of Practice. It did not arise from industry concern about standards of practice, public risk or improved services. Nor did it arise from the industry's own concerns for its ethical image or for the prevention of ethically questionable practices. Indeed, banking has been resistant to industry self-regulation. This suggests a failure to appreciate the benefits codes confer on business, as well as some indifference to stakeholder considerations.

The code of practice in the banking industry was a response to threats of government regulation. In 1993 the Federal Treasurer proposed a voluntary mechanism whereby banks could subscribe to a code that would be enforceable at law. This was not an attractive proposition for the banks because it made enforcement a matter for the courts rather than the industry, but it was preferable to direct government regulation.[14]

The report of the Federal Banking, Finance and Public Administration Committee of 1991 recommended a banking code of practice. In the following year a joint taskforce comprising the Treasury, the Trade Practices Commission and the Federal Bureau of Consumer Affairs prepared the draft Banking Industry Code of Practice.

In November 1992 the first draft code was released and circulated to banks and consumer groups for comment. Its stated objectives included the definition of 'standards of good banking practice and service which customers are entitled to receive', ensuring that the terms of contracts between banks and their customers are fair; the promotion of 'clarity in the relationship between institutions and their customers'; and the fair and rapid resolution of disputes between banks and customers.[15]

These provisions are typical of professional and industry codes. They protect the banking industry as well as its customers and other stakeholders, but the industry did not respond well to sustained stakeholder interest in an externally generated code. Although initiated by government, adoption of the code could have been embraced by the industry in a positive manner. This might have helped restore its tarnished reputation. Instead it was an opportunity lost. In addition, the story of the Banking Industry Code of Practice illustrates the point we made earlier: if business does not self-regulate, government will intervene. Enlightened self-interest in this matter can benefit stakeholders. If, however, there is a real divergence between the actual values of the industry (its *de facto* code), and the values embodied in a formal code, the imposition of the latter will fail to provide the ethos in which it has practical effect. In such circumstances it is better for the law to set operating conditions that will ensure compliance.

Clearly what is needed is a pro-active response to the spur of government regulation. The usefulness to business of embracing codes has to be promoted if their effectiveness is to be maximised. This is not a plea for ethical propaganda: in surveying 145 British companies with codes, Walter Manley found that senior management identified eighteen major benefits conferred by the adoption of codes of ethics.[16] His research supports the case we have made regarding the benefits of codes for business.

Institutionalising ethics

Codes of ethics are not a stand-alone treatment for the problems of organisational ethics. Together with training programs, mentoring, exemplary leadership, and structural incentives for ethical behaviour and disincentives for unethical behaviour, codes form part of the mutually supporting structures of an ethical organisation. As we have suggested, they can also be an excellent starting point in the process of reviewing the values of a business and devising other structures necessary for the development of an ethical climate.

There will always be temptations for people to do the wrong thing. Sometimes these temptations can be removed or made less attractive by a system of incentives and disincentives. Such organisational strategies are ways of institutionalising ethics. This involves focusing on the ethics of the organisation and what its members perceive its values to be, rather than on individual moral probity. As James Waters put it, 'Rather than ask "What was going on with those people to make them act that way?" we ask, "What was going on in that organization that made people act that way?"'[17] This is the question that needs to be answered in order to see why people who are morally decent in their private lives behave in unacceptable ways at work.[18] It is a question that organisations need to answer in order to create an ethical climate in which staff can develop professional excellences and shun improper conduct.

This is not to suggest that there are just two types of organisational culture: an ethical one, which produces good employees, and an unethical one, which produces bad ones.

There is no blueprint for an ethical organisation, and Waters's point is that the normal operations and structures of an organisation can unintentionally give rise to unethical behaviour. For example, while role modelling and mentoring are important means for initiating new employees into an organisation, they can also be used to induct people into unethical practices. Similarly, a strict hierarchy that allows an employee to report only to an immediate superior can prevent adequate feedback about the growth of unethical practices. A corporation that has successfully implemented many of these mechanisms for developing and sustaining an ethical culture is Honeywell.

Case 10.1   Honeywell – an ethical culture

As a United States based corporation, Honeywell falls under the *Federal Sentencing Guidelines*, but its practice nevertheless exemplifies how organisations can take ethics seriously. It clearly states its values; takes ethical leadership seriously; makes knowledge of ethics part of the normal expectations of all employees; audits this knowledge as well as the practice of ethics; requires reporting of code violations, and provides support and feedback for those reporting; and imposes penalties for violations.

As with the ICI Code, Honeywell's Code of Ethics and Business Conduct comes with a 'Message from the Chairman of the Board and Chief Executive Officer'. This message traces the principles and standards of the corporation back to its founding in 1885. It explains that, while observance of the code is mandatory, it cannot be comprehensive and does not replace common sense or conscience. It also warns that unethical conduct can sometimes arise from good but mistaken intentions. It stresses that 'In the conduct of Honeywell business, observance of the law and strict adherence to company policies and practices are requirements without exception. We clearly want to succeed, but never at the expense of our integrity. In everything we do, our ethics and our values must be the first consideration in our minds'. In other words, there is no room here for mixed messages from management. The code comes with a card that employees are required to sign to indicate their commitment to observance of its principles.

Because of the *Federal Sentencing Guidelines*, it is now common for United States corporations to include ethics compliance in management auditing, and this is the case at Honeywell. In the last quarter of each year, the external auditors obtain from managers at each level of the organisation a certificate that 'confirms that they and their key employees understand and comply with (ethics) policies'.[19] Managers are held accountable for ethical leadership.

The code contains Honeywell's 'Vision Statement' and a statement of its values. It is divided into sections that are clearly labelled for quick accessibility, and it is cross referenced to other corporate policies and procedures, which are briefly summarised. It should be difficult for an employee to plead ignorance of Honeywell's ethics policies.

At the conclusion of the code, options for reporting violations are given. Employees may report to a supervisor, the Office of General Counsel, a corporate compliance officer, an ethics hotline on a special number, or a designated vice-president at head office, or they may use an email address. The advice concludes: 'When you call the Hotline, the matter raised will be investigated promptly. The results will be reported back to you. If an anonymous call is placed, a process for a response to you will be established'. These options and the commitment to feedback make reporting of ethical failure less like snooping and more the routine expectation of a good employer, which Honeywell insists it is. It goes some way to removing the problem of whistle-blowing, while building employee confidence in the support of the organisation in acting conscientiously.

Discipline for breaches of the code includes cautions, suspensions or dismissal. Such discipline applies not only to direct breaches of the Code, but also to situations in which 'circumstances reflect a lack of supervision or diligence by a violator's superiors in enforcing Honeywell's policies'; in which a supervisor has directly or indirectly retaliated against an employee who suspects a violation of the code; and in which employees deliberately fail to report violations or withhold information.

Complementing the code and violation reporting mechanisms, Honeywell has a quick check on decision-making called 'Bell, Book and Candle'. This catchy title helps employees remember that they should be aware of warning signs of ethical infringements (Bell); check corporate policies to see if proposed actions would conflict with them or with relevant laws (Book); and consider how decisions would look under the 'light of day' test — say, public exposure by the media (Candle). Ethics evaluation of managers by subordinates and peers as well as superiors is part of the strategy for entrenching ethics into corporate life.

Honeywell exemplifies support of an ethical culture that goes beyond the minimum. The *Federal Sentencing Guidelines*[20] have been treated by some corporations as a checklist to be gone though by their lawyers: draw up a code, have employees sign it, have the CEO give an annual address on ethics, and the matter is taken care of. In other words, although such external pressures can offer some incentive to develop ethics programs, they can also lead to mere conformism,[21] or to a minimalism that has nothing to do with ethics and everything to do with insuring against a heavy sentence in the event of failure to comply.

Some of the mechanisms advocated for developing and sustaining an ethical culture are: publicly stated commitments to ethical practices emanating from top management; establishing an ethics officer or committee; ethics training programs for all staff at induction and updating this training periodically; channels for internal reporting of unethical conduct; and rewards (never penalties) for ethical behaviour and penalties (never rewards) for unethical behaviour, even if it improves the bottom line.[22] The main point here is to send unambiguous messages to all employees that what is expected of them is ethical behaviour first and last. There should be no hidden agenda about results at any cost. The expectations of employees should match those of the organisation. This means that staff are not placed in situations where competitive pressures can motivate unethical conduct. It also means making moral decisions collegially whenever possible, rather than placing ethical burdens on the shoulders of individuals.[23] This ensemble of measures to support an ethical culture in an organisation has the virtue of sustaining an open and sharing ethos that is self-correcting.[24]

Review questions

1   Why might a business want to develop a code of ethics?
2   What would be ways of introducing and maintaining systematic attention to good ethical decision-making by those people in an organisation who are authorised to make such decisions? What 'resources' could be available to these people?
3   What are the limits on codes of ethics? What won't they do?

International Business Ethics

11

Chapter outline

- Competition or trust?
- Ethics and cultural difference
- The global social responsibilities of business
- Business and human rights
- Affordability
- A double standard?
- Supportive institutions
- Review questions

International business dealings raise in a special way many of the ethical issues outlined at the beginning of this book. One kind of challenge is presented by the responsibilities of multinational corporations (MNCs) that operate in environments that are less regulated, that are not democratically governed, and in which corruption flourishes. Another challenge is respecting the cultural differences that MNCs encounter in the countries in which they operate. Another is the difficulty of regulating commerce in globalising markets. We shall consider just some of these issues in this chapter.

Competition or trust?

Competition in international business is such that ethics can appear to be a handicap, if not downright irrelevant. Too often, businesspeople argue in polarised terms, as though business had only two choices: to behave unethically or fail. It is easy to think of the standard slogans: 'It's kill or be killed'; 'It's a jungle out there'; 'It's dog eat dog'. Leaving aside the view that ethics is irrelevant, it can be argued that the survival of a firm should not be jeopardised in order to fulfil an ethical obligation when one's competitors are not ethical. A case could be made that paying a bribe to an official to secure a contract in a host country could mean the viability of the firm, help local employment, and even promote economic efficiency. Of course, making such a case is saying that paying the bribe is not really unethical (see chapter 2 on dirty hands). But how many cases are there in which the survival of a firm depends on a bribe? Just how inimical is ethics to international competitiveness? It is unconvincing, both in domestic and international business, to dramatise the difficulties of matching competitors ethically by claiming that the competitor's tactics are designed to destroy all rivals. The survival of most businesses does not depend on one decision, and if the matter is very serious, then being unethical in order to save the company simply changes the nature of the risk.

For a company to embark deliberately on unethical conduct under the guise of 'necessity' is morally indefensible. This might seem a harsh view, especially when the livelihood of a community is related to the survival of a business enterprise. In a time of economic restructuring, we are only too familiar with the human cost of business collapse. But the way to mitigate human tragedy is to appeal to public policy, not to go feral. Corporations are not natural persons who may legitimately steal when survival is on the line. A business conducted as though each sale is 'make or break' has serious problems, which breaches of ethics will only make worse, not resolve. But it is not only failing businesses that argue from necessity: as mentioned in chapter 2, necessity is often the excuse for a hard-nosed business culture that seeks to normalise indifference to moral principles in business — at least in relation to its own actions.

The link made between competition and survival is a parody of the work of Charles Darwin: Social Darwinism. It imagines a world where only the fit should survive. Interestingly, another great English thinker, Thomas Hobbes, suggests a different requirement for corporate survival in the arena of international competition. Hobbes believed that a world where people did whatever was required to maintain their own security was in a state of war. Such an unpredictable and unstable state is likely to result in an unpleasant life and an early death.[1] The remedy for this vulnerability is enforceable authority, which will bring people under the common regime of the state. By analogy, if international markets are to work, then a Hobbesian solution is needed. An international legal and normative infrastructure is necessary among states. The point that is often lost in analogies with war, however, is that a great deal of this infrastructure already exists in private and public international law. It enables the most complex kinds of global transactions to be conducted with a degree of trust and predictability that is often overlooked. Moreover, business itself has initiated a number of bodies to set standards of conduct internationally, which we will discuss in a later section.

Ethics and cultural difference

One of the difficulties of doing business internationally is the variety of social and legal standards that apply around the globe. What might be acceptable or legal in the home country of a business might be offensive or bring penalties in a host country. Whatever the differences between other cultures and Australia, the problem for business is arguably not primarily one of a conflict in basic values but of cultural, economic, and political differences. Corruption can exist in any context. It is the reaction of business to that corruption that matters. There are more safe exits for businesses faced with corrupt pressures in Australia than exist in some other countries, such as Thailand or Vietnam. But the lack of strong formal regulatory environments does not indicate an absence of values that we should respect and upon which the regulatory infrastructure of business can be built.

When we observe foreign cultures, we tend to be struck more by differences than by similarities. That is, after all, why we travel and take an interest in other peoples: to experience the breadth of human diversity. Ethical practices are among such differences in the customs and ways of life of our hosts. As we noted in chapter 1, the words 'ethics' and 'morals' originally referred to the standards of a culture: the social mores, understandings, conventions and norms by which conduct was judged. But there is a limit to the relevance of social and cultural difference. While we speak of the respective mores and norms of the French, Germans and Japanese, we do not usually speak of French ethics, German ethics and Japanese ethics. A particular emphasis on certain values in these countries need not suggest a different ethical universe. If multiple sets of ethics are applied — 'when in Rome … ' — then not only can one culture not criticise another, but there can be no real basis for one culture to learn from another's values. Each culture would have to reject the positive as well as the negative aspects of foreign societies. Not only does common experience contradict such cultural isolationism, but empirical work — such as that of the highly regarded mythographer Joseph Campbell — shows that the notion of a common humanity is not some Western ideal born of the eighteenth-century Enlightenment.[2]

It is not unreasonable, then, to suggest that ethics is universal as well as rooted in particular contexts. We expect some moral principles to transcend particular cultures. What values might these be? High on the list would be respectfulness, honesty, trust, integrity, sincerity, loyalty and diligence. Of course, these values are expressed in different and distinctive ways. Let us distinguish between primary and secondary values.[3] The list above identifies primary values. Secondary values would relate to the expression of these primary values in certain ways, such as marriage customs, social stratification, kinship obligations and so on. In the case of Japan, it would be important to understand the significance of harmony, consensus and loyalty within a group or company — *wa* — which could lead a subordinate, for example, to cover for a superior accused of accepting bribes. According to one research group, 'loyalty to one's group is a respected personal trait, which may be compared in importance to the personal integrity of Westerners'.[4] In China, trust — *xiyong* — is the fundamental value of business, much of which is conducted by verbal agreements in underregulated environments.[5] In Vietnam, Indonesia and Thailand, the reluctance to say 'no' directly to a request may seem evasive, when in fact it is a mark of respectfulness to those making the request. Understanding these differences can increase one's regard for those with whom one is doing business, especially if one recognises that many of the cultural mores of Asians and Australians rest upon the same primary values and, in terms of ethics, differ only in their secondary values. Ironically, if there were greater familiarity with Aboriginal culture among Australians, business people would be more sensitive to the Asian reluctance to give a blunt refusal.

Of course, the distinction between primary and secondary values does not help business in a situation where secondary values are the problem. The point of making the distinction, however, is that differences in secondary values might indicate cultural differences other than ethically divisive ones. It might be appropriate to give a gift as a matter of cultural sensitivity rather than to gain an uncompetitive advantage. So while we are not trying to reduce ethical questions to primary values shared universally, we would suggest that the traditions of a foreign culture are directed to preserving certain primary values and that when this is understood, unfamiliar customs become more intelligible and are not confused with ethical transgression. Moreover, this distinction between primary and secondary values helps us identify fundamental issues, and permits legitimate and sensitive criticism of practices that are believed to protect primary values but may not. Argument or discussion about primary values is more likely to come to a sudden halt: if there is disagreement, there may be nothing more to argue about. But secondary values thought to protect more fundamental goods through cultural and legal mechanisms invite the kind of discussion and dialogue that can benefit critics and defenders alike, and can invite imaginative solutions to differences.

Take the example of 'face', a crucial value common in many Asian societies. Causing a person to lose face in a business deal cuts through secondary values to primary values of respect and trust. Westerners do not like to be publicly embarrassed or to have their self-esteem or dignity damaged, so why should it be different for others? Given that Asian societies are more communal and relationship-based, and that family obligations extend beyond the nuclear and blood relationships familiar in the West, the nature of face needs to be examined on a case-by-case basis. The issue of face also illustrates how ethics must go beyond rules in order to be culturally sensitive. It takes an ethical imagination to do well in situations in which values collide. This sort of imagination was shown by a prominent Australian businessman who was managing an MNC in Thailand. At Christmas, a lavish gift of food and wine was given to him. He felt that it would be awkward to accept this gift but also awkward to refuse. His imaginative solution to this problem was to thank the gift-giver by saying how much his staff would enjoy it. The gift-giver's insistence that the gift was for the CEO was countered by a face-saving strategy of modesty and generosity: the staff must be permitted to share in the gift because they had worked hard. Dissipating the contents of the gift also dissipated the concern about the creation of a direct obligation to reciprocate by offering some business favour to the giver. Eventually the gifts stopped coming, perhaps indicating that their true purpose had not been achieved.

Is corruption acceptable in foreign cultures?

In December 1996, the German newspaper *Der Tagesspiegel* ran a story under the headline: 'Corruption part of traditional Thai culture'. This extraordinary claim was not made by the newspaper, however, but by the Thai Deputy Minister of the Interior, Mr Pairoj Lohsoonthorn, who publicly told officials that his department's policy was to accept bribes:

> *He had ordered staff of the land sales department of his ministry to accept any money offered to them, he told 'Matichon' newspaper. However, civil servants were not allowed to ask for bribes or to circulate price lists. 'This is part of traditional Thai culture,' Mr Pairoj said. The acceptance of bribes was justified by the low level of pay in the civil service.[6]*

From such reports, one might conclude that corruption is acceptable to the citizens of Asian countries or that their authorities are indifferent to it. This inference would be unjustified. First, as Johann Lambsdorff points out, alleging corruption in foreign business environments shifts responsibility from those who offer bribes to those who accept them: both sides of the equation need to be examined.[7] Second, although high levels of corruption are tolerated, the financial and political instability of 1997 has put new fight into anti-corruption programs already instituted by the Chinese, Thai, Malaysian and Vietnamese governments. Together with improved legal infrastructures and the economic resources to support them, these measures will lead to changes in the business cultures of these countries. If corruption were acceptable in Asia, it would follow that Westerners could engage in corruption in Asia without drawing comment. The hostile reaction of Indonesian commentators to a Canadian company's mining scam gives the lie to this.[8] Anti-corruption measures now reach into the elite ranks of Asian states. In Vietnam, the government has launched a campaign against corruption that involves the death penalty for some crimes. Some estimates put losses from corruption at over A\$180 million in 1996. Because corruption involves top party officials, there has been some scepticism about whether the new laws will be enforced diligently, but already two executives have been convicted and sentenced to death in absentia after fleeing to Cambodia with millions of dollars. Recently the director of an import–export company owned by the Vietnamese Communist Party, Tamexco, has been charged with fraud costing A\$33.2 million in a scheme involving nineteen others and a total of \$62 million. One of these is the former deputy of Vietnam's biggest state-owned bank, who faces charges of making illegal loans.[9]

Oddly enough, Japan, one of the world's most spectacular economies, is driven by an ethos that is not based on profit-maximisation but on values such as honour.[10] Corruption is consequently a great source of shame, even in the face of 'necessity'. In March 1997, Hideo Sakamaki, president of Nomura Securities, the largest stockbroking firm in the world, resigned because his vice president and two managing directors had complied with the demands of corporate extortionists.[11]

Would it be possible to splash the details of secret dealings over the front pages of local Asian newspapers and find approval among readers? Clearly not. Perhaps the most famous scandal involving an overseas company in corruption was Lockheed's channelling of money to the Japanese Liberal Democratic Party and the eventual charging of two former Japanese prime ministers. When one considers the magnitude of buying influence at the political summit of one of the world's leading economies, one wonders how such a thing could have happened.[12] The audacity of the company cannot be excused on the grounds of commercial necessity and the absence of regulation in the United States at the time. It was blatantly unethical, and Lockheed could not evade responsibility by shifting the blame onto the Japanese. This scandal should serve as a lesson for all those who wish to justify the payment of bribes by invoking its commercial necessity in an environment where bribery is alleged to be 'normal'. In 1977, the United States Congress passed the *Foreign Corrupt Practices Act*, which prohibits American corporations making payments to foreign governments to advance their business interests.

Scandals like the Lockheed bribe are not rare in Japan. Although they have brought leading businessmen and high-ranking politicians before the courts, the shame has not been sufficient to avert other corporate disgraces involving such major corporations as Nomura and Daiwa. Some might assume from cases such as these that Japanese business relies on fraud and corruption. If everybody is doing it, then it must be 'normal'. Hence, it is legitimate for foreign firms operating in Japan to give bribes or indulge in other forms of corruption. If home country laws forbid such corrupt practices, then a firm might form an alliance or partnership with an indigenous company, which will handle culturally and legally sensitive issues such as 'facilitation fees' and undisclosed commissions. Yet it is no more acceptable in Japan to offer or accept bribes than it is in the United States. In both countries, it is necessary to hide this conduct because it is shameful and unethical. When the Asahi newspaper reported that Osaka oil dealer Junichiro Izui, charged with tax evasion, had been a conduit for senior Mitsubishi Oil officials to channel several million dollars to Japanese politicians, there was a public outcry.[13] Again, the 'light of day' test makes the point: once bribery is publicly exposed, people are incensed.

Cultural relativism

The mere fact of cultural difference does not imply its acceptability. Although respect for persons is basic to civilised interaction, we are not obliged to respect every kind of belief that people might hold simply because we wish to show them due regard. On the contrary, while courtesy should prevail, we might on occasion feel obliged to criticise certain beliefs from what we believe is a stronger position in our own belief system. Were this not so, different peoples could never learn from each other. Examples of resistance to beneficial cross-cultural criticisms are common. Slavery flourished in the United States long after its abolition in Great Britain. Women's suffrage was achieved only gradually, after the example was set in the United States and Australia, with Switzerland granting women the vote as late as 1969. Respect for individuals does not mean sacrificing one's own values for those of others. Such respect is, however, likely to reveal that there is more common ground between cultures than is at first apparent.

In the early 1990s, a survey of 150 randomly chosen companies among Australia's 500 largest exporters identified the ten most commonly perceived ethical problems in international dealings. In order of frequency they were:[14]

1   gifts and favours: large sums of money, call girls, travel, lavish gifts
2   cultural differences: misunderstandings about cultural matters such as the significance of gifts and tokens of esteem
3   traditional small-scale bribery: for example, small sums of money to speed up a routine bureaucratic procedure
4   pricing practices: differential pricing, requests for invoices that do not reflect actual sums paid — for example, for dumping or price fixing
5   questionable commissions: large sums paid to middlemen, consultants, and so on.
6   tax evasion: transfer pricing
7   political involvement: political influence of multinationals, illegal technology transfers
8   large-scale bribery: political donations, sums paid to evade laws or influence policy
9   illegal or immoral activities in a host country: pollution of host country, unsafe working conditions, flouting patent and copyright provisions
10 inappropriate use of products: use of technology in a host country that is banned in the home country.

Ranked in order of importance, these problems were:

1 large-scale bribery
2 cultural differences
3 involvement in political affairs
4 pricing practices
5 illegal or immoral activities in a host country
6 questionable commissions
7 gifts or favours
8 tax evasion
9 inappropriate use of products
10 traditional small-scale bribery.

The dominant problem for businesses operating in Asia concerned bribes, gifts and commissions. But serious breaches need to be distinguished from minor ones. There is a difference between a payment to expedite business that is already in train and a payment to influence the awarding of a contract. While both involve departures from ethics, one is akin to queue jumping and the other is plain crooked. While small failings can lead to larger ones — for even small collusions have their costs — there are degrees of seriousness.

Australian perceptions of ethical problems in Asia are mirrored by the perceptions of Asian managers. Indonesia, for example, was perceived by nearly 17 per cent of Australian companies surveyed as the trading partner with which they experienced the greatest ethical difficulties, while China had a 10 per cent rating. In a survey of 280 Asian executives by Political and Economic Risk Consultancy Ltd (PERC) of Hong Kong, corruption was perceived as declining only in the Philippines and Singapore.[15] (See also the discussion of the Transparency International Corruption Perception Index on pp. 217–19.) Like the Australian survey, the PERC report found China to be near the top of the corruption list. South Korea (plagued by scandals such as the Hanbo collapse[16]) and Vietnam also ranked highly in the corruption stakes. According to PERC, control of corruption 'requires an institutional framework that is lacking in many countries ... and can take years to develop'. Vietnam's corruption problems have hampered the operations of business. A downturn in the property market and the consequent non-performance of many loans has badly affected the banking system. Poor management and corruption are to blame.[17]

A survey by the *Far Eastern Economic Review* in 1993 identified differences in the seriousness accorded to ethically dubious business practices in Asia and Australia. For example, according to this review, while Malaysians and Indonesians place little weight on pollution offences, Japanese and Australians regard pollution seriously. Indonesians and Thais will offer a bribe in order to retain a client far more readily than will Hong Kong Chinese and Australians. Koreans and Japanese will impose excessive working hours on staff in ways that Singaporeans and Australians would not. Koreans, Filipinos and Taiwanese are more likely to pay for escort services for business associates than Australians, Japanese and Hong Kong Chinese. Malaysians are most highly protectionist, and Hong Kong Chinese are least so. Koreans and Singaporeans are likely to pay a family man more than a single woman performing the same duties, something that Thais, Hong Kong Chinese and Australians will rarely do. Filipinos, Taiwanese and Koreans are more likely to favour family members for jobs than are Singaporeans and Hong Kong Chinese.[18]

Judgments about corruption are influenced by cultural factors, but what the surveys above reveal is a great deal of overlap among many cultures in what is regarded as unacceptable conduct. Crime and corruption in Australian and other Western business circles are often invisible,[19] while highly visible instances in other parts of the world can confirm certain stereotypes. A different reality might be hidden beneath such perceptions. One cross-cultural study of marketing ethics suggests that collectivist societies, such as those found in Asia, are more likely to conform to organisational ethical standards and requirements than are individualist societies such as Australia or the United States.[20] It is useful to issue such cautions in order to balance stereotypical judgments, and to point out that the problems Australian firms face in dealing with corruption and unethical conduct in Asia are often the very ones encountered by Asian firms as well.

It is not uncommon for a company to bring new skills and processes to a foreign country. If trained staff are not available, they are trained. If infrastructure is absent, it is built. With ethics, it is the same: insistence on certain standards of conduct, clear statements of guiding principles, and the introduction of values and priorities unfamiliar in the foreign environment are all part of building ethical infrastructure. If it is absent, it is built. The point is to do it reflectively and sensitively — that is, without imposing home country values as though they are some improvement on the host country's ethics. Foreign firms should consider the impact of their activities on local communities and build commercial and ethical infrastructure that respects the traditions and values of the host country.

These principles are easy to preach and hard to implement. In Indonesia, for example, the nobility (*priyayi*) of the Javanese majority divide the world into two: 'refined' or elevated elements and occupations, called *alus*, and the 'crude' or tainted elements and activities, called *kasar*. Tradition places business under *kasar*, which implies that it is inherently 'immoral'. The attitude that business is distasteful — familiar in the West until relatively recently — can make unethical conduct self-fulfilling: 'some businessmen ... show immoral conduct because they think that their activity is by definition immoral. Those who don't want to be dirty never ever enter business enterprises'.[21] An understanding of these values would help an MNC strategically but could also assist Indonesia in building culturally appropriate economic infrastructure. It would not excuse unethical conduct by the MNC in Indonesia.

Corruption is, by definition, not an ethical value for any country, and so, as long as the ways of minimising corruption are not offensive or culturally inappropriate, there is no reason to be anxious about shaping or enhancing the ethical environment of an overseas operation. This is well illustrated by the problem that confronted Julius Tahija, who was managing director of Caltex Pacific Indonesia from 1967 to 1977. When he was first approached with a kickback (which he rejected), Caltex had no formal training programs in ethics. Tahija believes that such programs can be an effective antidote to spurious claims of culturally relative standards:

> *Many people mistakenly believe, or convince themselves, that honesty and dishonesty translate differently in different parts of the world. This is self-deception. To be honest is to be honest... .*
> *If culture pressures people toward a certain type of business duplicity, then the transnational must counteract these pressures. Ethics classes should be integrated into training programs to strengthen each employee's personal sense of ethics and to clarify what the company expects.*[22]

Here the crucial goal is to meet the MNC's expectations, not to attempt wholesale reform of a foreign business environment. It is not unusual for MNCs to require consistency across corporate culture, no matter where it is located. If they are American corporations, the *Foreign Corrupt Practices Act* will support such requirements. For example, Honeywell's *Code of Ethics and Business Conduct* has, like those of all large American multinationals, specific provisions against overseas misconduct. In clear and direct terms, the code prohibits international price-fixing, bid-rigging, collusion, bribery, kickbacks or any kind of inducement to influence a transaction.[23] To the extent that such standards become global, the MNC is influencing the business environment of its hosts.

There is, however, some merit in the complaints of MNCs about competing ethically in an unfair market place. If all businesses are to be on a level footing, then public policy should enforce at least a rough equality among competitors. If this does not happen, how can people entering the market be expected to behave fairly? Why does any particular company have an obligation to put itself at a disadvantage in relation to its competitors? Any company doing so would go under in a market where the less scrupulous prevail. Such reasoning is a moral evasion, but one derived from a sound notion. We do not blame a bank teller for handing over cash when confronted by an armed robber. Whenever duress is applied, we reduce responsibility accordingly. In some environments, business can be confronted with operating conditions that are analogous to coercion, so no ethical blame should attach to them for conforming. The reason that it is an evasion nonetheless is that it makes an exception to the rule. In making necessity a virtue, it abandons reasonable responsibility. Companies can be caught in difficult situations, which may be exculpating, but to make the operating environment the justification for corrupt behaviour is unacceptable. General or stereotypical excuses will not convince. Corporations no less than individuals are required to make sacrifices at times: profits do not outrank morality, a point tacitly conceded by the necessity of reaching for excuses. The answer is not to deny the wrongfulness of the conduct, but to stop it. In the words of Richard De George: 'Some firms that operate in corrupt environments claim implicitly or explicitly that it is ethically justifiable for them to do whatever they must to stay in business. But their claim is too broad to be defensible. Ethics does not permit a company to capitulate to corruption'.[24]

Richard De George has specified moral guidelines for multinational corporations. The problem of doing business internationally is not only the relative underdevelopment of legal and commercial institutions in some countries, but also the absence of international background institutions, such as laws, shared norms, and social requirements. Rather than providing an excuse for substandard ethical practices, such differences place greater responsibilities on international business than those that apply at home. De George suggests that the most important criteria for responsible business operations abroad are for companies to:
- do no intentionally direct harm in the host country
- benefit the host country and contribute to its development
- respect the human rights of workers in the host country
- respect the values, culture and laws of the host country, as long as these do not involve moral inconsistency or the abridgment of human rights, as apartheid did
- pay their taxes
- assist the building of just background institutions in the host country and internationally.[25]

If a corporation cannot meet its responsibilities abroad, then De George suggests that an ethical manager might even have to consider sacrificing survival:

> At times, acting ethically takes some toll on a company, and it may even threaten its existence. Although we are told human life is sacred, it is sometimes right to lay down one's life for a friend, for one's family, for one's country … Similarly, might not a CEO justifiably lay down the life of the corporation for a cause or principle?[26]

This is a course that many writers on business ethics would find unacceptable because of the limited moral personality of the corporation. As an 'artificial person', it cannot lay down its life for others as natural persons (people) can. We discuss this issue below.

The global social responsibilities of business

Case 11.1   Kader Industrial Toy Company factory fire

On the afternoon of 10 May 1993, a fire broke out in a four-storey factory complex owned by Kader Industrial Toy Company in Nakhon Pathom Province near Bangkok in Thailand. Of the 188 workers killed in this tragedy, 174 were women and children. The Kader factory was a notorious sweatshop, but it supplied toys under sub-contract to some of the leading toy-makers in America.

Just before Christmas 1994, the *Australian* published a commentary on the fire by American journalist Bob Herbert. He did not mince words in apportioning responsibility:

> In the United States, toy company executives are immersed in the sweet season of Christmas. It is jackpot time and they do not want the holiday mood spoiled by reminders of the Kader horror. These executives know that their profits come from the toil of the poor and the wretched in the Far East; they can live with that — live well, in fact. But they do not want to talk about dead women and girls stacked in the factory yard like so much rubbish, their bodies eventually to be carted away like any other industrial debris.
>
> It is just for such occasions that God gave us the gift of denial. Much better to think of the happy American shoppers clutching the stuffed animals and other toys as they wait in line at the register … US executives keep the misery at a distance through the mechanism of contracts and subcontracts. They act as if they bear no responsibility for the exploitation of the men, women and children upon whom so much of their corporate profits rest.[27]

While Herbert concludes that corporations will always chase profits, no matter how tragic the circumstances in which they are generated, he hopes that consumers will be more ethically sensitive than corporate executives to scandals such as the Kader fire. He believes that when consumers realise that the lives and health of child labourers are at risk in the production of toys they buy for their own children, they will not buy them.

There are grounds for this belief, as successful campaigns against Nestlé and Shell have shown. Recently Nike has been targeted in campaigns by human rights organisations against foreign sweatshops.

Case 11.2   Nike 'sweatshop' allegations

According to a recent report, girls were being subjected to abuse by Vietnamese factories supplying footwear to Nike. 'Supervisors humiliate women, force them to kneel, to stand in the hot sun, treating them like recruits in boot camp,' Thuyen Nguyen, spokesman for Vietnamese Labor Watch, said after a sixteen-day inspection of four factories supplying Nike. Nguyen, an investment banker from New Jersey, has issued a report detailing abuses such as twelve-hour working days in overheated and noisy conditions; all-up labour costs of less than $US2 for items retailing for as much as $US149; wages of $US1.60 for eight hours work; and workers being allowed only one toilet break and two drinks of water in an eight-hour shift. At one subcontracting factory, the Taiwanese-owned Pou Chen Vietnam Enterprise, a manager forced fifty-six women to run in the hot sun as punishment for not wearing regulation shoes. Twelve women were hospitalised as a consequence. Nike has since instituted an inquiry and has suspended the manager. But Nguyen alleges that 'Nike clearly is not controlling its contractors, and the company has known about this for a long time'.[28] Nike denied this but was clearly spurred into damage control. The markets for its products are highly competitive and sensitive to the tarnishing of a clean, healthy, sporting image.

In Australia, too, this image has come under attack. Community Aid Abroad released its own report, *Sweating for Nike*, to coincide with that of Vietnam Labor Watch in launching a campaign for Australian consumers to boycott Nike products.[29] This was followed by a report by Perth academic, Peter Hancock, called 'Nike's Satanic factories in West Java'. Hancock spent eight months in Indonesia documenting sweatshop conditions, which mirror those in Vietnam. Employees worked an average of 11.5 hours a day, and 80 per cent of them were forced to work seven days a week; girls as young as 11 years old were employed; workers were sacked on the spot for taking sick leave; verbal abuse of female workers was endemic; and most workers earned the legal minimum wage of about $2.50 per day and some overtime. According to Hancock, this contrasted with the better conditions of Nike's competitors, such as Reebok. Nike's response to such allegations has been to deny control, and therefore responsibility, over its suppliers. Hancock rejects this defence. He claims to have observed two United States representatives of Nike working on the factory floor.[30]

The responsibilities of boards of directors and senior managers for offshore operations cannot be evaded by claims that cultural differences preclude intervention or that subcontractors are beyond their reach. Why, for example, do they deliberately locate in countries where unions are illegal? As the Bhopal disaster showed, it is easier to export the plant than responsibility. In the cases cited above, there was not even an attempt to assume a proper responsibility for work practices abroad until they were exposed. The 'light of day' test (as set out in the discussion of various decision-making models in Appendix 1) dictated a response from Nike: if the publicity does not subside, it could be forced to change its contracting terms to relieve public pressure. President Clinton introduced a code of practice for corporations operating overseas and, while this will not eliminate sweatshops — and might even give a façade of respectability to some companies that use them — it is a necessary first step in mobilising public opinion against oppressive labour conditions.[31]

Business and human rights

In 1993, representatives of Asian governments met in Bangkok prior to the Vienna conference on human rights. In a joint declaration they claimed that 'While human rights are universal in nature, they must be considered in the context of a dynamic and evolving process of international norm-setting, bearing in mind the significance of national and regional peculiarities and various historical, cultural and religious backgrounds'.[32] Chris Patten, last British governor of Hong Kong, read this equivocal endorsement of human rights as a camouflaged attack on their universality. Specifically, he believes that the rhetoric hides a belief that human rights hamper economic development: they are bad for business.

Yet Hong Kong exemplifies, he maintains, the constructive role of the rule of law and 'a proper regard for human rights' in the creation of prosperity. He takes the Hong Kong experience to be 'living proof' that human rights are as relevant to Asia as they are to the West. They are not some colonial relic or a new imperialism. Patten believes that if the critics had had their way, Hong Kong should have reached a certain undefined level of affluence before starting to take human rights seriously. Otherwise rights might have got in the way of economic progress, much as the Bangkok delegates implied.

Patten's polemic is a welcome change from the weasel words of conditional supporters of human rights, even though there is no more evidence for his claims than there is for the belief that ethical business people will prosper. Moreover, his position seems to suggest that human rights are cost-free. Human rights that mean anything in practice are not without costs.[33] At the very least they require the removal of negative externalities, and sometimes considerably more. Rights that rely on non-interference and governmental forbearance (often called negative rights) seem to be what Patten had in mind. The protection of negative rights is not free, but is less costly than protecting positive rights, which entail the allocation or redistribution of resources. Acknowledging such costs up front, even though this might seem to subject rights to an affordability test, is important if the role of business in human rights protection is to be serious. We discuss this further in connection with South Africa and arguments about affordability below.

Patten is on firmer ground in demanding evidence to support the view that human rights retard the material development of peoples. This demand does not address the question of whether material prosperity should be pursued at the expense of human rights — a question that the Bangkok conference probably had on its mind. It is a question that is much on the minds of businesspeople in the West as well: it would be wrong to suggest that Australia has problems of business ethics and less developed countries have problems of human rights. Economic justifications for ignoring human rights problems in the conduct of business are as familiar in Australia as anywhere around the globe. The labour conditions of outworkers in the clothing industry in this country are as much a human rights matter as those in China or India. Confronted with the need to rectify abuses in the outworker system in the garment industry, the president of the Council of Textile and Fashion Industries of Australia, Tim Todhunter, remarked, 'I don't know anyone in the industry who has the capacity to absorb significant increases in costs. Some garments will go back into factory situations. Some garments will still be made at home but with award rates [paid] … Some garments will go offshore and jobs will be lost'.[34] It would be easy to dismiss Todhunter's remarks as irrelevant to the ethics of exploitation, but the rigours of competition can make ethical considerations seem unattainable. If offshore competitors have lower labour costs, Australian producers are in a difficult position and the use of outworker labour can assume the colour of necessity.

In April 1996, Don Mercer, chief executive of the ANZ Banking Group, addressed the Australian–British Chamber of Commerce on a number of topics, including the issue of human rights and trade. Mercer found recent moves to link environmental issues, labour standards and human rights to international trade 'disturbing'.[35] In the same month, John Moore abolished the Outworker Project, aimed at identifying exploitative employers of outworkers in order to save $400,000. While it is easy to be glib about government docility, this does seem a genuine failure on the part of the Australian government in an area where setting a good example is part of setting the agenda for reform in other countries in our region.[36]

In November 1996, the Deputy Prime Minister, Tim Fischer, ruled out sanctions against Burma on the grounds that they would be ineffective and therefore do nothing for human rights. Despite calls from the Burmese democracy leader, Aung San Suu Kyi, for economic sanctions against the military dictatorship, Fischer rejected such a course: 'They are not practical with regard to the Burma situation. It is, therefore, the view of Australia that they are not practical'. The United States and the European Union had threatened to impose trade and investment sanctions if political repression worsened. Fischer's response provided a telling contrast: 'I've been to Burma many times, including Mandalay and elsewhere. It's, err, I'm watching developments very closely'.[37] Business leaders have been too ready to treat questions of human rights in host countries as internal matters that have nothing to do with them, even when their operations and investments are enmeshed with rights issues. Political leaders have shown a similar reluctance to confront rights abuses squarely when trade might be jeopardised by such action. The only reasonable conclusion that may be drawn is that human rights are taken to be less important than profits.

In a series of influential works, Thomas Donaldson has argued that multinational corporations ought not to deprive workers in host countries of their rights and should even assist in protecting some rights — minimal education and subsistence — but that they have no duty to provide direct aid to those whose rights have been abridged.[38] The reason is that such direct aid 'would be unfair [to the] profit-making corporation [which] is designed to achieve an economic mission and as a moral actor possesses an exceedingly narrow personality'.[39] The economic mission of the business corporation makes it a poor substitute for a government in dispensing welfare. It is neither a real (moral) person nor a democratic institution and has no mandate to render more than minimal assistance except in unusual circumstances (Donaldson gives the example of an earthquake). It is not within the moral capacity of a corporation to rectify deficiencies in human rights, such as minimal education and subsistence, even if it is notionally within its resource capacity. Quite simply, argues Donaldson, the languages of personal morality, of virtue and vice, of personal perfection and the maximisation of human welfare are inappropriate to considerations of corporate responsibility. The business corporation is a very restricted, artificial person, and only restricted moral responses may be expected of it. These are not responses that presuppose a human psychology, but those that relate to legal and contractual duties and rights, responsibilities and benefits.[40]

The application of such reasoning to concrete cases can be complicated as the following case study shows.

Case 11.3   Shell and Nigeria

Geraldine Brooks, a journalist on the *Wall Street Journal*, was arrested by the Nigerian Security Service for delving too deeply into the fate of the Ogoni, among whom she found conditions far worse than she expected:

> I suppose that 10 years of working on a conservative pro-business paper had taught me that self-interest, if nothing else, usually prompts corporations to behave with a measure of decency. Oil companies, dogged by poor records in developing nations, have tried in recent years to better their image.

But three days in Nigeria's Ogoniland had quickly revealed a picture much grimmer than anything the Ogoni leader, Sari Wewa, had described. Since Shell struck oil there in 1958, an estimated $US 30 billion … worth had been extracted and sold. Yet the poverty of the 500,000 Ogoni remained desperate, even by the harsh yardstick of the poor world.

As subsistence farmers dug for yams with sticks, their naked children drank from streams polluted by the toxic chemicals of neglected oil spills. Oil pipelines snaked hard up against the farmers' mud brick huts, even though current industry practice is to site them far from human habitation. I spoke to a woman burned in one of the inevitable oil fires that had resulted from this perilous practice. Still in pain almost three months later, she lay on the earthen floor of a traditional healer's hut, her burns wrapped in poultices of leaves. When I asked a Shell spokesman about her, he said the company was 'hazy' on the details of the accident, and couldn't investigate because of tensions in the area.[41]

Is it inappropriate to make an adverse moral judgment about a company such as Shell, which has had an appalling environmental record in Nigeria and a disastrous effect on the Ogoni people?

Can a multinational be an innocent bystander when it operates in a country ranked next-to-last (one hundred thirty-second) on Transparency International's 2003 Corruption Perception Index?[42]

And what is Shell's position when that oppressive regime executes dissenters such as Ogoni leader Ken Sari Wewa?

A supporter of Donaldson's view might argue that Shell is responsible for the evils it causes, but should not be expected to become involved in supplying remedies for rights violations for which it is not responsible. To impose such obligations would not only mistake the purpose of corporations and their restricted moral personality, but also commit the additional error of believing that they were fitted for such a role. On Donaldson's analysis of corporate duties, it would seem that Shell should assist the Ogoni people in overcoming the hardship inflicted upon them from oil drilling, but should avoid the political questions arising from protests against drilling on their land. But such a position, while plausible on paper, would be absurd in practice. Shell is producing oil with government approval but without the consent of the Ogoni. The political question is inseparable from the business issue, just as the economic and political issues in slavery were entwined. Moreover, the hardships of these people are not exceptional: they are an everyday occurrence; they are 'normal'. And Shell, by taking the posture of innocent bystander, helped to normalise them.

To argue otherwise would be to partition one kind of public institution in one sector of social life — the business corporation in the economy — from the kinds of burdens and costs that have to be carried by others. Whatever the limitations on the corporate personality, it cannot be suggested that it is incapable of conferring and enjoying political benefits, of being criminal or of behaving justly. Ultimately it is reductionist to hold that, because the business corporation has limited purposes, its moral accountability can be described only in terms of these purposes; that it is such a restricted vehicle for economic advantage that it cannot be responsible for matters that are not its legal or causal responsibility; and that deviations from such conceptions of the business corporation are warranted only in exceptional circumstances, such as natural disasters. Corporations do not behave according to such a limited conception of their (moral) capabilities, and the public clearly expects more than a minimal standard of conduct from business in circumstances less unusual than an earthquake. As Kevin Jackson has remarked, given the widespread nature of poverty and disease in less developed countries where multinationals operate profitably, 'The Donaldsonian exception ought ... to be the rule'.[43] Specifying the extent of the moral obligation is not easy, but that does not amount to an objection in principle. Shell's conduct subsequent to the Ogoni disasters, which included the execution of prominent dissidents by the government, shows that corporations are not immune from moral responsibility. As noted in chapter 8, Shell took seriously the impact of its actions on the peoples and environments in which it operated and adopted corporate social responsibility, winning a British Social Reporting Award for its 1999 Report in 2001.

The test of business probity is not only observance of procedure in the matter of basic rights (such as the law), but also respect for human goods more generally. In the words of George Brenkert, 'morally significant human rights [cannot be obtained] by appealing to utterly minimal duties'.[44] Some conception of the goods necessary to human flourishing is also required, and no society, government or business is entitled to trade them for more general benefits, as some forms of utilitarianism would allow. It took decades of argument and hard campaigning to get rid of slavery, to secure fair wages and conditions for workers, and to abolish child labour. These are matters that, at one time or another, were opposed on the grounds that they were unaffordable — that is, on grounds that claimed exemption from moral appraisal. An unwillingness among those who benefit from the exploitation of others to recognise their moral responsibilities is not a sufficient ground on which to pronounce an issue non-moral. Such an unwillingness betrays a move from the view that the corporation has severely limited moral capacities to the view that those who benefit from the corporation have similarly limited moral responsibilities. The thin moral personality of the corporation can be a very thick barrier between its beneficiaries and the moral problems encountered in producing earnings.

It will be difficult for those businesses that differ with the hostile policies of host governments to stand up for human rights, and the decisions will be made on a case-by-case basis. Each case has to be argued, not merely proclaimed. This is a large demand to place on human rights activists: moral argument is difficult enough in a community that seems to accept cultural relativism and moral pluralism unreflectively. But moral argument of various kinds does go on. The case of BHP's mining activities in Ok Tedi was argued by that company and its critics, and was resolved when BHP acknowledged its responsibilities in a fashion too rarely seen among transnational corporations. The questions it faced were not simple. The case was not just about investment and tailings in a river. It was also one of the different aspirations of the peoples who work in that region; of just compensation for losses; of the costs and benefits, the losers and beneficiaries from mining. The BHP decision to compensate says something about the moral community in which the company's owners live, and may signal the effect of ethical investment and moral suasion on such global businesses.

Ethical questions such as those surrounding the involvement of BHP in Ok Tedi are difficult: they require argument about the issues mentioned above. Whether companies should cooperate with evil is one of the most significant and common questions faced by businesses based in countries that claim to uphold human rights. If business is to further human rights, mere withdrawal from the site of conflict might not always be the ethical thing to do. It might be better to leave, as Levi's did in China (see p. 212); on the other hand, it may be better to stay and prevent things from becoming worse for the host population. Such decisions, like Oskar Schindler's reversal of support for the German cause when he witnessed atrocities in Nazi-occupied Cracow, are not made because of slogans, but by uniting an appreciation of context with principle.

Realistically business will not lead the way on human rights. Indeed, it would be enough if business were to follow in the wake of human rights activism and support its advances. At the very least, business may be forced to protect its interests (that is, its reputation) in the face of pressure from ethical investment organisations[45] and public interest groups. This is the argument from self-interest.[46] It is not to be despised, particularly if it assists the recognition of human rights in practice. Ultimately the argument for international business ethics must be in terms of humanity, not commercial advantage, but at a less sublime level, self-interest is an aspect of the work of organisations dedicated to ethical standards in global business, such as Transparency International and the Caux Round Table (see pp. 216–20).

Affordability

According to Donaldson, one of the three conditions for a human right is that 'the obligations or burdens imposed by the right must satisfy a fairness–affordability test'.[47] This is simply the familiar moral requirement that agents must be capable of realising or preventing an action for which they are to be held responsible. If they were not in a position to act, then they could not be held accountable. So too with rights: corporations that are not able to prevent breaches of human rights are not to be blamed. And, because of their limited moral personalities, business corporations are less able to give effect to rights claims than real persons, governments or aid organisations. Donaldson does not adequately distinguish between the possession of a right and the blame attributable to those who do not, or cannot, recognise it. That is what the affordability condition is really about: blameworthiness in cases where rights are not observed, not the possession of a right.[48] Even if corporations cannot afford to act positively in defence of rights in a particular context, and so cannot reasonably be blamed for this, it does not follow that the people making the rights claims do not have a legitimate case.

The failure to make this distinction clearly could have unfortunate consequences for the defence of human rights. It also underlines the importance of giving an unambiguous sense to 'fairness' and 'affordability' in this context. The danger is that ethics might be seen as tradeable, something that Donaldson does not endorse. Nevertheless, moral rights will appear to be expensive and perhaps unaffordable in situations where rights are regarded as having equal standing with economic development, profits, property and the exploitation of a resource. Objections to mining, bridge-building, forest-felling, tourism development, child labour, less regulated labour markets, self-regulation of occupational health and safety, and so on, could well be met with the response that choices that protect human rights are too costly, that they destroy competitive advantage, and that they will cause the loss of jobs or the flight of capital.

Questions of economic benefits should take into account who is being asked to bear the costs: For whom is the business activity affordable? Are social costs being fairly compensated? In concrete terms, this means questions such as these: What if the Ogoni told Shell that they could not afford to have petroleum drilling in their midst? What if the people of Ok Tedi told BHP that they could not afford mining because it increased effluent in their river? What if outworkers were to ask Tim Todhunter why he thought we could afford the current system and why we could not afford fair wages for all workers in the garment industry? What if the same questions were put to Don Mercer?

The notion of affordability suggests that we can decide when and where human rights will have currency, rather than determining the answer to the different question of whether particular rights claims can be met. The notion that, in argument, morals are trumps implies that other factors should carry less weight in governing action. If that is so, then decisions about what can be afforded by a business — as distinct from a society — have already shifted ground to the detriment of human rights. If affordability is an issue for a corporation, it might have to forego operations in a particular country. It is not entitled to evade human rights to prevent this outcome. There is a maxim in ethics that 'ought' implies 'can' — that is, that we should only ask someone to do something if they are able to do it. In the case of business, as with individuals, this means — among other things — that some ethical actions are subject to an affordability criterion. But affordability is a slippery notion, which can easily slide over into suggesting that human rights are conditional on profitability — that we can decide when and where human rights will operate or, worse still, that we can decide when and where human rights exist at all. Peter Drucker has expressed the matter soundly:

> An organization has full responsibility for its impact on community and society … It is irresponsible of an organisation to accept, let alone to pursue, responsibilities that would seriously impede its capacity to perform its main task and mission. And where it has no competence it has no responsibility … But — and it is a big 'but' — organisations have a responsibility to try to find an approach to basic social problems which fits their competence and which, indeed, makes the social problem into an opportunity for the organisation.[49]

There are, however, many instances of businesses refusing to compromise ethically and prospering nonetheless, as the following cases show.

Cae 11.4   Levi Strauss leaves China

Because of systematic human rights violations in Myanmar and China, Levi's pulled out of these countries. The decision to leave China has been described as one of the most difficult for Levi's to make because it meant sacrificing large market opportunities. Explaining the decision, Levi's communications manager, Linda Butler, said:

Last year we issued our global sourcing guidelines, which help us make decisions about what countries we should be in and what business partners we should be doing business with. There is a provision in those guidelines concerning human rights violations, and in light of that and in light of the current human rights situation in China, we have decided that we will not pursue a direct investment at this time and that we will begin a phased withdrawal of our contract sewing and finishing work in China.[50]

Despite the potential costs, Levi Strauss CEO, Bob Hass, said that 'never has an action by the company been met with such immediate, spontaneous, large and mainly supportive reaction from people all over the world'.[51]

Another MNC that has moved beyond an ethics of minimal duty to take a more proactive role in securing the goods necessary to human development — often called corporate citizenship — is Grand Metropolitan, a leader in the international consumer goods market.

Case 11.5   Grand Met and corporate citizenship

Grand Met has taken an expansive view of affordability because 'It shows that the company is not content just to comply with high standards of behaviour; we also want to contribute actively to the community. This pro-active approach to corporate citizenship … sees (it) as a two-way street where value flows to the company as well as from it'.[52]

A stakeholder approach, similar to that advocated by the Caux Round Table (see pp. 216–17), underlies Grand Met's model of corporate relationships.[53] In India, for example, Grand Met's managers were faced with the problem of being accepted in a host society, not just in a legal sense, but also in a social sense:

They wanted Grand Met to be clearly seen to be adding value to Indian society and to be setting an example to other firms, both foreign and Indian. More specifically, they wanted to be in tune with the transcendent Indian goal of sarbodaya (moral and material well-being) and were keen to focus mainly on the needs of the most disadvantaged members of Indian society.[54]

Accordingly, they sponsored community-development programs that could become self-sustaining.

Although Grand Met describes such activities in terms of charity or philanthropy, leading advocates of corporate citizenship, such as Chris Marsden relate them to self-interest. Marsden, like many of those who are impressed by Milton Friedman's argument that managers have no business giving their owners' money to worthy causes,[55] sees so-called 'corporate philanthropy' as strategic. So Grand Met's corporate citizenship in India could, in Marsden's terms, be described as 'earning its "licence to operate"'. It is a strategic move by a business that benefits its operating environment but also, and intentionally, benefits other stakeholders in that environment.[56] It goes beyond ethics, in the minimalist sense of avoiding wrongdoing, and attempts to do good. But this is not the disinterested good of the philanthropist. In the words of Julius Tahija, 'Promoting goodwill in a host country is critical to a transnational's survival. But for corporate development programs to be more than stopgap measures, transnational managers must make a serious commitment to the more ambitious long-term goal of transferring business, technical, and social competencies to people in the developing world'.[57]

Caltex Pacific Indonesia is another example of active international corporate citizenship.

Case 11.6   Caltex Pacific Indonesia

Caltex Pacific Indonesia spent thirty years repairing damage done during drilling in the Indonesian province of Riau in Sumatra. But, in building infrastructure, they went beyond the expected minimum. They built bridges that could also be used by local people; drained swampy land, which then became available for agriculture; promoted local businesses so that Caltex could be supplied by the people among whom it operated; avoided environmental destruction at monetary cost but a gain in good will; and provided a relatively high standard of living to Indonesian workers so that they would not feel uncomfortable working beside better favoured American expatriates.[58]

The decisions to provide benefits to local stakeholder groups must have been taken not only in the light of ethics, but also with some vision — perhaps the belief that such actions would enhance Caltex's long-term fortunes in Indonesia, that these decisions were afford-able in terms of investment.

A double standard?

Richard De George has argued persuasively that the same standards are not always appli-cable to small entrepreneurs and MNCs in international business.[59] His argument is based on a fundamental principle of moral philosophy: we are morally responsible only if we are able to act (once again, the moral 'ought' implies the practical 'can'). If, for example, you say that I ought to pay my debt to you now, I must have the money to do so. It makes no sense to impose a duty on a person who is unable to undertake it for reasons beyond their control. De George argues that this consideration applies to relative assessments of multi-national and domestic business operations.

De George argues that context changes the application of ethical principles. In the case of apartheid, the Sullivan Code (see pp. 215–16) was an effective brake on United States companies using a structurally unjust political system to their commercial advantage. International outrage at the appalling racism of South Africa at least restricted the exploita-tion of Blacks by MNCs. But what of the case of a White South African businessperson employing Blacks: is that person guilty of exploitation in a similar manner to the multina-tional that takes advantage of cheap labour? De George regards placing the local enterprise and the MNC on the same level as 'both logically necessary and too strong'.[60] Any Whites who wished to remain ethical would be precluded from engaging in business. Paradoxically this would mean that Blacks could only work for Whites who were unethical. Even living in such an unjust environment would make one a party to the unjust system — a participant in Black exploitation. Hence the position of the White in South Africa seems to have been 'necessarily unethical': 'But any doctrine that says that people are necessarily unethical is too strong because one can only be held responsible for doing what it is possible for them to do'.[61]

Bribery poses another challenge to De George's position. There seems to be a clear distinction between the obligations of international businesses and those of local business operations. In many countries — such as Indonesia, Russia and Thailand — bribes, favours, 'gifts' or secret commissions are commonplace. There is no question that each individual payment of this kind reinforces the corruption of the system and introduces injustice at personal, market, and probably political levels. But the system is not primarily the individual's responsibility. Systemic corruption is a collective responsibility, and the individual can only be asked to do so much to remove it.[62] While multinationals have the option of resisting demands for bribes and even of moving their operations elsewhere, local entrepreneurs might have no real choice. If a local business refuses to comply with corrupt practices, it might go out of business. Then the field will be left to those who do not mind paying bribes, and the chances of reform will be lessened. If a local business pays bribes, it is complicitous in corruption, but De George argues that this is the lesser of two evils. At least the ethically disposed local business can try to change the system; something not to be expected of businesses that do not even recognise that bribery is a problem.[63]

In the cases of both apartheid and bribery, the contexts of operation for local and multinational operators differ, even in the same country. Both practices are wrong, but responsibility differs for the local and the multinational company. The local operator has limited resources and nowhere else to go; the multinational has extensive resources and other locations. The multinational could — like Levi's — challenge corruption in a host country; the local company would be unlikely to succeed and is therefore unlikely to try. It is true that some local entrepreneurs are condemned in their own countries as exploiters, but can this judgment be generalised in countries where corruption is systemic? De George argues that it cannot. While a multinational might be embarrassed about offering bribes in a country notorious for this form of corruption, the same judgment would probably not apply to the local owner of a small transport company or retail outlet or factory. While rejecting relativism, he argues with some force that the same judgments cannot be applied to both types of business:

Of course it would be better to change the system and to make it fair and just. But if 'ought' implies 'can', then the small entrepreneurs, just as the individual workers, may plead that they cannot change the system. The conclusion that it is better for them to suffer injustice than to try to improve their lot, if this means engaging in the system, is a harsh doctrine indeed.[64]

Supportive institutions

Too often, campaigns against business decisions are driven by external interests. This type-casts business as reactive rather than responsive. Initiatives such as the Sullivan Code, the Caux Round Table and Transparency International (see below) are important because they model a more engaged and responsive form of business conduct. Sometimes businesses can surprise themselves by taking the initiative on issues such as the environment.[65]

Institutional support for the ethical conduct of international business is important in both the domestic and international arenas. Most of that support is not in a legal form, although important legislation such as the *Foreign Corrupt Practices Act 1977* obliges United States multinationals to avoid corruption. As yet, there is no parallel legislation applying to Australian companies, although the Australian government announced in May 1997 that it would comply with OECD recommendations that member countries should criminalise the bribery of foreign public officials by 1 April 1998.[66] Nevertheless, informal support exists in the institution of international business, fragmented as it is, and in more-or-less formal institutions born of a growing need for international standards of ethical business. The Sullivan Code, The Caux Round Table and Transparency International all illustrate the work of international business to support ethical international transactions.

The Sullivan Code

In 1977 Leon Sullivan, a Black minister from Philadelphia and a board member of General Motors, drafted a set of principles for investment and operation in South Africa by United States companies, which came to be known as 'the Sullivan Code'. The code was an attack on apartheid through the morality of American investors, corporate directors and managers. According to the code, Black workers in South Africa required equal pay, opportunity, facilities and respect. Unions were to be recognised and living conditions improved. The stability of the South African government, the cheapness of Black labour, the natural resources of the country and the expanding market for American products in a nation of 28 million people were powerful incentives for over 300 United States companies to operate there. Perhaps surprisingly, many United States firms voluntarily adopted the Sullivan Code, thereby lessening their profits but keeping their investors happy and their image at home clean. Critics argued that the code allowed apartheid to continue with sanitised American support. Eventually Sullivan agreed with the critics and set a deadline of 1987 for the removal of apartheid, just a few years before Nelson Mandela's release from prison. When that deadline passed, he vigorously opposed investment in South Africa, and many American firms either pulled out or sold off their interests to South African concerns. Lost products from American sources were replaced by those from other countries, but even so, there were important moral victories as a result of the code. Some firms, like Kodak, not only pulled out of South Africa but also refused to sell any of their products there. Hindsight has shown the Sullivan Code to have been more constructive as a challenge to injustice than its critics believed. Although limited, it added to the accumulation of world opinion and translated that opinion into action. Considering the way sanctions against Rhodesia were evaded, the Sullivan Code was a strategy that immediately did away with bottom-line justifications for breaches. The code required companies to take a cut in profits in South Africa. That was up-front.

The principles of the Caux Round Table

The Caux Round Table (CRT) evolved from a meeting of Japanese, American and European business leaders in the Swiss mountain retreat of Caux in 1986.[67] The meeting had been called by Frederik Philips, the Dutchman who rebuilt Philips Electrical Industries after the Second World War. Philips had had extensive contacts with Japan since 1950, and was concerned about growing anti-Japanese sentiment in the light of successful Japanese car and electronics exports to Europe and the United States. Japan's high-quality and low-priced exports had placed enormous pressure on European and American industries, and now the Japanese were accused of using protectionism, dumping, theft and blackmail to expand their international market share. Philips was concerned that these accusations would lead to trade wars, or worse, and contacted his Japanese friends to propose a meeting at Caux.

The first meeting was marked by frankness and openness, and these became the founding principles for the continuing forum. Jean-Loup Dherse, chair of the CRT steering committee, compares its meetings to chemical reactions 'in which the experience of being honest over real conflicting situations has allowed trust to develop to such an extent that there now is a common philosophy'.[68] From this beginning, an informal institution emerged. The informality arises from the friendships among the members of the group, who are senior executives from such major MNCs as Philips, Canon, Matsushita, Chase Manhattan Bank, Prudential Insurance, Mitsubishi, Toshiba, Proctor and Gamble, Nissan, Schock, Ambrosetti, Medtronic and Royal Dutch Petroleum. These are not, however, just social gatherings. The members meet twice yearly, once in Caux and once elsewhere, and sometimes invite guests. These meetings seek to advance the aims of the CRT.

A basic aim of the CRT is to encourage business to contribute to global economic and social development. Ryuzaburo Kaku, Chairman of Canon Inc. and a founder of the CRT, has focused its attention on the global responsibilities of business to foster world peace and economic stability. Hence, the CRT 'emphasises the development of continuing friendship, understanding and cooperation, based on a common respect for the highest moral values and on responsible action by individuals in their own spheres of influence'. Underlying this aspiration are two basic ethical principles: *kyosei*, a Japanese term coined by Kaku meaning 'working together for the common good', and respect for human dignity in the Kantian sense.

In 1994 the CRT published its 'Principles for Business' as 'a world standard against which business behaviour can be measured'. This is, in effect, the first international code of business ethics. The principles are not new, but the attitude of the CRT is distinctive. While publishing principles that they believe have global application, the members 'place their first emphasis on putting one's own house in order, and on seeking to establish what is right rather than who is right'. In other words, they have emphasised leadership by good example and responsibility, and have tried to avoid moralising. Corporations that want to grow ethically will put their own houses in order according to *kyosei*, rather than waiting to be regulated. (The 'Principles for Business' are set out in Appendix 3.)

The CRT identifies six sets of stakeholders — customers, employees, owners or investors, suppliers, competitors and communities — but seeks to move business beyond even these towards a new international perspective. This is in keeping with Kaku's vision of *kyosei* and the fullest conception of stakeholder responsibility in a global community. To respect these stakeholders and secure the place of business in the global economy, the CRT enjoins business to observe the principles of business ethics and 'to go well beyond the requirements of the law'.[69] The Caux principles set out the basic requirements of fairness, integrity, social responsibility, obligations to stakeholders, and observance of the law and human rights, which one would expect of a company operating under the rule of law in any country, and then applies them internationally. There is no blueprint for the future in the CRT principles. Their strength derives from the authority of those who devised and endorse them, and from their appeal to the moral sense of ethical business leaders.

Transparency International (TI)

TI was founded in 1993 and commenced its work against international corruption in 1994. It has chapters all around the world, including an active Australian chapter, which convened TI's first Asian regional meeting in 1995. It is best known for its annual *Corruption Perception Index* (CPI), which scores countries across a range of criteria. Based on a number of surveys, the CPI ranks countries according to the propensity of public officials to accept bribes. Although it has a strong focus on developing nations, TI's strongest criticisms are reserved for multi-national companies that indulge in corrupt practices that would be condemned at home, such as bribery. In the words of TI's Chairman, Peter Eigen, the index is 'a measure of lost development opportunities as an empirical link has now been established between the level of corruption and foreign direct investment. Every day the poor scores in the CPI are not being dealt with means more impoverishment, less education, less health care'.[70]

TI-Australia began in March 1995 to assist in the exposure of, and fight against, international business corruption in Australia. Among its corporate members are BHP and Telstra, two of Australia's largest companies. TI-Australia also enjoys the support of the accounting and legal professions, law enforcement agencies, academics, political leaders, non-government organisations and concerned citizens. TI has state councils in New South Wales and Victoria, and intends to establish councils in other states. In the first year of its existence, TI-Australia began implementing the mission statement of its parent organisation to forge alliances against corruption. It did so by convening, in association with TI-Philippines, TI's first regional meeting in Asia. This meeting attracted delegates from fourteen Asian countries, Europe and North America, who discussed how civil society might combat corruption.

Selected countries in Transparency International's *Corruption Perception Index* 2003

Rank	Country	Score out of 10
1	Finland	9.7 (evaluated best in terms of its public officials being unlikely to accept bribes)
2	Iceland	9.6
3	Denmark	9.5
	New Zealand	
5	Singapore	9.4
6	Sweden	9.3
7	Netherlands	8.9
8	Australia	8.8
	Norway	
	Switzerland	
11	Canada	8.7
	Luxembourg	
	United Kingdom	
14	Austria	8.0
	Hong Kong	
16	Germany	7.7
17	Belgium	7.6
18	Ireland	7.5
	USA	
20	Chile	7.4
21	Israel	7.0
	Japan	
23	France	6.9
	Spain	
25	Portugal	6.6
26	Oman	6.3

27	Bahrain	6.1
	Cyprus	
29	Slovenia	5.9
30	Botswana	5.7
	Taiwan	
35	Italy	5.3
	Kuwait	
37	Malaysia	5.2
	United Arab Emirates	
43	Cuba	4.6
46	Saudi Arabia	4.5
48	South Africa	4.4
50	Greece	4.3
	South Korea	
66	China	3.4
70	Thailand	3.3
86	Russia	2.7
92	Pakistan	2.5
100	Vietnam	2.4
122	Indonesia	1.9
132	Nigeria	1.4
133	Bangladesh	1.3

Since 1999, TI has also compiled a *Bribe Payers Index* (BPI). This is an index of the propensity of businesses in developed countries to offer bribes in order to gain or keep business in developing countries: '835 business experts in 15 leading emerging market countries were asked: In the business sectors with which you are most familiar, please indicate how likely companies from the following countries are to pay or offer bribes to win or retain business in this country? A perfect score, indicated zero perceived propensity to pay bribes, is 10.0.'[71]

Countries in Transparency International's *Bribe Payers Index* 2002

1	Australia	8.5 (evaluated as best in terms of businesses being least likely to offer bribes)
2	Sweden	8.4
	Switzerland	
4	Austria	8.2
5	Canada	8.1

6	Netherlands	7.8
	Belgium	
8	United Kingdom	6.9
9	Singapore	6.3
	Germany	
11	Spain	5.8
12	France	5.5
13	United States	5.3
	Japan	
15	Malaysia	4.3
	Hong Kong	
17	Italy	4.1
18	South Korea	3.9
19	Taiwan	3.8
20	People's Republic of China	3.5
21	Russia	3.2

The mission of Transparency International (TI) is to forge coalitions internationally; to combat corruption through law reform and anti-corruption policies; to build public support for anti-corruption measures; to promote transparency and accountability in public administration and international business; and to encourage all involved in international business to adhere to high standards of ethics, such as those proclaimed in TI's *Standards of Conduct*. The main instrument used to pursue this mission is the global building of coalitions of like-minded individuals and organisations. TI was heavily involved in the International Anti-Corruption Conference in Lima, Peru, in 1997 (the Chairman of TI, Peter Eigen, was secretary; New South Wales MP Peter Nagle was chairman) and the *Lima Declaration*, which issued from it.[72] TI sponsors conferences and studies, and publishes information about the costs of corruption in international business.

International norms of business conduct are very much like those that prevail at the domestic level: many who know of them observe them in the breach, many are cynical about the notion for self-interested reasons, and some have yet to make their acquaintance. Efforts to build a global business culture have begun and have the strong support of some of the largest MNCs, as well as a host of governments. But all of these efforts must be based on sound reasoning about the issues. That is what this chapter has tried to elicit.

Review questions

1   Is ethics a handicap to successful international business? Does the nature of international business mean that it must be? Is *this* the right way to look at it?
2   Does the distinction between primary and secondary values itself have any practical value in dealing with apparently different and conflicting ethical practices?

3   If we can speak of being 'tolerant' and even 'accepting' of some cultural and ethical differ-
    ences, can we also speak of a limit to such toleration and acceptance? Can we identify
    criteria for determining whether and where such lines should be drawn?

4   In Transparency International's *Corruption Perception Index* of 113 countries, roughly the
    bottom 50 per cent of the countries listed are poor countries. So, the poor countries are
    those in which public officials are most likely to take bribes. From this fact, should we
    conclude, 'Ethics is OK, but, really, it is a luxury that only the wealthy can afford'?

Conclusion

Business has a clear interest in minimising government regulation. It is therefore counter-productive for managers to take the position that if something is not illegal then it is not immoral. Such a position simply invites interest groups to lobby government to enact more legislation. Because the law cannot cover every wrong, businesses that persist in regarding only the letter of the law become the cause of ever more detailed regulation. Business as a whole becomes tangled in the red tape set to trap unethical practitioners.

It would be more practical and more responsible for business to devise strategies to reassure stakeholders that it is sensitive and responsive to ethical issues. In terms of general policy, this would mean:

- awareness of the importance of ethical conduct as an integral part of everyday business operations so that ethical implications become a normal part of decision-making
- recognition of a business's stakeholders and the need to listen to them
- awareness of the specific ethical responsibilities which are entailed in business operations
- promotion of an ethical culture within business organisations, including an enforceable code of conduct and attendant training; and policies and procedures for dealing with ethical problems and ethical failure
- recognition of the requirements, obligations, and benefits of being accountable to society for business operations
- active monitoring of the social and business environments to anticipate or respond to emerging ethical demands before they threaten the normal operations of the business
- regarding ethics not as a punishment or as correction, but as best practice.

If these responsibilities were embraced individually and collectively, not only would business be in a position to ask for less regulation, but it would also be well placed to advise government on appropriate and constructive legislation when it is needed. Such advice would carry more weight than self-interest and protection, and would be likely to find community support. In short, claims for self-regulation would be more successful if business could demonstrate that it was pro-active ethically.

These admonitions seem to us to be moderate. But, having said this, we wish to caution against ethical puritanism, a position that makes ethical purity itself the focus of activity, and that sees clearly and rigidly defined ethical results as the ultimate goal of human activities. Adoption of such an extreme, sweeping, and single-minded position causes sensible and workable proposals for ethical improvement to be dismissed as insignificant and as missing the point of the complete ethical transformation of society.[1] We are not urging that the pursuit of ethical excellence should itself be the aim of business. Business is not essentially about ethics but about business. Still, business can and should be conducted ethically. Neither do we contend that business can be altogether purged of unethical conduct. We are not attempting to provide a blueprint or a route to achieve such an idealistic end. Increased regulation and oversight or the adoption of the morally pure high ground in pursuit of some pre-defined plan about the place of business in society are not the task of business ethics. On the contrary, we believe that ethical consideration about matters of business and business conduct must allow for interplay between important values and principles, and the presence of liberty, which will always risk and sometimes damage those values and principles.

Freedom is the environment in which ethical conduct occurs. Ethical conduct is not a matter of conformity to some preset plan. It is more concerned with acceptable and desirable parameters of conduct. Ethics demands responsibility, and a sense of justice and compassion. There will always be ethical failures. There will always be conduct that pushes at the edges of toleration, and conduct that is far removed from altruism and even from goodwill. Being unrealistic and puritan about ethics will do more harm than good, cast ethics into a purely negative light, and invite a reaction of the order of 'ethics might be interesting, maybe even intriguing, as a pastime, but I've got a business to run and a real world to deal with'.

This brings us to our final point. If ethics offers nothing positive, then it will be of little interest to business. We have suggested from the outset that ethics is about excellence as well as failure. In the film 'Bill and Ted's Excellent Adventure', the motto of the eponymous heroes is to be excellent to each other. Excellence is the development of talents to the highest level possible, and inasmuch as work is one of humanity's primary modes of self-expression, the ethics of work should be less of a duty to produce than an invitation to excel. Being excellent is an ethical matter, not solely a matter of preference. Our whole lives, as well as the lives of others, ought to be enriched by the development of our excellences, and this is as much a matter of personal responsibility as performing one's duties or conforming to a code of conduct. Needless to say, such excellences will be deformed if they are achieved at the expense of others: we must also be excellent to other people. Central to such a notion is treating other people with respect, treating them as persons who have value in and of themselves, and not merely as instruments to be of use towards the achievement of other goals and values.

Ethics at both the personal and institutional level is, then, about ways of life that develop rather than deny or exploit human excellences. It is better to seek justice as a mode of business excellence than to succeed as a ruthless tycoon who seeks a gilded memory or a seat in heaven by philanthropy from the edge of the grave.

Appendix 1:
Ethical Decision-Making Models

An 'ethical decision-making model' is a suggested device for use in working through ethical problems and reaching a decision about a course of action in a structured and systematic way. In recent years, a great number of ethical decision-making models have been proposed, and various models have been officially adopted or endorsed by several professional and business organisations. A number of decision-making models are reproduced here for your consideration. These models are not provided as the only ways to go about dealing with ethical issues. Indeed, some people have expressed concern about the wisdom of using decision-making models at all. The concern has largely been that decision-making models can give the impression that ethical decision-making is an algorithmic and mechanical process when, in fact, it is usually much more complex and subtle than that. In addition, the fact of there being so many different decision-making models can give the impression that just any old decision procedure, involving any considerations, will do, as long as it can be represented as steps that can be followed in reaching a decision. Ethical decision-making models do, however, have the important characteristic of representing ethical deliberation as a systematic process, rather than simply as a 'touchy-feely' experience or as a matter of one's gut reaction to a situation. Ethical decision-making models emphasise that there is, in fact, deliberation associated with making ethical decisions — there is something to deliberate about, and the various contributing factors can be articulated and dealt with.

In considering the following proposed ethical decision-making models, you should give some thought to the appearance of common elements in some or most of them (for instance, they almost all include a 'light of day' test, a suggestion that you imagine how you would feel if the proposed action came to be widely known). You should also give some thought to whether any of the steps or elements in these models seems to be particularly insightful, potentially fruitful or helpful in dealing with ethical matters systematically. You will notice that all the models allow for what was earlier referred to as 'ethical pluralism'; none of them is couched in terms of a purported correct moral theory.

1 The American Accounting Association model: seven steps

In 1990, the American Accounting Association (AAA) published a casebook, *Ethics in the Accounting Curriculum: Cases and Readings*. These cases illustrate ethical issues that accountants may encounter in the context of their professional activities. Each case is analysed using a seven-step decision-making model.[1]

1 Determine the facts — What, who, where, when, how.
   What do we know or need to know, if possible, that will help define the problem?
2 Define the ethical issue.
   a List the significant stakeholders.
   b Define the ethical issues.
   Make sure you know precisely what the ethical issue is — e.g., conflict involving rights, question over limits of an obligation, etc.
3 Identify major principles, rules, values — e.g., integrity, quality, respect for persons, profit.
4 Specify the alternatives.
   List the major alternative courses of action, including those that represent some form of compromise or point between simply doing or not doing something.
5 Compare values and alternatives. See if a clear decision is evident.
   Determine if there is one principle or value, or combination, which is so compelling that the proper alternative is clear — e.g., correcting a defect that is almost certain to cause loss of life.
6 Assess the consequences.
   Identify short and long, positive and negative consequences for the major alternatives. The common short run focus on gain or loss needs to be measured against long run considerations. This step will often reveal an unanticipated result of major importance.
7 Make your decision.
   Balance the consequences against your primary principles or values and select the alternative that best fits.

2 The Laura Nash model: twelve questions[2]

Nash wants to make decision-making more practical, rather than relying on abstract philosophical concepts.

1 Have you defined the problem accurately?
   Gain precise facts and many of them.
2 How would you define the problem if you stood on the other side of the fence?
   Consider how others perceive it; alternatives?
3 How did this situation occur in the first place?
   Consider the history, problem or symptoms.
4 To whom and what do you give your loyalties as a person and as a member of the corporation?
   Private duty *v* corporate policy or norms.
5 What is your intention in making this decision?
   Can you take pride in your action?

6   How does this intention compare with the likely results?
     Are results harmful even with good intentions?
7   Whom could your decision or action injure?
     A good thing resulting in a bad end? Wanted A; got B.
8   Can you engage the affected parties in a discussion of the problem before you make
     your decision?
     Example: talk to workers before closing the plant.
9   Are you confident that your position will be valid over a long period of time as it
     seems now?
     Look at long-term consequences.
10   Could you disclose without qualm your decision or action to your boss, your CEO, the
     board of directors, your family or society as a whole?
     Would you feel comfortable with this on TV?
11   What is the symbolic potential of your action if understood? If misunderstood?
     Sincerity and the perceptions of others.
12   Under what conditions would you allow exceptions to your stand?
     Speeding to a hospital with a heart attack victim.

3 The Michael Rion model: six questions[3]

1   Why is this bothering me?
     • Is it really an issue? Am I genuinely perplexed, or am I afraid to do what I know
       is right?
2   Who else matters?
     • Who are the stakeholders who may be affected by my decisions?
3   Is it my problem?
     • Have I caused the problem or has someone else? How far should I go in resolving
       the issue?
4   What is the ethical concern?
     • Legal obligation, fairness, promise-keeping, honesty, doing good, avoiding harm?
5   What do others think?
     • Can I learn from those who disagree with my judgment?
6   Am I being true to myself?
     • What kind of person or company would do what I am contemplating? Could I
       share my decision 'in good conscience' with my family? with colleagues? with public
       officials?

4 Mary Guy: values, rules and a decision-making model[4]

Before offering a decision-making model, Guy suggests that one might keep 'ten core
values' in mind: 'By evaluating how these values relate to an issue under consideration, and
by analyzing who the stakeholders are in the decision, the ethical implications of an action
become clearer'.

Caring — treating people as ends in themselves, not as means to ends. This means having
    compassion, treating people courteously and with dignity, helping those in need, and
    avoiding harm to others.

Honesty — being truthful and not deceiving or distorting. One by one, deceptions undermine the capacity for open exchange and erode credibility.

Accountability — accepting the consequences of one's actions and accepting the responsibility for one's decisions and their consequences. This means setting an example for others and avoiding even the appearance of impropriety. Asking such questions as 'How would this be interpreted if it appeared in the newspaper?' or 'What sort of person would do such a thing?' brings accountability dilemmas into focus.

Promise keeping — keeping one's commitments. The obligation to keep promises is among the most important of generally accepted obligations. To be worthy of trust, one must keep one's promises and fulfil one's commitments.

Pursuit of excellence — striving to be as good as one can be. It means being diligent, industrious, and committed; and become well informed and well prepared. Results are important, but so is the manner and the method of achievement.

Loyalty — being faithful and loyal to those with whom one has dealings. This involves safeguarding the ability to make independent professional judgments by scrupulously avoiding undue influence and conflicts of interest.

Fairness — being open-minded, willing to admit error, and not overreaching or taking undue advantage of another's adversities. Avoiding arbitrary or capricious favouritism; treating people equally and making decisions based on notions of justice.

Integrity — using independent judgment and avoiding conflicts of interest, restraining from self-aggrandisement, and resisting economic pressure; being faithful to one's deepest beliefs, acting on one's conviction, and not adopting an end-justifies-the-means philosophy that ignores principle.

Respect for others — recognising each person's right to privacy and self-determination and having respect for human dignity. This involves being courteous, prompt, and decent, and providing others with information that they need to make informed decisions.

Responsible citizenship — having one's actions in accord with societal values. Appropriate standards for the exercise of discretion must be practiced.

Guy also suggests five rules, which integrate these values, and which might be of assistance in codifying one's ethical decision-making:

Rule 1 Consider the well-being of others, including nonparticipants. This rule emphasises caring and respect for others.

Rule 2 Think as a member of the community, not as an isolated individual. This emphasises loyalty, integrity, respect for others, and responsible citizenship.

Rule 3 Obey, but do not depend solely on the law. This emphasises integrity and responsible citizenship.

Rule 4 Ask, 'What sort of person would do such a thing?' This emphasises all the values by calling each into question.

Rule 5 Respect the customs of others, but not at the expense of your own ethics. This emphasises accountability, fairness, integrity, and respect for others.

Guy's decision-making model:

1 Define the problem.
   Isolate the key factors in question and diagnose the situation to define the basic problem and to identify the limits of the situation. This step is critical, because it prevents solving the wrong problem.

2   Identify the goal to be achieved.

If you do not know where you are going, you will never know when you get there. For this reason, it is essential that a goal is clearly declared.

3   List all possible solutions to the problem.

All alternatives that will address the problem and achieve the goal are placed under consideration.

4   Evaluate each alternative to determine which one best meets the requirements of the situation.

This requires a thorough analysis of each alternative. The analysis involves measuring the benefits, costs, and risks of each, as well as identifying the likely intended and unintended consequences of each. This step provides information about the utility of each alternative in terms of the efficiency with which it maximises desired values and still achieves the goal.

5   Identify the one course of action that is most likely to produce the desired consequences within the constraints of the situation.

This requires selecting the alternative that maximises the most important values and holds the most promise of achieving the goal, while solving the problem as effectively as possible.

6   Make a commitment to the choice and implement it.

This requires converting the decision into action.

Guy further suggests that a slightly larger, ten-step, model is more appropriate for complex problems:

1   Define the problem.
2   Identify the goal to be achieved.
3   Specify all dimensions of the problem.
4   List all possible solutions to each dimension.
5   Evaluate alternative solutions to each dimension regarding the likelihood of each to maximise the important values at stake.
6   Eliminate alternatives that are too costly, not feasible, or maximise the wrong values when combined with solutions to other dimensions.
7   Rank the alternatives to each dimension according to which are most likely to maximise the most important values.
8   Select the alternative to each dimension that is most likely to work in the context of the problem while maximising the important values at stake.
9   Combine the top ranking alternatives for each dimension of the problem in order to develop a solution to the problem as a whole.
10 Make a commitment to the choice and implement it.

5 The Kent Hodgson model: the three-step process[5]

1   Examine the situation.
   •   Get the critical facts.

What does the situation look like? What has happened? What are the circumstances involved?

- Identify the key stakeholders.

Who are the significant players? Include all the key stakeholders significantly affected by the situation and by any decisions you might make.

- Identify each stakeholder's options (what each stakeholder wants done).

State the options for action that represent each stakeholder's interest. Put yourself in the stakeholders' shoes and think from their point of view. This is not the time to make final judgments or slant stakeholder options from your own perspective.

2   Establish the dilemma.

- Identify the working principles and norms that drive each option (why each stake-holder wants it done).

Pinpoint, as best you can, the business reasons for each option. Why is this stakeholder in favour of this option for action? The answers show you what the stakeholders' value and the working principles that flow from those values.

- Project the possible outcomes (consequences) of each stakeholder option.

Do any violate your principles, or those of your organisation? What will each stake-holder option cause to happen? You are trying to discover what the stakeholder wants to have happen in this situation. Then ask, 'Do any of the outcomes resulting from these options violate my principles, or those of my organisation?'

- Determine the actions (means) necessary to produce each outcome.

Do any violate your principles, or those of your organisation? What will stakeholders have to do to get the result they want? What steps will they take to make their desired options happen? Then ask, 'Do any of the actions they will take to make their options happen (means to the end) violate my principles, or those of my organisation?'.

- State the dilemma.

Through the activities completed, you know the stakeholders, the options they repre-sent, the validity of the working principles behind their options, and the validity of the means to implement their options. You are now in a position to decide if what you are facing is a true dilemma (balanced opposite interests). You are now able to state, even write down, the dilemma exactly.

3   Evaluate the options.

- Identify the General Principle(s) behind each stakeholder option

Is the option driven primarily by dignity of human life, autonomy, honesty, loyalty, fairness, humaneness, or the common good (the 'magnificent seven')? The answer is not automatic or expedient; rather, it is a matter of honest judgment on your part.

- Compare the General Principle(s) behind each option.

Which is the most responsible General Principle(s) in this situation? In your mind, in this situation, which of the 'magnificent seven' holds top priority as an ethical reason for this or that option? The object is to choose an option for action that represents the most responsible General Principle (or Principles) for you, now, in this situation.

- The option with the most responsible General Principle(s) is your choice for action.

Your decision is not a guess, a choice from ignorance, or a choice from expediency. It is choice for action derived from principles. And it is a decision that is defensible on the grounds of principle and an attitude of cooperative responsibility.

6 The Cottell and Perlin model: five steps[6]

1   Describe all the relevant facts in the case. Be certain to note any assumptions not directly presented in the case.
2   Describe the ethical and legal perspectives and responsibilities of the parties. Try to distinguish between legal and ethical responsibilities. Take note of potential value conflicts among participants in the case.
3   State the principal value conflicts in the case.
4   Determine possible courses of action. Note both short- and long-term consequences. Describe the principles affirmed or abridged in projected courses of action. Distinguish utilitarian (consequences) from deontological (principles) justifications in each case. Would ethical realism as it exists in the accounting profession assist in resolving the dilemma?
    ['Ethical realism' is an important notion for Cottell and Perlin. Basically, it means trying to consider what the leaders in the profession would think is right or wrong. This relies on the premise that 'the leadership has an ethical insight'. By 'leaders', they mean the 'intellectual authorities … the big guns. Each of us can name the national leaders in the profession. They are the managing partners of large firms, the heads of professional bodies, the members of standard-setting boards. In short, they are the men and women who have risen up through the ranks to positions of respect'.]
5   Choose and defend a decision. State why one value (or set of values) was chosen over another in the case. Discuss the result of such a choice for participants in the case, for the accounting profession, and for society in general.

7 David Mathison: the synthesis model[7]

First, understand three foundational concepts:

Obligations — restrictions on behaviour, things one must do or must avoid. E.g., business relationships, fidelity in contracts, gratitude, justice.

Ideals — notions of excellence, the goal of which is to bring greater harmony to self and others. E.g., concepts as profit, productivity, quality, stability, tolerance, and compassion all fit here.

Effects — the intended or unintended consequences of a decision. E.g., oil rigs on the high seas, a spillage.

This requires a three-step process:

1   Identify the important issues involved in the case using obligations, ideals, or effects as a starting point. The goal here is to expand one's view.
2   Decide where the main emphasis or focus should lie among the five or so issues generated in Step 1. Which is the major thrust of the case? Is it a certain obligation, ideal, or effect? E.g., it may be a choice of remaining silent about a wing design defect with the effect of people dying in a plane accident versus going to the media with the effect of damaging a plane manufacturer's credibility on a personal 'hunch'.
3   With the well-focused issue worked out in Step 1, now you apply the 'Basic Decision Rules':
    a   When two or more obligations conflict, choose the more important one.
    b   When two or more ideals conflict, or when ideals conflict with obligations, choose the action which honours the higher ideal.

c   When the effects are mixed, choose the action which produces the greatest good or lesser harm. E.g., in the case of the questioning engineer, clearly saving human lives is the greater good over saving a manufacturer's image.

8   Anthony M. Pagano: six tests[8]

Pagano proposes six tests, rather than outlining a particular approach or model. His idea is that these tests can provide useful insights into the ethical perspective of a proposed action:

1   Is it legal?
    This is the core starting point.
2   The benefit–cost test.
    This is the utilitarian perspective.
3   The generalisation test.
    Do you want this action to be a universal standard? If it's good for the goose, it's good for the gander.
4   The light of day test.
    What if it appeared on TV? Would you be proud?
5   Do unto others — The Golden Rule test.
    Do you want the same thing to happen to you?
6   Ventilation test.
    Get a second opinion from a wise friend with no investment in the outcome.

Appendix 2: AANA Advertiser Code of Ethics[1]

Advertiser Code of Ethics

This Code has been adopted by AANA to be applied as a means of advertising self-regulation in Australia and is intended to be applied to 'advertisements' as defined in this code.

The object of this Code is to ensure that advertisements are legal, decent, honest and truthful and that they have been prepared with a sense of obligation to the consumer and society and fair sense of responsibility to competitors.

In this Code, the term 'advertisement' shall mean matter which is published or broadcast, other than via internet, direct mail, point of sale or direct distribution to individuals, in all of Australia or in a substantial section of Australia for payment or other valuable consideration and which draws the attention of the public, or a segment of it, to a product, service, person, organisation or line of conduct in a manner calculated to promote or oppose directly or indirectly that project, service, person, organisation or line of conduct.

1. Section 1

1.1 Advertisements shall comply with Commonwealth law and the law of the relevant State or Territory.

1.2 Advertisements shall not be misleading or deceptive or be likely to mislead or deceive.

1.3 Advertisements shall not contain a misrepresentation that is likely to cause damage to the business or goodwill of a competitor.

1.4 Advertisements shall not exploit community concerns in relation to protecting the environment by presenting or portraying distinctions in products or services advertised in a misleading way or in a way that implies a benefit to the environment that the product or services do not have.

1.5 Advertisements shall not make claims about the Australian origin or content of products advertised in a manner that is misleading.

2. Section 2

2.1 Advertisements shall not portray people in a way that discriminates against or vilifies a person or section of the community on account of race, ethnicity, nationality, sex, age, sexual preference, religion, disability or political belief.

2.2 Advertisements shall not present or portray violence unless it is justifiable in the context of the product or service advertised.

2.3 Advertisements shall treat sex, sexuality and nudity with sensitivity to the relevant audience and, where appropriate, the relevant program time zone.

2.4 Advertisements which, having regard to the theme, visuals and language used, are directed primarily to children aged 14 years or younger and are for goods, services and facilities which are targeted toward and have principal appeal to children, shall comply [sic] with the AANA's *Code of Advertising to Children* and section 2.6 of this Code shall not apply to advertisements to which AANA's *Code of Advertising to Children* applies.

2.5 Advertisements shall only use language that is appropriate in the circumstances and strong or obscene language shall be avoided.

2.6 Advertisements shall not depict material contrary to prevailing community standards on health and safety.

2.7 Advertisements for motor vehicles shall comply with the Federal chamber of Automotive Industries Code of Practice relating to Advertising for Motor Vehicles and section 2.6 of this Code shall not apply to advertisements to which the Federal Chamber of Automotive Industries Code of Practice applies.

Appendix 3: The Caux Round Table Principles for Business[1]

Principle 1

The Responsibilities of Businesses: Beyond Shareholders toward Stakeholders

The value of a business to society is the wealth and employment it creates and the marketable products and services it provides to consumers at a reasonable price commensurate with quality. To create such value, a business must maintain its own economic health and viability, but survival is not a sufficient goal.

Businesses have a role to play in improving the lives of all their customers, employees, and shareholders by sharing with them the wealth they have created. Suppliers and competitors as well should expect businesses to honor their obligations in a spirit of honesty and fairness. As responsible citizens of the local, national, regional and global communities in which they operate, businesses share a part in shaping the future of those communities.

Principle 2

The Economic and Social Impact of Business: Toward Innovation, Justice and World Community

Businesses established in foreign countries to develop, produce or sell should also contribute to the social advancement of those countries by creating productive employment and helping to raise the purchasing power of their citizens. Businesses also should contribute to human rights, education, welfare, and vitalisation of the countries in which they operate.

Businesses should contribute to economic and social development not only in the countries in which they operate, but also in the world community at large, through effective and prudent use of resources, free and fair competition, and emphasis upon innovation in technology, production methods, marketing and communications.

Principle 3

Business Behavior: Beyond the Letter of Law Toward a Spirit of Trust

While accepting the legitimacy of trade secrets, businesses should recognise that sincerity, candor, truthfulness, the keeping of promises, and transparency contribute not only to their own credibility and stability but also to the smoothness and efficiency of business transactions, particularly on the international level.

Principle 4

Respect for Rules

To avoid trade frictions and to promote freer trade, equal conditions for competition, and fair and equitable treatment for all participants, businesses should respect international and domestic rules. In addition, they should recognise that some behavior, although legal, may still have adverse consequences.

Principle 5

Support for Multilateral Trade

Businesses should support the multilateral trade systems of the GATT/World Trade Organization and similar international agreements. They should cooperate in efforts to promote the progressive and judicious liberalisation of trade and to relax those domestic measures that unreasonably hinder global commerce, while giving due respect to national policy objectives.

Principle 6

Respect for the Environment

A business should protect and, where possible, improve the environment, promote sustainable development, and prevent the wasteful use of natural resources.

Principle 7

Avoidance of Illicit Operations

A business should not participate in or condone bribery, money laundering, or other corrupt practices: indeed, it should seek cooperation with others to eliminate them. It should not trade in arms or other materials used for terrorist activities, drug traffic or other organised crime.

Notes

Introduction

1 Richard De George, *Business Ethics*, 3rd edn (New York: Macmillan, 1990), pp. 3–5.
2 Ross Gittens, 'The best practice is to accentuate the positive', *Sydney Morning Herald*, 25 April 1994, p. 21.
3 Stephen Cohen, *Moral Reasoning: The Framework and Activities of Ethical Deliberation, Argument and Decision-Making* (Melbourne: Oxford University Press, 2004).

1 Ethical Reasoning in Business

1 Aristotle, *The Ethics of Aristotle*, trans. J. A. K. Thomson et al. (Harmondsworth: Penguin Books, 1976), pp. 64–5.
2 James Rachels, *The Elements of Moral Philosophy*, 2nd edn (New York: McGraw-Hill, 1993), p. 13.
3 Lawrence M. Hinman, *Ethics: A Pluralistic Approach to Moral Theory* (Orlando, Florida: Harcourt Brace Jovanovich, 1994), p. 4.
4 Peter Singer (ed.), *Ethics* (New York: Oxford University Press, 1994), pp. 4, 10.
5 Peter Singer, *Practical Ethics*, 2nd edn (New York: Cambridge University Press, 1993), pp. 10, 12.
6 *New York Times*, 23 September 1969, p. 34.
7 Albert Jonsen & Stephen Toulmin, *The Abuse of Casuistry* (Berkeley: University of California Press, 1988).
8 John Rawls, *A Theory of Justice* (Cambridge, Mass.: Harvard University Press, 1971).
9 Roger P. Ebertz, 'Is reflective equilibrium a coherentist model?', *Canadian Journal of Philosophy*, 23, 1993, p. 194.
10 J. S. Mill, *Utilitarianism* (Indianapolis: Bobbs-Merrill, 1957), p. 22.
11 Deontological theories of ethics have been invigorated in two very different theories by philosophers John Rawls and Robert Nozick. Although they argue for radically differing views concerning the role of government in a just society, both take a strong position on respect for persons as a matter which is independent of concern for consequences. See Rawls's *A Theory of Justice* and Nozick's *Anarchy, State and Utopia* (New York: Basic Books, 1974).
12 Immanuel Kant, *Foundations of the Metaphysics of Morals*, trans. L. W. Beck (New York: Macmillan, 1990).
13 ibid., p. 38.
14 ibid., p. 46.
15 Depending on how they are counted, Kant offers five or six formulations of the categorical imperative.
16 Adam Smith, *The Theory of Moral Sentiments* (Indianapolis: Liberty Press, 1982). See also E. W. Coker, 'Adam Smith's concept of the social system', *Journal of Business Ethics*, 9, 1990, pp. 139–42.

17   William Frankena, *Ethics*, 2nd edn (Englewood Cliffs, NJ: Prentice-Hall, 1973), p. 47.

18   See Edmund L. Pincoffs, *Quandaries and Virtues* (Lawrence, Kansas: University of Kansas Press, 1986).

19   Mill, p. 30.

20   This is discussed more in Stephen Cohen, *The Nature of Moral Reasoning*, pp. 84–7.

21   Cicero, *De officiis*, trans. Walter Miller (Cambridge, Mass. & London: Loeb edn, 1913), vol. 3, pp. 99–101.

22   For a recent and accessible presentation of a variety of positions concerning relativism, see *Social Philosophy and Policy*, 11, no. 1, 1994.

23   Marcus G. Singer, *Generalization in Ethics* (New York: Russell & Russell, 1971), pp. 327–34; John Finnis, *Natural Law and Natural Rights* (Oxford: Clarendon Press, 1980), pp. 81–5.

24   Although at this point a very important question can sometimes be asked concerning whether and why such-and-such convention is itself worthy of respect. It is not worthy of respect just because it is a group's convention.

25   Royal Commission into Productivity in the Building Industry in New South Wales, *Reports of Hearings* (Sydney: Government of New South Wales, 1992).

26   Walt W. Manley II & William A. Shrode, *Critical Issues in Business Conduct* (New York: Quorum Books, 1990), ch. 14.

27   Adam Smith, *An Enquiry into the Nature and Causes of the Wealth of Nations* (New York: Modern Library, 1937). See, for example, p. 423.

28   Cicero, vol. 3, p. xiii.

29   Peter Drucker, 'What is "business ethics"?', *Public Interest*, 63, 1981, pp. 18–36.

30   Milton Friedman, 'The social responsibility of business is to increase its profits', *New York Times Magazine*, 13 September 1970, reprinted in T. Donaldson & P. Werhane (eds), *Ethical Issues in Business: A Philosophical Approach*, 2nd edn (Englewood Cliffs, NJ: Prentice Hall, 1983), pp. 239–42.

31   Jonathan Dancy, *Moral Reasons* (Oxford: Blackwell, 1993), p. 211.

32   See, for instance Lawrence Hinman, *Ethics: A Pluralistic Approach to Moral Theory*, 3rd edition (Belmont, California: Wadsworth/Thompson, 2003). Hinman also maintains a website that includes references to and discussions about moral pluralism. http://ethics.acusd.edu/, and, in particular, http://ethics.acusd.edu/theories/Pluralism/index.html

33   Geoffrey Barker, 'Ethics: the glove that tempers the iron fist', *Australian Financial Review Magazine*, 7 July 1995, pp. 14–20.

34   Much of the following discussion of 'good ethics is good business' is revised from Stephen Cohen, 'Good Ethics is Good Business – Revisited', *Business and Professional Ethics Journal* (18) 2, (1999), pp. 57–68.

35   Barker, particularly p. 20.

36   Paul Simons, Chairman of Woolworths Ltd, is in this camp. See, for instance, Paul Simons, 'Be interested in the people you serve and your life will be happy', Fourth Annual Lecture, St James Ethics Centre, Sydney, November 1994.

37   We realise that, strictly speaking, an enhanced bottom line is not identical to, and is sometimes not a good indicator of, enhanced self-interest. For convenience here, however, we will use the expressions as though they are equivalent.

38   Thomas Hobbes (1588–1679) argued in *Leviathan* (1651) that ethics is founded on self-interest, which provides the sole motivation for behaving ethically.

39   Padraic P. McGuinness is one who holds this view. See his 'Elusive ethics', *Sydney Morning Herald*, 17 November 1994, p. 20.

40   Kant argued in *Foundations of the Metaphysics of Morals* (1785) that the nature of ethics is such that it necessarily involves a conflict with self-interest.

41   Simons, 'Be interested in the people you serve and your life will be happy'.

42   In New South Wales, Australia, this statutory body extends over the public sector. The authority of the ICAC in Hong Kong extends over the private sector, as well as the public sector.

43   We will return to this example again, and in greater detail, in chapter 9.

44   The Body Shop is also a good example of how it is that when you trumpet your virtues, you can get very severely criticised for not living up to them.

45   *Australian Financial Review Magazine*, 7 July 1995, p. 16.

46   This has also been discussed on pp. xi–xv and will be discussed again at pp. 51–5 under the heading 'Good ethics is good business — again'.

47   St Thomas Aquinas (1224–74). Questions 90–97 of his *Summa Theologica* are referred to as the *Treatise on Law*. In the *Treatise on Law*, Aquinas argues that, although one should focus on advancing the common good for its own sake (an ethical requirement), it is nevertheless the case that if one were trying to further one's own interest, the best way to do it would be to focus on trying to advance the common good, rather than by trying directly to advance one's own interest.

48   We will refer to these features more systematically later on in this chapter, particularly in the section entitled 'Defining ethics'. There is nothing unusual or peculiar about nominating these features as formal characteristics of an ethical opinion. See, for example, James Rachels, *The Elements of Moral Philosophy*, 2nd edn (New York: McGraw-Hill, 1993), p. 13; Lawrence M. Hinman, *Ethics: A Pluralistic Approach to Moral Theory* (Orlando, Florida: Harcourt Brace Jovanovich, 1994), p. 4; Peter Singer (ed.), Ethics (New York: Oxford University Press, 1994), pp. 4, 10; Peter Singer, *Practical Ethics*, 2nd edn (New York: Cambridge University Press, 1993), pp. 10, 12.

49   Ethical egoism is a view according to which the proper gauge for judging an action to be morally right is that it advances one's own interest: actions are right if they benefit *numero uno*. Psychological egoism is a view about how people do, in fact, behave, and what they take into account. According to psychological egoism people care most about themselves. Ethical egoism, but not psychological egoism, is a normative view, a view about how people should behave.

50   Milton Friedman offers this view in a number of publications, such as 'The social responsibility of business is to increase its profits', *New York Times Magazine*, 13 September 1970, reprinted in T. Donaldson & P. Werhane (eds), *Ethical Issues in Business: A Philosophical Approach*, 2nd edn (Englewood Cliffs, NJ: Prentice-Hall, 1983), pp. 239–42; *Capitalism and Freedom* (Chicago: University of Chicago Press, 1962).

51   For a brief and clear discussion of egoism and self-interest, see Rachels, chapters 5 and 6.

52   *Business Review Weekly*, 23, no. 4, 1993, p. 39.

53   In 1995, the Australian Securities Commission warned about approaches from Country Estate to shareholders in Bridgestone Australia to buy their shares: 'The ASC is concerned that the information set out by Country Estate & Agency could cause Bridgestone shareholders to suffer substantial losses'; 'Warning over Country Estate', *Age*, 17 June 1995, p. 17.

2   Dirty Hands

1   Albert Z. Carr, 'Is business bluffing ethical?', *Harvard Business Review*, January– February 1968.

2   Milton Friedman, *Capitalism and Freedom* (Chicago: University of Chicago Press, 1962).

3   T. J. Peters & R. H. Waterman, *In Search of Excellence* (Sydney: Harper & Row, 1984).

4   ibid., p. 39.

5   J. Ladd, 'Morality and the ideal of rationality in formal organisations', *Monist*, 54, 1970, pp. 488–516.

6   ibid., p. 50.

7   Peter Heckman, 'Business and games', *Journal of Business Ethics*, 11, 1992, pp. 933–8.

8   As quoted in Timothy Blodgett, 'Showdown on "business bluffing"', *Harvard Business Review*, May–June 1968, pp. 162–70.

9   ibid.

10   ibid.

11   Thomas Nagel, 'Ruthless in public life', in Stuart Hampshire (ed.), *Public and Private Morality* (New York: Cambridge University Press, 1978), pp. 75–92.

12   See Blodgett, pp. 168–70.

13   ibid., p. 169.

14   Lord Patrick Devlin, 'Morals and the Criminal Law', originally published in 1959. The essay has been reprinted in a number of places. We have cited it from Richard A. Wasserstrom, *Morality and the Criminal Law* (Belmont, Calif.: Wadsworth, 1971), pp. 24–48, at p. 46.

15   H. L. A. Hart, 'Immorality and treason', first presented as a British radio broadcast on the BBC in 1959, then published in the *Listener*, 62, 30 July 1959, pp. 162–3. Reprinted in Wasserstrom, pp. 49–54. Professor Hart explores this issue more fully in his book *Law, Liberty, and Morality* (London: Oxford University Press, 1963).

16   Gerald Dworkin, 'Lord Devlin and the enforcement of morals', *Yale Law Journal*, 75, 1966, pp. 986–1005.

17 In this connection see the sensible and timely argument of Max Charlesworth, 'Ethical reflection and business practice', in C. A. J. Coady & C. J. G. Sampford (eds), *Business, Ethics and the Law*, (Sydney: Federation Press, 1993), pp. 187–205.

18 Sir Adrian Cadbury, 'Ethical managers make their own rules', *Harvard Business Review*, September–October 1987, reprinted in F. K. Kellar (ed.), *Ethical Insight, Ethical Action* (Washington: ICMA, 1988), pp. 51–8. Sir Adrian's whole essay can be read as a discussion of the problem of dirty hands.

19 Bernard Williams, 'Politics and moral character', in Stuart Hampshire (ed.), *Public and Private Morality* (New York: Cambridge University Press, 1978), pp. 55–74.

20 ibid., p. 63.

21 Thomas More, *Utopia*, ed. G. Logan & R. M. Adams (Cambridge: Cambridge University Press, 1989), p. 36.

22 Raimond Gaita, *Good and Evil: An Absolute Conception* (London: Macmillan, 1991), pp. 72–3.

23 See, for example, Williams' 'Politics and Moral Character' in S. Hampshire (ed.) *Public and Private Morality* (New York: Cambridge University Press, 1978) and also in the same volume, Thomas Nagel, 'Ruthlessness in Public Life', pp. 75–92. See also Alan Donagan, *The Theory of Morality* (Chicago: University of Chicago Press, 1979), pp. 180–8, and Damian Grace and Stephen Cohen, *Business Ethics: Australian Problems and Cases*, 2nd edition (Sydney: Oxford University Press, 1998), chap. 2, pp. 37–56.

24 This example is quite like one offered by Bernard Williams in presenting a critique of utilitarianism: 'A critique of utilitarianism', in J. J. C. Smart & Bernard Williams, *Utilitarianism: For and Against* (London: Cambridge University Press, 1973), pp. 98–9, but that is not the point here.

25 See, for example, Julian Disney et al., *Lawyers*, 2nd edn (Sydney: Law Book Company, 1986), pp. 660–5.

26 There have been recent changes to the specific requirements of this client privilege. For the point here, however, it does not matter.

27 This is a case in which we are using 'ethical' and 'moral' to mean different things. 'Ethical' here has a narrow meaning, referring only to that which is required by the code of ethics of the profession.

28 See, for example, Williams, 'Politics and moral character'.

29 'Blame shared in Bond case: Lucas', *Sydney Morning Herald*, 20 April 1992, p. 22.

3 Stakeholders

1 Norman Bowie & Ronald Duska, *Business Ethics*, 2nd edn (Englewood Cliffs, NJ: Prentice Hall, 1990), p. 40. For a history of the concept and its background, see R. Edward Freeman, *Strategic Management: A Stakeholder Approach* (Boston: Pitman, 1984), ch. 2.

2 Dennis Pratt, *Aspiring to Greatness* (Sydney: Business & Professional Publishing, 1994), p. 58 (our emphasis), and more generally, ch. 1.

3 Freeman, p. vi (our emphasis).

4 James E. Liebig, *Business Ethics: Profiles in Civic Virtue* (Golden, Colo.: Fulcrum, 1990), p. 217.

5 Kenneth Goodpaster, 'Business ethics and stakeholder analysis', *Business Ethics Quarterly*, 1, 1991, pp. 53–71.

6 Perhaps this is not a good thing to do. Perhaps it could never be justified. Nevertheless, if it were the case, there would be no point in taking further account of the group whose interests were to be sacrificed. Nothing more could be learned about that group.

7 Robert Nozick, *Anarchy, State and Utopia* (Oxford: Blackwell, 1974), ch. 7.

8 Richard Titmuss, *Social Policy: An Introduction*, ed. Brian Abel-Smith & Kay Titmuss (London: Allen & Unwin, 1974), pp. 137ff.

9 Information about this case is taken from Paul Barry, *The Rise and Fall of Alan Bond* (Sydney: Bantam, 1990), ch. 15.

10 ibid., p. 171.

11 Tony Grant-Taylor, 'Greyhound hardly shareholder's best friend', *Sydney Morning Herald*, 25 March 1994, pp. 21 and 25.

12 Brad Norrington, 'Unions against job-saving deal', *Sydney Morning Herald*, 12 December 1990, p. 3; 'SPC to go ahead with wage cutting plan at cannery', *Australian Financial Review*, 14 December 1990, p. 5; Mark Davis, 'SPC row: workers paying for company's strategy', *Australian Financial Review*, 17 December 1990, p. 5; Mark Davis, 'SPC meeting on wages', *Australian Financial Review*,

19 December 1990, p. 4; Mark Davis, 'Furphies ripe for canning in SPC deal', *Australian Financial Review*, 29 December 1990, p. 11; Sue Neales, 'High stakes as SPC treads in union preserve', *Australian Financial Review*, 2 January 1991, p. 6; Mark Skulley, 'SPC agrees to compromise pay cut deal', *Sydney Morning Herald*, 3 January 1991, p. 4; Mark Davis, 'SPC deal cuts costs, leaves award intact', *Australian Financial Review*, 3 January 1991, p. 1; Mark Davis, 'SPC workforce agrees', *Australian Financial Review*, 4 January 1991, p. 5; Mark Davis, 'Enterprise bargaining masters at the cannery', *Australian Financial Review*, 4 January 1991, p. 4.

13   *Sydney Morning Herald*, 3 October 1992, pp. 41 and 44.

14   Dollar *Sweets Pty Ltd v. Federated Confectioners Association of Australia and Others* (1986), VR, 383.

15   ibid., Murphy J., at 386–7 and 388.

16   Malcolm Brown, 'Study lists dangerous injuries', *Sydney Morning Herald*, 24 March 1993, p. 4.

17   *Weekend Australian*, 12–13 March 1994, p. 58.

18   ibid.

19   Cited in Bowie & Duska, p. 90.

20   The information for this case is drawn from 'Mistral's ill wind', *Choice*, April 1992, pp. 7–11.

4   Ethics in the Marketplace: Generosity, Competition and Fairness

1   This distinction mirrors that made by Tönnies in 1887 between *Gesellschaft* and *Gemeinschaft*. who said: 'The corporation or joint stock company … which is liable only for itself, represents, in its exclusive concentration on profit making, the perfect type of all legal forms for an association based on rational will. This is because it is from its very origin a relationship of *Gesellschaft* (ie. an enterprise association), without any admixture of elements of *Gemeinschaft* (community), and thus does not allow, as in other cases, any misconception as to its real character.' Ferdinand Tönnies, *Community and Association*, trans. C.P. Loomis, (London: Routledge and Kegan Paul, 1955), p. 227.

2   William S. Laufer, 'Integrity, diligence, and the limits of good corporate citizenship', *American Business Law Journal*, 34, 2 Winter 1996, pp. 157-181.

3   See the United States Sentencing Commission Website at http://www.ussc.gov/GUIDELIN.HTM

4   Denning L.J in *H.L. Bolton (Engineering) Co. Ltd. v T.J. Graham & Sons Ltd* [1951] 1 Q.B. 159 at 172, quoted in Paul Redmond, *Companies and Securities Law*, 2nd edn. (North Ryde: The Law Book Company, 1992) p. 214.

5   Milton Friedman, 'The Social Responsibility of Business is to Increase its Profits', *The New York Times Magazine*, 13 September 1970.

6   Christine Parker's work, *The Open Corporation*, (Cambridge: Cambridge University Press, 2002) shows why the assumption is simplistic and inaccurate.

7   Mark Lawson, 'Just don't invite the chief executive out to play golf', *Australian Financial Review*, 5 December, 2002.

8   Mark Lawson, 'The ethical dilemma of corporate generosity', *Australian Financial Review*, Dec 5, 2002.

9   Mel Wilson, 'Corporate Reputation and the Triple Bottom Line: The Social Responsibilities of Business', *Risky Business*, Issue 2, 2001 http://www.pwc.com/extweb/manissue.nsf/DocID/C00115084F24343E852569E600656A08.

10   Kate Legge, 'Humble hero of the operating theatre', *The Weekend Australian*, 23–4 June 2001, p. 10.

11   Colleen Ryan, 'The hard yard', *The Australian Financial Review Magazine*, July 2003, 18–25.

12   ibid. p. 22.

13   ibid. p. 22.

14   Elaine Sternberg, *Just Business*, (London: Warner Books, 1995) p. 42.

15   Elizabeth Vallance, *Business Ethics at Work*, (Cambridge: Cambridge University Press, 1995) pp. 9–10.

16   Milton Friedman & Rose Friedman, *Free to Choose* (London: Secker & Warburg, 1980), esp. ch. 4; and for a succinct rejoinder, Colin Grant, 'Friedman fallacies', *Journal of Business Ethics*, 10, 1991, pp. 907–14.

17   For a highly readable discussion of these issues see Thomas C. Schelling, *Choice and Consequence: Perspectives of an Errant Economist* (Cambridge: Harvard University Press, 1984).

18   Cf. John Finnis, *Natural Law and Natural Rights* (Oxford: Clarendon Press, 1980), pp. 174–7.

19   See Edward Coker, 'Adam Smith's concept of the social system', *Journal of Business Ethics*, 9, 1990, pp. 139–42.

20 Karl Marx, *Capital*, vol. 1 (New York: International Pubs, 1967, Foreign Languages Publishing House, 1959), ch. 32.

21 Dwight Lemke & Marshall Schminke, 'Ethics in declining organizations', *Business Ethics Quarterly*, 1, 1991, pp. 235–48.

22 Anthony Hughes 'Beware, a low offer for IAG', *Sydney Morning Herald*, 20 May 2002.

23 David Elias 'The secretive life of a market opportunist', *Age*, 9 November 2002.

24 *Business Review Weekly*, 23, no. 4, 1993, p. 39.

25 In 1995, the Australian Securities Commission warned about approaches from Country Estate to shareholders in Bridgestone Australia to buy their shares: 'The ASC is concerned that the information set out by Country Estate & Agency could cause Bridgestone shareholders to suffer substantial losses'; 'Warning over Country Estate', *Age*, 17 June 1995, p. 17.

26 Elias, 'The secretive life of a market opportunist'.

27 ibid.

28 ibid.

29 ASIC Media and information release 03-165 'National Exchange must declare market price,' 26 May 2003, accessed at http://www.asic.gov.au/asic/asic_pub.n.../03-165+National+Exchange+must+declare+market+price?openDocumen.

30 Christopher Webb,'Make sure you read both sides of letter', *Age*, 6 September 2002.

31 David Elias, 'Accidental hero defeats David Tweed', *Sydney Morning Herald*, 24 October 2003.

32 *Sydney Morning Herald*, 13 November 1993, p. 33.

33 The relevant sections of the carefully worded minutes read as follows:
'Meeting of 12 February, 1976. / Similar Transport Brokerage Agencies had appeared in the industry at various times in the past and previous experience showed that it was better for the Client and Operator to deal direct.
'Meeting of 20 May, 1976./ ... Similar "Transport Brokerage Agencies" had appeared in the industry at various times in the past and that experience showed that it was better for the Client and Operator to deal direct.
'Meeting of 4 August, 1976. / A letter from Tradestock Pty Ltd was tabled and noted. The Meeting reaffirmed its opinion that it is in each Company's best interests to deal directly with its own clients.' TPC v. T.N.T. Management Pty Ltd & Ors (1985), ATFR, paras 40–512, at 46, 087, 46, 099–100, 46, 105.

34 Before 1 July 1977, the relevant sections of the *Trade Practices Act* read as follows:
'Section 45(2). A corporation shall not —
(a) make a contract or arrangement, or enter into an understanding, in restraint of trade or commerce ...
(b) give effect to a contract, arrangement or understanding to the extent that it is in restraint of trade or commerce, whether the contract or arrangement was made or the understanding entered into before or after the commencement of this subsection.
'Section 45(4). A contract, arrangement or understanding ... is not in restraint of trade or commerce for the purposes of this Act unless the restraint has or is likely to have a significant effect on competition between the parties to the contract, arrangement or understanding or on competition between those parties or any of them and other persons.'

35 Tim Treadgold, 'Lady Bountiful turns nasty', *Business Review Weekly*, 1 October 1993, pp. 24–8.

36 Mark Lawson & Ian Howarth, 'WMC mauled in Savage engagement', *Australian Financial Review*, 27 July 1993, p. 24.

37 M. Smith & I. Howarth, 'WMC cuts back power of managing director', *Australian Financial Review*, 1 September 1993, p. 20.

38 M. Smith, 'Western's code of conduct for its employees', *Australian Financial Review*, 10 November 1993, p. 21.

5 Marketing and Advertising Ethics

1 See, for example, Robert Arrington, 'Advertising and behavior control', *Journal of Business Ethics*, 1, no. 1, February 1982, pp. 3–12; and Alan Goldman, 'Ethical issues in advertising', in Tom Regan (ed.), *Just Business: New Introductory Essays in Business Ethics* (New York: Random House, 1984), pp. 235–69.

2 Richard De George has also suggested that advertising can be considered as a transaction: 'the transaction is fair if both parties have adequate, appropriate information about the product, and if

they enter into the transaction willingly and without coercion'; *Business Ethics*, 2nd edn (New York: Macmillan, 1986), p. 273.

3   De George, *Business Ethics*, 2nd edn, p. 283.

4   This was announced by a spokesperson for the U.S. Department of Consumer Affairs. Apparently over 60 per cent of email advertisements violate some law or other with respect to untrue or fraudulent or insufficiently informative claims.

5   These were the Therapeutic Advertising Code, Alcoholic Beverages Advertising Code, Cigarette Advertising Code, and Slimming Advertising Code.

6   The fourteen constituent members of the Media Council were: The Federal Capital Press of Australia, Eastern Suburbs Newspapers, Australian Accreditations Bureau, Australian Consolidated Press, David Syme, News Limited, Regional Dailies of Australia, Country Press Australia, Federation of Australian Commercial Television Stations, Federation of Australian Radio Broadcasters, Outdoor Advertising Association of Australia, Perth Newspapers Publishers' Association, Sun Newspapers, and The News (SA). Additionally, there were six associate members: Australian Rural Publishers' Association, Peter Isaacson Group, Independent Magazine Publishers, Australian Cinema Advertising Council, I. M. Publishing, and Eastern Express.

7   Much of the dissatisfaction concerned matters not particularly related to the ASC, but rather matters of fees to be paid and the control of the industry.

8   To pursue any further the rationale for the change of regulatory regimes in Australia here would be beside the point.

9   From the Advertising Standards Bureau website: http://www.advertisingstandardsbureau.com.au.

10   International Advertising Association, 'Advertising. It makes the difference', *Sydney Morning Herald*, 5 June 1993, p. 13.

11   *Bulletin*, 3 August 1993, p. 72.

12   Bowie & Duska, p. 54.

13   Catharine Lumby, 'Sexist or sexy?', *Independent Monthly*, November 1993, p. 33.

14   *Australian*, 12 May 1993, pp. 1–2.

15   This description is taken from the Advertising Standards Council's seventeenth report, 1993, p. 48.

16   Seventeenth report, p. 49.

17   Lumby, p. 33.

18   Of course, such a view would also favour a much more liberal approach to what products or services should be legally available.

19   *Australian Business Monthly*, June 1992, pp. 103–4.

20   *Australian*, 16 April 1993, p. 20.

21   *Sydney Morning Herald*, 6 May 1993, p. 38.

22   This is taken from David Braybrooke, *Ethics in the World of Business* (Totowa, NJ: Rowman & Allanheld, 1983), pp. 94–5.

23   Le Winter's lost in the first instance, but the decision was reversed on appeal (Supreme Court of New York, Appellate Division, Second Department, 1939).

24   *Sydney Morning Herald*, 14 June 1993, p. 1.

25   'Optus bites into Telecom', results of Time Morgan Poll on preferred telecommunications carrier in coming ballot, *Time Australia*, 21 June 1993, p. 10.

26   *Sydney Morning Herald*, 7 June 1993, p. 15.

27   *Sydney Morning Herald*, 18 June 1993, p. 1.

28   John Millard (reporter), *The Investigators*, 2 March 1993, ABC Television.

29   Reported on the Saturn website, April, 2004: http://www.saturn.com/aboutus2/news/a02press1.jsp] 'In the history of the study, the only other brand that earned both top achievements simultaneously was Lexus in 1994.' Reported on the Saturn website, April, 2004: http://www.saturn.com/aboutus2/news/a02press3.jsp]. Further, 'the no-haggle, no-hassle sales approach and respectful treatment of customers earned Saturn retailers the top spot in J.D. Power and Associates' sales satisfaction index for six of the past seven years'. Reported on the Saturn website, April, 2004: http://www.saturn.com/aboutus2/news/a01press4.jsp].

30   The claims in this case were made by the independent Australian Consumers' Association, 'Cigarette tar levels questioned', *Sydney Morning Herald*, 7 June 1993, p. 7. On 7 June 1993 A Current Affair broadcast a story about a former testing officer for the Australian Government Analytical Laboratories who had tested the cigarettes and recommended the removal of low tar cigarettes from the market until warning labels were placed on them.

6 Equal Opportunity, Discrimination and Affirmative Action

1   'Back entry into shops not bias', *Sydney Morning Herald*, 18 March 1993, p. 3.
2   Bronwyn Young, 'Sex bias decision upheld', *Australian Financial Review*, 6 December 1989, p. 3.
3   A reasonable question, of course, is why specific guidelines would be called for in the first place. But that is a topic that we do not pursue here.
4   *C. M. and S. v. Australian Telecommunications Corporation, Human Rights and Equal Opportunity Commission* (16 December 1991).
5   Duncan Graham, '$92,000 damages for porn in workplace harassment', *Sydney Morning Herald*, 22 April 1994, p. 3.
6   ibid.; see also Mark Irving, 'Women in workplace porn case get $92,000', *Australian*, 22 April 1994, p. 3.
7   See for example Ian Palmer, "Email Abuse & Misuse", Insight accessed at http://www.insight-mag.com/insight/03/08/col-5-pt-1-WorkForce.asp and the NSW Department of Commerce, Office of Industrial Relations at http://www.industrialrelations.nsw.gov.au/pubs/July2003/email.html.
8   *Nowland v. Skypak & Anor* (1993), EOC 92–509; 'Sexist attitude costs $20,000', *Sydney Morning Herald*, 9 June 1993, p. 5.
9   Cathy Bolt, 'Pregnancy sacking damages $12,000', *Australian Financial Review*, August 1993, p. 6.
10 *Why Don't You Ever See a Pregnant Waitress?*, Summary Report of the Findings of the Inquiry into Pregnancy Related Discrimination, New South Wales Anti-Discrimination Board, 1993, pp. 1–2.
11 ibid., p. 6.
12 ibid., p. 7.
13 ibid., p. 8.
14 ibid., p. 9.
15 *Sydney Morning Herald*, 9 September 1993, p. 34.
16 Patrick Kelly, 'Conducting a glass ceiling self-audit now', *HR Magazine*, October 1993, p. 76.
17 ibid., pp. 77–8.
18 ibid., pp. 77–8.
19 *Australian Financial Review*, 27 August 1993, p. 1 and *Weekend Review*, p. 3.
20 Cyndee Miller, 'Women at ad agencies say top pay, positions denied them', *Marketing News*, 27, 13, 21 June 1993, pp. 1–2.
21 *Australian Financial Review*, 27 August 1993, p. 33.
22 ibid., *Weekend Review*, p. 3.
23 'Breaking the glass ceiling: another perspective', *Women In Management Series*, Paper no. 15, Faculty of Commerce, University of Western Sydney, Nepean, July 1992.
24 *Sydney Morning Herald*, 14 September 1993, p. 9.
25 ibid.
26 'The glass ceiling' in A. P. Iannone (ed.), *Contemporary Moral Controversies* (New York: Oxford University Press, 1989), pp. 181–3.
27 *Australian Financial Review*, 27 August 1993, p. 1.
28 Mark Pickering, 'Minority applies for start-up finance', *Australian*, 2 March 1994, p. 38.
29 *Australian*, 7 April 1993, p. 3.
30 The information on disability is taken from Mark Bagshaw, 'Ready, willing and able', *Australian Business Monthly*, July 1992, pp. 138–40.
31 See for example, the Web site of the Disability Service Reforms Branch at http://www.facs.gov.au/internet/facsinternet.nsf/who/branches-disability_service_reforms.htm case based funding for people with disabilities at http://www.facs.gov.au/internet/facsinternet.nsf/aboutfacs/programs/disability-cbf_job_in_jeopardy.htm and the provisions for disability employment in the 2003–4 budget at http://www.facs.gov.au/internet/facsinternet.nsf/aboutfacs/budget/budget2003-wnwd_a.htm.
32 See the FACS Web site at http://www.facs.gov.au/internet/facsinternet.nsf/content/nrdc.htm.
33 The information on disability is taken from Mark Bagshaw, 'Ready, willing and able', *Australian Business Monthly*, July 1992, pp. 138–40.
34 The Victorian law provides that people with HIV must not be treated less favourably than others. It does not oblige employers to treat people with HIV more favourably than other people.

7 The Ethics of Accounting

1   As quoted in Elizabeth Wolgast, *Ethics of an Artificial Person* (Stanford, California: Stanford University Press, 1992), p. 23.

2   Time Morgan Poll, *Time Australia*, 25 April 1994, p. 12.
3   Philomena Leung & Barry Cooper, *Professional Ethics: A Survey of Australian Accountants* (Melbourne: ASCPA, 1995), p. 10. The authors sent their survey to 7000 members and obtained useable responses from 1500.
4   ibid., pp. 12, 18.
5   Adapted from Leung & Cooper, p. 16.
6   R. L. Whitelaw, as quoted in Mike W. Martin & Roland Schinzinger, *Ethics in Engineering*, 2nd edn (New York: McGraw-Hill, 1989), p. 168.
7   ibid., pp. 168–9.
8   As quoted in Jack Maurice, *Accounting Ethics* (London: Pitman Publishing, 1996), p. 30.
9   Adapted from the British Statement on the Ethical Responsibilities of Members in Business, as quoted in Maurice, p. 31.
10   OnlineNewshour, 'Enron: After the Collapse', accessed at http://www.pbs.org/newshour/bb/business/enron/player6.html.
11   See Barbara Ley Toffler with Jennifer Reingold, *Final Accounting: Ambition, Greed and the Fall of Arthur Andersen*, Broadway Books, 2003.
12   Kurt Eichenwald, 'Ex-Accounting Chief at Enron Is Indicted on 6 Felony Charges', *New York Times*, 23 January 2004, accessed at http://www.nytimes.com/2004/01/23/business/23enron.html?ex=1077339600&en=7bee0e9c177fec7a&ei=5070.
13   Kurt Eichenwald, 'Audacious Climb to Success Ended in a Dizzying Plunge', *New York Times*, 13 January 2002 accessed at http://www.nytimes.com/2002/01/13/business.html. 12.
14   Frank Clarke and Graeme Dean, 'Corporate collapses analysed' in *Collapse Incorporated* (North Ryde: CCH, 2001), p. 86.
15   ibid. pp. 72–6.
16   Eichenwald, 'Ex-Accounting Chief at Enron Is Indicted...'; Kristen Hays, 'Causey May Be Key In Enron Prosecutions', *Chicago Tribune* Online Edition, January 24, 2004, http://www.chicagotribune.com/business/sns-ap-enron-causey,1,7140173.story?coll=sns-business-headlines.
17   Joseph Kahn 'Californians Call Enron Documents the Smoking Gun' May 8, 2002.
18   See 'Summary of SEC Actions and SEC Related Provisions Pursuant to the Sarbanes-Oxley Act of 2002' July 30, 2003, http://www.sec.gov/news/press/2003-89a.htm.
19   IFAC, 'Proposed Revision to Code of Ethics for Professional Accountants' Exposure Draft, 2003 accessed at http://www.ifac.org/Guidance/EXD-Details.php?EDID=0027.
20   Clarke and Dean, 'Corporate collapses analysed' in *Collapse Incorporated* (North Ryde: CCH, 2001), p. 86.
21   ibid. p. 91.
22   The Institute of Chartered Accountants in Australia, *Code of Professional Conduct* (Sydney, 1997).
23   For example, The Code of Ethics of the New Zealand Institute of Chartered Accountants (Wellington: ICANZ, 2003) requires accountants to display integrity, objectivity and independence, competence, quality performance, and professional behaviour.
24   To make the distinction clear, think of the rules of football. They are there to 'constitute' the game of football, not to regulate the conduct of people kicking a ball around a paddock. Anyone can do the latter, but only those who know the rules of football can play the game. Sprinting, handball and hockey are not football; each game is distinguished by the rules that constitute it. It makes no sense to say that the rules of football or hockey are oppressive or that the recipe for soufflé is over-regulated. These rules are the conditions that allow the activity — be it a game, cooking or professional activity — to happen.
25   See the discussion of the spirit of a 'true and fair' account in F. L. Clarke, G. W. Dean & K. G. Oliver, *Corporate Collapse* (Cambridge: Cambridge University Press, 1997), pp. 246–7.
26   ibid., p. 23.
27   See these recent discussions of this point: Frank Clarke and Graeme Dean, 'Legislators and regulators have failed to get the principles right', *Australian Financial Review*, November 7, 2002, p. 71; Stephen Cohen, 'Ethics is judgement, not rules', *Australian Financial Review*, November 26, 2002, p.71; Stephen Cohen, 'Regulations are not the answer', *Australian Financial Review*, January 15, 2003.
28   In the 'Legislators and regulators have failed to get the principles right', Frank Clarke and Graeme Dean make a point very similar to this one.
29   Michael West, 'BT sues auditors for $60m', *Sydney Morning Herald*, 31 January 1996, p. 25.

30 Mark Westfield, 'Longest running trial puts blowtorch on auditors', *Australian*, 9 September 1997, p. 25.

31 George Sutton, 'Accountability brings with it all sorts of limits', *Australian*, 9 December 1994, p. 22.

32 Peter Jubb, 'Confidentiality in a professional context with especial reference to the accounting profession in Australia', in M. Hoffman, J. Brown Kamm, R. E. Frederick & E. S. Petry (eds), *The Ethics of Accounting and Finance* (London: Quorum Books, 1996), p. 77.

33 ibid.

34 Clarke, Dean & Oliver, p. 254.

35 'Financial reports review program', *Charter*, February 1994, pp. 55–6.

36 ibid., p. 55.

37 For example, the journal of The Institute of Chartered Accountants, Charter, now includes a regular ethical problem and articles on ethics. The same body has also launched videos of ethical hypotheticals and founded the Academics Ethics Network, with its own newsletter, *Focus on Ethics*.

8 The Environment

1 Naomi Klein, *No Logo* (Hammersmith, London: Flamingo: 2001).

2 Elizabeth Becker, 'Animal Fans' Secret Recipe Is to Boycott Restaurant', *New York Times*, 6 January, 2003.

3 A fuller argument is developed in S. Cohen and D. Grace, 'Ethics and Sustainability: Looking beyond basic legal requirements', *Australian master OHS and environment guide 2003*, (Sydney: CCH, 2002).

4 Henry Bosch, *Bosch on Business* (Melbourne: Business Library, 1992), p. 14.

5 De George, *Business Ethics*, 2nd edn, p. 283.

6 'The tragedy of the commons', *Science*, 162, December 1968, pp. 1234–8.

7 Manuel Velasquez, *Business Ethics*, 3rd edn (Englewood Cliffs, NJ: Prentice Hall, 1992), p. 231.

8 Manuel Velasquez provides an excellent discussion of this point in *Business Ethics*, pp. 238–41.

9 William T. Blackstone, 'Ethics and ecology', in William T. Blackstone (ed.), *Philosophy and the Environmental Crisis* (Athens, Ga.: University of Georgia Press, 1974).

10 Michael Hoffman, 'Business and environmental ethics', *Business Ethics Quarterly*, 1, no. 2, 1991, pp. 169–84.

11 Peter Singer, *Animal Liberation*, 2nd edn, (New York: Thorsons, 1991), p. 6.

12 More, p. 73.

13 See Raimond Gaita's excellent discussion in *The Philosopher's Dog* (Melbourne: Text Publishing, 2002).

14 Ted Trainer, for example, argues that economies based on ever-increasing consumption are both unsustainable and irrational. There are alternative possible economies not based on geometric consumption. For Trainer, affluence is the problem; *Abandon Affluence* (London: Zed Books, 1985).

15 H. Daly & J. Cobb, *For the Common Good* (London: Greenprint, 1989), p. 450.

16 John Rawls, *A Theory of Justice* (Oxford: Clarendon Press, 1972), p. 289.

17 ibid., pp. 285–9.

18 For a list of explicit principles which give effect to Rawls's point see Holmes Rolston III, 'Just environmental business', in Tom Regan (ed.), *Just Business* (New York: Random House, 1984), ch. 11.

19 Christopher Pearson, 'Green errors began with DDT', *The Weekend Australian*, 24–5 January 2004, 16.

20 Michael Crichton, 'Remarks to the Commonwealth Club San Francisco', September 15, 2003, http://www.crichton-official.com/speeches/speeches_quote05.html.

21 This information may be accessed at http://www.shell.com/home/Framework?siteId=royal-en&FC2=/royal-en/html/iwgen/environment_and_society/making_it_happen/our_approach/zzz_lhn.html&FC3=/royal-en/html/iwgen/environment_and_society/making_it_happen/our_approach/our_approach.html.

22 Mel Wilson 'Corporate Reputation and the Triple Bottom Line: The Social Responsibilities of Business', *Risky Business*, Issue 2, 2001 http://www.pwc.com/extweb/manissue.nsf/DocID/C00115084F24343E852569E600656A08.

23 Accessed at http://www.igc.apc.org/habitat/agenda21/rio-dec.html. See also the Wingspread Statement, http://www.gdrc.org/u-gov/precaution-3.html.

24 'Wingspread Statement' accessed at http://www.gdrc.org/u-gov/precaution-3.html.

25 ibid.

26   Frank Cross, 'Paradoxical Perils of the Precautionary Principle', 53 *Washington and Lee Law Review*, 851 (1996).

27   Gerard Ryle, 'Industrial waste sold as fertilizer', *Sydney Morning Herald*, 6 May 2002, p. 1.

28   Quoted by Duff Wilson, 'Fear In The Fields — How Hazardous Wastes Become Fertilizer — Spreading Heavy Metals On Farmland Is Perfectly Legal, But Little Research Has Been Done To Find Out Whether It's Safe', *Seattle Times*, 3 July 1997 accessed at http://archives.seattletimes.nwsource.com/cgi-bin/texis.cgi/web/vortex/display?slug=2547772&date=19970703.
The series of articles by Duff Wilson may be accessed at http://seattletimes.nwsource.com/news/special/fear_fields.html.

29   M. Wade, 'Petrol importing fuels bitter debate over retail ethics', Sydney Morning Herald, 10 July 2002, p. 6.

30   Jan Mayman, 'The stink of uncle Al', *The Weekend Australian*, 11-12 May 2002, pp. 19–22.

31   ibid. p. 19.

32   ibid.

33   For evidence presented at the inquiry see http://www.parliament.wa.gov.au/parliament/commit.nsf/(InqByName)/AEED11314738B6B148256B610023EA99?opendocument.

34   ibid.

35   Christine Parker, *The Open Corporation* (Melbourne: Cambridge University Press, 2000), pp. 68-83.

36   Parker, p. 77.

37   ISO statistics accessed at http://www.ecology.or.jp/isoworld/english/analy14k.htm.

38   See the SustainAbility website for more on Elkington at http://www.sustainability.com/home.asp.

39   See http://www.globalreporting.org/about/brief.asp.

40   Information on the Valdez Principles is drawn from Rajib Sanyal & Joao Neves, 'The Valdez Principles: implications for corporate social responsibility', *Journal of Business Ethics*, 10, December 1991, pp. 883–90.

41   A decade earlier, American business had responded to another challenge – racial discrimination in South Africa – with the Sullivan Code. The Sullivan Code was initially a voluntary code designed to prevent American firms from exploiting non-white South Africans, and its success made it a model for the Valdez Principles.

42   R. Hawke, *Our Country, Our Future* (Canberra: AGPS, 1989).

43   World Commission on Environment and Development, *Our Common Future* (London: Oxford University Press, 1987).

44   Ecologically Sustainable Development Working Group Chairs, *Intersectoral Issues Report* (Canberra: AGPS, 1992), p. 2.

45   Ecologically Sustainable Development Working Group Chairs, p. 3.

46   ibid., p. 13.

47   John Davis, 'Paper price falls dents recyclers', *Sydney Morning Herald*, 25 June 1993, p. 3.

48   *BHP and Ok Tedi: The Facts*, BHP publicity, 28 September 1995, p. 3.

49   Rowan Callick, 'Green codes drawn up for doing business overseas', *Australian Financial Review*, 2 November 1995.

50   Cameron Forbes & Matthew Stevens, 'BHP considers PNG mining solutions', *Australian*, 24 May 1994.

51   *BHP and Ok Tedi*, p. 8.

52   ibid., p. 1.

53   Cited in Geoffrey Barker, 'Dead fish, ethics and Ok Tedi', *Australian Financial Review*, 9 October 1995, p. 15. Barker also quotes BHP's then head of minerals, Jerry Ellis, who rejects the proposition that his company has bullied rather than courted the PNG government: 'When you are in competition, you do everything you possibly can to win people's hearts and minds, not to bully them. As soon as you become a bully, they look elsewhere'.

54   ibid.

55   Barry Fitzgerald, 'BHP in deal on Ok Tedi compo', *Age*, 8 May 1997.

56   See BHP Billiton *Health Safety Environment & Community Report 2003* at http://www.bhpbilliton.com/hsecReport/2003/home/home8 .html.

9   Whistleblowing

1   Norman Bowie & Ronald Duska, *Business Ethics*, 2nd edn (Englewood Cliffs, NJ: Prentice Hall, 1990), p. 37.

2   Norman Bowie & Ronald Duska, *Business Ethics*, 2nd edn (Englewood Cliffs, NJ: Prentice Hall, 1990), p. 37.

3   Mike Martin & Roland Schinzinger, *Ethics in Engineering*, 2nd edn (New York: McGraw-Hill, 1989), pp. 43–4.

4   Norman Bowie & Ronald Duska, p. 37.

5   ibid., p. 210.

6   See Roger Boisjoly's first-hand account of the decision to launch Challenger in the face of indications of high risk, in 'The Challenger disaster; moral responsibility and the working engineer', in Deborah G. Johnson, *Ethical Issues in Engineering* (Englewood Cliffs, NJ: Prentice-Hall, 1991), pp. 6–14.

7   'Persons of the Year', *Time*, December 30–January 6, 2003, pp. 34-57.

8   ibid. p. 57.

9   Quentin Dempster, *Whistleblowers* (Sydney: ABC Books, 1997), p. 3.

10   See Howard Whitton, 'Ethics and principled dissent in the Queensland public sector: A response to the Queensland whistleblower study', *Australian Journal of Public Administration*, 54, 1995, pp. 455–61.

11   Sissela Bok, 'Blowing the whistle', in J. Fleishman et al. (eds), *Public Duties: The Moral Obligations of Government Officials* (Cambridge: Cambridge University Press, 1982), pp. 208–9.

12   De George, *Business Ethics*, 3rd edn, pp. 208–14.

13   See, for example, Bowie, pp. 138–49, and Bowie & Duska, pp. 72–7.

14   Ross Webber, 'Whistleblowing', *Executive Excellence*, July 1990; see Westin's 'Conclusion', in Allen Westin (ed.), *Whistleblowing: Loyalty and Dissent in the Corporation* (New York: McGraw-Hill, 1981), pp. 160–3.

15   Bowie & Duska, p. 74.

16   A. Gorta & S. Forell, 'Corruption: consensus, cognisance or confusion?', paper presented to the 9th Annual Conference of the Australian and New Zealand Society of Criminology, Sydney, September–October 1993.

17   Michael Keeley & Jill Graham, 'Exit, voice and ethics', *Journal of Business Ethics*, 10, 1991, pp. 350–1.

18   Bok, pp. 215–17.

19   Westin, pp. 151–60, makes some suggestions about such protections that partly apply in Australia through industrial legislation — for example, laws against unfair dismissals.

20   Sharon Beder, 'Engineers, ethics and etiquette', *New Scientist*, 25 September 1993, pp. 36–41.

21   See Dempster, *Whistleblowers*, for ten representative case studies.

22   Colleen Ryan, 'Whistleblower is out in the cold', *Sydney Morning Herald*, 20 March 1993, p. 33.

23   ibid.

24   ibid.

25   The Martin Committee had much to say about the supervisory role of the Reserve Bank, not just in relation to private banks but also state banks. See section III, recommendations 22–30 of House of Representatives Standing Committee on Finance and Public Administration, *A Pocket Full of Change: Banking and Deregulation* (Canberra: AGPS, 1991).

26   ibid., recommendation 62, p. 351.

27   Information for this case is taken from Ryan, 'Whistleblower is out in the cold', and Bill Mellor, 'Integrity and ruined lives', *Time Australia*, 21 October 1991, pp. 46–51.

28   The information in this case comes from Julian Cribb, 'Committed to truth', *Australian*, 8 September 1993, p. 8.

29   ibid.

30   Vince Neary, 'Second Report on Victimisation and Harassment in My Employment Situation in the State Rail Authority', personal submission to the State Rail Authority of New South Wales, February 1993, p. 2.

31   ibid., pp. 14–15.

32   Office of the NSW Ombudsman, *Special Report to Parliament: The Neary–SRA Report*, 03/93, 12 October 1993.

33   Fred P. Clark, 'Unfounded "whistle blower" suit can kill a small defense company', *Aviation Week and Space Technology*, 2 March 1992, pp. 65–6.

34   See for example, William De Maria, 'Quarantining dissent: The Queensland public sector ethics movement', *Australian Journal of Public Administration*, 54, 1995, pp. 443–54. Although De Maria's

critique is directed to the public sector, it could equally be directed to the private sector. De Maria's article is rebutted by Howard Whitton, 'Ethics and principled dissent in the Queensland public sector: A response to the Queensland whistleblower study'; compare Noel Preston, 'Public sector ethics in Australia: A review', *Australian Journal of Public Administration*, 54, 1995, pp. 462–70.

10 Codes of Ethics and Institutional Ethics

1 ' For an illuminating discussion of the supposed differences among types of codes, see Conal Condren, 'Code types: Functions and failings and organizational diversity', *Business and Professional Ethics Journal*, 14, no. 4, 1995, pp. 69–90.

2   Bowie & Duska, p. 85.

3   Adrian Lynch, 'Get integrity back into management', *Rydges*, December 1985, p. 49.

4   See Amanda Sinclair, 'Codes in the workplace: Organisational versus professional codes', in Margaret Coady & Sidney Bloch (eds), *Codes of Ethics and the Professions* (Melbourne: Melbourne University Press, 1996) for a comparison of professional and organisational codes that take up some of the issues mentioned here.

5   Some qualification is required here. For example, chartered accountants advertise in terms of their profession as being better able to do a number of things (e.g., income tax returns) perhaps, impliedly, not merely because of their expertise but also because of their commitment to a code of conduct. There are other examples as well; but as a general point, it does seem correct to say that the profession operates as a monopoly, and so would usually have no reason to offer the presence of a code of ethics as competitive advertising.

6   Robert Howard, 'Values make the company', *Harvard Business Review*, September–October 1990, pp. 133–44.

7   Alan Farnham, 'State your values, hold the hot air', *Fortune*, 19 April 1993, p. 54.

8   ibid., p. 54.

9   Under the NSW *Independent Commission Against Corruption Act*, s. 8, corrupt conduct is defined as '(a) any conduct of any person … that adversely affects, or that could adversely affect, either directly or indirectly, the honest or impartial exercise of official functions by any public official …; (b) any conduct of a public official that constitutes or involves the dishonest or partial exercise of any of his or her official functions …; (c) any conduct … that constitutes or involves a breach of public trust; or (d) any conduct of a public official or former public official that involves a misuse of information or material that he or she has acquired in the course of his or her official functions …'. If the references to public officials and official functions were replaced by company officers and corporate functions, these definitions could as easily apply to the private sector.

10   On enforcement of codes, see Ian Freckelton, 'Enforcement of ethics' in Coady & Bloch, pp. 130–65.

11   Norman Bowie, 'Business codes of ethics: window dressing or legitimate alternative to government regulation?', in Tom L. Beauchamp & Norman E. Bowie (eds), *Ethical Theory and Business* (Englewood Cliffs, NJ: Prentice-Hall, 1979), pp. 234–9.

12   Bruce N. Kaye, 'Codes of ethics in Australian business corporations', *Journal of Business Ethics*, 11, 1992, pp. 857–62.

13   This is available at the ASX website: <http://www.asx.com.au/about/CorporateGovernance_AA2. shtm>.

14   Office of Regulation Review, 'Recent developments in regulation and its review', *Information Paper*, Canberra, November 1993, p. 35.

15   Steve Lewis, 'Govt. moves to shake up banks with new code', *Australian Financial Review*, 25 November 1992, p. 37.

16   Walter W. Manley II, *Handbook of Good Business Practice* (London: Routledge, 1992), pp. 4–13. According to Manley's research, the British managers found that codes help establish the ethical tone of the organisation, state its values and facilitate the imparting of these values to employees; give a commonly accepted basis to a company's policies and employee understandings of them; underpin a company's strategic direction; prepare staff for external scrutiny and help avoid intrusive attention from interest groups and the media; set clear standards for dealings with other businesses and third parties; clarify the rights and responsibilities of the company, its management and its employees; respond to government pressure for greater external regulation; improve a company's image and public confidence in it; reduce exposure to law suits; improve performance and profits;

enhance corporate pride; build excellence across the company's operations; set benchmarks for performance; reassure shareholders as to the company's integrity; sustain public confidence in the market system; foster a business culture of openness and free communication; facilitate the integration of the cultures of merged companies; deter unethical behaviour throughout a company.

17   James A. Waters, 'Catch 20.5: corporate morality as an organizational phenomenon', in A. P. Iannone (ed.), *Contemporary Moral Controversies* (New York: Oxford University Press, 1989), p. 152.

18   For an interesting and readable discussion of this point, see C. A. J. Coady, 'Ethos and ethics in business', in Coady & Sampford, pp. 149–71.

19   *Honeywell, Code of Ethics and Business Conduct* (Minneapolis: Honeywell, 1995), p. 4.

20   The Guidelines require that: (i) a code of ethics and organisational standards be developed; (ii) responsibility for ethics programs should be vested in a senior executive; (iii) persons with a record of sharp practice or misconduct be excluded from positions of authority; (iv) employees are properly informed about the code of ethics and organisational standards; (v) monitoring, auditing and safe reporting mechanisms be instituted; (vi) fair and firm disciplinary measure be taken against misconduct; (vii) measures be taken to prevent recurrences of misconduct.

21   The issue of conformism to external pressures is a serious objection to organisational ethics programs. For a discussion of the problem, see C. A. J. Coady, 'On regulating ethics', in Coady & Bloch, pp. 269–87.

22   Ronald R. Sims, 'The institutionalization of organizational ethics', *Journal of Business Ethics*, 10, 1991, p. 504.

23   ibid., passim; and Waters, pp. 159–61.

24   Amanda Sinclair has argued that ethical cultures can be established through treating an organisation as a single culture or as a number of co-existing sub-cultures, but we believe that ethical failure is more likely to result from fragmentation. See Sinclair's 'Improving ethics through organisational culture: a comparison of two approaches', in Coady & Sampford, pp. 128–48.

11   International Business Ethics

1   In a famous passage, Hobbes characterised such a life as 'solitary, poor, nasty, brutish, and short'; *Leviathan* (1651), part I, ch. 13.

2   Campbell writes, 'Now in every human being there is a built-in human instinct system, without which we should not even come to birth. But each of us has also been educated to a specific local culture system'; *Reflections on the Art of Living: A Joseph Campbell Companion*, selected and edited by Diane K. Osbon (New York: Harper Perennial, 1991), p. 126.

3   Here we follow John Kekes, *The Morality of Pluralism* (Princeton, NJ: Princeton University Press, 1993), pp. 38–44.

4   Robert Armstrong et al., 'Business Ethics', in Anthony Milner & Mary Quilty (eds), *Australia in Asia: Comparing Cultures* (Melbourne: Oxford University Press, 1996), p. 24.

5   Ibid., p. 26. In a brief but pointed way, Armstrong et al. set out some of the core values of Japanese, Chinese, Thai, Indonesian and Korean cultures.

6   Reported in 'Excerpts from the International Press', *TI Newsletter* <http://www.transparency.de/ newsletter/> March 1997.

7   Johann Lambsdorff, 'The question of responsibility' <http://gwdu19.gwdg.de/ %7Ejlambsd/bribery/ node4.htm> 26 September 1997.

8   Louise Williams, 'Bre-X scam sparks attacks on foreigners', *Sydney Morning Herald*, 6 May 1997, p. 28.

9   Nicholas Cumming-Bruce, 'Chief of State-owned firm in $62m graft case', *Sydney Morning Herald*, 25 January 1997, p. 22.

10   Amartya Sen, 'Does business ethics make economic sense?', *Business Ethics Quarterly*, 3, 1993, p. 50.

11   Robert Garran, 'Nomura president falls on his sword', *Weekend Australian*, 15–16 March 1997, p. 53; 'Nomura bosses resign en masse', *Australian*, 23 April 1997, p. 23. When the rest of the senior management of Nomura resigned in April 1997, they retained their rights as 'advisers', with the power to continue to do business in the company's name. In this way, public honour is saved, but Nomura did not face a sudden loss of corporate knowledge and the individuals did not have to pay the full price of resignation.

12   For details of the Lockheed scandal, see Velasquez, pp. 207–8; Martin & Schinzinger, pp. 261–2.

13   *Sydney Morning Herald*, 18 November 1996, p. 38.

14   Robert W. Armstrong, 'An empirical investigation of international marketing ethics: problems encountered by Australian firms', *Journal of Business Ethics*, 11, 1992, pp. 161–71.

15   The Asian Intelligence Report, cited in 'Indonesia "most corrupt"', business survey, *Sydney Morning Herald*, 31 March 1997, p. 7.

16   Hanbo, one of Korea's largest steel makers and US$6 billion in debt, allegedly obtained loans it would not otherwise have got from government-controlled banks at the behest of the ruling New Korea Party. Hanbo chairman, Chung Tae-soo, has a history of bribing government officials. He was convicted of paying former President Roh Tae-woo US$23 million in bribes during his 1988–92 term.

17   'Dud loans dog Vietnam's banks', *Sydney Morning Herald*, 24 March 1997, p. 38.

18   'Managing in Asia: ethics and other issues', *Far Eastern Economic Review*, 16 September 1993, pp. 33–53.

19   On 7 March 1997, the *Australian Financial Review* reported on its front page that the east coast criminal milieu had assumed all the trappings of legitimate business in order to pursue criminal activities — such as money laundering — more efficiently. In the United States, the Mob has infiltrated the securities industry; 'Mob muscles into brokers' offices', *Sydney Morning Herald*, 24 March 1997, p. 38.

20   S. J. Vitell, S. L. Nwachukwu & J. H. Barnes, 'The effects of culture on ethical decision-making: an application of Hofstede's typology', *Journal of Business Ethics*, 12, 1993, pp. 753–60. They distinguish two types of culture: individualist and collectivist. In individualist cultures, it is acceptable to give primacy to the interests of individuals, their families and connections. In collectivist cultures, the individual's identity is determined by a group of some kind, and the interests of the group are accorded primacy. Collectivist societies emphasise loyalty more than individualist ones. The authors suggest that in collectivist societies (they cite Japan), individuals are more likely to be guided by the norms and values of their industrial, business or professional group. In contrast with this alignment, the individual in an individualist society (they cite the United States) will be less influenced by organisational norms, even when formally stated, as in codes of ethics. Moreover, they suggest that business practitioners in individualistic societies are more likely than those in collectivist societies to consider themselves as more important stakeholders than other employees or the owners (pp. 754–6).

21   Alois A. Nugroho, 'The myth of immoral business: a specific challenge of business ethics in Indonesia', *International Society of Business, Economics and Ethics Papers*, Tokyo 1996 <http://www.nd.edu/~isbee/p_nugroh.htm> 15 September 1997.

22   Julius Tahija, 'Swapping business skills for oil', *Harvard Business Review*, September–October 1993, p. 113.

23   'All employees are expected to comply with antitrust/competition laws throughout the world, ie., no price fixing, bid rigging, criminal collusion. Marketing and selling efforts must conform to highest ethical standards … It is Honeywell's policy to comply with FCPA laws which prohibit the bribery of foreign government or political officials and establish mandatory internal record keeping standards … No employee will provide or accept kickbacks … No employee will give, offer or promise to give, or ask for or accept anything of value to or from an employee or other representative of any current or potential customer, supplier, or regulatory authority, in exchange for assistance or influence in a transaction'; Honeywell, *Code of Ethics and Business Conduct* (Honeywell: Minnesota, 1995), pp. 1–2.

24   Richard De George, *Competing with Integrity in International Business* (New York: Oxford University Press, 1993), p. 114.

25   ibid, pp. 46–56. De George also offers ten 'strategies' or counsels of perfection for dealing with corruption in international business. The first and probably hardest is to remain ethical, even if competitors do not. The others include: using an imaginative response to ethical difficulty; avoidance of over-reaction and maintenance of a sense of proportion; development of background legal institutions at home and abroad; exposure of unethical practices in the media where possible; combining with other parties to reform social, legal, and political institutions; and requiring strict accountability of MNCs and those who work within them. See also pp. 114–20.

26   Ibid., p. 112.

27   Adapted from Herbert's report, reprinted in K. Woldring (ed.), *Business Ethics in Australia and New Zealand* (Melbourne: Nelson, 1996), pp. 191–2.

28   Verena Dobnik, 'Nike accused of allowing "boot camp" factories', *Sydney Morning Herald*, 29 March 1997, p. 17.

29   Brad Norington, 'Nike protests urged over "appalling" work conditions', *Sydney Morning Herald*, 1 April 1997, p. 6.

30   Peter Hancock, 'Satan's factory: Nike attacked by researcher', *Sydney Morning Herald*, 4 April 1997, p. 10.

31   Brad Norington, 'The shoe fits here as well', *Sydney Morning Herald*, 18 April 1997, p. 15.

32   Chris Patten, 'Synergy of Robust Rights and Robust Development' *Sydney Morning Herald*, 24 November 1993, p. 15.

33   Although the costs can be overstated: see the argument that ethical knowledge is an asset in Norman E. Bowie & Paul Vaaler, 'Some arguments for universal moral standards', *International Society of Business, Economics and Ethics Papers*, Tokyo 1996 <http:// www.nd.edu/~isbee/ p_bowie.htm> 28 August 1997.

34   Diane Stott & Helen Greenwood, 'Shoppers "must wear" outworker reforms', *Sydney Morning Herald*, 15 April 1996, p. 6. It is worth noting that, in the same article, Senator Sid Spindler reported a visit to a Brookvale manufacturer who paid up to 40 per cent above award rates and was still profitable.

35   James Kirby, 'ANZ rules out merger changes', *Australian*, 4 April 1996, p. 27.

36   ABC TV news report for 5 April 1996. The glibness takes the form of simple blame attribution. For example, although Country Road has asked its suppliers not to use outworkers, this request is difficult to enforce. In April 1996, the Senate's inquiry into outworkers in the garment industry was told that some outworkers could receive as little as $1 for work on a garment retailing for $500.

37   Mark Baker, 'Fischer rules out sanctions on Burma', *Sydney Morning Herald*, 4 November 1996, p. 11.

38   Thomas Donaldson, 'Multinational decision-making: reconciling international norms', in Anthony Fllis (ed.), *Ethics and International Relations* (Manchester: Manchester University Press, 1986), pp. 127–40; *The Ethics of International Business* (New York: Oxford University Press, 1989), ch. 5; and 'The language of international corporate ethics', *Business Ethics Quarterly*, 2, 1992, pp. 271–81.

39   Donaldson, *The Ethics of International Business*, p. 84. Compare Donaldson's 'The perils of multi-nationals' largess', *Business Ethics Quarterly*, 4, 1994, pp. 367–71.

40   As Donaldson puts it, 'the corporation, if indeed it is a moral agent at all, has limited moral capacities and a decidedly non-human psychology. It is often taller and richer than most of us: but it is morally peculiar. It strives for nothing except economic objectives, or, if it [does strive for other objectives,] its striving has none of the psychological characteristics of human moral striving. It does not weep at funerals, struggle with its appetite, or enjoy wedding parties'; 'the language of international corporate ethics', pp. 275–6. Compare, for example, Robert Ewin, 'The moral status of the corporation', *Journal of Business Ethics*, 10, 1991, p. 755,: 'Because they are artificial people and not 'natural' people, corporations lack the emotional makeup necessary to the possession of virtues and vices. Their moral personality is exhausted by their legal personality'.

41   Geraldine Brooks, 'They hang writers don't they?', *Weekend Australian*, 30–31 December 1995, features, p. 5.

42   Found at http://www.transparency.org/surveys/index.html .

43   Kevin Jackson, 'Global distributive justice and the corporate duty to aid', *Journal of Business Ethics*, 12, 1993, p. 550. See Donaldson's reply in 'The perils of multinational's largess'.

44   George C. Brenkert, 'Can we afford international human rights?', *Journal of Business Ethics*, 11, 1992, pp. 517.

45   These have been growing in number internationally. For Australian ethical investment services, see Ross Knowles (ed.), *Ethical Investment* (Sydney: Choice Books,1997); and the World Wide Web sites of ethical investment advisers Terry Pinnell <http:// www.peg. apc.org/~dei>, Australian Ethical Investment Ltd <http://www. austethical.com.au>, and Ecobusiness Consultants Pty Ltd <http://www.ecobusiness. com.au>.

46   For an elaboration of the argument from self-interest, see Bowie & Vaaler.

47   *The Ethics of International Business*, p. 75. Donaldson nominates ten fundamental human rights: the right to freedom of physical movement; the right to ownership of property; the right to freedom from torture; the right to a fair trial; the right to nondiscriminatory treatment; the right to physical security; the right to freedom of speech and association; the right to minimal education; the right to political participation; the right to subsistence.

48   This criticism is discussed at length in Brenkert, pp. 515–21.

49   Peter Drucker, *Post-Capitalist Society* (New York: Harper Business, 1993), p. 102.

50   As quoted in Sam North, 'Human rights concerns pull Levi's out of China', *Sydney Morning Herald*, 8 May 1993, p. 15.

51   Robert Waterman, *Frontiers of Excellence* (Sydney: Allen & Unwin, 1994), pp. 166–7. For a discussion of the Levi's Aspiration Statement, its emphasis on ethics, and its attempt to globalise its values, see ch. 7 of Waterman, as well as Rhymer Rigby, 'Jeans genius', *Management Today*, November 1996, pp. 56–60. Rigby's article shows just how tough, in a business sense, Levi's is, but also just how seriously it takes ethics. In Bangladesh and Turkey, Levi's pays contractors to keep their children in school until they are 14 years old. This ensures that those who are potentially the main income-earners for families, children in sweatshops, are instead given an education and, of course, that Levi's is not open to charges of using child labour. According to Rigby, this is an expensive option for Levi's, but the company takes a long-term view and believes in adhering to its published ethical stance. Elaine Sternberg argues that Levi's can do these things legitimately because it is not in the position of a listed company, which must increase shareholder value and would not be at liberty to disperse profits in this manner. This point is a fair one, but overlooks the fact that Levi's' shareholders choose to set an example through their corporation to shareholders in public companies.

52   Grand Metropolitan, *Report on Corporate Citizenship 1997* (London: Grand Metropolitan, 1996), p. 15.

53   Grand Met's model is based on corporate relationships with employees, government, investors, brand consumers, business partners, and communities.

54   Grand Metropolitan, pp. 19–20.

55   Friedman, 'The social responsibility of business is to increase its profits'.

56   Chris Marsden, 'Corporate citizenship', unpublished discussion paper, BP Corporate Citizenship Unit, Business School, University of Warwick, 1997, p. 15.

57   Tahija, p. 5.

58   Tahija, pp. 5–9.

59   Richard De George, 'Entrepreneurs, multinationals, and business ethics', paper given at the International Society of Business, Economics and Ethics, Tokyo, 1996.

60   ibid., p. 2.

61   ibid., p. 2.

62   Systems do not absolve individuals of personal responsibility for acting ethically. But not all corruption is of equal seriousness, and individuals cannot be required to display ethical behaviour out of proportion to the likely benefits. Although this cannot be required, it might still be freely given (for instance, by whistleblowers) and exact our moral admiration and gratitude.

63   De George also argues that bribes harm those paying them: they suffer the injustice, 'but [do] not impose it on others' (*Entrepreneurs, multinationals, and business ethics*, p. 5). This is not strictly true: bribes impose a direct cost on customers and on those who must bear the costs of policing corruption. Bribery distorts markets, disadvantages competitors, and tends to drive up prices. This is not always the case, particularly in maturing economies, where, as Michael Backman argues, corruption 'can enable bad government to be frustrated, and incompetent or slothful bureaucracies can be cut through'. This does not answer the ethical objections, but as De George shows, even this requires discrimination; Backman, 'Putting a kick back into business', *Australian Financial Review*, 27 October 1997, p. 15.

64   ibid., p. 4.

65   In 1996, in a first for Australia, WMC produced the report of an audit of the company's environmental performance. The audit identified problems and potential savings of which the company was previously unaware — for example, in water consumption. The CEO of WMC, Hugh Morgan, says the company has 'a very strong self-interest in getting it right. I try to make it clear that this environmental activity is not a function of something imposed from outside. This is very much in our own self-interest'; Mark Davis, 'WMC compiles its own green report card', *Business Review Weekly*, 10 June 1996, pp. 20–2.

66   Reported in TI Australia NEWS <http://www.transparency.de/chapters/Oceania/ Australia/ news/july97.html> 11 July 1997.

67   The background history of the CRT is to be found at 'Caux Round Table: History and Meetings' <http://www.cauxroundtable.org/History.htm> 2 November 1997, extracted in part from Michael Henderson, *The Forgiveness Factor: Stories of Hope in a World of Conflict* (Salem, Oreg.: Grosvenor Books, 1996), pp. 181–93.

68   ibid.

69   Charles M. Denny, one of the authors of the Caux Principles, as quoted in Henderson.

70   J. Lambsdorff, TI Newsletter <http://www.transparency.de/newsletter/997index. html> September 1997.

71   http://www.transparency.org/surveys/index.html#bpi.
72   *Lima Convention* http://www.transparency.de/iace/council.html 2 November 1997.

Conclusion

1   This point is by no means new. St Thomas Aquinas, quite a campaigner for significant ethical reform throughout society, urged a very similar caution in the thirteenth century.

Appendix 1

1   William W. May (ed.), *Ethics in the Accounting Curriculum: Cases and Readings* (Sarasota, Florida: American Accounting Association, 1990). This model was adapted by the AAA from an eight-step model suggested by H. Q. Langenderfer and J. W. Rockness, 'Integrating ethics into the accounting curriculum: Issues, problems and solutions', *Issues in Accounting Education*, 4, 1989, pp. 58–69.

2   Laura Nash, 'Ethics without the sermon', *Harvard Business Review*, 59, November– December 1981, pp. 79–90.

3   Michael Rion, *The Responsible Manager: Practical Strategies for Ethical Decision Making* (San Francisco: Harper & Row, 1990), pp. 13–14, and then applied throughout the book.

4   Mary Guy, *Ethical Decision Making in Everyday Work Situations* (New York: Quorum Books, 1990), pp. 14–19, 28–30.

5   Kent Hodgson, *A Rock and a Hard Place: How to Make Ethical Business Decisions When the Choices are Tough* (New York: American Management Association, 1992), pp. 93–4, 97–9, 103–4, 129–30.

6   Philip G. Cottell Jr. & Terry M. Perlin, *Accounting Ethics: A Practical Guide for Professionals* (New York: Quorum Books, 1990), pp. 10, 12–13.

7   David Mathison, 'Business ethics cases and decision models: A call for relevancy in the classroom', *Journal of Business Ethics*, 7, 1988, p. 780.

8   Anthony M. Pagano, 'Criteria for ethical decision making in managerial situations', *Proceedings of the National Academy of Management*, New Orleans, 1987, pp. 1–12.

Appendix 2

1   This material is available from Australian Association of National Advertisers, Suite 2, Level 5, 99 Elizabeth Street, Sydney, NSW, 2000. It is also available on the Internet at http://www.advertising-standardsbureau.com.au/industry/aana_code_ethics.html.

Appendix 3

1   The CRT Principles may be found at <http://www.cauxroundtable.org>. They are largely based on principles developed by the Minnesota Centre for Corporate Responsibility, which may be found at <http://www.stthomas.edu/mccr>.

Bibliography

Aristotle. *The Ethics of Aristotle*, trans. J. A. K. Thomson et al. (Harmondsworth: Penguin Books, 1976).

Armstrong, Robert W. 'An empirical investigation of international marketing ethics: problems encountered by Australian firms', *Journal of Business Ethics*, 11, 1992, pp. 161–71.

Armstrong, Robert, et al. 'Business Ethics', in Anthony Milner & Mary Quilty (eds), *Australia in Asia: Comparing Cultures* (Melbourne: Oxford University Press, 1996).

Arrington, Robert. 'Advertising and behavior control', *Journal of Business Ethics*, 1, no. 1, February 1982, pp. 3–12.

Bagshaw, Mark. 'Ready, willing and able', *Australian Business Monthly*, July 1992, pp. 138–40.

Barker, Geoffrey. 'Ethics: The glove that tempers the iron fist', *Australian Financial Review Magazine*, 7 July 1995, pp. 14–20.

Barker, Geoffrey. 'Dead fish, ethics and Ok Tedi', *Australian Financial Review*, 9 October 1995, p. 15.

Barry, Paul. *The Rise and Fall of Alan Bond* (Sydney: Bantam, 1990).

Becker, Elizabeth, 'Animal Fans' Secret Recipe Is to Boycott Restaurant', *New York Times*, 6 January 2003.

Beder, Sharon. 'Engineers, ethics and etiquette', *New Scientist*, 25 September 1993, pp. 36–41.

BHP and Ok Tedi: The Facts, BHP publicity, 28 September 1995.

BHP Billiton *Health Safety Environment & Community Report 2003* at http://www.bhpbilliton.com/hsecReport/2003/home/home.html.

Blodgett, Timothy. 'Showdown on "business bluffing"', *Harvard Business Review*, May–June 1968, pp. 162–70.

Bok, Sissela. 'Blowing the whistle', in J. Fleishman et al. (eds), *Public Duties: The Moral Obligations of Government Officials* (Cambridge: Cambridge University Press, 1982).

Bosch, Henry. *Bosch on Business* (Melbourne: Business Library, 1992).

Bowie, Norman. 'Business codes of ethics', in Tom L. Beauchamp & Norman E. Bowie (eds), *Ethical Theory and Business* (Englewood Cliffs, NJ: Prentice Hall, 1979).

Bowie, Norman & Duska, Ronald. *Business Ethics*, 2nd edn (Englewood Cliffs, NJ: Prentice Hall, 1990).

Bowie, Norman E. & Vaaler, Paul. 'Some arguments for universal moral standards', *International Society of Business, Economics and Ethics Papers*, Tokyo 1996 <http://www.nd. edu/~isbee/p_bowie.htm> 28 August 1997.

Braybrooke, David. *Ethics in the World of Business* (Totowa, NJ: Rowman & Allanheld, 1983).

Brenkert, George C. 'Can we afford international human rights?', *Journal of Business Ethics*, 11, 1992, pp. 517.

Brooks, Geraldine. 'They hang writers don't they?', *Weekend Australian*, 30–31 December 1995, features, p. 5.

Business Council of Australia. *Principles of Environmental Management* (Melbourne: Business Council of Australia, 1992).

Cadbury, Sir Adrian. 'Ethical managers make their own rules', *Harvard Business Review*, September–October 1987, reprinted in E. K. Kellar (ed.), *Ethical Insight, Ethical Action* (Washington: ICMA, 1988).

Campbell, Joseph. *Reflections on the Art of Living: A Joseph Campbell Companion*, selected and edited by Diane K. Osbon (New York: Harper Perennial, 1991).

'Caux Round Table: History and Meetings' <http://www.cauxroundtable.org/History. htm> 2 November 1997.

Cicero. *De officiis*, trans. Walter Miller (Cambridge, Mass. & London: Loeb, 1913).

Clark, Fred P. 'Unfounded "whistle blower" suit can kill a small defense company', *Aviation Week and Space Technology*, 2 March 1992, pp. 65–6.

Clarke, F. L., Dean, G. W., & Oliver, K. G. *Corporate Collapse* (Cambridge: Cambridge University Press, 1997).

Clarke, Frank and Dean, Graeme. 'Corporate collapses analysed' in *Collapse Incorporated* (North Ryde: CCH, 2001).

C., M. and S. v. Australian Telecommunications Corporation, Human Rights and Equal Opportunity Commission (16 December 1991).

Coady, C. A. J. 'Ethos and ethics in business', in C. A. J. Coady & C. J. G. Sampford. *Business, Ethics and the Law* (Sydney: Federation Press, 1993).

Coady, Margaret & Bloch, Sidney (eds). *Codes of Ethics and the Professions* (Melbourne: Melbourne University Press, 1996).

Cohen, S and Grace, D. 'Ethics and Sustainability: Looking beyond basic legal requirements', *Australian master OHS and environment guide 2003* (Sydney: CCH, 2002).

Cohen, Stephen. *The Nature of Moral Reasoning: The Framework and Activities of Ethical Deliberation, Argument, and Decision-making* (Melbourne: Oxford University Press, 2004).

Coker, Edward. 'Adam Smith's concept of the social system', *Journal of Business Ethics*, 9, 1990, pp. 139–42.

Condren, Conal. 'Code types: Functions and failings and organizational diversity', *Business and Professional Ethics Journal*, 14, no. 4, 1995, pp. 69–90.

Cottell, Philip G., Jr. & Perlin, Terry M. *Accounting Ethics: A Practical Guide for Professionals* (New York: Quorum Books, 1990).

Crichton, Michael. 'Remarks to the Commonwealth Club San Francisco', 15 September 2003 at http://www.crichton-official.com/speeches/speeches_quote05.html.

Cross, Frank. 'Paradoxical Perils of the Precautionary Principle', 53 *Washington and Lee Law Review*, 851 (1996).

Daly, H. & Cobb, J. *For the Common Good* (London: Greenprint, 1989).

Dancy, Jonathan. *Moral Reasons* (Oxford: Blackwell, 1993).

Davis, Mark. 'WMC compiles its own green report card', *Business Review Weekly*, 10 June 1996, pp. 20–2.

De George, Richard T. *Business Ethics*, 2nd edn (New York: Macmillan, 1986).

De George, Richard. *Competing with Integrity in International Business* (New York: Oxford University Press, 1993).

De George, Richard. 'Entrepreneurs, multinationals, and business ethics', paper given at the International Society of Business, Economics and Ethics, Tokyo, 1996.

De Maria, William. 'Quarantining Dissent: The Queensland Public Sector Ethics Movement', *Australian Journal of Public Administration*, 54, 1995, pp. 443–54.

Dempster, Quentin. *Whistleblowers* (Sydney: ABC Books, 1997).

Devlin, Lord Patrick. 'Morals and the criminal law', in Richard A. Wasserstrom, *Morality and the Criminal Law* (Belmont, Calif.: Wadsworth, 1971).

Disney, Julian, et al. *Lawyers*, 2nd edn (Sydney: Law Book Company, 1986).

Dollar Sweets Pty Ltd v. Federated Confectioners Association of Australia and Others (1986), VR, 383.

Donaldson, John. *Key Issues in Business Ethics* (London: Academic Press, 1989).

Donaldson, Thomas. 'Multinational decision-making: reconciling international norms', in Anthony Ellis (ed.), *Ethics and International Relations* (Manchester: Manchester University Press, 1986), pp. 127–40.

Donaldson, Thomas. *The Ethics of International Business* (New York: Oxford University Press, 1989).

Donaldson, Thomas. 'The language of international corporate ethics', *Business Ethics Quarterly*, 2, 1992, pp. 271–81.

Downie R. S. *Roles and Values: An Introduction to Social Ethics* (London: Methuen, 1971).

Drucker, Peter. 'What is "business ethics"?', *Public Interest*, 63, 1981, pp. 18–36.

Drucker, Peter. *Post-Capitalist Society* (New York: Harper Business, 1993).

Dworkin, Gerald. 'Lord Devlin and the enforcement of morals', *Yale Law Journal*, 75, 1966, pp. 986–1005.

Ebertz, Roger P. 'Is reflective equilibrium a coherentist model?', *Canadian Journal of Philosophy*, 23, 1993.

Ecologically Sustainable Development Working Group Chairs. *Intersectoral Issues Report* (Canberra: AGPS, 1992).

Eichenwald, Kurt. 'Audacious Climb to Success Ended in a Dizzying Plunge', *New York Times* , 13 January 2004.

Eichenwald, Kurt. 'Ex-Accounting Chief at Enron Is Indicted on 6 Felony Charges', *New York Times*, 23 January 2004.

Elias, David. 'The secretive life of a market opportunist', *Age*, 9 November 2002.

Elias, David. 'Accidental hero defeats David Tweed', *Sydney Morning Herald*, 24 October 2003.

Ewin, Robert. 'The moral status of the corporation', *Journal of Business Ethics*, 10, 1991, pp. 749–56.

Farnham, Alan. 'State your values, hold the hot air', *Fortune*, 19 April 1993, p. 54. 'Financial Reports Review Program', *Charter*, February 1994, pp. 55–6.

Frankena, William. *Ethics*, 2nd edn (Englewood Cliffs, NJ: Prentice-Hall, 1973).

Freeman, R. Edward. *Strategic Management: A Stakeholder Approach* (Boston: Pitman, 1984).

Freckelton, Ian. 'Enforcement of ethics', in Margaret Coady and Sidney Bloch (eds), *Codes of Ethics and the Professions* (Melbourne: Melbourne University Press, 1996).

Friedman, Milton. *Capitalism and Freedom* (Chicago: University of Chicago Press, 1962).

Friedman, Milton. 'The social responsibility of business is to increase its profits', *New York Times Magazine*, 13 September 1970, reprinted in T. Donaldson & P. Werhane (eds), *Ethical Issues in Business: A Philosophical Approach*, 2nd edn (Englewood Cliffs, NJ: Prentice-Hall, 1983), pp. 239–42.

Friedman, Milton & Friedman, Rose. *Free to Choose* (London: Secker & Warburg, 1980).

Gaita, Raimond. *Good and Evil: An Absolute Conception* (London: Macmillan, 1991).

Gaita, Raimond. *The Philosopher's Dog* (Melbourne: Text Publishing, 2002).

Goldman, Alan. 'Ethical issues in advertising', in Tom Regan (ed.), *Just Business: New Introductory Essays in Business Ethics* (New York: Random House, 1984).

Goodpaster, Kenneth. 'Business ethics and stakeholder analysis', *Business Ethics Quarterly*, 1, 1991.

Gorta, A. & Forell, S. 'Corruption: consensus, cognisance or confusion?', paper presented to the 9th Annual Conference of the Australian and New Zealand Society of Criminology, Sydney, September–October 1993.

Grand Metropolitan. *Report on Corporate Citizenship 1997* (London: Grand Metropolitan, 1996).

Guy, Mary. *Ethical Decision Making in Everyday Work Situations* (New York: Quorum Books, 1990).

Hart, H. L. A. *Law, Liberty, and Morality* (London: Oxford University Press, 1963).

Hart, H. L. A. 'Immorality and treason', in Richard Wasserstrom (ed.), *Morality and the Criminal Law* (Belmont, Calif.: Wadsworth, 1971).

Hawke, R. *Our Country, Our Future* (Canberra: AGPS, 1989).

Hays, Kristen. 'Causey May Be Key In Enron Prosecutions', *Chicago Tribune Online Edition*, 24 January 2004.

Heckman, Peter. 'Business and games', *Journal of Business Ethics*, 11, 1992, pp. 933–8.

Henderson, Michael. *The Forgiveness Factor: Stories of Hope in a World of Conflict* (Salem, Oreg.: Grosvenor Books, 1996).

Hinman, Lawrence M. *Ethics: A Pluralistic Approach to Moral Theory* (Orlando, Florida: Harcourt Brace Jovanovich, 1994).

Hodgson, Kent. *A Rock and a Hard Place: How to Make Ethical Business Decisions When the Choices are Tough* (New York: American Management Association, 1992).

Hoffman, Michael. 'Business and environmental ethics', *Business Ethics Quarterly*, 1, no. 2, 1991, pp. 169–84.

Honeywell. *Code of Ethics and Business Conduct* (Minneapolis: Honeywell, 1995).

House of Representatives Standing Committee on Finance and Public Administration. *A Pocket Full of Change: Banking and Deregulation* (Canberra: AGPS, 1991).

Hughes, Anthony. 'Beware, a low offer for IAG', *Sydney Morning Herald*, 20 May, 2002.

Hymowitz, Carol & Shellhardt, Timothy. 'The glass ceiling', in A. P. Iannone (ed.), *Contemporary Moral Controversies* (New York: Oxford University Press, 1989).

Jackson, Kevin. 'Global distributive justice and the corporate duty to aid', *Journal of Business Ethics*, 12, 1993, p. 550.

Jamrozik, Wanda. 'Women on top', *Independent Monthly*, February 1994.

Jonsen, Albert & Toulmin, Stephen. *The Abuse of Casuistry* (Berkeley: University of California Press, 1988).

Jubb, Peter. 'Confidentiality in a professional context with especial reference to the accounting profession in Australia', in M. Hoffman, J. Brown Kamm, R. E. Frederick, & E. S. Petry (eds), *The Ethics of Accounting and Finance* (London: Quorum Books, 1996).

Kant, Immanuel. *Foundations of the Metaphysics of Morals*, trans. L. W. Beck (New York: Macmillan, 1990).

Kaye, Bruce N. 'Codes of ethics in Australian Business Corporations', *Journal of Business Ethics*, 11, 1992, pp. 857–62.

Keeley, Michael & Graham, Jill. 'Exit, voice and ethics', *Journal of Business Ethics*, 10, 1991.

Kekes, John. *The Morality of Pluralism* (Princeton, NJ: Princeton University Press, 1993).

Kelly, Patrick. 'Conducting a glass ceiling self-audit now', *HR Magazine*, October 1993.

Knowles, Ross (ed.). *Ethical Investment* (Sydney: Choice Books, 1997).

Ladd, John. 'Morality and the ideal of rationality in formal organisations', *Monist*, 54, 1970, pp. 488–516.

Lambsdorff, Johann. *TI Newsletter* <http://www.transparency.de/newsletter/997index. html> September 1997.

Lambsdorff, Johann. 'The question of responsibility' <http://gwdu19.gwdg.de/%7Ejlambsd/ bribery/node4.htm> 26 September 1997.

Langenderfer, H. Q. & Rockness, J. W. 'Integrating ethics into the accounting curriculum: Issues, problems and solutions', *Issues in Accounting Education*, 4, 1989, pp. 58–69.

Laufer William S. 'Integrity, diligence, and the limits of good corporate citizenship', *American Business Law Journal*, 34, 2 Winter 1996, pp 157–81.

Lawson, Mark. 'Just don't invite the chief executive out to play golf', *Australian Financial Review*, 5 December, 2002.

Lawson, Mark. 'The ethical dilemma of corporate generosity', *Australian Financial Review*, 5 December 2002.

Legge, Kate. 'Humble hero of the operating theatre', *The Weekend Australian*, 23–4 June 2001.

Lemke, Dwight & Schminke, Marshall. 'Ethics in declining organizations', *Business Ethics Quarterly*, 1, 1991, pp. 235–48.

Leung, Philomena & Cooper, Barry. *Professional Ethics: A Survey of Australian Accountants* (Melbourne: ASCPA, 1995).

Liebig, James E. *Business Ethics: Profiles in Civic Virtue* (Golden, Colo.: Fulcrum, 1990).

Lima Declaration <http://www.transparency.de/iacc/council.html> 2 November 1997.

Lumby, Catharine. 'Sexist or sexy', *Independent Monthly*, November 1993.

Lynch, Adrian. 'Get integrity back into management', *Rydges*, December 1985.

McMillan, John. 'Legal protection of whistleblowers', in S. Prosser, R. Wear & J. Nethercote (eds), *Corruption and Reform* (St Lucia, Qld: University of Queensland Press, 1990).

'Managing in Asia: ethics and other issues', *Far Eastern Economic Review*, 16 September 1993, pp. 33–53.

Manley II, Walter W. *Good Business Practice* (London & New York: Routledge, 1992).

Marsden, Chris. 'Corporate citizenship', unpublished discussion paper, BP Corporate Citizenship Unit, Business School, University of Warwick, 1997.

Martin, Jane. 'The ethical advantage in business strategy', MBA dissertation, Graduate School of Business, University of Sydney, 1990.

Martin, Mike & Schinzinger, Roland. *Ethics in Engineering*, 2nd edn (New York: McGraw-Hill, 1989).

Marx, Karl. *Capital*, vol. 1 (New York: International Publishing, 1967).

Mathison, David. 'Business ethics cases and decision models: A call for relevancy in the classroom', *Journal of Business Ethics*, 7, 1988, pp. 777–82.

Maurice, Jack. *Accounting Ethics* (London: Pitman Publishing, 1996).

May William W. (ed.). *Ethics in the Accounting Curriculum: Cases and Readings* (Sarasota, Florida: American Accounting Association, 1990).

Mayman, Jan. 'The stink of uncle Al', *The Weekend Australian*, 11–12 May 2002.

Mellor, Bill. 'Integrity and ruined lives', *Time*, 21 October 1991.

Miller, Cyndee. 'Women at ad agencies say top pay, positions denied them', *Marketing News*, 27, no. 13, 21 June 1993, pp. 1–2.

More, Thomas. *Utopia*, ed. G. Logan & R. M. Adams (Cambridge: Cambridge University Press, 1989).

Nagel, Thomas. 'Ruthless in public life', in Stuart Hampshire (ed.), *Public and Private Morality* (New York: Cambridge University Press, 1978), pp. 75–92.

Nash, Laura. 'Ethics without the sermon', *Harvard Business Review*, 59, November–December 1981, pp. 79–90.

New South Wales Anti-Discrimination Board. *Why Don't You Ever See a Pregnant Waitress?*, Summary Report of the Findings of the Inquiry into Pregnancy Related Discrimination, Sydney, 1993.

Nowland v. Skypak & Anor (1993), EOC 92–509.

Nozick, Robert. *Anarchy, State and Utopia* (Oxford: Blackwell, 1974).

Nugroho, Alois A. 'The myth of immoral business: a specific challenge of business ethics in Indonesia', *International Society of Business, Economics and Ethics Papers*, Tokyo 1996 <http://www.nd.edu/~isbee/p_nugroh.htm> 15 September 1997.

Office of Regulation Review. 'Recent developments in regulation and its review', Information Paper, Canberra, November 1993.

Pagano, Anthony M. 'Criteria for ethical decision making in managerial situations', *Proceedings of the National Academy of Management*, New Orleans, 1987, pp. 1–12.

Palmer Ian, 'Email Abuse & Misuse', Insight at http://www.insight-mag.com/insight/03/08/col-5-pt-1-WorkForce.asp.

Parker, Christine. *The Open Corporation* (Cambridge: Cambridge University Press, 2002).

Pearson, Christopher. 'Green errors began with DDT', *The Weekend Australian*, 24–5 January 2004.

Pratt, Dennis. *Aspiring to Greatness* (Sydney: Business & Professional Publishing, 1994).

Preston, Noel. 'Public sector ethics in Australia: A review', *Australian Journal of Public Administration*, 54, 1995, pp. 462–70.

Rachels, James. *The Elements of Moral Philosophy*, 2nd edn (New York: McGraw-Hill, 1993).

Rawls, John. *A Theory of Justice* (Cambridge, Mass.: Harvard University Press, 1971).

Redmond, Paul. *Companies and Securities Law*, 2nd edn. (North Ryde: The Law Book Company, 1992).

Rigby, Rhymer. 'Jeans genius', *Management Today*, November 1996, pp. 56–60.

Rion, Michael. *The Responsible Manager: Practical Strategies for Ethical Decision Making* (San Francisco: Harper & Row, 1990).

Robert, Howard. 'Values make the company', *Harvard Business Review*, September–October 1990, pp. 133–44.

Rolston III, Holmes. 'Just environmental business', in Tom Regan (ed.), *Just Business* (New York: Random House, 1984).

Ryan, Colleen. 'The hard yard', *Australian Financial Review Magazine*, July 2003.

Ryle, Gerard. 'Industrial waste sold as fertilizer', *Sydney Morning Herald*, 6 May 2002.

Sanyal, Rajib & Neves, Joao. 'The Valdez Principles: implications for corporate social responsibility', *Journal of Business Ethics*, 10 December 1991, pp. 883–90.

Sen, Amartya. 'Does business ethics make economic sense?', *Business Ethics Quarterly*, 3, 1993, p. 50.

Simons, Paul. 'Be interested in the people you serve and your life will be happy', fourth annual lecture, St James Ethics Centre, Sydney, November 1994.

Sims, Ronald R. 'The institutionalization of organization ethics', *Journal of Business Ethics*, 10, 1991.

Sinclair, Amanda. 'Improving ethics through organisational culture', in C. A. J. Coady & C. J. G. Sampford (eds), *Business, Ethics and the Law* (Sydney: Federation Press, 1993).

Sinclair, Amanda. 'Codes in the workplace: Organizational verses professional codes', in Margaret Coady and Sidney Bloch (eds), *Codes of Ethics and the Professions* (Melbourne: Melbourne University Press, 1996).

Singer, Peter. *Animal Liberation*, 2nd edn (New York: Thorsons, 1991).

Singer, Peter. *Practical Ethics*, 2nd edn (New York: Cambridge University Press, 1993).

Singer, Peter (ed.). *Ethics* (New York: Oxford University Press, 1994).

Smart, J. J. C. & Williams, Bernard. *Utilitarianism: For and Against* (London: Cambridge University, 1973).

Smith, Grant. 'Does ethics pay?', *Marketing*, September 1993, pp. 14–15.

Sternberg, Elaine. *Just Business* (London: Warner Books, 1995).

Still, Leonie. 'Breaking the glass ceiling: another perspective', *Women In Management Series, paper no. 15*, Faculty of Commerce, University of Western Sydney, Nepean, July 1992.

Tahija, Julius. 'Swapping business skills for oil', *Harvard Business Review*, September–October 1993, p. 113.

Titmuss, Richard. *Social Policy: An Introduction*, ed. Brian Abel-Smith & Kay Titmuss (London: Allen & Unwin, 1974).

Toffler, Barbara Ley with Reingold, Jennifer. *Final Accounting: Ambition, Greed and the Fall of Arthur Andersen* (Broadway Books, 2003).

Tönnies, Ferdinand. *Community and Association*, trans. C.P. Loomis (London: Routledge and Kegan Paul, 1955).

TPC v. T.N.T. Management Pty Ltd & Ors (1985), ATFR, paras 40–512.

Trainer, Ted. *Abandon Affluence* (London: Zed Books, 1985).

Treadgold, Tim. 'Lady Bountiful turns nasty', *Business Review Weekly*, 1 October 1993, pp. 24–8.

Vallance, Elizabeth, *Business Ethics at Work* (Cambridge: Cambridge University Press, 1995).

Velasquez, Manuel. *Business Ethics*, 3rd edn (Englewood Cliffs, NJ: Prentice Hall, 1992).

Vitell, S. J., Nwachukwu, S. L., & Barnes, J. H. 'The effects of culture on ethical decision-making: an application of Hofstede's typology', *Journal of Business Ethics*, 12, 1993, pp. 753–60.

Wade, M. 'Petrol importing fuels bitter debate over retail ethics', *Sydney Morning Herald*, 10 July 2002.

Waterman, Robert. *Frontiers of Excellence* (Sydney: Allen & Unwin, 1994).

Waters, James A. 'Catch 20.5: corporate morality as an organizational phenomenon', in A. P. Iannone (ed.), *Contemporary Moral Controversies* (New York: Oxford University Press, 1989).

Webb, Christopher. 'Make sure you read both sides of letter', *Age*, 6 September 2002.

Webber, Ross. 'Whistleblowing', *Executive Excellence*, July 1990.

Westin, Allen (ed.). *Whistleblowing: Loyalty and Dissent in the Corporation* (New York: McGraw-Hill, 1981).

Whitton, Howard. 'Ethics and principles dissent in the Queensland public sector: A response to the Queensland whistleblower study', *Australian Journal of Public Administration*, 54, 1995, pp. 455–61.

Williams, Bernard. 'Politics and moral character', in Stuart Hampshire (ed.), *Public and Private Morality* (London: Cambridge University Press, 1978).

Wilson, Duff. 'Fear In The Fields — How Hazardous Wastes Become Fertilizer — Spreading Heavy Metals On Farmland Is Perfectly Legal, But Little Research Has Been Done To Find Out Whether It's Safe', *Seattle Times*, 3 July 1997 at http://archives.seattletimes.nwsource.com/cgi-bin/texis.cgi/web/vortex/display?slug= 2547772&date=19970703.

Wilson, Mel. 'Corporate Reputation and the Triple Bottom Line: The Social Responsibilities of Business', *Risky Business*, Issue 2, 2001 at http://www.pwc.com/extweb/manissue.nsf/DocID/C00115084F24343E852569E600656A08.

Woldring, K. (ed.). *Business Ethics in Australia and New Zealand* (Melbourne: Nelson, 1996).

Wolgast, Elizabeth. *Ethics of an Artificial Person* (Stanford, California: Stanford University Press, 1992).

World Commission on Environment and Development. *Our Common Future* (London: Oxford University Press, 1987).

Index